Games, Changes, and Fears

The **ISEAS – Yusof Ishak Institute** (formerly Institute of Southeast Asian Studies) is an autonomous organization established in 1968. It is a regional centre dedicated to the study of socio-political, security, and economic trends and developments in Southeast Asia and its wider geostrategic and economic environment. The Institute's research programmes are grouped under Regional Economic Studies (RES), Regional Strategic and Political Studies (RSPS), and Regional Social and Cultural Studies (RSCS). The Institute is also home to the ASEAN Studies Centre (ASC), the Singapore APEC Study Centre, and the Temasek History Research Centre (THRC).

ISEAS Publishing, an established academic press, has issued more than 2,000 books and journals. It is the largest scholarly publisher of research about Southeast Asia from within the region. ISEAS Publishing works with many other academic and trade publishers and distributors to disseminate important research and analyses from and about Southeast Asia to the rest of the world.

Games, Changes, and Fears

The Philippines from Duterte to Marcos Jr.

EDITED BY
ARIES A. ARUGAY
JEAN ENCINAS-FRANCO

ISEAS YUSOF ISHAK INSTITUTE

First published in Singapore in 2024 by
ISEAS Publishing
30 Heng Mui Keng Terrace
Singapore 119614
E-mail: publish@iseas.edu.sg
Website: http://bookshop.iseas.edu.sg

All rights reserved. No part of this publication may be reproduced, stored in a retrieval system, or transmitted in any form or by any means, electronic, mechanical, photocopying, recording or otherwise, without the prior permission of the ISEAS – Yusof Ishak Institute.

© 2024 ISEAS – Yusof Ishak Institute, Singapore

The responsibility for facts and opinions in this publication rests exclusively with the authors and their interpretations do not necessarily reflect the views or the policy of the publisher or its supporters.

ISEAS Library Cataloguing-in-Publication Data

Name(s): Arugay, Aries A., editor. | Franco, Jean Encinas-, editor.
Title: Games, changes, and fears : the Philippines from Duterte to Marcos Jr. / edited by Aries A. Arugay and Jean Encinas-Franco.
Description: Singapore : ISEAS – Yusof Ishak Institute, 2024. | Includes bibliographical references and index.
Identifiers: ISBN 978-981-5203-17-2 (soft cover) | ISBN 978-981-5203-18-9 (PDF) | ISBN 978-981-5203-19-6 (epub)
Subjects: LCSH: Philippines—Politics and government.
Classification: LCC DS686.614 G19

Cover and section photos by Mr Basilio Sepe
Cover design by Lee Meng Hui
Index compiled by Sheryl Sin Bing Peng
Typesetting by International Typesetters Pte Ltd
Printed in Singapore by Markono Print Media Pte Ltd

Contents

List of Tables vii

List of Figures ix

Acknowledgements x

About the Contributors xii

1. Introduction: Change and Continuity Narratives in the Philippines from Duterte to Marcos Jr. 1
   Aries A. Arugay, Jean Encinas-Franco, and Justin Keith A. Baquisal

2. Much a Duterte about Nothing: Continuity, Complacency, and Crisis in the Philippine Economy (2016–23) 33
   Jan Carlo Punongbayan

3. From Entrepreneur to Saboteur: How the Philippines Won and Lost the South China Sea on Social Media 59
   Charmaine Misalucha-Willoughby

4. Course Correction from Over-Militarization: National Security from the Duterte to the Marcos Jr. Administration 84
   Julio S. Amador III and Deryk Matthew Baladjay

5. Duterte's Federalism and Constitutional Change Project: From Campaign Promise to Abandoned Reform 119
   Maria Ela L. Atienza

6.	Experiencing Grief: Duterte's Lethal Drug War and Its Widows *Bianca Ysabelle E. Franco*	149
7.	*Tsek.ph* and the Media's Pushback against Digital Disinformation *Ma. Diosa Labiste*	171
8.	A Quixotic Quest? Electoral and Political Reforms from Duterte to Marcos Jr. *Cleo Anne A. Calimbahin and Luie Tito F. Guia*	203
9.	The Changing Local Political Dynamics during the COVID-19 Pandemic: The Philippine Experience under Duterte (and Marcos Jr.) *Jan Robert R. Go*	229
10.	An Unchanging Terrain? Environment and Climate Change in the Philippines from Duterte to Marcos Jr. *Ruth R. Lusterio-Rico*	255
11.	Mitigating Risks, Fostering Resilience: Human Security and Disaster Response Policy from Duterte to Marcos Jr. *Cherry Ann Madriaga*	273
12.	Understanding Gendered Disinformation in the Philippines and Its Implications to Women in Politics *Jean Encinas-Franco*	303
13.	(Dis)continuities and Disruptions in Labour Migration Governance: The Philippines from the Duterte to the Marcos Jr. Administration *Bubbles Beverly Asor and Rizza Kaye Cases*	327
Index		348

List of Tables

1.1	Vote Share of Leading Presidential Candidates in the 2016 and 2022 Presidential Elections	7
1.2	Philippine Democracy Scores through the Years	12
4.1	Partial List of Retired Military Personnel Occupying Civilian Positions under Duterte	93
4.2	Cabinet Appointments of the Marcos and Duterte Administrations	98
5.1	Awareness of Proposals to Change the 1987 Philippine Constitution (2014–18)	132
5.2	Opinion on the Appropriateness to Amend the 1987 Philippine Constitution (2018)	133
5.3	Knowledge of the 1987 Philippine Constitution (2018)	133
5.4	Knowledge of the Proposed Federal System of Government (2018)	134
7.1	List of *Tsek.ph* Fact-Checking Partners	189

7.2	Fact-Checked Claims on Martial Law and the Marcoses	191
11.1	Ranking of the Most Destructive Calamities in the Philippines (2016–23)	279
11.2	Ranking of the Highest Number of Affected due to Calamities in the Philippines (2016–23)	280
11.3	Total Damages and Losses from Major Disasters (2016–23)	281
11.4	NDRRMC Budget and Total Philippine Budget (2016–23)	284

List of Figures

2.1	Annual GDP Growth Rate (1960–2022)	41
2.2	Monthly Inflation in the Philippines (January 2016–July 2023)	42
2.3	Debt-GDP Ratio	46
5.1	Awareness of the Federal System of Government (March 2018)	134
5.2	Agreement or Disagreement on the Federal System of Government (March 2018)	135
7.1	Positive and Negative Fact-Checked Content/Messaging	193
9.1	Duterte's Net Satisfaction Rating (2016–22)	242

Acknowledgements

Doing a book about the Philippines since 2016 is not an easy task. We had to patiently wait until the end of the Duterte administration in 2022 for us to have a very clear picture of how this firebrand leader has changed Philippine politics and society. The benefit of hindsight allowed us to do this with humility, sobriety, and reflexivity.

As they say, scholarship is a collective endeavour. Indeed, this volume would not have been possible without the support of many people and organizations. Primarily, we thank the chapter authors, all of whom are respected colleagues but also dear friends, who trusted us with their insightful take on Philippine politics, economics and society, at the crossroads of one administration to another. The time and effort they spent on this publication indicate their great interest in expressing their voices not merely to inform, but to advocate necessary reforms, even as they know that the road might be difficult and contentious. May more academic publications about the Philippines be spearheaded by locally based Filipino scholars who rigorously undertake serious research and navigate the complexities and risks of academe and public engagement.

The Department of Political Science at the University of the Philippines Diliman, our institutional home, deserves to be mentioned, not only because of its staff and our colleagues' immense support, but also because we were its products at some points in each of our academic journeys. Its nurturing environment allowed us to informally discuss the book in its inception, bringing along some of our colleagues to contribute their chapters. Apart from Filipinos worldwide, it is to our department, which turned 109 years old in 2024 that we dedicate this book.

We also would like to thank the ISEAS – Yusof Ishak Institute for believing in the value of this project. In particular, Hoang Thi Ha and Sue-Ann Lee had unwavering faith in the promise of this academic publication to contribute towards Philippine studies. The Konrad-Adenauer-Stiftung-Singapore has also been a vital partner in this endeavour through its financial and institutional support. Special thanks are given to Julio Amador III, executive director of the Philippine-American Educational Foundation, for graciously hosting the hybrid workshop that allowed us to work collectively in revising the chapters.

Many scholars lent their time and expertise in reviewing the draft chapters. We thank Pamela Cajilig, Ronald Holmes, Sol Iglesias, Adoracion Navarro, Thaemar Tana, and Edson Tandoc, Jr. for their invaluable feedback and sharp comments for the improvement of the chapters.

Our heartfelt gratitude also goes to one of our most brilliant graduate students, Justin Baquisal, whose excellent research, analytical and writing skills, immensely helped in the book's conceptualization and production—not to mention his good coordination and great rapport with the authors, thus assisting us in updating everyone, amidst our busy schedules. Needless to say, we were fortunate to have him. We also thank Basilio Sepe, the photographer whose images are presented in the book, for producing pictures that will help readers visually capture some of the book's arguments.

Aries A. Arugay and *Jean Encinas-Franco*

About the Contributors

Julio Amador III is CEO of Amador Research Services, Interim President of the Foundation for the National Interest, and Founder and Trustee of the non-profit FACTS Asia. He regularly participates in Tracks 1.5 and 2 events and occasionally writes on national security and foreign affairs for various publications. Julio was a civil servant in the Philippine government for more than a decade and worked on foreign affairs and national security issues. He was a Fulbright Graduate Scholar at the Maxwell School of Citizenship and Public Affairs, Syracuse University, and an Asia Studies Visiting Fellow and EWC-Korea Foundation Visiting Scholar at the East-West Center in Washington D.C. Julio has published peer-reviewed journal articles, book chapters, and op-eds/commentaries in online news media.

Aries A. Arugay is Visiting Senior Fellow and Coordinator of the Philippine Studies Programme at the ISEAS – Yusof Ishak Institute. He is also Professor and Chair of the Department of Political Science at the University of the Philippines Diliman. Aries is the Editor-in-Chief of *Asian Politics & Policy*, a Scopus-indexed journal in political science and international relations published by Wiley-Blackwell and the US-based Policy Studies Organization. He has published in *Asian Perspective, Pacific Affairs, Journal of East Asian Studies, American Behavioral Scientist*, and the *Journal of Current Southeast Asian Affairs*, among others. Aries obtained his PhD in political science from Georgia State University as a Fulbright Fellow.

Maria Ela L. Atienza is Professor and former Chair of the Department of Political Science, University of the Philippines (UP) Diliman. She is also the Editor of the *Philippine Political Science Journal*, the Scopus journal of the Philippine Political Science Association, and Co-Convenor of the Program on Social and Political Change of the UP Center for Integrative and Development Studies. She is currently the President of the Pi Gamma Mu International Honor Society in the Social Sciences – University of the Philippines (Philippine Alpha) Chapter. She also served as Director of the UP Third World Studies Center (2010–13) and President of the Philippine Political Science Association (2007–9). She obtained her PhD in political science from Kobe University. Her research interests and international refereed publications focus on local politics and devolution, health policy, human security and charter change.

Bubbles Beverly Asor is the Academic Coordinator of the Initiative for the Study of Asian Catholics (ISAC) at De La Salle University Manila. She received her PhD in Sociology at the National University of Singapore in 2016. Her research interests include migrant organizations, faith-based organizations, urban diversity, border studies, everyday life, international migration to South Korea, and Philippine migration. She also holds a Research Fellow position with the Border Studies Cluster, Faculty of Humanities at the Airlangga University, Surabaya, Indonesia. She is the Editor-in-Chief of the *Philippine Sociological Review*, the flagship journal of the Philippine Sociological Society. She had teaching posts as Assistant Professor at the University of the Philippines Diliman, De La Salle University, Manila, and the University of the Philippines Los Baños.

Deryk Matthew Baladjay is Lecturer at the International Studies Department of the De La Salle University, Manila. He is also Assistant Editor at FACTS Asia and a consultant for Amador Research Services where he serves as its Research Manager. He is also a member of the Young Leader cohort of Pacific Forum, a think tank based in Hawai'i specializing in Indo-Pacific affairs. He has a master's degree in international studies with specialization in Asian studies from De La

Salle University, Manila. His key research interests include Philippine strategic foreign relations and East and Southeast Asian affairs and writes extensively on Philippine security and strategic interests. He recently authored a piece titled "The Nuclear Discourse after the Invasion of Ukraine: Insights from the Philippines" (2023) and a peer-reviewed journal article titled "Modernizing or Equalizing? Defence Budget and Military Modernization in the Philippines, 2010–2020" (2022).

Justin Keith Baquisal is a Resident National Security Analyst at FACTS Asia and a Southeast Asia Young Leader at the International Institute for Strategic Studies' Shangri-La Dialogue. He has a degree in political science (*magna cum laude*) from the University of the Philippines Diliman and is currently a graduate student in the same institution. He has published policy briefs, op-eds, and academic articles on Philippine national security, foreign policy, and autocratization, which have appeared in *Southeast Asian Affairs*, *Pacific Affairs*, *Palgrave*, *The Diplomat*, *Fulcrum*, and *Asialink*.

Cleo Anne A. Calimbahin is Professor of Political Science specializing in elections, corruption, and democracy studies in the Department of Political Science and Development Studies at De La Salle University, Manila (DLSU). She completed her PhD at the University of Wisconsin-Madison as a Fulbright Fellow. Dr Calimbahin was a Research Associate with RAND, a Visiting Scholar at Stanford's Asia-Pacific Research Center (APARC), the Global South Scholar in Residence at the Graduate Institute of International and Development Studies (IHEID) in Geneva, and a Visiting Research Fellow for the Institute of Developing Economies (IDE-JETRO) in Japan. Dr Calimbahin provides technical assistance and research to international organizations and foundations. She is currently the Chair of the Department of Political Science and Development Studies, DLSU and a Social Weather Stations (SWS) board member.

Rizza Kaye Cases is Assistant Professor at the Department of Sociology, College of Social Sciences and Philosophy, University of the Philippines Diliman. She obtained her PhD in Sociology and Social Research from the University of Trento, Italy in 2018. Her research interests include migration studies, sociology of health and illness, social network analysis, social capital, and relational and comparative sociology. Her methodological works focus on the innovative applications of network methods in understanding migration processes and outcomes. Apart from migration research, she is also engaging in collaborative works such as the multi-country survey research project on trust in science and scientists and qualitative content analyses of social media groups of various genetic disorders and conditions.

Jean Encinas-Franco is Professor and Assistant Chair of the Department of Political Science, University of the Philippines Diliman. Her research interests are on gender and politics, and the politics of international migration. Her work on gender and politics has been published in various local and international journals. Some of her recent publications include "Filipino Women's Substantive Representation in Electoral Politics", a chapter in the book *Substantive Representation of Women in Asian Parliaments* and "Migrant Filipino Nurses: Gendered Nationalism and Ontological (In)Security during the COVID-19 Pandemic", a chapter in *Nurse Migration in Asia: Emerging Patterns and Policy Response*. Before she entered the academe, she worked at the Senate of the Philippines, where she was Director III of the Senate Economic Planning Office. In 2022, she received an honourable mention award in the category of the Feminist from the Global South Award of the International Studies Association (ISA).

Bianca Ysabelle Franco holds a master's degree in sociology from the University of the Philippines Diliman and formerly served as a research associate at Ateneo de Manila University's Development Studies Program, focusing on human rights, deliberative democracy, and conflict studies. Her written contributions have been featured on prominent academic blogs and news platforms worldwide. In March 2023, she co-authored a chapter titled "Anticriminality and Democracy in Southeast Asia" in the book *Regional Identities in Southeast Asia: Contemporary Challenges, Historical Fractures*.

Jan Robert R. Go is Associate Professor of Political Science at the University of the Philippines Diliman. He is also the President of the Philippine Political Science Association (2023–25). He received his PhD in political theory from Central China Normal University in Wuhan, China in 2022. He is interested in local politics and decentralization in the Philippines, urban and rural grassroots politics, the construction of power, participation theory, and Chinese domestic politics.

Luie Tito Guia is a former election commissioner in the Philippines, having served in the Commission on Elections (COMELEC) until 2 February 2020 after completing a seven-year term of office. He is currently a Senior Professional Lecturer at the Tañada-Diokno School of Law and the Department of Political Science and Development Studies of De La Salle University, Manila. He is also a Professorial Lecturer and a member of the Constitutional Law Committee of the Philippine Judicial Academy. Recently, he co-founded Democratic Insights Group Inc., a non-profit organization to promote competitive and voter-centred approach to elections. He now shares his knowledge and experience on election processes and right to political participation. He obtained his Bachelor of Arts in Political Science (1986) and Bachelor of Laws (1991) degrees from the University of the Philippines.

Ma. Diosa Labiste is Associate Professor in the Department of Journalism of the College of Mass Communication, University of the Philippines Diliman. A former community journalist, she earned her Doctor of Philosophy (DPhil) from the University of Birmingham in the United Kingdom, with a focus on media, culture, and society. Her latest work are the book chapters, "Punitive Populism and Disinformation as Legacies of Duterte" and "Critical Incidents and Auto Analysis: Photojournalists' Introspection while Covering the Drug War in the Philippines", published in 2023 and 2021 respectively. She has co-authored a book on land reform, *Stories of Struggles* (2018), and had written book chapters and journal articles on journalism, disinformation and hate speech, and the COVID-19 infodemic. In 2021, she co-wrote and edited the book *COVID-19 Journals*, on women's experiences during the first year of the COVID-19 pandemic in the Philippines.

Ruth R. Lusterio-Rico is Professor of Political Science and Dean of the College of Social Sciences and Philosophy (CSSP) at the University of the Philippines Diliman. She served as Chair of the Department of

Political Science from November 2010 to October 2013 and as Associate Dean for Academic Affairs of CSSP from July 2017 to August 2023. She obtained her PhD in political science from the University of the Philippines Diliman. Her research interests are environment and politics, policymaking, indigenous peoples' rights, and migration. Professor Lusterio-Rico was formerly a Visiting Professor/Researcher at the Department of Political Science and Center for East Asian Studies, University of Montreal, Quebec, Canada.

Cherry Ann D. Madriaga holds a PhD in international development studies from the National Graduate Institute for Policy Studies in Tokyo, Japan. Her research primarily focuses on maritime security, disaster risk, environment, and other policy issues. She is co-host of the *Usapang Econ* podcast and has tackled issues on micro, small, and medium enterprises, agriculture, and land reclamation.

Charmaine Misalucha-Willoughby is Associate Professor in the Department of International Studies at De La Salle University. She is a Nonresident Fellow at Carnegie China and at Agora Strategy, the Senior Editor of *Asian Politics & Policy (Wiley)*, and Co-Editor of *Bandung: Journal of the Global South (Brill)*. Her work on the Philippines' conception of international order appeared in the July 2023 issue of *International Affairs*. Outside academia, she is on the Board of Trustees of the Foundation for the National Interest and a member of the Friedrich Ebert Stiftung Asia-Pacific's Asia Strategic Foresight Group. Her areas of specialization are alliances, maritime security, security cooperation, and critical international relations theory. She received her PhD from the S. Rajaratnam School of International Studies at the Nanyang Technological University in Singapore.

Jan Carlo Punongbayan is Assistant Professor at the University of the Philippines School of Economics (UPSE). He earned his PhD from UPSE in 2021, where he also graduated *summa cum laude* and valedictorian in 2009 and was awarded the José Encarnación Jr. Award for Excellence in Economics and the Gerardo P. Sicat Award for Best Undergraduate Thesis. He previously worked at the Securities and Exchange Commission, the World Bank Office in Manila, the FEU

Public Policy Center, and the National Economic and Development Authority. His current research interests are macroeconomics, Philippine economic history, and education economics. Jan Carlo writes a weekly economics column for Rappler.com. He is also co-host of the Usapang Econ podcast. His first book, *False Nostalgia: The Marcos "Golden Age" Myths and How to Debunk Them*, was published by Ateneo University Press in February 2023.

1

Introduction: Change and Continuity Narratives in the Philippines from Duterte to Marcos Jr.

Aries A. Arugay, Jean Encinas-Franco, and Justin Keith A. Baquisal

> *Since 2016, the Philippines underwent profound policy changes under the leadership of firebrand and populist leader Rodrigo Duterte. Within the span of six years, these sea changes had widespread ramifications for the country's democratic regime as well as economic and social conditions that include a bloody war on drugs, a massive terrorist attack in Mindanao, a pivot away from orthodox foreign policies, a gripping global pandemic, and economic hardship, among others. Side by side with these changes are the reinforcement of strongman rule, militarized governance, and dynastic dominance in the political sphere of Asia's oldest democracy. This chapter introduces this edited volume by discussing the three*

narratives that currently describe the state of Philippine state and society since Duterte took power: games, changes, and fears. Games represent the continuity of elite competition and collusion at the expense of the public welfare and the difficulty to assert the republic's national interest given the superpower rivalry between the United States and China. On the other hand, the changes brought about by Duterte's populist playbook have further weakened institutions and perniciously polarized society. This in turn generated multiple fears of Duterte's legacies of autocratic politics, militarization, social violence, and economic uncertainty given the advent of the Marcos Jr. administration.

Keywords: Duterte; democracy; Marcos Jr.; political change; Philippines

INTRODUCTION

Since 2016, the Philippines underwent profound policy and political changes under the leadership of firebrand and populist leader Rodrigo Duterte. These include major modifications in the country's foreign policy through a more accommodationist stance towards China while undermining the military alliance with the United States. Beyond this foreign policy shift, Duterte has also instigated major assaults on the Philippines' liberal and democratic institutions and the public sphere. His populist rhetoric mobilized a broad political coalition that directly attacked the opposition, independent media, and civil society. The country's major media network was deprived of a franchise to operate, a Supreme Court Chief Justice was removed from office, Duterte's political opponents were incarcerated, and political dissidents and critics were labelled as communists and terrorists. By all metrics of democratic quality, the Philippine democratic regime underwent further erosion under the Duterte administration.[1]

Without the benefit of hindsight, the rise of Duterte was welcomed by the country's elites and masses. Similar with other populist strongmen such as Hugo Chávez, Thaksin Shinawatra, Recep Tayyip Erdogan, Victor Orban, Donald Trump, among others, Duterte's capture of presidential power at the outset was a welcome change given the excesses and limitations of the Philippine liberal-democratic regime brought by the inspirational people power revolution of 1986.[2] There was no umbrella coalition of political forces that could have effectively prevented Duterte's electoral victory. On the contrary, the Duterte era in Philippine politics ushered a swift and rapid concentration of power within the presidency unmatched since the martial law period. With supermajority support in the legislature, Duterte was able to pass draconian policies, pounce the opposition, and had the fortunate timing of appointing critical positions in the judiciary and independent constitutional bodies that were supposed to safeguard democracy and the rule of law.[3] The results of the 2019 midterm elections for national and local political positions revealed Duterte's domineering position in the political arena as the opposition failed to secure a seat in the twenty-four-member Senate, an institution historically known as a check to presidential power.[4]

As the country entered a critical juncture with the May 2022 national elections, the legacies of the Duterte administration underwent an informal referendum from the Filipino electorate. The national campaign centred on whether Duterte's mode of governance and political style should be continued or not. Among the major presidential candidates, the tandem of Ferdinand Marcos Jr., the son and namesake of the country's late dictator, and Sara Duterte, President Duterte's scion, committed to continuing the changes Duterte has started. On the other hand, leading opposition candidate and Vice President Leni Robredo promised to recalibrate Philippine democracy to its more liberal-democratic version by reversing the country's democratic regression. In the end, the elections delivered a majority mandate to Marcos Jr. as president and Sara Duterte as vice president, an electoral outcome unseen since Marcos Sr. got re-elected in the 1969 presidential elections. History for the Philippines has indeed come full circle.

This edited volume is situated within this peculiar context. It analyses the policy legacies of the entire Duterte administration (2016–22) to the country's society and politics on relevant themes such as economic policy, party politics, foreign policy, civil-military relations, civil society, social media, national security, and others. Second, it discusses the implications of the 2022 Philippine elections and the victory of the Marcos-Duterte alliance to the country's democracy and provides an evidence-based examination of the new government's policies and agenda. This project both looks back by examining the Duterte administration and looks forward by providing some insights into the continuities and changes in the country during the early part of Marcos Jr. administration.

The introductory chapter of this volume sets the tone for the interrelated narratives depicting the state of Philippine politics and society since Duterte took power in 2016. The *game* narrative represents the continuity of both elite competition and/or collusion that has defined the country's contemporary political landscape. The games played by dynastic and oligarchic elites have reinforced their dominance, narrowing the space for alternative leadership, opposition figures, and even civil society. They can be seen in the three electoral cycles (2016, 2019, and 2022) where the Duterte and Marcos dynasties captured state power with overwhelming mandates. On the one hand, it demonstrated the resilience of electoral democracy (see Table 1.1) in the Philippines. Unlike other Southeast Asian countries, elections remain the sole legitimate means of conferring legitimacy to political leaders in the country. However, political science scholarship also cautioned that excessive reliance on elections (irrespective of their quality and integrity) and majoritarianism can also erode other important elements of a democratic regime such as human rights, rule of law, and pluralism.[5] Marcos Jr. represents the third progeny of a former president to become the country's highest political leader in the Philippines with Sara Duterte posing perhaps to be the fourth. To a certain extent, the country's democratic regime might as well be a "hereditary republic".

Apart from the games at the domestic level, this narrative can also be extended in the foreign policy front as the country is caught in the intensifying rivalry between the United States and China in the Indo-Pacific region. This superpower contest has far-reaching repercussions on small powers like the Philippines. Foreign policy "pendulum swings" have occurred within a short period of time with President Duterte's pivot to China and Marcos Jr.'s embrace of the United States. How the country traverses this international game is both a function of domestic politics within its elites, bureaucracy, and even the public. But the US-China rivalry will also have consequences for the Philippines as it deals with several political, security, and economic challenges.[6]

The second narrative of *change* is the outcome of Duterte's campaign promise that has captivated the Filipino public. However, many did not anticipate how rapid and deep these changes are. His populist playbook has further weakened institutions and perniciously polarized society. Duterte's legacies were quite clear. By engaging in a multifront war against illegal drug addicts, terrorists, communists, and civil society, the country saw a return to violence. Duterte also deeply entrenched the military in policymaking and implementation with a heavily militarized cabinet that securitized issues, including the COVID-19 pandemic response.[7] The disinformation that propped his legitimacy but also undermined social cohesion and collective memory was rigorously implemented by outsourced agents of fake news. These changes are now heavily woven into the nation's socio-political fabric as Duterte maintained high popularity ratings unseen in post-martial law Philippines.[8]

Finally, the narrative of *fear* resonates deeply given the political succession occasioned by the 2022 national elections with the restoration of the Marcos dynasty at the zenith of power. The sources of the fears stem from the fact that Marcos Jr. campaign platform revolved around reinforcing Duterte's policies. The appointments of Duterte allies and supporters further solidify his alliance with Sara Duterte, the inheritor of Duterte's strongman legacies. But fear also represents strategic, economic, and political uncertainty emanating from the country's weak economy, polarized society, and weakened institutions.[9] Will the Filipino majority that provided a very strong mandate to the Marcos-Duterte government prove themselves correct in entrusting the custodianship of the nation to the two most powerful political dynasties in the country? Or will the Philippines enter another vicious downward political and economic spiral and deprive itself again of realizing its supposed potential and free itself from being known as "Asia's greatest underachiever"?[10] The burden ultimately lies in the shoulders of the formidable Marcos-Duterte coalition to deliver on their promises for a better future for the Philippines.

GAMES: THE ENDURING DYNAMICS OF PHILIPPINE POLITICS

Since the fall of the Marcos dictatorship in 1986, there is a major political consensus that democracy is the "only game in town". Apart from this two-decade authoritarian interlude, the Philippines stayed with popular elections as the only means to confer procedural legitimacy to any government. Despite having more than a century of democratic elections, much is to be desired in terms of their freedom, fairness, competitiveness, and integrity. Comparatively, neighbouring countries like Indonesia with barely three decades of election experience, have better electoral integrity than the Philippines.[11] Even with the deficient nature of its elections, there is overwhelming voter turnout of its ballot exercises that could be the envy of mature democracies around the world. Of all eligible voters, 83 per cent participated in the 2022 national elections, a record-breaking turnout from the 2016 elections which had 82 per cent.[12]

In the Philippines, while electoral politics is a game skilfully mastered by the country's political class, it still has to be conducted within a competitive and minimally democratic framework. The 2016 national elections that catapulted Rodrigo Duterte to the presidency was a shock to the country's trajectory towards a more liberal-democratic regime. While emanating from a local political dynasty, Duterte's image, idiosyncrasies, and political style veered from the usual stereotype of the Philippine chief executive, characteristics that attracted the electorate enough to make him the first president to come from Mindanao.[13] In many ways, it was a rebuke of an unresponsive and insensitive government that did not allow democracy to work for the ordinary Filipino.

Despite not getting a majority, Duterte secured a convincing victory with an estimated 16.6 million of the 44 million votes cast for president (see Table 1.1). With only an almost moribund party and support from a handful of local oligarchs, he propped a presidential bid against candidates with extensive national political experience, solid political pedigree, and the state machinery from the outgoing administration. His tough image, no-nonsense posturing, and sheer political will seemed sufficient for Filipinos desperate for leadership with a vision.[14] And in Philippine politics, timing is everything.

TABLE 1.1
Vote Share of Leading Presidential Candidates in the 2016 and 2022 Presidential Elections

2016 Elections		2022 Elections	
Presidential Candidate	Vote Share	Presidential Candidate	Vote Share
DUTERTE, Rodrigo	39%	MARCOS, Ferdinand Jr.	58%
ROXAS, Mar	23%	ROBREDO, Leni	28%
POE, Grace	21%	PACQUIAO, Manny	7%
BINAY, Jejomar	13%	DOMAGOSO, Isko Moreno	4%
SANTIAGO, Miriam	3%	Others	3%

The conventional wisdom on Philippine politics is that "outsiders" like Duterte have fewer barriers to entry given the lack of strong representative institutions that filter political competition and ensure leadership recruitment conducive for policy continuity and stability. Political parties, particularly, are neither credible nor cohesive enough, to organize politics, offer meaningful political alternatives, and temper radical dispositions. Instead, this extremist brand of politics is immediately thrown into the populace for their consideration. Moreover, programmatic vision and shared principles are not the glue that holds political elites together. They are instead attracted to patronage and particularistic factors that usually end up with corruption and abuse of authority. These insights on electoral politics were first established almost six decades ago and reinforced by new research of political scientists.[15] The enduring qualities of the game played by Filipino political elites are equally fascinating from a scholarly perspective and disturbing for a supposedly experienced democratic country.

Some expected that Duterte and his campaign for change would entail revising the rules of the political game of Philippine democracy. After all, similar initiatives from other populist leaders were successful in redistributing power through, for example, constitutional change.[16] Instead of disrupting the political status quo, Duterte did the opposite by reinforcing dynastic politics. Similar to previous presidents, he started to build his own powerful political dynasty and even revived the political careers of other dynasties by including them in his coalition. Perhaps unintentionally, the populist leader who promised change is ironically the president who became the catalyst for the "cartelization" of dynasties in the Philippines.

The outcome of the 2019 midterm elections, with the embarrassing defeat of the political opposition in the Senate elections in particular, clearly showed the enduring dynastic character of Philippine politics. Not only was it a convincing referendum on the legitimacy of Duterte's government, but it also showed the political power of his daughter, Sara Duterte. Her alliance with the Marcos dynasty as well as former president Gloria Macapagal-Arroyo became the dominating force in the Philippine political arena.[17]

The Duterte father-daughter combo also contributed a huge deal in paving the road for the restoration of the Marcos dynasty through a mix of deliberate actions. Rodrigo Duterte conditioned the mind of his coalition as well as the Filipino public that the Marcos dictatorship was a glorious era in Philippine history. Duterte's strongman proclivities made this type of leadership palatable to a supposedly pro-democracy public. By presidential fiat, he allowed the burial of Marcos Sr. in the National Heroes Cemetery that symbolically redeemed the dictator's sins against the republic.[18] In the end, Duterte boosted the political stock of the Marcoses and made it easy for them to recapture state power.

The 2022 election cycle, however, revealed the hubris of some dynastic elites in believing that they have full control over political succession. Rodrigo Duterte's original plan was for Sara to succeed him. Through a combination of internal dynamics within the Duterte dynasty and the successful pact-making between Marcos Jr. and Sara Duterte to promiscuously share power, the 2022 elections seemed to have been a foregone conclusion even before its campaign period even started. By deciding to settle as vice-presidential candidate, the other Duterte agreed to form a "dynasty cartel" and handed the presidency back to the Marcoses on a silver platter.[19] For the first time since democracy was restored in 1986, the winning president and vice president secured a majority mandate from the Filipino electorate (see Table 1.1). After more than 120 years of existence and almost twenty-five years of contemporary democratic experience, the country has a Marcos again as its president. Politics may change but dynasties are forever in the Philippines.

CHANGES: THE DANGEROUS LEGACIES OF RODRIGO DUTERTE

For better or worse, presidents after the 1986 Philippine "People Power" revolution tried and failed to meaningfully transform the trajectory of Philippine politics. General-turned-president Fidel Ramos (1992–97) failed to secure charter change to prolong his term. The populist Joseph Estrada (1997–2001) was ousted in another EDSA people power uprising. The Machiavellian Gloria Arroyo (2001–10) held on to power for nine years—the longest of any post-democratization presidency—but never enjoyed popular support, which sidetracked her agenda to that of political survival. Benigno Aquino III (2010–16), whose liberal-reformist agenda was a breath of fresh air after the "lost decade of democracy" under Arroyo, saw his legacy demolished like a sandcastle on the beach—swept aside by the tidal wave of support for the tough-talking, openly illiberal, and human rights-hating Rodrigo Duterte in 2016. The liberal opposition did not win a single Senate seat in 2019. Filipinos voted in 2022—for the first time in thirty years—for a continuity ticket under the tandem of Ferdinand Marcos Jr. and Sara Duterte as president and vice president, respectively.

In hindsight, there is now little doubt that the Duterte presidency was an "electoral earthquake" and that the last six years had been a series of aftershocks shaping the state of Philippine democracy, its foreign policy, and its domestic politics.[20] That Duterte was a maverick was obvious from the start. As a candidate, he promised this presidency will be "bloody because we'll order the killing of all criminals, drug-users, and drug lords" in what could be characterized as an "order over law" approach.[21] He also called then US President Barack Obama a "son of a whore", going off in lengthy diatribes against US colonial mentality while praising China and Russia, which are historically distrusted by Manila's bureaucrats and political elite.

What is more consequential, however, is that Duterte managed to make his brand "stick": he "ended his six-year presidential term in June 2022 with the highest late-term approval rating among Philippine presidents in recent history" and uncertainties surrounding US-Philippine relations have never been exorcised despite the changing of the guard.[22] Democratic civil-military relations also continue to deteriorate, with many retired security officials being appointed in key positions and "confidential and intelligence funds" becoming more commonplace in the executive branch's budget allocations. Indeed, as Deinla and Dressel argue, the Duterte administration was a "rapture" in Philippine politics.[23] We posit that while much of this is due to Duterte's *sui generis* policy agenda, Philippine politics was transformed because Duterte created structural conditions that allowed his legacies to be resilient and gain longevity. Of note here are his attacks on media institutions, empowerment of alternative and openly partisan media (a process dubbed as the "Fox News-ification of Philippine media"), co-optation of favourable civil society groups, and the politicization of the security establishment.[24]

From Careening to Democratic Backsliding

There is broad consensus that the Duterte presidency was a period of democratic backsliding for the Philippines, particularly on civil-political liberties and limits of executive power. Various indices from Freedom House to Varieties of Democracy saw the Philippines under Duterte decline on the liberal aspects of liberal democracy.[25] Notably, there were significant declines in the country's human rights observance, freedom of the press and expression, rule of law, and the efficacy of its guardrails against executive concentration of power. All these aspects of democracy were steadily and gradually eroded over time. Duterte, however, was not the first Philippine post-democratization president to attack the press or to try to break free from institutional checks and balances. What made him a critical juncture in Philippine post-1986 history was that he was the first to systematically attack liberalism as a political credo and his shift in priorities:

> The novelty of Duterte is not so much in his illiberal approach to politics but his exclusive focus on the goal of state-building fundamentals (e.g., public order, infrastructure, and services) over a values-based agenda (e.g. human rights and anti-corruption) that previous administrations have not openly challenged. As the Philippines enters its critical period

of economic take-off, the reality is that it is beginning to confront more questions of "stateness"—levels of street crime, the presence of vital infrastructure, and issues of social services—which precisely reinforce the logic of Duterte—over high-brow, values-based reformism.[26]

But as Ding and Slater argue, democracy is not an institutional monolith: some aspects are more prone to backsliding than others.[27] When comparing the Duterte administration in historical perspective, Baquisal and Arugay argue, "Varieties of Democracy data show that the Philippines is not autocratizing or backsliding if based on the Electoral Democracy Index, but it has shown a severe erosion of civil rights using the Liberal Democracy Index, indicating that democracies components erode asymmetrically. Electoral quality has remained the same under Duterte, whilst civil society and rights-based indicators of democratic quality have severely worsened." The same holds true for Freedom House. The Philippines' political rights and electoral democracy scores under Duterte were not significantly different under Arroyo—a presidency that presided over the so-called "lost decade of democracy" where indicators merely stagnated or "careened". The Philippines' scores on the Liberal Democracy Index, however, significantly differed between the two, making Duterte *sui generis* in terms of new lows for liberalism in the Philippines (see Table 1.2). In the same vein, Duterte's economic development planning and migration policies were not as singularly revolutionary as his pet policies on law and order, foreign policy, and defence. Democracy in the Philippines took a beating under Duterte, but it is worth explaining how, in what form, and to what extent.

In many ways, Duterte's popular appeal sharpened conceptual tensions between two pillars of democracy: vertical accountability—those relating to direct popular mandate—and horizontal accountability or the restraints on concentrations of power, particularly in the executive. But with such significant attacks on liberal components of democracy in the Philippines, more scholars have now labelled the Philippines as "backsliding" rather than merely "careening" or muddling through an electoral democracy wrought with many defects. This volume also highlights the indirect ways in which electoral competitiveness may even erode residually from attacks on civil liberties, such as from the drug war and the militarization of the civilian government.

TABLE 1.2
Philippine Democracy Scores through the Years

	Freedom House		Varieties of Democracy	
	Political Rights	Civil Liberties	Electoral Democracy Index	Liberal Democracy Index
2004			0.497	0.36
2005			0.476	0.355
2006			0.475	0.352
2007			0.473	0.357
2008			0.472	0.358
2009			0.473	0.359
2010			0.531	0.413
2011			0.558	0.439
2012			0.558	0.439
2013			0.554	0.435
2014	26	37	0.552	0.433
2015	26	37	0.553	0.432
2016	27	38	0.518	0.368
2017	27	36	0.506	0.346
2018	27	35	0.483	0.317
2019	26	35	0.454	0.297
2020	25	34	0.425	0.284
2021	25	31	0.436	0.28
2022	25	30	0.431	0.283
Change (2015 vs 2022)	−1	−7	−0.122	−0.149
Change (2004 vs 2022)			−0.066	−0.077

Source: Compiled by the authors.

At the same time, Duterte's "authoritarian allure" should be contextualized in terms of the substance of his policies: his infrastructure spending spree known as "Build, Build, Build", his War on Drugs, and what surveys show to be a consistent historical demand for strong executive leadership in a country often characterized in the literature as having a weak state and a strong society.[28] More than any lofty ideal, Duterte's unsuccessful pitch to amend the Philippine constitution to transition from a unitary to a federal form of government was also anchored in the concrete idea of fiscal and political decentralization to fund basic services. This volume evaluates changes brought about by Duterte's style of governance and the substance of his policy agenda that deviated from the status quo.

Structural and Policy Changes

Much has been said of "Dutertismo"—the melange of leadership style and policies that made Duterte the maverick that he is—as a form of "performative populism". While true, there also needs to be a deeper understanding of the substance of his political agenda. Duterte's "authoritarian project" is a *programmatic* agenda; one that will reverberate beyond his presidency.[29] It goes beyond individual misogynistic statements and inflammatory rhetoric. For example, the legacy of the drug war has reinforced longstanding cultures of impunity and vertical violence between the Philippine state and its citizens, but also took them to new heights unprecedented in recent decades.[30]

Chief among the Duterte presidency's legacy is the securitization of governance in the Philippines. This took a myriad of forms under his tenure, including the appointment of retired security sector personnel in civilian leadership posts and the penchant for coercion-heavy rule even when it was inappropriate, such as during the COVID-19 pandemic.[31] In making the security sector so critical to the country's governance, Duterte's legacy stands to undo decades of efforts since 1986 to put the military back in the barracks.[32] Presently, the military continues to be a key backer of the Duterte family and an institution torn in its loyalties between the allied but ultimately rival Duterte and Marcos families, not to mention to the Constitution and the people. Only time will tell whether political elites can maintain civilian supremacy over the military and police forces; after all, the Philippine military is now consistently one of the most trusted government agencies, while the Supreme Court and the legislature continue to be perceived negatively.[33]

Despite Duterte being the most popularly supported president in the Philippines post-democratization history, the irony was that he increasingly relied on non-elected elements to form his elite coalition. This led to another major change in Philippine politics: the diversification of elite composition. Many ascendant elites—be they in the opposition and the ruling Marcos-Duterte dynastic cartel—did not come from the ranks of oligarchs and entrenched political families. Duterte loyalists such as his former aide and his former police chief topped the 2019 senatorial elections, besting even traditional political dynasties. While the Liberal Party lost again in the 2022 elections, it undoubtedly found a rationale for a rejuvenation and return to the grassroots. The electoral campaign of development lawyer-turned-politician Maria Leonor "Leni" Robredo proved that the popular yearning for liberalism was down but not out, raking in 30 per cent of the popular vote on election day despite starting only at 7 per cent preference in the pre-election polls.

This edited volume discusses emerging political actors who were the main characters in the struggle for democracy under Duterte. The chapters cover actions by security personnel-turned-politicians, social media influencers, state functionaries, and the democratic pushback from community organizers, liberal-reformists, and advocates holding the line against outright authoritarian takeover. Philippine politics today continues to experience a polarizing struggle between two extreme political persuasions, but the players of the game are more diverse than ever.

Another notable change brought about by Duterte was his widely unpopular rapprochement with China and virulent anti-Americanism. Duterte's presidency was a diplomatic coup handed to China. At many times in his presidency, Duterte threatened to review the 1951 Mutual Defense Treaty, cancel the Visiting Forces Agreement, and pledged to join China and Russia "against the world". However, Duterte was less successful in this endeavour, with much of his foreign policy being undone by his successor Ferdinand Marcos Jr. in the first year of his presidency.[34] The public's distrust of China and the bureaucracy's historic working-level ties to the United States proved to be robust ballasts against a strategic reorientation of the Philippines. Duterte's China policy proves that populism has its limits and the people's support is not unconditional.

But to be fair, the "China question" was something that was bound to be confronted by any Philippine president given the middle kingdom's growing economic clout. Even before Duterte, China was on track to be the Philippines' largest trading partner.[35] The problem, however, was that Duterte's answer was to use "independent foreign policy" as a rhetorical cover for what was essentially a move into China's strategic orbit. This cost Duterte political capital and became a defining political divide between him and the Marcoses. Yet, there is reason to believe that US-Philippine relations will never be the same again. Duterte's anti-Americanism became a lightning rod for historic grievances from strange bedfellows composed of the radical Left, Duterte's supporters keen on justifying his policy, and business interests who perceive the future economic gravity of the country to lean towards Beijing rather than Washington.[36] Some politicians—driven by China's growing investments in their provinces—have imbibed Duterte's talking points. In this context, the Philippines has become an important case study for how great power competition today permeates developing countries' national and subnational politics from aid support, defence and security, economics, and even elections.

From Disinformation to Influence Operations

Another important development under Duterte was a two-pronged assault on the information and civic education ecosystem: the proliferation of disinformation-driven polarizing rhetoric in politics and the assault on traditional media. Disinformation, or the use of false, incomplete, or misleading information, has been closely linked to Duterte's electoral campaign in 2016 and his popularity-retention strategy while in office. Numerous studies show that disinformation networks in the Philippines propagated pro-Duterte content and attacked opposition figures.[37] In this sense, disinformation is as much a coercive tool for Duterte, in that it makes civic space toxic for pluralism of thought, as is merely a vote-getting tool.

Critically, Duterte made good on his promise to curtail what he portrayed as oligarch-controlled traditional media. In 2020, his allies in Congress voted to not renew the franchise of ABS-CBN, one of the country's largest television networks which was last shut down when Ferdinand Marcos Sr. declared martial law in 1972.[38] The Philippines has long been at an impasse: it is historically one of the deadliest places for journalists in the world, but it also has an active media role in "fiscalizing" politicians. Duterte's unprecedented move against ABS-CBN sent a chilling effect down the spine of media networks to tone down criticism of the government or be forced to close shop.

But Duterte did not stop at just neutralizing traditional media. His political machinery also expanded to co-opt social media content creators. Beginning in mid-2019, many of the pro-Duterte Facebook pages and YouTube channels rebranded their usernames claiming to be "news", "live", and "TV" channels, "signalling an intent to eventually replace traditional media as sources of information".[39] For this reason, fact-checking has increasingly been salient under Duterte to keep up with the swell of disinformation that has carved out a critical place in political discourse.

Finally, Duterte's pivotal legacy has also been the politicization of the information ecosystem, which is not all about disinformation. Rather, there has been a growth in the lucrative industry of political punditry catering *specifically* to Duterte's supporters. Much of this is due to monetization of content on social media and Filipinos' own world-leading usage of social media when measured by the number of hours spent per day.[40] Many of his supporters gained a livelihood from being pro-administration commentators and were critical in Duterte's strategy of perpetual campaigning of agitation against the opposition, including disclosures of unsubstantiated coup-plotting matrices and McCarthyist witch hunts against opposition figures by linking them to the opposition. Prominent social media talking heads such as Mocha Uson and Lorraine Badoy were appointed to high government posts. This transition from mere disinformation to broader political influence operations—the collection of information and their dissemination in pursuit of a competitive advantage—became the norm under Duterte and has transformed civic education in the Philippines.[41] Partisan political punditry, once made profitable, locks a country in a cycle of pernicious polarization.

Like any Machiavellian leader, Duterte's governance style—which had often been described as an "authoritarian project", "executive imperialism", or Dutertismo's "illiberalism"—was a product of both *virtu* (virtue) and *fortuna* (fortune), namely Duterte's own policies and the socio-political and historical milieu that he inherited and benefitted from without much effort. Coming in after years of "People Power fatigue" and resurgent authoritarian nostalgia, Duterte benefitted from the alignment of political stars.[42] Philippine politics is unlikely to be the same in the foreseeable future again.

FEARS: PORTENT OF THINGS TO COME OR DISCONTINUITIES?

The advent of the Duterte administration ushered in a "politics of fear" not felt since Ferdinand Marcos Sr.'s dictatorship. The war on drugs, the militarized COVID-19 response and resulting economic downturn, along with his pivot to China did not make a dent on his popularity. His occasional threat to declare martial law or a revolutionary government makes it clear that he has no qualms about democratic norms.[43] Yet, his approval and trust ratings at the end of his term was the highest among post-1986 presidents. The most potent indicator of this popularity is his daughter's victory as vice president in the 2022 elections. Its concomitant large support base among Filipinos provides reason that it can reverberate in the next administrations.

As the lynchpin of his administration, Duterte's violent drug war established his notoriety to his domestic critics and before the international community, including the United Nations. While the extra-judicial killings have been feared by those who became police targets, high public approval for the war on drugs further emboldened the administration, three years after Duterte assumed office.[44] The opposition's massive loss in the 2019 senatorial elections likewise suggests its weakness and the administration's victory in owning and winning the narrative against the drug war. Without a viable opposition, however, it will be difficult to address perennial problems of corruption, warlordism, and state capture that have characterized Philippine politics.

In responding to the COVID-19 pandemic, Duterte did not completely depart from his drug war strategy. By employing a militarized response to the pandemic, the prolonged lockdowns were justified, including an emergency power law that was deemed to have encroached on legislative power. By blaming the *pasaway* (hardheaded) citizens and threatening to shoot them, Duterte employed a war-like stance in addressing the pandemic, thereby further amplifying his authoritarian tendencies.[45] The aftermath of the pandemic yielded one of the country's biggest economic setbacks since 1946,[46] aided in no small part to excessive lockdowns resulting in business closures and job losses. While economic recovery seems to be promising at the beginning of 2023, massive inflation is feared to further bring down poverty levels.[47] If this is the case, then the much-vaunted goal to reach middle-income status, as stated in the current and previous development plans, may remain elusive.

Meanwhile, Duterte's penchant for silencing his critics by violent threats engendered a culture of fear and became his currency for stifling any means of dissent and seeking accountability on his administration's actions. But its impact has been far-reaching. For instance, the closure of the country's biggest network discussed above has transformed Filipinos viewing and information-seeking behaviour. More importantly, Philippine media's political economy structure has also been transformed by the shutdown. With the rise of unaccountable vloggers and a demoralized traditional media, one of the country's pillars of democracy may be facing a decline just like its counterparts in the rest of the world. This situation is unfortunate, as the country's democratization history would attest, the media plays an important role as an accountability mechanism, especially at crucial moments.

Duterte is not just notorious for his threats and violent rhetoric but also for his misogynist remarks against his critics. The hypermasculine, sexist, and misogynist rhetoric that marked his administration not only made headlines worldwide but have also earned him the moniker, "Trump of the East".[48] But one big casualty of his rhetoric is women's political participation. As Asia's first democracy, the Philippines boasts of having granted women the right to vote as early as 1937 and has been a forerunner in legislating gender equality laws since 1987. Nonetheless, in both 2019 and 2022 elections, only 20 per cent of candidates are women. If misogyny gets to be a norm in targeting political opponents, then women and sexual minorities may be further discouraged to join the political fray.

Aside from domestic issues, Duterte's pivot to China was a defining characteristic of his term. A small-town mayor, with an obvious lack of foreign policy experience, dared to turn back against the Philippine-US alliance. This significant shift was met with much alarm and criticisms, foremost of which are countries threatened by China's increased activities in the West Philippine Sea. At the same time, his decision to ignore the 2016 Arbitral Award was consistent with his disrespect of the rule of law. However, though this pivot was not necessarily supported by the military who is wary of Chinese encroachment on Philippine territory, others argue that Duterte's move was meant to court China's Belt and Road Initiative that can benefit much-needed Philippine infrastructure projects.[49] Though Marcos Jr. revitalized the country's military alliance with the United States, Russia's war in Ukraine has raised the spectre of China reclaiming Taiwan, thereby potentially ushering in a war practically at the country's doorsteps.

Arguably, Duterte's political style and legacy helped fuel the Marcoses' restoration project. When Duterte assumed power, many were surprised that thirty years after the much-celebrated democratic restoration in 1986, someone with authoritarian tendencies like Marcos Sr. was elected. It was then unsurprising that the Marcos Jr.–Sara Duterte's tandem won in 2022, as both the legacies of their fathers reinforced their electoral narrative. While it is too early to tell how the political arena will play out in the next few years, some of the fears identified in the discussion above may or may not be realized, depending on the extent to which vertical accountability initiatives can be successfully launched, and the realization of the tandem's promise to uplift the lives of Filipinos.

STRUCTURE OF THE BOOK

Following the introductory chapter that discusses the three main narratives that defined the country during the entirety of the Duterte administration (2016–22) into the early years of the Marcos Jr. government, the subsequent chapters probe into the specific policy legacies and other political dynamics within the country that shape the political, economic, and social conditions of the Philippines. The chapter authors are scholars and/or practitioners who come from different disciplinary backgrounds including political science, international relations, sociology, communication, economics, law, public policy, and development studies. The tie that binds all the contributors is the fact that they are Filipino specialists and are all based in Philippine academic institutions and research organizations.

Each chapter focuses on a particular policy area and examines the major contemporary developments as well as the policy changes and transformation that occurred since 2016. Unlike previously published scholarship on the same topic, this collection of chapters had the benefit of assessing the Duterte administration in its entirety. Moreover, the chapters also interrogate the future prospects of the country within each respective policy theme and identify main reform proposals and policy actions needed to generate better outcomes for the Philippine state and its society.

In Chapter 2, Jan Carlo Punongbayan examines the state of the Philippine economy under Duterte and his legacies for the Marcos Jr. administration. By and large, the Duterte administration continued the macroeconomic policies of the Aquino (2010–16) administration, enshrining the promise of policy continuity in Duterte's ten-point economic agenda. Punongbayan argues that the administration yielded mixed economic results, notably skyrocketing inflation—which was a non-issue under Aquino given consistently low rates in previous years—and presiding over a 50 per cent increase in the debt-to-GDP ratio before and after his presidency—from 40 per cent in 2016 to 60 per cent in 2022. Part of this can be attributed to Duterte's tax-and-spend economic priorities. Duterte deviated from Aquino's development strategy by pouring huge sums of money and debt into infrastructure spending but still fell below his own spending-to-GDP targets. That said, the Duterte administration presided over a period of expansion for the Filipino middle class and continued economic growth until 2020 which translated to unemployment and underemployment statistics reaching fourteen-year lows before the COVID-19 pandemic.

Despite his initial anti-elite rhetoric, the populist president has shown "a level of comfort to preserve the status quo he promised to meaningfully change". By tinkering with some welfare programmes like free tertiary education, limited universal healthcare, pension increases defying expert advice, and increasing salaries for military and uniformed personnel, his presidency avoided going deep into contentious social redistribution. For all his tough talk, Duterte presided over cosmetic changes in matters of social redistribution but did so in ways that still create serious fiscal problems for future presidential administrations. However, Punongbayan writes that the COVID-19 pandemic not only threw a wrench in Duterte's plans but also exposed the unsustainable aspects inherent in his economic policy to begin with. Agriculture, education, and reproductive health policies fell by the wayside while foreign direct investments decreased.

Chapter 3 focuses on the most pressing strategic issue of the country—the South China Sea (SCS). Charmaine Misalucha-Willoughby puts Duterte's pivot to China under the microscope to uncover one of its most critical consequences: the inability of the Philippine government to assert its territorial and maritime interests in the West Philippine Sea, a portion of the SCS belonging to the country by international law. This chapter argues that ironically, Duterte's strongman rhetoric was selective at best—brutish against the United States and yet defeatist and accommodationist towards China. Using discourse analysis, her chapter posits that the Duterte administration's disinformation strategy helped justify the inability of the country to leverage the favourable 2016 Arbitral Award in its dealings with China. This chapter not only provides a compelling account of Duterte's pivot to China but also shows that state-sponsored disinformation can be used to frame dangerous and myopic adventures in foreign policy.

National security policy and civil-military relations are the themes pursued by Julio S. Amador III and Deryk Matthew Baladjay in Chapter 4. Both security practitioners analysed the factors that drove Duterte's prioritization of national security, specifically its domestic dimensions. They pointed out his heavy reliance on retired generals de facto militarized his cabinet and therefore his government's national security policy. This was seen in his war fighting mode against what was identified as enemies of the state. Duterte's violent war on drugs, against terrorism, and vis-a-vis the communist insurgency entailed a heavy-handed approach that wreaked tremendous collateral damage and arguably, negative outcomes despite their popularity to the general public. They provide a glimpse of hope since early indications reveal that Marcos Jr.—by focusing more on external defense, demilitarizing security policy, and ending draconian measures that curtail civil liberties—may not necessarily follow the security policies of his predecessor.

Duterte also tried to tinker with the country's constitution and specifically, its political set-up, albeit a marked failure of his administration. His much-vaunted campaign promised to institute federalism-generated media mileage but fizzled out. It is this attempt that Maria Ela L. Atienza carefully examined in Chapter 5. Among others, she argues that the bid to change the charter failed due to several factors. She reasons that Duterte's lack of direction as to its specificities, his administration's top-down approach to the process, and economic problems at the national and regional levels may be exacerbated by a poorly conceptualized federalism arrangement. Ultimately, due to the country's weak political parties, Duterte's party mates and "supermajority" in both Houses of Congress did support his proposal. According to Atienza, this challenges the dominant view of Duterte's supposed strong leadership. Meanwhile, in contrast to Duterte, Marcos Jr. hardly focused on charter change as an electoral issue. Curiously, however, the House of Representatives, headed by his cousin, Speaker Martin Romualdez, endorsed constitutional change, focusing on economic provisions. Nonetheless, while a higher percentage (41 per cent) of Filipinos agree to charter change according to recent surveys, Atienza contended that a public information campaign is still crucial. During Marcos Jr.'s first year in office, attempts at charter change as noted by Atienza, suffer from similar constraints as those of Duterte's, foremost of which is the dismal post-pandemic economic picture.

In Chapter 6, Bianca Ysabelle E. Franco examines the micropolitics of Duterte's ultimate legacy—his bloody war on drugs. While extant accounts focus on the structural, policy, and institutional dimensions of this state-sponsored violence, this collection of in-depth and personal accounts allowed Franco to weave the narratives of the war's victims through the relatives and loved ones they left behind. Apart from the war's fatalities and the fear it conjured, this systematic purge of mostly the poor and marginalized members of Philippine society left widows and orphans who likewise became victims of stigma and other forms of social isolation and political exclusion. Franco reminds that the collateral damage of Duterte's drug war reflects the lingering reality that violence remains imprinted in the country's political culture and is less likely to be discontinued under the Marcos Jr. administration.

Disinformation in social media and the attempts to curb it through fact-checking was the focus of Ma. Diosa Labiste in Chapter 7. As a communication scholar and one of the founders of *tsek.ph*, a multi-sectoral civil society initiative that conducted fact-checking in the 2019 and 2022 elections, Labiste exposes the main contours of disinformation in the Philippines. Her chapter argues that a highly polarized social sphere coupled with state-sponsorship and toleration of fake news made fact-checking extremely challenging. Election-related disinformation focused on revising and white-washing the Marcos dictatorship, the "red-tagging" of prominent individuals and institutions as communist sympathizers, and hate speech towards the opposition. The chapter ends with a gloomy note that Duterte has left a systematized disinformation architecture that aided the electoral victory of the Marcos-Duterte coalition and further deepened political polarization in the country. Fact-checking must be strengthened in the succeeding elections at the very least but policy interventions that seek to improve media literacy and critical thinking among the populace should also be implemented.

In Chapter 8, Cleo Anne A. Calimbahin and Luie Tito F. Guia detail electoral initiatives that have not seen the light of day in the Duterte administration, from the bid to change the constitution, to pushing for overall electoral reforms such as strengthening political parties. In their account, the authors reason that the president was not interested in building political parties but was instead focused on creating parties supporting the administration. However, Calimbahin and Guia argue that the Bangsamoro Organic Law, approved under Duterte, was a step in the right direction and can be a model for future attempts to redesign national-level political institutions. Under the Marcos Jr. administration, the authors express "cautious optimism" given that the current head of the Commission on Elections seems to be open to civil society inputs to enhance the election body's capability in election management. Key amendments to the country's electoral code have also been filed in Congress, albeit moving at a snail's pace. Key recommendations include expanding the proportional representation system and abolishing the split-ticket voting rule for president and the vice-president.

Chapter 9 by Jan Robert R. Go discusses the Philippines' response to the COVID-19 pandemic as a case study for local governance. In the 2016 campaign trail, Duterte rallied the country to promises of federalism and decentralization. Being the first local mayor-turned-president in recent decades, Duterte was torn from the beginning between his populist-authoritarian reflexes and his vision of local government empowerment. Go writes that it is ironic that Duterte inevitably showed his centralizing tendencies full throttle after 2018 primarily because he governed like a local Philippine mayor who was accustomed to having many organs of the government directly under his command. First, local governments were increasingly subordinated to the national government beginning with the nationwide drug war that started in 2016 when there was immense pressure for local chief executives to comply and deliver body counts. Second, Duterte's immense popularity allowed him to exact compliance from local politicians even on matters that should have been within the purview of local governments according to the 1991 Local Government Code. Go cites the COVID-19 pandemic as a pivotal period that expanded the scope of the national government's emergency powers.

In Chapter 10, Ruth R. Lusterio-Rico underscores the Duterte administration's early promise to protect the environment but did not lead to concrete and beneficial outcomes in the end. The author claims that overall, the president was distracted by his focus on the drug war and did not really make a significant legacy in terms of environmental and climate change issues. Accordingly, the lifting of the mining permit moratorium, the lack of support for a pro-environment minister when the latter was rejected by the Commission on Appointments, coupled with reports of a rise in killings of environment defenders, prove this point. Like Duterte, Marcos Jr. has made token statements that he will address climate change but maintains the same stance on mining. With what seems to be a status quo even with the new administration, the author suggests that environmentalists and civil society organizations' role in exacting accountability on the government must be sustained.

In Chapter 11, Cherry Ann Madriaga evaluates human security and disaster response policies from Duterte to Marcos Jr., particularly the implementation of the Disaster Risk Reduction and Management Act. Climate change, extreme weather events, and natural hazards continually batter the Philippines across administrations. Duterte is no stranger to the importance of disaster response, having catapulted himself into the national spotlight when he was on ground-zero in Tacloban City after Typhoon Haiyan in 2013—an issue used in the 2016 presidential election to criticize the Aquino administration. Madriaga's chapter assesses the Duterte administration's handling of disaster response mechanisms and fund disbursement between 2016 and 2022, and several critical incidents such as the 2020 Taal Volcano eruption and the COVID-19 pandemic. Madriaga concludes that the Duterte administration has done little to move the needle on the consolidation of various government agencies handling disaster response, which often leads to coordination issues, turfing, policy incoherence, and response lags. Despite Duterte's urging, the Philippine legislature failed to pass a new Department of Disaster Resilience.

Chapter 12 focuses on how sexism and misogyny pervaded Duterte's politics and policies through disinformation. Jean Encinas-Franco argued that fake news had a multiplier effect in reinforcing gender stereotypes that marginalize Filipino women. Using case studies of female opposition politicians, Leila de Lima and Leonor "Leni" Robredo, who became the object of Duterte's misogynistic gaze, the chapter identified the nature of a very specific type of disinformation that focuses on gender. Apart from direct assaults on the opposition, Duterte also mobilized agents of disinformation that painted unfair, scathing, and harmful narratives against female political leaders brave enough to criticize the populist president. In her conclusion, Encinas-Franco recommends for critical policy interventions that can protect women and afford equal opportunities in the political arena.

As an important contributor to the country's socio-economic situation, international migration of Filipinos continues to play a vital role in both the Duterte and Marcos Jr. administrations. In Chapter 13, Bubbles Beverly Asor and Rizza Kaye Cases highlight that despite the common assumption of a radical shift in migration governance due to the COVID-19 pandemic, economic recession, and other supposed rupture-causing events, migration practices remain tethered to past programmes and policy positions. In giving substance to this argument, the authors explore government initiatives (bans, repatriations, health assessments) at the height of the pandemic, and the establishment of the Department of Migrant Workers—a newly created government agency that consolidates the migration functions that used to be scattered among other ministries. Among others, Asor and Cases argue that such interventions do not necessarily signify a marked or transformative change in terms of migration governance. Rather, such steps are incremental ones that have acquired the nature of taken-for-granted. Further, the authors point out that such practices will likely continue under the Marcos Jr. administration.

Notes

1. Sol Iglesias, "Violence and Impunity: Democratic Backsliding in the Philippines and the 2022 Elections", *Pacific Affairs* 95, no. 3 (2022): 575–93; Varieties of Democracy, "The V-Dem Dataset", 2023, https://v-dem.net/data/the-v-dem-dataset/.
2. Moses Naim, "The Dictator's New Playbook: Why Democracy Is Losing the Fight", *Foreign Affairs* 101, no. 1 (2022): 144–54.
3. Arjan Aguirre, "The Philippines in 2018: A Year of Disruption and Consolidation", *Philippine Political Science Journal* 40, nos. 1–2 (2019): 100–123.
4. Julio C. Teehankee and Yuko Kasuya, "The 2019 Midterm Elections in the Philippines: Party System Pathologies and Duterte's Populist Mobilization", *Asian Journal of Comparative Politics* 5, no. 1 (2020): 69–81.
5. Dan Slater, "Democratic Careening", *World Politics* 65, no. 4 (2013): 729–63; Dan Slater and Aries A. Arugay, "Polarizing Figures: Executive Power and Institutional Conflict in Asian Democracies", *American Behavioral Scientist* 62, no. 1 (2018): 92–106.
6. Renato Cruz de Castro, "The Philippines' Hedging between the United States and China: Can the Biden Administration Tip the Balance?" *Asia Policy* 28, no. 4 (2021): 115–23.
7. Aries A. Arugay, "Militarizing Governance: Informal Civil–Military Relations and Democratic Erosion in the Philippines", in *Asian Military Evolutions: Civil–Military Relations in Asia*, edited by Alan Chong and Nicole Jenne (Bristol: Bristol University Press, 2023), pp. 68–89.
8. Geoffrey M. Ducanes, Steven Rood, and Jorge Tigno, "Sociodemographic Factors, Policy Satisfaction, Perceived Character: What Factors Explain President Duterte's Popularity?" *Philippine Political Science Journal* 44, no. 1 (2023): 1–42.
9. Justin Keith A. Baquisal and Aries A. Arugay, "The Philippines in 2022: The 'Dance' of the Dynasties", in *Southeast Asian Affairs 2023*, edited by Thi Ha Hoang and Daljit Singh (Singapore: ISEAS – Yusof Ishak Institute, 2023), pp. 234–53.

10. Steven Rogers, "Philippine Politics and the Rule of Law", *Journal of Democracy* 15, no. 4 (2004): 111–25.
11. Max Grömping, "The Integrity of Elections in Asia: Policy Lessons from Expert Evaluations", *Asian Politics & Policy* 10, no. 3 (2018): 527–47.
12. Dwight de Leon, "Philippines Logs Record Voter Turnout for 2022 Polls", *Rappler*, 19 May 2022, https://www.rappler.com/nation/voter-turnout-philippines-2022-polls/.
13. Mark R. Thompson, "Bloodied Democracy: Duterte and the Death of Liberal Reformism in the Philippines", *Journal of Current Southeast Asian Affairs* 35, no. 3 (2016): 39–68.
14. Jonathan Miller, *Duterte Harry: Fire and Fury in the Philippines* (Melbourne: Scribe Publications, 2018).
15. Carl Lande, *Leaders, Factions and Parties: The Structure of Philippine Politics* (New Haven: Yale University, 1965); Allen Hicken, Edward Aspinall, and Meredith Weiss, eds., *Electoral Dynamics in the Philippines: Money Politics, Patronage and Clientelism at the Grassroots* (Singapore: National University of Singapore Press, 2019); Julio C. Teehankee and Cleo Anne A. Calimbahin, eds., *Patronage Democracy in the Philippines: Clans, Clients, and Competition in Local Elections* (Quezon City: Bughaw, 2022).
16. Maxwell A. Cameron, "Latin America's Left Turns: Beyond Good and Bad", *Third World Quarterly* 30, no. 2 (2009): 331–48.
17. Yuko Kasuya and Julio C. Teehankee, "Duterte Presidency and the 2019 Midterm Election: An Anarchy of Parties?" *Philippine Political Science Journal* 41, nos. 1–2 (2020): 106–26.
18. David G. Timberman, "Philippine Politics under Duterte: A Midterm Assessment", Carnegie Endowment for International Peace, 10 January 2019, https://carnegieendowment.org/2019/01/10/philippine-politics-under-duterte-midterm-assessment-pub-78091.
19. Aries A. Arugay, "The 2022 Philippine Elections: Like Father, like Daughter-te", *Fulcrum*, 17 November 2021, https://fulcrum.sg/the-2022-philippine-elections-like-father-like-daughter-te/.
20. Aries A. Arugay, "The Philippines in 2016: The Electoral Earthquake and Its Aftershocks", in *Southeast Asian Affairs 2017*, edited by Daljit Singh and Malcolm Cook (Singapore: ISEAS – Yusof Ishak Institute, 2017), pp. 277–96.
21. Patricia L. Viray, "Duterte Admits to Bloody Presidency If He Wins", *Philstar*, 21 February 2016, https://www.philstar.com/headlines/2016/02/21/1555393/duterte-admits-bloody-presidency-if-he-wins; Thomas Pepinsky, "Southeast Asia: Voting against Disorder", *Journal of Democracy* 28, no. 2 (2017): 120–31.

22. Sharmila Parmanand, "Democratic Backsliding and Threats to Human Rights in Duterte's Philippines", in *Populism and Human Rights in a Turbulent Era*, edited by Alison Brysk (United States: Edward Elgar Publishing, 2023), pp. 105–25.
23. Imelda Deinla and Björn Dressel, "Introduction: From Aquino II to Duterte (2010–2018): Change, Continuity – and Rapture", in *From Aquino II to Duterte (2010–2018): Change, Continuity – and Rapture*, edited by Imelda Deinla and Björn Dressel (Singapore: ISEAS – Yusof Ishak Institute, 2019), pp. 1–36.
24. Jasmin Lorch, "Elite Capture, Civil Society and Democratic Backsliding in Bangladesh, Thailand and the Philippines", *Democratization* 28, no. 1 (2021): 81–102; Mark R. Thompson, "Explaining Duterte's Rise and Rule: Penal Populist Leadership or a Structural Crisis of Oligarchic Democracy in the Philippines?" *Philippine Political Science Journal* 41, nos. 1–2 (2020): 5–31.
25. Varieties of Democracy, "The V-Dem Dataset"; Freedom House, *Freedom in the World 2022* (2022).
26. Lowell Bautista, "The Ones Who Don't Walk Away from the Philippines", in *Southeast Asian Affairs 2020*, edited by Malcolm Cook and Daljit Singh (Singapore: ISEAS – Yusof Ishak Institute, 2020), pp. 274–92.
27. Iza Ding and Dan Slater, "Democratic Decoupling", *Democratization* 28, no. 1 (2021): 63–80.
28. Matthew D. Ordoñez and Anthony L. Borja, "Philippine Liberal Democracy under Siege: The Ideological Underpinnings of Duterte's Populist Challenge", *Philippine Political Science Journal* 39, no. 2 (2018): 139–53.
29. Cleve Arguelles, "The Populist Brand Is Crisis: Durable Dutertismo amidst Mismanaged COVID-19 Response", in *Southeast Asian Affairs 2021*, edited by Daljit Singh and Malcolm Cook (Singapore: ISEAS – Yusof Ishak Institute, 2021), pp. 257–74.
30. Vicente L. Rafael, *The Sovereign Trickster: Death and Laughter in the Age of Duterte* (Durham: Duke University Press, 2021); Human Rights Watch, "Philippines: No Letup in Drug War under Marcos", 12 January 2023.
31. Baquisal and Arugay, "The Philippines in 2022: The 'Dance' of the Dynasties", pp. 234–53.
32. Terence Lee, "The Philippines: Civil-Military Relations, from Marcos to Duterte", *Oxford Research Encyclopedia of Politics* (2020), https://doi.org/10.1093/acrefore/9780190228637.013.1845.
33. Priam Nepomuceno, "AFP Gets Excellent Rating in Latest SWS Survey", Philippine News Agency, 23 January 2023.
34. Charmaine Misalucha-Willoughby, "The Philippines' Security Outlook", *RSIS Commentaries* 027-23 (2023).

35. World Integrated Trade Solution, "Philippines Trade Summary 2016", 2016, https://wits.worldbank.org/CountryProfile/en/Country/PHL/Year/2016/Summarytext.
36. Aries A. Arugay, "Fall from Grace, Descent from Power? Civil Society after Philippine Democracy's Lost Decade", in *From Aquino II to Duterte (2010–2018)*, pp. 285–308.
37. Rossine Fallorina, Jose Mari Hall Lanuza, Juan Gabriel Felix, Ferdinand Sanchez II, Jonathan Corpus Ong, and Nicole Curato, "From Disinformation to Influence Operations: The Evolution of Disinformation in Three Electoral Cycles", Internews, June 2023; Jonathan Corpus Ong, Rossine Fallorina, Jose Mari Hall Lanuza, Ferdinand Sanchez II, and Nicole Curato, "Parallel Public Spheres: Influence Operations in the 2022 Philippine Elections", *The Media Manipulation Case Book* (Internews and Harvard Kennedy School Shorenstein Center, 2022); Jonathan Corpus Ong and Ross Tapsell, "Demystifying Disinformation Shadow Economies: Fake News Work Models in Indonesia and the Philippines", *Asian Journal of Communication* 32, no. 3 (2022): 251–67.
38. Ross Tapsell, "Divide and Rule: Populist Crackdowns and Media Elites in the Philippines", *Journalism* 23, no. 10 (2022): 2192–207.
39. Aries Arugay and Justin Keith A. Baquisal, "Mobilized and Polarized: Social Media and Disinformation Narratives in the 2022 Philippine Elections", *Pacific Affairs* 95, no. 3 (2022): 549–73.
40. Rossine Fallorina et al., "From Disinformation to Influence Operations: The Evolution of Disinformation in Three Electoral Cycles".
41. Fatima Gaw, Jon Benedik A. Bunquin, Samuel I. Cabbuag, Jose Mari H. Lanuza, Noreen H. Sapalo, and Al-Habbyel B. Yusoph, "Political Economy of Covert Influence Operations in the 2022 Philippine Elections", Internews, 31 July 2023.
42. Aries A. Arugay and Dan Slater, "Polarization without Poles: Machiavellian Conflicts and the Philippines' Lost Decade of Democracy, 2000–2010", *The ANNALS of the American Academy of Political and Social Science* 681, no. 1 (2019): 122–36.
43. Bjorn Dressel and Cristina Regina Bonoan, "Duterte versus the Rule of Law", *Journal of Democracy* 30, no. 4 (2019): 134–48.
44. "Filipinos Give Thumbs Up to Duterte's 'Excellent' Drugs War: Poll", Reuters, 23 September 2019, https://www.reuters.com/article/us-philippines-drugs-idUSKBN1W803M.
45. Karl Hapal, "The Philippines' COVID-19 Response: Securitising the Pandemic and Disciplining the Pasaway", *Journal of Current Southeast Asian Affairs* 40, no. 2 (2021): 224–44.
46. Rajiv Biswas, "Philippines Economy Hit by Rising COVID-19 Wave", *S&P Global Market Intelligence*, 9 April 2021, https://www.spglobal.com/

marketintelligence/en/mi/research-analysis/philippines-economy-hit-by-rising-covid19-wave-apr21.html.

47. Cai U. Ordinario, "Inflation Seen to Hit Growth, Poverty Goal", *BusinessMirror*, 8 September 2021, https://businessmirror.com.ph/2021/09/08/inflation-seen-to-hit-growth-poverty-goal/.
48. Charlie Campbell, "Rodrigo Duterte: Trump of the East", *Time*, 12 May 2016, https://time.com/4327421/rodrigo-duterte-the-trump-of-the-east/.
49. Renato de Castro, "Preventing the Philippines from Pivoting toward China: The Role of the US–Japan Security Alliance", *Asian Journal of Comparative Politics* 8, no. 1 (2023): 381–99.

2

Much a Duterte about Nothing: Continuity, Complacency, and Crisis in the Philippine Economy (2016–23)

Jan Carlo Punongbayan

In 2016, President Rodrigo Duterte inherited an economy with years of steady growth, low inflation, a lower debt burden, an influx of investments, and robust consumer and business confidence. In some ways, the Duterte administration (2016–22) kept that momentum. But this period also saw the reversal of some of these beneficial macroeconomic outcomes, as evidenced by slowing growth, a spell of high inflation, the steady decline of foreign direct investments, and the deep recession wrought by the pandemic (exacerbated by Duterte's inept pandemic response). The subsequent Marcos Jr.

administration will have to contend with the deep economic scars left by the pandemic. But early signals suggest that Marcos Jr. is more interested in efforts to rehabilitate his family's image and rehash old programmes and policies of the late dictator, Marcos Sr.

Keywords: Philippine economy, economic policies, COVID-19 pandemic

The economic environment that prevailed during the Rodrigo Duterte administration (2016–22)—and extended into the early part of the succeeding Ferdinand Marcos Jr. administration—is largely the by-product of the cumulative economic reforms and momentum spurred by previous administrations, notably the Benigno Aquino III administration (2010–16). Based on all major macroeconomic indicators, Aquino III left a legacy of stability and growth. From 2010 to 2015, annual gross domestic product (GDP) grew at an average rate of 6.26 per cent—the highest average growth in a post-war administration since the time of former president Ramon Magsaysay. Meanwhile, inflation averaged 3.1 per cent, the lowest since the administration of Carlos P. Garcia.[1] The unemployment rate dropped from 8 per cent before Aquino III took office to 6.1 per cent right before he stepped down.

As for public finances, government revenues as a share of GDP rose from 13.4 per cent in 2010 to 15.8 per cent in 2015. The higher net revenues resulted in rare budget surpluses in 2013 and 2015. This, however, is also a function of government underspending brought about by several factors, including protracted contract reviews for public works (partly due to Aquino's thrust towards greater transparency), persistent right-of-way issues, as well as the long-standing lack of absorptive capacity in many government agencies to spend their budget and pump-prime the economy. At any rate, the lack of major fiscal deficits eased pressures for the government to borrow: the debt-to-GDP ratio went down from about 50 per cent to a little over 40 per cent. The commitment to good governance also led to a significant increase in business confidence, which manifested in a variety of indicators: a significant rise of the stock market index; improvements in credit ratings from S&P, Fitch, and Moody's; and an influx of foreign direct investments (FDIs). There were also marked improvements in global rankings such as the World Economic Forum Global Competitiveness

Index Ranking, Heritage Economic Freedom Ranking, World Bank Ease of Doing Business Ranking, and Transparency International Corruption Perceptions Index. Progress was also seen in some social welfare indicators: self-rated hunger abated, the poverty rate went down from a fourth of the population in 2009 to a fifth in 2015 (further dropping to a sixth in 2018), and the number of beneficiaries of the flagship anti-poverty programme, called 4Ps or Pantawid Pamilyang Pilipino Program, also more than quadrupled. Growth was not only fast, it was also somewhat inclusive.[2]

When Rodrigo Duterte, the long-time mayor of Davao City in southern Philippines, became president in 2016, the challenge was how to maintain that economic momentum. Mere days after the 2016 presidential elections, Carlos Dominguez III—Duterte's childhood friend who would later become the finance secretary—bared an eight-point economic agenda. That later evolved into a ten-point economic agenda, whose primary thrust was to "continue and maintain current macroeconomic policies, including fiscal, monetary, and trade policies".[3] In a way, this was a tacit acknowledgement of the economic policies and reforms of previous administrations. Apart from this, Duterte's ten-point agenda promised to pursue tax reform programmes, improve the nation's competitiveness and ease of doing business, beef up infrastructure spending (focusing at first on public-private partnerships, but relying more on official development assistance later on), promote rural and agricultural productivity, push for land reform, invest in human capital development (education, training, and health), promote science and technology and the creative arts, improve social protection programmes (notably the conditional cash transfer programme called 4Ps), and strengthen the implementation of the reproductive health law.[4]

This chapter examines the economic record of the Duterte administration before and during the COVID-19 pandemic, his legacy in terms of key economic and social indicators, and how the state of the economy shaped the 2022 Philippine presidential election. It then provides an assessment of the early part of the Marcos Jr. administration. Lastly, this chapter identifies policy reforms that could contribute to long-term economic development in the Philippines.

TAXES AND INFRASTRUCTURE: DUTERTE'S ECONOMIC PRIORITIES

Among the most significant of Duterte's economic reforms was the passage of tax reform laws, collectively known as the Comprehensive Tax Reform Program (CTRP). The first of these measures was the TRAIN (Tax Reform for Acceleration and Inclusion) Law. Enacted in November 2017, TRAIN was touted as the Duterte government's "best Christmas and New Year's gift" for Filipinos that year. Essentially, the TRAIN Law lowered personal income taxes, but this was offset with increases in excise taxes on several products, such as petroleum and sugar-sweetened beverages. Ostensibly, TRAIN served to fix long-standing problems in the tax system, including the fact that it has been too complex, not progressive enough, and many taxes are not indexed to inflation (e.g., petroleum excise taxes have been fixed for too long despite rising prices, resulting in huge foregone revenues). TRAIN also supposedly widened the tax base (i.e., taxed more products in a bid to lower average tax rates) and nudged certain behaviours that reduced negative externalities (e.g., it disincentivized the consumption of sugary drinks for public health reasons). Apart from TRAIN, the Duterte administration also passed two other sin tax laws. Supposedly, this was the first administration that was able to raise sin taxes thrice on alcohol, tobacco, and e-cigarettes.

However, it remains to be seen whether TRAIN made the tax system significantly more progressive. For instance, there were previous studies showing that TRAIN could exacerbate poverty and inequality by raising the prices of public transportation services and sugary drinks, which are disproportionately consumed by lower-income groups.[5] Indeed, TRAIN was seen as a major contributor to the rise of inflation in 2018 to a nine-year high (coinciding with a rise in global oil prices and the local mismanagement of rice supplies, mainly the depletion of subsidized rice sold by the National Food Authority or NFA).[6] Moreover, it is not obvious that TRAIN was pro-poor and anti-rich. For instance, a considerable segment of the poor population did not benefit from the lower personal income taxes of TRAIN, because they did not pay such taxes to begin with, being in the informal sector. Another study showed that even if TRAIN did impose a higher top marginal tax rate (from 32 per cent to 35 per cent), this affected only the super-rich, and by itself it did not make the tax system significantly more progressive.[7] At any rate, more comprehensive economic studies have yet to be made for a proper reckoning of the aftermath of TRAIN.

Besides TRAIN (Package 1 of CTRP), the Duterte administration also passed the CREATE (Corporate Recovery and Tax Incentives for Enterprises) Law in March 2021 amid the COVID-19 pandemic. Called Package 2 of CTRP, CREATE lowered the corporate income tax (CIT) rate of micro, small, and medium enterprises (MSMEs) from 30 to 20 per cent, and the CIT of other businesses from 30 to 25 per cent. This was meant to attract investments and boost economic activity, especially right after the historic pandemic recession in 2020 wherein annual GDP shrank by 9.5 per cent (and in the second quarter of that year, GDP contracted by 16.9 per cent). Also, the Philippines' CIT rate had been the highest in the ASEAN region and was considered a strong disincentive for potential investors. CREATE also "rationalized" the fiscal incentives given to investors by making such incentives "performance-based, time-bound, targeted, and transparent". The historical problem was that many investors—especially those located in economic zones—have benefitted for too long from generous perks from the government, and this became a huge drain on the public coffers. However, as one might expect, the removal of these perks met a lot of opposition from investors and business groups, and even the Philippine Economic Zone Authority (PEZA).[8] Also, CREATE was passed just when the government lost significant tax revenues from businesses due to the pandemic.

Another successful component of CTRP is the Tax Amnesty Act (Package 1B), which was also passed into law. Other proposals that ran out of time before Duterte's term ended include a proposal regarding motor vehicle user's charge (MVUC), a bill on the real property valuation system (Package 3), and a bill on passive income and financial intermediary taxes (Package 4). Interestingly, Duterte himself showed little interest in pushing for tax reforms; instead, the programme was spearheaded by Finance Secretary Carlos Dominguez III together with Finance Undersecretary Karl Kendrick Chua, a former World Bank economist who was eventually appointed the Socioeconomic Planning Secretary in April 2021.

Apart from CTRP, the "flagship" economic programme of the Duterte administration was the infrastructure spending mechanism called "Build, Build, Build" (BBB). Inaugurated in April 2017, BBB was called the "economic and development blueprint" of the Duterte administration and promised to deliver PHP 8.4 trillion worth of infrastructure projects by 2022—supposedly bringing about a "golden age" of infrastructure. Again, like CTRP, BBB was backed by a sound rationale: infrastructure spending during past administrations has been lacklustre and paled compared with the country's ASEAN neighbours. In addition, urban areas—especially Metro Manila, which accounts for a third of GDP—have been increasingly choking from traffic congestion. In 2018, the Japan International Cooperation Agency (JICA) estimated that the country lost PHP 3.5 billion daily due to Metro Manila traffic. Later they said that, with the status quo, such costs may rise to PHP 5.4 billion per day by 2035.[9] There was an urgent need to unclog the roads and revamp other types of infrastructure like roads, bridges, seaports, and airports.

In addition, BBB was repeatedly touted as a way to boost economic activity. For instance, the Department of Finance said in press releases that BBB would result in a government spending multiplier of about two (i.e., for every PHP 1 spent on BBB projects, the return to the economy would be an additional PHP 2). BBB was also complemented by a spin-off programme called "Jobs, Jobs, Jobs", an online portal that was supposed to post job openings related to BBB.[10]

The financing style was different as well: whereas the Aquino III administration relied on public-private partnerships (PPP), the Duterte administration leaned heavily on official development assistance (ODA) to finance BBB. This strategy came from claims that PPP stymied the execution of projects in past administrations. Duterte also relied on promises from the Chinese government to finance some BBB projects, as part of Duterte's foreign policy pivot to China (indeed, China would come to finance two bridges in Metro Manila, and a Chinese state-owned company won the bid for the construction of Kaliwa Dam, touted as a solution to Metro Manila's increasing water demand).[11]

As good as its intentions were, BBB was met with mixed success. Throughout Duterte's tenure, the BBB master list of projects kept on changing. All in all, the frequent changes in BBB's master list amounted to moving goalposts that made it difficult to assess the effectiveness of BBB by the end of Duterte's term. There were many reasons for this. First, some projects later turned out to be not feasible, such as bridges between the Visayas Islands that needed to be built on waters that turned out to be too deep. Second, possibly to make up for the slow execution of projects, the Duterte administration included projects that were carryovers from previous administrations (e.g., LRT-1 Cavite Extension, MRT-7, and NLEX-SLEX Connector Road). Third, the administration lengthened the list of projects to include those that are not normally infrastructure projects. Some notable examples include the National Identification System, the Virology Science and Technology Institute of the Philippines, and the Safe Philippines Project Phase 1—where the Chinese government helped to set up CCTV cameras across Metro Manila and Davao City. Fourth, Duterte added projects related to the reconstruction of war-torn Marawi City. It came to the point that Congress programmed BBB budgets in 2018 and 2019 that were smaller than what the economic managers had originally envisioned. Then, during the pandemic, BBB was touted as a way to prop up the economy from the recession. However, public spending on construction could not grow significantly during that time because spending bottlenecks remained unresolved.[12]

Among the perennial constraints in infrastructure spending in the Philippines is the chronic lack of "absorptive capacity" in many infrastructure-related agencies, especially the Department of Public Works and Highways (DPWH) and the Department of Transportation (DOTr). Simply, this means that these agencies could not spend their allocated budgets because of, say, the lack of technical staff to manage and oversee projects. To be fair, this problem existed even before the Duterte administration. But once in office, Duterte was able to do little to mitigate it. Unsurprisingly, the administration failed to meet its original target for infrastructure spending of 5 per cent of GDP annually (revised later to 5.3 per cent in 2017, to as much as 7.4 per cent come 2022). Data show that from the third quarter of 2016 to the second quarter of 2022, the share of public construction in GDP averaged only 4.44 per cent.

Other than his tax reform measures and infrastructure programme, Duterte made little headway into his ten-point agenda. For instance, in 2018, he signed the Ease of Doing Business and Efficient Government

Service Delivery Act, which was supposed to make it easier and faster for businesses to transact with the government (e.g., in securing permits and clearances). However, the success of this measure has yet to be properly evaluated in studies. FDI actually declined steadily even before the pandemic. Other items in the ten-point agenda fell by the wayside. Agricultural productivity continued to languish throughout Duterte's term. International assessments uncovered a dire education crisis.[13] The COVID-19 pandemic highlighted long-standing and myriad problems in the health sector. The coverage of the 4Ps programme did not significantly expand during his watch. And other objectives—like improvements in land titling, science and technology, and the implementation of the Reproductive Health Law—were simply beyond the radar of Duterte, who was extraordinarily obsessed with his war on drugs, leaving all other issues for his cabinet to deal with.

Regarding regional development, the Duterte administration was able to implement the Bangsamoro Organic Law, passed in 2018 and ratified through a plebiscite in 2019. It provided economic provisions that allowed the new region, the Bangsamoro Autonomous Region in Muslim Mindanao (BARMM), to achieve fiscal autonomy, provide for its own budget, and establish intergovernmental relations. At the same time, however, the siege of Marawi City in 2017 by jihadist terrorists brought about incalculable economic and social damage. As of this writing—and despite an influx of economic aid from here and abroad—many families dispossessed and displaced by the conflict have not been able to return to their homes.[14]

RIDING ON ECONOMIC MOMENTUM: DUTERTE'S ECONOMIC LEGACY

Near the tail-end of the Duterte administration, there was a conscious effort from the cabinet secretaries—notably from Finance Secretary Carlos Dominguez III—to highlight Duterte's achievements pre- versus post-COVID-19.

In terms of total production, the Duterte government was able to sustain the growth momentum laid down by his predecessor. From 2016 to 2019, annual GDP growth averaged 6.64 per cent—even higher than average growth during the term of Aquino III. However, such growth steadily declined across those years, from 7.15 per cent in 2016 to 6.12 per cent in 2019 (see Figure 2.1). Moreover, Duterte and his economic team did not meet their growth targets in 2018 and 2019. Annual inflows of FDIs also drastically went down despite the passage of the Ease of Doing Business Act.

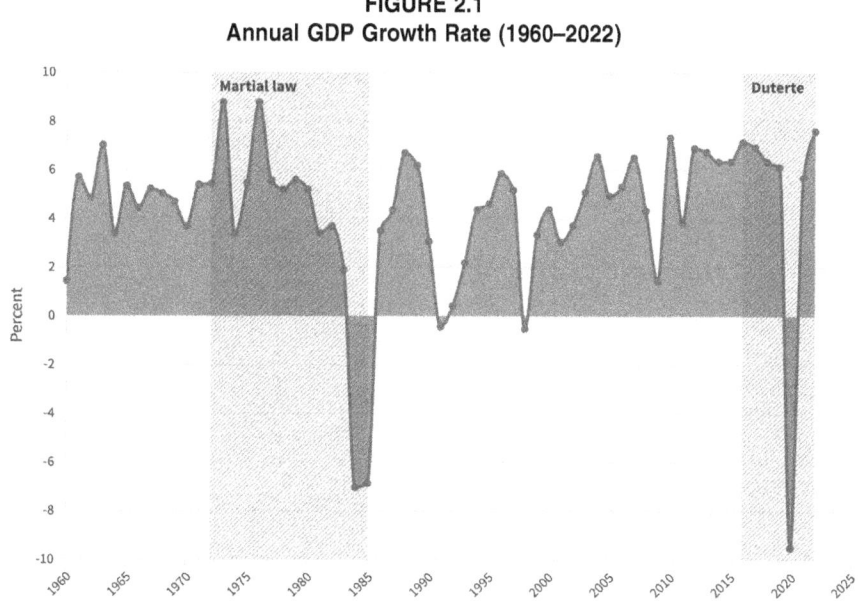

FIGURE 2.1
Annual GDP Growth Rate (1960–2022)

Source: Philippine Statistics Authority

Meanwhile, when it comes to prices of goods and services, the Duterte administration was able to keep annual inflation within the 2 to 4 per cent target in 2017 and 2019, but not in 2018 when inflation rose to a nine-year high, peaking at 6.7 per cent in September 2018 (see Figure 2.2). This was because of a global rise of oil prices, coupled with higher excise taxes borne by the TRAIN Law, as well as a shortage of government-subsidized rice that led to high rice and food inflation. Data show that inflation as felt by the poorest 30 per cent of households also shot up way above the headline inflation rate. This was unsurprising since food inflation was also off-target in 2018, and food accounts for a huge portion of poor households' budgets. There was a tendency among the economic managers at the time to dismiss rising inflation as something "transitory", which it did turn out to be, but not without much cost to poor households. This inflation episode paved the way for the passage of the Rice Tariffication Act, which liberalized rice imports and removed the rice importation monopoly of the National Food Authority. This was a game-changing reform that has languished in the legislative mill for decades, and eventually led to the negative contribution of rice by 2019, albeit temporarily.[15]

FIGURE 2.2
Monthly Inflation in the Philippines (January 2016–July 2023)

Source: Philippine Statistics Authority • Base year 2018.

Even though there was a decline in the unemployment rate from 5.7 per cent in 2017 to 5.1 per cent in 2019, it was off target in 2017 and on the higher end of the 2018 target. The number of new jobs generated was also off target in 2017 and 2018: the economy *lost* rather than gained 664,000 jobs in 2017, and the 823,000 new jobs in 2018 were below the government's 900,000 to 1.1 million target. In 2019, though, the economy generated 1.27 million new jobs, higher than the 1.1 million upper target. Meanwhile, youth unemployment increased during the pre-pandemic period and was consistently above the targets. Despite the mixed labour market performance, the quarterly unemployment and underemployment data reached fourteen-year lows by end-2019. This can be partially attributed to the economic growth momentum.[16]

There was also a rapid decline in poverty from 23.3 per cent in 2015 to 16.6 per cent in 2018. In just three years, nearly six million Filipinos were lifted out of poverty. This would turn out to be the fastest decline of poverty on record. On the face of it, this development would suggest that Duterte's anti-poverty policies worked. However, it could also be possible that this impressive record was the by-product of years of high growth starting in the early 2010s, and the long-standing anti-poverty programmes of the government like 4Ps.[17] In contrast, many of the pet policies of Duterte, notably the war on drugs, were considered anti-poor by many human rights groups and could not have helped reduce poverty. Arguably, then, the reduction in poverty in 2018 could have been even greater if such anti-poor policies had not been pushed.[18]

COVID-19 AND HOW IT UNDID DUTERTE'S ECONOMIC GAINS

Many of Duterte's putative economic gains were, alas, undone by COVID-19. Contrary to the expectations of many Filipinos, Duterte ended up imposing one form of lockdown or another for more than two years—amounting to one of the longest (if not the longest) lockdowns in the world.[19] This contributed to the record recession in 2020, when GDP dropped by 9.5 per cent (see Figure 2.1)—even worse than the economic recession in 1984 and 1985 during the martial law period. In April 2020, according to a World Bank study, about 77 per cent of firms closed; in July this went down to 40 per cent, but by then 15 per cent had already permanently closed. Unsurprisingly, an Asian Development Bank study found that about 84 per cent of households experienced income declines, and more than half of households said that if they lost their income sources, they would not last for two weeks.[20] Moreover, the proportion of households with any savings at all dropped from 37.8 per cent in the first quarter of 2020 to 24.7 per cent in the second quarter.[21]

This would turn out to be the worst pandemic recession among major ASEAN countries, and it also permanently pulled down the Philippines' economic trajectory. Various think tanks, and even the National Economic and Development Authority, estimated that it would take at least a decade for the Philippines to get back to its pre-pandemic trajectory.[22] A large part of the drastic decline was due to the services sector, which is the biggest sector in the economy (accounting for about 60 per cent of total output) and also the most reliant on in-person interactions (think arts and entertainment, tourism, transportation, and education). Industry dropped as well, while agriculture turned out to be robust because its gross value added dropped only slightly. Another reason for the severe output drop was the equally severe mobility decline in public places owing to Duterte's draconian and protracted lockdowns.

Meanwhile, from 5.07 per cent in 2019, the unemployment rate more than doubled to 10.41 per cent in 2020 (the highest in ASEAN then) and remained high at 8.02 per cent in 2021. The biggest jump in unemployment occurred in April 2020, when it reached a record 17.6 per cent, or more than triple the previous quarter's unemployment rate of 5.32 per cent. This was occasioned by a severe drop in the labour force participation rate, especially among women. Meanwhile, underemployment increased, but only slightly: from 14 per cent in 2019 to 16.36 per cent in 2020; this would increase further to 17.58 per cent in 2021. (Previous studies have argued that in the Philippines, underemployment—which has long stayed in the double digits—is the more apt welfare indicator than unemployment.) As for overseas Filipino workers (OFWs), who have long been a valuable source of remittances and foreign exchange for the country, at least 2.24 million were repatriated between March 2020 and June 2022.[23]

Amid the pandemic recession, one area that grew tremendously was the online economy. From 2019 to 2020, the total value of e-commerce transactions grew by a whopping 55 per cent (according to e-Conomy SEA 2020), food deliveries grew by 48 per cent, and online media by 27 per cent. This was due in part to the lockdowns and mobility restrictions, but also because the online economy became an adaptation for people who had lost their jobs or sources of livelihood. Many Filipinos also worked in the gig economy as delivery personnel for Grab, Foodpanda, and other services.[24]

Duterte pursued expansionary policies to boost the economy but with limited effect. For instance, Duterte signed the Bayanihan to Heal as One Act in March 2020. The law included "emergency subsidies" for about 18 million households nationwide.[25] The aid distribution was also too slow: near the end of 2020, the government was still not finished distributing aid that was supposed to tide over households in April and May that year. Finally, because of the lack of a robust system for handing out aid at such a massive scale, the distribution was highly politicized and left to the devices of local government units (LGUs). Many reports indicated that aid was prioritized for people who had close working or even familial ties with local leaders in *barangay*s (the smallest political unit). The government was committed to a shift to digitized distribution of aid (through, say, online transfers and apps). However, this did not push through and the government largely resorted to manual distribution until the end of Duterte's term. There was also a lot of clamour for the Duterte administration to give assistance for small businesses. But only a small portion of businesses received such aid: distribution was largely stymied by numerous documentary requirements that micro and small enterprises, especially those in the informal sector, could not produce.[26]

Even with the limited aid distribution, the Duterte government touted their pre-pandemic programmes (like BBB and CTRP) as ways to shore up the economy. Finance Secretary Dominguez said BBB would "fuel our bounce back" and claimed that infrastructure spending was the "best driver of economic growth".[27] However, this had limited effect because problems regarding underspending and lack of absorptive capacity were still unresolved at that time. Meanwhile, the CREATE Law was also touted as an expansionary measure, so much so that Dominguez said it would be "one of the largest economic stimulus measures in the country's history".[28] But again, this did not amount to much. GDP in 2021 was still well below its pre-pandemic (i.e., 2019) level.

At any rate, government spending more than doubled in April 2020 from the previous year, owing to spending requirements for the pandemic response. This led to a significant increase in debt. From a little under 40 per cent in 2019, the debt-to-GDP ratio rose to 54.6 per cent in 2020, and further rose to 60.4 per cent in 2021 and 60.9 per cent in 2022 (see Figure 2.3). The good news is that, unlike martial law, more than two-thirds of borrowings these days are domestic, and just under a third are external. Still, even Secretary Dominguez acknowledged that "fiscal consolidation" would be required in the form of, say, new taxes, and suggested this to the next administration.[29]

FIGURE 2.3
Debt-GDP Ratio

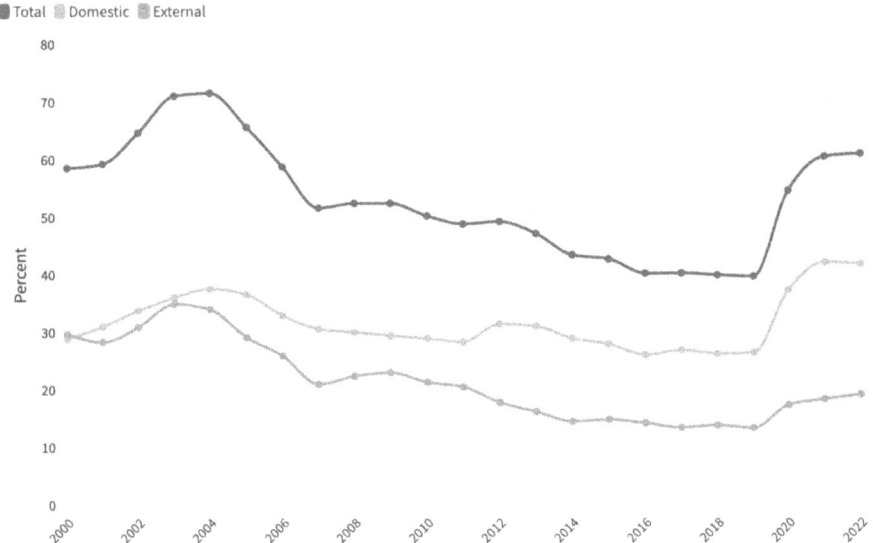

Source: Bureau of the Treasury

The pandemic also posed structural and long-term effects on the economy. For instance, it exacerbated the country's long-standing education crisis. Even before the pandemic, a number of international assessments showed that the Philippines ranked dead last (or nearly dead last) in standardized reading, science, and math tests. The Southeast Asia Primary Learning Metrics study showed that only one in ten Grade 5 students was able to achieve reading proficiency (in Malaysia and Vietnam, the corresponding proportions were 58 per cent and 82 per cent, respectively). The pandemic almost certainly worsened learning poverty, especially since the Philippines experienced the world's longest school closures. Moreover, access to the Internet and gadgets for online learning was enjoyed by some privileged students but not their poorer counterparts.[30] This resulted in huge inequality in learning capabilities amid the pandemic (i.e., better learning outcomes for those who were able to cope with the demands of online learning), and this will likely exacerbate future inequality in labour market outcomes. The severe rate of learning poverty before and after the pandemic presents a huge challenge for future growth and will certainly have a bearing on the productivity of today's children when they grow up and eventually join the labour force.

DISCONNECT BETWEEN GUT ISSUES AND DUTERTE'S POPULARITY

Interestingly, Duterte remained extremely popular as reported by reputable opinion polls despite the Duterte administration's economic troubles (e.g., the spell of high inflation in 2018), the mixed performance of flagship economic programmes, and the singular focus on the bloody war on drugs which killed thousands, as Bianca Franco's chapter shows. This may be attributed to the fact that the economy continued to grow rather robustly, and whatever economic hardship that befell the country (especially the poor) was counteracted by economic growth which benefitted the majority of Filipinos, including the ballooning middle class.[31] In the aftermath of the 2019 elections, no opposition bets won, and Duterte's closest allies—like the former chief of police who implemented the war on drugs, as well as a long-time personal aide—won coveted Senate seats on the back of Duterte's popularity.

Even more surprisingly, despite the significant gaps in his administration's pandemic response, Duterte kept his sky-high ratings. His approval ratings (based on Pulse Asia data) peaked at a whopping 91 per cent in September and November 2020, smack in the middle of the lockdowns. Then by March 2022, his approval rating was 73 per cent—abnormally high for an administration already in its closing months.[32]

This is not to say that economic issues were unimportant or sidelined. Some of the possible reasons for Duterte's durable popularity are explained in this volume, including the role of disinformation and control over the media. In the surveys of Pulse Asia, economic issues consistently were top-of-mind throughout the Duterte years.

For example, in their September 2018 survey regarding "Most Urgent National Concerns", the top issues were economic in nature: "controlling inflation", "improving/increasing the pay of workers", "reducing the poverty of many Filipinos", and "creating more jobs".[33] Nearly four years later, in June 2022, the same issues made it to the top four. Interestingly, Duterte's pet issues—as well as other important issues like the West Philippine Sea—were not top-of-mind: in 2018, "fighting criminality" came in at rank 5, "defending the integrity of Philippine territory against foreigners" came in at 14th place, and "changing the constitution" ranked 15th. In 2022, "controlling the spread of COVID-19" came in at just rank 18. Economic issues also dominate another Pulse Asia survey about the "Most Liked Issue to be Discussed by President Duterte in His Coming SONA (State of the Nation Address)". In 2019 the top three were increasing salaries, lowering prices of commodities, and job/livelihood creation.[34] In 2021, before Duterte's last SONA, it was "creating more jobs or livelihood", "improving the national economy", and "controlling inflation".[35]

"GOLDEN AGE" OF THE ECONOMY 2.0? THE MARCOS JR. ADMINISTRATION

The same issues that hounded Duterte surfaced in the 2022 campaign trail. But rather than engage in debates, Duterte's successor, Ferdinand Marcos Jr., banked on authoritarian nostalgia surrounding the contested legacy of his father, the former president and dictator Ferdinand Marcos Sr. Specifically, Marcos Jr. promoted myths about the supposed "golden age" brought about by his father's regime.[36] Although such myths have long existed since the days of the dictatorship, they have been amplified by disinformation and propaganda networks in social media. Throughout his 2022 campaign, Marcos Jr. constantly brought up names of his father's old policies and projects like Kadiwa (rolling stores where government subsidized food items and basic necessities can be bought), Masagana 99 (agricultural credit programme), Nutribun (bread fortified with nutrients), and the Bataan Nuclear Power Plant (which did not produce a single kilowatt of electricity).[37] Many of these programmes bled the public coffers and created many fiscal problems for the Philippines in the 1980s.

Apart from this, Marcos Jr. also tended to stick to simple messages, including a call for "unity" and "Babangon Muli" [We Shall Rise Again], which imperfectly derives from his initials BBM. Finally, Marcos Jr. made lofty but memorable promises that resonated and tickled the imagination of the masses, such as bringing down the price of rice to PHP 20/kg or US$0.37/kg. This, alongside many other factors (identity politics, regionalism, an education crisis, and the popularity of his running mate Sara Duterte, among others), led to a landslide win for Marcos Jr. in the May 2022 polls.[38] He ended up with the first majority vote in the post-EDSA era, garnering 59 per cent of the vote (31.6 million votes).

Just like Duterte before him, Ferdinand Marcos Jr. began his presidency by articulating an eight-point economic agenda which included healing the economic scars left by the pandemic: abating inflation and the cost-of-living crisis, ensuring sound macroeconomic fundamentals and fiscal management, creating more jobs, ensuring energy security, promoting research and development, supporting the green and blue economy, upholding peace and order, and ensuring a level playing field among businesses.

The need to accelerate the economy's recovery coming from the COVID-19 pandemic was a key priority. Luckily for Marcos Jr., the pandemic had already begun to subside, and it was relatively safe to relax masking and social distancing requirements outdoors and indoors to return businesses to their pre-pandemic postures. By November 2022, Vice President Sara Duterte, who concurrently serves as the Education Secretary, ordered all public schools to go back to in-person classes. Coupled with other factors such as pent-up demand or "revenge spending" by the private sector, these developments led to the near-full reopening of the economy. By end-2022, GDP had gone back to its pre-pandemic level.

But the side effect of this flurry of economic activity was demand-pull inflation[39] that coincided with a global rise of inflation brought about by logistics bottlenecks in major economies, as well as the Russian invasion of Ukraine in February 2022 which later led to oil, fertilizer, and cereal price hikes worldwide.[40] Throughout 2022, inflation in the Philippines rose steadily. By January 2023 it reached a fourteen-year high of 8.7 per cent. Despite the inclusion of inflation issues in the eight-point agenda, Marcos Jr. failed to abate inflation. At first, he even denied the alarming July 2022 statistics by saying "we're not that high"—only to be corrected by the national statistician who stood by the official numbers.

Marcos Jr.'s inaction against inflation is also more baffling given his assumption of the post of agriculture secretary at the very beginning of his term. He did so ostensibly to signal to the people his commitment to boost agriculture and address its long-standing problems, such as chronic low productivity, insufficient investments, and poor research and development. But the early portion of Marcos Jr.'s term was marked by a "sugar fiasco" where he surprisingly blocked the importation of sugar, resulting in high sugar inflation and food inflation. Later, in February 2023, he would allow sugar imports, but there were allegations that some importers were favoured, and some imports were allowed to arrive in the country despite a lack of permits. This raised suspicions of "government-sponsored smuggling" and "government-sponsored cartels" in the words of an opposition senator. A similar problem beset onions: a failure to import them in time led to a whopping 200 per cent inflation of red onions by end-2022. Onions came to be a symbol of Marcos Jr.'s failure to control inflation.[41] In September 2023, Marcos Jr. imposed price ceilings on rice (reminiscent of his father's policies during martial law). But this quickly led to rice shortages and fears among suppliers that may eventually drive-up hoarding, as one might expect from textbook economics.

Marcos Jr. also took many foreign trips in too short a time. His justification was that such trips (including one in Singapore to watch the Grand Prix) were necessary to introduce the Philippines (or maybe the Marcoses, for many of his family members joined the junkets) on the world stage, and also to attract investments.[42] In Marcos Jr.'s second State of the Nation Address to Congress in July 2023, he claimed that all his foreign trips had brought back investment pledges to the tune of PHP 3.9 trillion (US$72.2 billion). But many critics were careful to point out that, as of writing, none of the investment pledges came in as actual investments, and that many things need to be fixed in the domestic investment scene before waves of investment can come through, such as ease of doing business, rule of law, infrastructure, high cost of power.[43] Without a clear good governance agenda that addresses these bottlenecks—which are often connected to corruption—it remains to be seen how Marcos Jr. will bring about the transformation he has promised.

Marcos Jr. was most keen to create a sovereign wealth fund, dubbed as Maharlika Investment Fund—yet another play at the martial law iconography by referencing "Maharlika", a precolonial term for a warrior class which was used as propaganda during his father's dictatorship. Touted by the economic managers as a way by which the government can raise funds for various projects, Maharlika was initially proposed by six lawmakers, half of whom are the president's relatives. However, critics said that, unlike many other sovereign wealth funds, Maharlika is not a legitimate sovereign wealth fund since it will not be (and cannot be) funded using any government surplus, unlike in other countries where their sovereign funds are funded using windfalls from, say, oil revenues.[44] In 2022, the government ran a deficit of PHP 1.6 trillion (nearly US$30 billion) or 7.3 per cent of GDP.[45]

Moreover, there were questions about the source of funds. Initially, Maharlika was supposed to get billions from pension funds, but this was aborted after severe public backlash. Still, it will get about PHP 75 billion (US$1.38 billion) from state banks—a move expected to compromise the leverage ratios (and financial health) of such banks. Maharlika is also set to take money from the dividends remitted by the Bangko Sentral ng Pilipinas (BSP) to the Treasury—a move that will invariably delay the much-needed capital-raising activities of the BSP. In total, when Marcos Jr. signed the Maharlika law in July 2023, the fund's authorized capital is PHP 500 billion (US$9.26 billion)—a hefty sum in a country with huge deficits and mounting debt.[46] Finally, many questions surrounded the governance structure of the corporation that will handle Maharlika. As of writing, the economic managers have published the implementing rules and regulations for the Maharlika law, and they are also shortlisting people who will populate the board of the Maharlika Investment Corporation.[47]

In Marcos Jr.'s first year in office, the economic thrust of his administration has been largely swayed by the technocrats, most of whom are recognized economists. Despite initial delays in forming such a team, many congratulated the president for hiring the "best and brightest". Indeed, these economists have had several decades of government service under their belt, and are renowned economists themselves, having been long-time academics at the University of the Philippines. The stellar credentials and long years of government service, however, were no assurance of sound policymaking. For instance, despite the hesitations of many private sector and academic economists regarding Maharlika—as well as the Fund's lack of economic sense—Marcos Jr.'s economic team strongly supported the push for the Maharlika Investment Fund. The economic managers also supported the rice price ceilings introduced in September 2023, despite opposition from rice retailers and economists outside of government. In many other instances, the economic team also omitted to chime in on other important issues of the day: for instance, the sugar and onion fiascos, as well as allegations of agricultural smuggling and cartels—this, despite "[ensuring] a level playing field by strengthening market competition" being the last in the eight-point agenda. The hiring of top-notch economists in the cabinet has led some to remark that such a move served, more than anything else, to "deodorize" the Marcos Jr. administration and to provide the president's policies and projects an undeserved veneer of legitimacy. This claim may have been prompted by the fact that in the 1970s and 1980s, Marcos Sr. himself was notorious for hiring technocrats with doctorate degrees but who were eventually used as front men for the regime's wanton borrowing from multilateral organizations such as the World Bank and the International Monetary Fund.[48] The reliance on subservient technocrats would be another thing Marcos Jr. got straight from his father's playbook.

CONCLUSION

The task that befell the Duterte administration in 2016 was to maintain the economic momentum and build on its predecessors' reforms. And in a real sense, Duterte was able to do that. However, one can argue that it was possible for his government to see through even better economic outcomes, had his governance style been different. For instance, GDP growth could have been faster if agencies on the frontlines of BBB were able to overcome underspending problems. Inflation could have been lower in 2018 if the timing of TRAIN's excise taxes were better, and if rice supplies were not allowed to deplete. Also, the record poverty reduction from 2015 to 2018 could have been larger had the administration not pursued anti-poor programmes like the war on drugs. FDI inflows could also have increased—rather than decreased—if the Ease of Doing Business Act, alongside other reform measures, had become more effective in improving the country's business environment.

Unfortunately, many of the economic gains achieved from 2016 to 2019 were erased by the COVID-19 pandemic and, more crucially, the Duterte government's inept pandemic response. The economy endured permanent scars which will stay with Filipinos for decades to come and will likely frustrate the Marcos Jr. administration's objectives of meeting their economic targets (on top of current global economic headwinds including elevated inflation and interest rates). For instance, data show that for GDP to get back to its pre-pandemic trajectory by 2028 (the final year of the Marcos Jr. administration), GDP will have to grow by more than 9 per cent annually, certainly a tall order. In 2022, growth clocked in at only 7.6 per cent and continues to be below-target in 2023. Among the things that will continue to pull down growth include a protracted cost-of-living crisis which the Marcos Jr. government failed to abate using the Kadiwa stores and sloppy importation policies; the continued stagnation of the agriculture sector (Marcos Jr. will have to push for reforms more aggressively, although the benefits will take some time to manifest); and a potential energy crisis come 2027 with the impending depletion of the natural gas reserves in the Malampaya, which in 2019 accounted for about 29 per cent of power generation in Luzon, and 21 per cent of the country's total power supply. Rather tellingly, promoting human capital investments in education and health is not part of Marcos Jr.'s eight-point economic agenda. By contrast, it was part of Duterte's ten-point agenda. At the beginning of his term, Marcos Jr. also appointed Vice President Sara Duterte—who is not an educator—to helm the Department of Education.

To ensure long-run growth and development, the government will do well to focus on the following policy reform areas. In the short and medium terms, there needs to be a strong commitment towards reforming the broken military and uniformed personnel pension system, which, if left unaddressed, will lead to a future fiscal crisis and crowd out crucial public programmes and projects.⁴⁹ The government will also need to veer away from car-centric infrastructure and promote mass and active transportation to promote productivity. Social protection systems also need to be beefed up in order to minimize poverty and reduce the still sizable "vulnerable" population of the country. In the long term, much more effort will need to be expended for, say, education reforms as well as investments on renewable energy that could avert future energy crises and lower the cost of electricity.

In the end, there are few indications that President Marcos Jr. will be as reform-minded as his predecessors, or that he will pay greater attention to economic issues that pose threats to future Philippine growth. Right now, the Maharlika Investment Fund is the only notable economic project that has received intense personal focus from the president. But Maharlika stands to weaken government financial institutions and pose significant risks on the public coffers. Marcos Jr. also seems dead set on rehashing some of his father's old programmes, in an ongoing bid to rehabilitate his family's political image and clout—something which they stated as an overt political goal. But with such a massive mandate, and with the stakes so high for the country, he will have to do more than rely on false nostalgia for his father's dictatorship. In the eyes of the Filipino public, the performance of Marcos Jr. in Malacañang might put to the test the perception or myth of a Marcosian "golden age".

Notes

1. JC Punongbayan, "[ANALYSIS] PNoy's Legacy: We Were No Longer the 'Sick Man of Asia'", *Rappler*, 30 June 2021, https://www.rappler.com/voices/thought-leaders/analysis-pnoy-legacy-we-were-no-longer-sick-man-of-asia/.
2. Punongbayan, "[ANALYSIS] PNoy's legacy: We Were No Longer the 'Sick Man of Asia'".
3. Trisha Macas, "Duterte's Economic Team Reveals 10-point Socioeconomic Agenda", *GMA News Online*, 20 June 2016, https://www.gmanetwork.com/news/money/economy/570703/duterte-s-economic-team-reveals-10-point-socioeconomic-agenda/story/.
4. Macas, "Duterte's Economic Team Reveals 10-point Socioeconomic Agenda".
5. For instance, see Czar Joseph Castillo, Ramon Clarete, Marjorie Muyrong, Philip Tuaño, and Miann Banaag, "Assessing the TRAIN's Coal and

Petroleum Excise Taxes: Macroeconomic, Environmental and Welfare Effects", Philippine Institute for Development Studies Discussion Paper 2018-41 (December 2018).
6. JC Punongbayan, "[ANALYSIS] Why Is Philippine Inflation Now the Highest in ASEAN?" *Rappler*, 6 September 2018, https://www.rappler.com/voices/thought-leaders/211285-analysis-reasons-philippine-inflation-now-highest-asean/.
7. Rosario G. Manasan, "Assessment of Republic Act 10963: The 2017 Tax Reform for Acceleration and Inclusion", Philippine Institute for Development Studies Discussion Paper 2018-17 (2018), https://pidswebs.pids.gov.ph/CDN/PUBLICATIONS/pidsdps1827.pdf.
8. See for example, *ABS-CBN News*, "TRABAHO Bill Could Lead to Job Losses, Exporters Fear", 18 July 2019, https://news.abs-cbn.com/business/07/18/19/trabaho-bill-could-lead-to-job-losses-exporters-fear.
9. *CNN Philippines*, "PH Traffic May Worsen, to Cost ₱5.4 Billion Daily – JICA", 19 September 2018, https://www.cnnphilippines.com/news/2018/09/19/JICA-study-traffic-5-billion.html.
10. Ian Nicolas Cigaral, "Gov't Opens 'Jobs, Jobs, Jobs' Portal to Bolster Building Boom", *Philstar.com*, 29 May 2018, https://www.philstar.com/business/2018/05/29/1819756/govt-opens-jobs-jobs-jobs-portal-bolster-building-boom.
11. Ben Cal, "P12.2-B Kaliwa Dam Project to Augment Metro Manila Water Supply", Philippine News Agency, 8 November 2018, https://www.pna.gov.ph/articles/1053324.
12. JC Punongbayan and Zy-za Suzara, "[ANALYSIS] Why We Can't Build, Build, Build Our Way Out of This Pandemic", *Rappler*, 14 May 2020, https://www.rappler.com/voices/thought-leaders/analysis-why-we-cannot-build-our-way-out-of-coronavirus-pandemic/.
13. JC Punongbayan, "[ANALYSIS] Dismal PISA Rankings: A Wake-Up Call for Filipinos", *Rappler*, 4 December 2019, https://www.rappler.com/thought-leaders/246384-analysis-dismal-programme-international-student-assessment-rankings-wake-up-call-filipinos.
14. Froilan Gallardo, "Six SONAs Later, Displaced Marawi Families Still Barred from Returning Home", *Rappler*, 26 July 2023, https://www.rappler.com/nation/mindanao/displaced-marawi-families-still-barred-returning-homes-2023/.
15. JC Punongbayan, "[ANALYSIS] Plummeting Rice Prices: How Will Our Rice Farmers Cope?" *Rappler*, 5 September 2019, https://www.rappler.com/voices/thought-leaders/239392-analysis-plummeting-rice-prices-how-will-our-rice-farmers-cope/.

16. JC Punongbayan, "[ANALYSIS] Making Sense of the Surprisingly Good Jobs, Poverty Stats", *Rappler*, 11 December 2019, https://www.rappler.com/voices/thought-leaders/246984-analysis-making-sense-surprisingly-good-jobs-poverty-statistics/.
17. The *Pantawid Pamilyang Pilipino* Program (4Ps) is a conditional cash transfer programme that was piloted during the administration of former president Gloria Macapagal-Arroyo, and it expanded significantly during the Aquino administration; see https://www.officialgazette.gov.ph/programs/conditional-cash-transfer/.
18. Punongbayan, "[ANALYSIS] Making Sense of the Surprisingly Good Jobs, Poverty Stats".
19. Aie Balagtas See, "Rodrigo Duterte Is Using One of the World's Longest COVID-19 Lockdowns to Strengthen His Grip on the Philippines", *Time*, 15 March 2021, https://time.com/5945616/covid-philippines-pandemic-lockdown/.
20. Peter J. Morgan and Long Q. Trinh, "Impacts of COVID-19 on Households in ASEAN Countries and Their Implications for Human Capital Development", ADBI Working Paper Series No. 1226 (2021), https://www.adb.org/sites/default/files/publication/688271/adbi-wp1226.pdf.
21. Bangko Sentral ng Pilipinas, "Consumer Expectations Survey, Third Quarter 2020", https://www.bsp.gov.ph/Lists/Consumer%20Expectation%20Report/Attachments/17/CES_3qtr2020.pdf.
22. Agence France-Press, "Philippine Economy to Take 10 Years to Recover from Virus — NEDA", *Philstar.com*, 2 October 2021, https://www.philstar.com/business/2021/10/02/2131293/philippine-economy-take-10-years-recover-virus-neda.
23. Lawrence Agcaoili, "More OFWs Seen Going into Businesses", *Philstar.com*, 8 February 2023, https://www.philstar.com/business/2023/02/08/2243279/more-ofws-seen-going-businesses.
24. Asian Development Bank, "Gig Economy Employment during the Pandemic: An Analysis of GrabFood Driver Experiences in the Philippines", ADB Briefs No. 251 (2023), https://www.adb.org/sites/default/files/publication/894231/adb-brief-251-gig-economy-employment-pandemic-philippines.pdf.
25. Every beneficiary family would receive an amount ranging from PHP5,000 to PHP8,000 (US$92.6 to US$148) a month for two months (April and May), but this turned out to be a lot smaller compared with the poverty lines across all regions. Throughout this chapter we assume an exchange rate of PHP54/USD.
26. Cherrie Regalado, "Undisbursed and Underutilized: Here's What Happened to the P10-B Covid-19 Loan Program for Small Businesses", Philippine

Center for Investigative Journalism, 7 December 2022, https://pcij.org/article/9710/what-happened-coronavirus-loan-program-for-small-businesses.
27. Department of Finance, Philippines, "Dominguez Proposes 5 Priority Measures to Restart Economy", 12 May 2020, https://www.dof.gov.ph/dominguez-proposes-5-priority-measures-to-restart-economy.
28. Ben O. de Vera, "Dominguez: Create Is 'One of Largest Economic Stimulus Measures' in PH History'", *Inquirer.net*, 21 May 2020, https://business.inquirer.net/297819/dominguez-create-is-one-of-largest-economic-stimulus-measures-in-ph-history.
29. Ralf Rivas, "DOF Urges Marcos: Postpone Income Tax Cuts, Slap New Taxes, Slash VAT Exemptions", *Rappler*, 25 May 2022, https://www.rappler.com/business/department-finance-proposals-marcos-jr-new-taxes-slash-vat-exemptions/.
30. JC Punongbayan, "[ANALYSIS] Why the PH Economy's Recovery Will Be K-shaped", *Rappler*, 8 January 2021, https://www.rappler.com/voices/thought-leaders/analysis-why-ph-economy-recovery-k-shaped/.
31. Emmanuel S. de Dios, "The Economy Fifty Years since Martial Law: Changing Landscapes, Unchanged Views", in *Martial Law in the Philippines: Lessons and Legacies, 1972–2022*, edited by Edilberto C. de Jesus and Ivyrose S. Baysic (Quezon City: Ateneo de Manila University Press, 2023). Evidence of pro-poor growth was also seen by Joseph J. Capuno, "Growth with Redistribution, Finally: Regional Poverty and Inequality in the Philippines, 2000–2018", *Asia and the Global Economy* 2, no. 2 (2022), https://doi.org/10.1016/j.aglobe.2022.100039.
32. Llanesca T. Panti, "Duterte Approval Stayed High through Six Years — Pulse Asia Data", *GMA News Online*, 28 June 2022, https://www.gmanetwork.com/news/topstories/nation/836404/duterte-approval-stayed-high-through-six-years-pulse-asia-data-show/story/.
33. Jess Diaz, "Soaring Prices Worry Filipinos Most — Pulse Asia", *Philstar.com*, 28 September 2018, https://www.philstar.com/headlines/2018/09/28/1855450/soaring-prices-worry-filipinos-most-pulse-asia.
34. Mia Gonzales, "Filipinos' Top SONA 2019 Issues: Pay Hike, Lower Prices, Philippine Sovereignty", *Rappler*, 19 July 2019, https://www.rappler.com/nation/235780-filipinos-top-issues-sona-2019-pulse-asia-survey/.
35. Gaea Katreena Cabico, "Filipinos Want Duterte to Discuss Jobs, Economy in Final SONA — Pulse Asia", *Philstar.com*, 26 July 2021, https://www.philstar.com/headlines/2021/07/26/2115324/filipinos-want-duterte-discuss-jobs-economy-final-sona-pulse-asia.
36. JC Punongbayan, *False Nostalgia: The Marcos "Golden Age" Myths and How to Debunk Them* (Quezon City: Ateneo de Manila University Press, 2023).

37. JC Punongbayan, "[ANALYSIS] Mga palpak na proyekto ng tatay na Marcos, bakit ibabalik ni Junior?" *Rappler*, 11 March 2022, "https://www.rappler.com/voices/thought-leaders/analysis-why-would-ferdinand-bongbong-marcos-jr-bring-back-father-failed-projects/.
38. Lian Buan, "36 Years after Ousting Marcos, Filipinos Elect Son as President", *Rappler*, 10 May 2022, "https://www.rappler.com/nation/elections/ferdinand-bongbong-marcos-jr-wins-president-philippines-may-2022/.
39. JC Punongbayan, "[ANALYSIS] Fastest Economic Growth in 46 Years? Some Context and Caveats", *Rappler*, 27 January 2023, https://www.rappler.com/voices/thought-leaders/analysis-fastest-economic-growth-46-years-context-caveats/.
40. Ralf Rivas, "Philippine Inflation Leaps to 4% as Russia-Ukraine War Sends Oil Soaring", *Rappler*, 5 April 2022, https://www.rappler.com/business/inflation-rate-philippines-march-2022/.
41. For instance, see Chad de Guzman, "In the Philippines, Onions Are Now More Expensive Than Meat. Here's Why", *Time*, 9 January 2023, https://time.com/6245568/philippines-onions-shortage-inflation/.
42. Bea Cupin, "Marcos Defends Cost of Foreign Trips: It's About Return on Investment", *Rappler*, 24 January 2023, https://www.rappler.com/nation/marcos-jr-defends-cost-foreign-trips-return-on-investment/.
43. See, for example, US Department of State, "2022 Investment Climate Statements: The Philippines", https://www.state.gov/reports/2022-investment-climate-statements/the-philippines/.
44. JC Punongbayan et al., "Maharlika Investment Fund: Still Beyond Repair", UP School of Economics Discussion Paper, 2023.
45. Bureau of the Treasury, "Full-Year NG Budget Deficit Narrows to P1.6 Trillion in 2022", 28 February 2023, https://www.treasury.gov.ph/?p=52816.
46. JC Punongbayan, "[ANALYSIS] The Economy during Marcos' First Year", *Rappler*, 30 June 2023, https://www.rappler.com/voices/thought-leaders/analysis-philippine-economy-marcos-jr-administration-first-year-office-2023/.
47. Ronnel W. Domingo, "Search On for Maharlika Fund Managers as IRR Issued", *Inquirer.net*, 30 August 2023, https://newsinfo.inquirer.net/1823732/search-on-for-maharlika-fund-managers-as-irr-issued.
48. Teresa S. Encarnacion Tadem, *Philippine Politics and the Marcos Technocrats: The Emergence and Evolution of a Power Elite* (Manila: Ateneo de Manila University Press, 2019).
49. JC Punongbayan, "[ANALYSIS] Did You Know You're Paying for Police, Military Pensions?" *Rappler*, 4 August 2023, https://www.rappler.com/voices/thought-leaders/analysis-did-you-know-you-are-paying-for-police-military-pensions/.

3

From Entrepreneur to Saboteur: How the Philippines Won and Lost the South China Sea on Social Media

Charmaine Misalucha-Willoughby*

> *Social media in the Philippines is critical in disseminating information, shaping narratives, and solidifying discourses regarding the South China Sea. This issue makes for a compelling study on how the state can be a purveyor and a consumer of information campaigns. The argument is that strong undercurrents hidden by President Duterte's strongman stance can explain why the Philippines could not leverage the 2016 Arbitration Award. Three narratives are germane: entrapment, cooperation, and* utang na loob *(debt of gratitude). This chapter diagnoses defeatism in the South China Sea issue during the Duterte years (2016–22). What were the manifestations of this stance? How did Duterte's pursuit of an "independent foreign policy" fit his pivot to China? Following that, the chapter offers a prognosis, and the implications of Duterte's policy turn to the trajectory of*

the Philippines' international relations from Marcos onwards. This chapter draws from original research and data collection where the discourse analysis identifies three interrelated narratives that emerged, circulated, and took root during Duterte's six-year term in office. In closing, the chapter highlights the critical role of information campaigns in shifting a state's foreign policy.

Keywords: South China Sea; Duterte; foreign policy; pivot to China; information campaigns

INTRODUCTION

Based on current values from the World Bank, the Philippines' total population is estimated at 113 million as of 2021.[1] Of this number, 85 million are Internet users at the start of 2023, 84 million of whom use social media.[2] These numbers reveal that a vast percentage of the population is active on social media platforms such as Facebook, YouTube, and Twitter, and spend an average of more than three hours online daily. Facebook alone has about 80 million users in the Philippines, making it the platform of choice for communication, information, and commerce. Social media use in the Philippines has been so pervasive that it became a mobilizing factor in the last two national elections.[3] In fact, President Rodrigo Duterte relied heavily on social media to magnify his strongman stance during the 2016 elections. He declared in a press conference, "I will ask the Navy to bring me to the nearest point in [the] South China Sea that is tolerable to them, and I will ride a jet ski. I will carry a flag, and when I reach [the] Spratlys, I will erect the Filipino flag. I will tell [China], *suntukan o barilan* (fistfight or gunfight)?"[4] Running on a platform of purging the country of illegal drugs and criminality, he also vowed to solve these perennial problems within six months of his holding office.[5] When the United States and other Western countries criticized his war on drugs, he called President Barack Obama a "son of a whore" for raising human rights concerns with him.[6] Meanwhile, the 2022 elections that led to the victory of Ferdinand "Bongbong" Marcos Jr., the son of the former dictator and his namesake, tapped into TikTok, YouTube, and messaging apps like Facebook Messenger and Viber.[7]

In this context, social media in the Philippines plays a critical role in disseminating information, shaping narratives, and solidifying discourses. The Philippines-China disputes over the South China Sea are another area that makes for a compelling study on how the state can be both a purveyor and a consumer of information campaigns. First, the Philippines displays little confidence that China would "do the right thing" in upholding global peace, security, prosperity, and governance. This mistrust contrasts with the high confidence rating towards the United States as a strategic partner and provider of regional security.[8] The Philippines' negative perceptions of China can be attributed to the latter's economic and military power that threatens the Philippines' interests and sovereignty.[9] The deep mistrust that the Philippines displays towards China is compounded by its unceasing occupation of features in the West Philippine Sea and its notorious reliance on grey zone tactics, including information and influence campaigns.

In 2012, the Philippines and China engaged in a standoff in Scarborough Shoal, which culminated in the Philippines' filing of an arbitration case against China under the United Nations Convention on the Law of the Sea over China's occupation of several features within the Philippines' Exclusive Economic Zone. Likewise, China built artificial islands and militarized those at the expense of the ecological integrity of the marine and coastal environments. China has also been known to use its maritime militia to chase Filipino fisherfolk away from traditional fishing grounds in parts of the South China Sea, affecting their catch volume. In January 2023, Marcos visited Beijing and attracted numerous investment pledges. He ran on a platform of not making territorial disputes the defining factor of Philippines-China relations. But a month later, the Chinese Coast Guard's aiming of a military-grade laser at a Philippine Coast Guard vessel carrying food and supplies to troops stationed in Second Thomas Shoal (Ayungin Shoal) highlighted the inconsistency of China's position, as well as intractable tensions between the two countries. All these contribute to the Philippines' high distrust towards China.[10]

With the general population relying heavily on social media, this chapter examines the impact of this information ecosystem on the Philippines' foreign policy stance in the South China Sea. During the

Duterte presidency, what explains the Philippines' shift from a staunch supporter of international law—in this case, a norm entrepreneur that lobbied and won its case against China at the Permanent Court of Arbitration (PCA)—to a saboteur that caved into China's demands and downplayed the significance of the arbitral award? The administration of President Benigno Aquino III filed a case against China following the impasse in Scarborough Shoal in 2012. The Philippines eventually won the case in 2016, just when Duterte came to power. Instead of using the arbitral ruling to advance the Philippines' national interest, Duterte's foreign policy pivoted towards China, translating to closer bilateral ties and deeper economic engagements in exchange for China's support for Duterte's controversial drug war, which the then-Obama administration in the United States criticized. The arbitration award was effectively set aside under Duterte. Although there are early signs that the incumbent Marcos administration can balance the country's relations with the United States and China, it remains to be seen if such a move is sustainable.

The Philippines' inability to leverage the 2016 arbitration award can be explained by powerful undercurrents obscured by Duterte's strongman stance. In particular, underlying insecurity in the Philippines manifested in chronic defeatism, which Duterte tried to offset using strongman tactics. Over time, scholars have elaborated on the psychological or socio-structural origins of Duterte's populism. But where this chapter contributes is the impact of these dynamics on the country's foreign policy, specifically as it applies to pervasive social media narratives in the Philippines during the Duterte administration about the country's South China Sea policy.[11]

Three narratives in social media are germane and instrumental in effecting Duterte's foreign policy direction: entrapment, cooperation, and *utang na loob* (debt of gratitude). The narrative on entrapment focuses on the Philippine-US alliance. It posits that the Americans "duped" the Filipinos into a military alliance, which would only lead the latter into sticky situations in the future such as being embroiled in a US-China conflict. This trajectory aligns with Chinese thinking that the United States is containing China by fomenting anti-China security policies and defence postures across Asia and provokes China into a defensive position. Meanwhile, the cooperation narrative highlights the benefits the Philippines can gain from closer relations with China. Here, the Philippines acquiesces to the idea that being friends with China can prevent a military confrontation in the West Philippine Sea, a line of thinking that supports Chinese projections of being a benign power in the region. Finally, the *utang na loob* (debt of gratitude) narrative became acute in the early stages of the COVID-19 pandemic when Duterte leaned on China's vaccine diplomacy. These three complementing narratives suggest that underneath the Duterte administration's bravado, deep-seated insecurity is propped up and exacerbated by massive online information campaigns, resulting in a widespread defeatist attitude.

The chapter investigates defeatism in the South China Sea issue during the Duterte years (2016–22). What were the manifestations of this stance? How did Duterte's pursuit of an "independent foreign policy" fit his pivot to China? Following that, the chapter offers a prognosis and the implications of Duterte's foreign policy turn to the Philippines' international relations from Marcos onwards. This section draws from original research and data collection where the discourse analysis identifies three interrelated narratives that emerged, circulated, and took root during Duterte's six-year term in office. In closing, the chapter highlights the critical role of information campaigns in shifting a state's foreign policy.

MANIFESTATIONS OF DEFEATISM IN THE SOUTH CHINA SEA

Four instances during the Duterte administration were symptomatic of a defeatist foreign policy in the South China Sea. The first stemmed from his announcement almost immediately upon his assumption that his administration would pursue an "independent foreign policy". Considering the strongman stance that was highly palpable during the campaign, this announcement resonated with Filipinos. After all, a country led by a strong leader would not shy away from pursuing a foreign policy that might be perceived as unpopular by more traditional international partners. In this regard, Duterte declared during his visit to Beijing in October 2016 that he was "separating" from the United States and reinvigorating relations with China, which garnered the

Philippines US$24 billion worth of deals and thirteen government-to-government agreements.[12] The pivot towards China was executed early in Duterte's presidency in 2016 when he faced heavy criticism from the international community—particularly the United States and the European Union—for his controversial drug war. In this context, moving closer to China afforded the Philippines the needed support from an external actor who could replace the United States and the European Union as investors and financial backers. One of Duterte's centrepiece programmes was his flagship "Build, Build, Build" infrastructure spending spree which promised a breakneck pace of construction of airports, road networks, bridges, and other vital infrastructure to spur economic development. Deeper relations with China meant more financing for his infrastructure projects.

The pledges notwithstanding, the actual outcomes were lacking. By 2020, China's Official Development Assistance (ODA) to the Philippines was US$620.74 million, a far cry from the US$9 billion in pledges accrued during the Duterte years.[13] Moreover, the supposed economic gains resulted in a sharp increase in the number of visitors from China: from 675,663 arrivals in 2016 to 1.7 million in 2019.[14] Chinese foreign direct investment (FDI) likewise grew significantly under Duterte, from around 500 to 600 firms in 2010–16 to 1,257 by 2017.[15] The bulk of the recipients of Chinese FDIs was the offshore gambling industry, which required the acquisition of small hotels and resorts in prime locations to operate. The boom of Philippine offshore gaming operators (POGOs) benefitted the economy. At their height in 2019, they contributed an estimated US$1.9 billion (PHP 104 billion) and accounted for 0.67 per cent of the Philippines' gross domestic product.[16] The social costs, however, were controversial. Chinese POGOs were linked to crimes and syndicates involving kidnapping, murder, human trafficking, and prostitution—a policy issue in the Philippines that continues to be debated today and was one of the political opposition's rallying issues in the 2022 Philippine elections. POGOs also changed the social dynamics in local communities as Chinese nationals more visibly took over commercial establishments and residential areas, especially in the National Capital Region.

Despite these, improved bilateral relations were also beneficial for China. In particular, the Duterte administration downplayed the 2016

Permanent Court of Arbitration's ruling on the South China Sea. The optimism about diplomatic rapprochement at the time was not entirely unfounded, but later on, many now perceive the costs to have been too great, not least because discussions on the South China Sea were marginalized during the Philippines' chairmanship of the Association of Southeast Asian Nations (ASEAN) in 2017, grey zone incidents involving China's maritime militia have been understated, and the patrols and presence of the Armed Forces of the Philippines (AFP) and the Philippine Coast Guard (PCG) in the West Philippine Sea have been severely constrained. Duterte himself often spoke of any manner of standing up against China as provoking war—a slippery slope fallacy that endures in the Philippines presently.

The tit-for-tat strategy—a function of Duterte's pivot to China—was only one side of pursuing the Philippines' independent foreign policy. The other side was abrogating the Visiting Forces Agreement (VFA) with the United States. The Philippines' alliance with the US was founded on the 1951 Mutual Defense Treaty (MDT) and supplemented by the 1999 VFA and the 2014 Enhanced Defense Cooperation Agreement (EDCA). The alliance has had its share of ups and downs. Still, its lowest point was when Duterte initiated the VFA's abrogation in early 2020 after his chief of police's US visa was cancelled. The abrogation was suspended when the COVID-19 pandemic hit and was cancelled altogether by mid-2021, right after US Secretary of Defense Lloyd Austin visited Manila. But by then, it was clear that China's massive investment pledges would not materialize. It was also towards the end of Duterte's term when he started warming up to the alliance with the United States, albeit half-heartedly.

One of the symptoms of the Philippines' defeatist stance in the South China Sea is the misapplication of the pursuit of an independent foreign policy. Rather than diversifying the country's external relations, which could have entailed reaching out to partners like Australia and South Korea, Duterte's definition was to be independent of the United States and turn to China. This move exacerbated the Philippines' security dilemma and contributed to further entrenching feelings of resignation and futility.

Another instance where the defeatist stance manifested was the country's involvement in China's Belt and Road Initiative (BRI).

Although the Philippines only joined the BRI in 2018, it signed on to the China-led Asian Infrastructure Investment Bank (AIIB) in 2015, which is the funding source of the BRI. Joining the AIIB was expected to boost Duterte's infrastructure programme. Accordingly, the AIIB co-financed a transportation project in the Philippines with the Asian Development Bank and a flood-control project with the World Bank in 2016. Infrastructure connectivity, however, is only one of the five major priorities of the BRI. The others include policy coordination, increased trade, financial integration, and people-to-people links.

Running concurrently with the decision to pivot towards China, infrastructure projects under the BRI progressed under Duterte, although many ran into controversies. Among these is the Kaliwa Dam, whose contractor is the China Energy Engineering Corporation, and which proceeded with the construction without government offices' necessary permits. Duterte wanted the project to advance as the dam was Metro Manila's "last resort" for its diminishing water supply. Apart from the lack of permits, the dam's construction would cause the displacement of an estimated 1,465 indigenous families.[17] The Chico River Pump Irrigation Project is a similar endeavour, with a funding agreement with the China Exim Development Bank. It aims to increase national rice production and save on rice imports. The project required a pump house, substation, transmission line, canals, and access roads. It was anticipated to benefit farmers in Kalinga province and create jobs during construction. Still, indigenous people's groups and environmentalists opposed the project because of its impact on forests and rivers in the mountainous region of the Cordillera.[18] The risks of debt traps and social costs became almost synonymous with the BRI, but the fact that signing up for it meant financing infrastructure projects implied that the Duterte administration thought that the short-term benefits outweighed the long-term costs.[19] Such a perception indicates the Philippines' recognition that as beggars cannot be choosers, a suboptimal situation under the BRI is better than nothing.

A third symptom of defeatism is the joint exploration between the Philippines and China in the West Philippine Sea. Under President Gloria Arroyo's watch in 2005, the Philippines signed the Joint Marine Seismic Undertaking (JMSU) with China and Vietnam to jointly explore areas in the South China Sea. State-owned oil companies—the

Philippine National Oil Corporation and the China National Offshore Oil Corporation—led to a joint search of about 140,000 square kilometres of sea, including areas under Philippine territory and other contested areas with China, Vietnam, Malaysia, Brunei, and Taiwan. The JMSU was later found to be steeped in corruption and kickbacks. Arroyo had acted less in favour of Philippine national interests in that more concessions over the country's waters were granted to China.[20] The agreement expired in 2008 but was revived under Duterte in 2018. The fact that Duterte tried to restore an agreement mired with corruption to keep in line with his pivot to China policy can be perceived more as serving Chinese interests. Like many of the infrastructure projects under the BRI, talks on joint exploration failed, and Duterte terminated the negotiations towards the end of his term. At the onset of 2023, the Philippine Supreme Court deemed the 2005 pact unconstitutional, arguing that the state-owned companies of China and Vietnam were not supposed to undertake joint oil exploration in Philippine waters.[21]

Finally, widespread defeatism was palpable during the height of the COVID-19 pandemic, as the Philippines' response initially relied heavily on China. Like the war on drugs, the pandemic response was framed as a "war" against the virus, violators of quarantine rules, and critics of the government. From the onset of the virus in early 2020, Duterte placed the country under a state of public health emergency and eventually under a state of calamity, while the capital Manila was placed under a series of lockdowns that entailed severe restrictions on people's movement such as strict home quarantine, social distancing, and the mandatory use of face masks and face shields. Land, domestic air, and domestic sea travel to and from Manila were suspended. Quarantine passes were issued to authorized persons outside their residences, and failure to produce them at checkpoints could result in unfavourable situations. Curfews were likewise imposed, with corresponding penalties for violators. The police and military were tasked to enforce the quarantine and to deal with violators accordingly. The highly securitized response was prone to "pandemic backsliding", or the extent to which the Philippines stayed within democratic standards for emergency response.[22]

China donated testing kits, surgical masks, and personal protective equipment to many countries worldwide, including the Philippines, and sent a team of Chinese experts to the Philippines to advise on controlling the spread of the disease.²³ For these reasons, Duterte thanked Chinese President Xi Jinping on several occasions while downplaying US support.²⁴ Many observers note, however, that China's pandemic diplomacy was a way to deflect criticism for its handling of the first cases in Wuhan. Moreover, it later appeared that China's test kit donations were defective.²⁵ Regarding vaccine procurement, the Philippines signed a deal for 25 million doses of China's Sinovac, the first shipment of which arrived in the country in February 2021, despite scientific evidence of Sinovac's lesser efficacy than other vaccines.²⁶

Duterte's defence of purchasing Chinese vaccines indicates his continuing desire to favour China against all odds.²⁷ For example, the Commission on Audit flagged the Department of Health for mismanaging US$1.2 billion (PHP 67.323 billion) in pandemic funds, where US$89 million (PHP 5.038 billion) lacked documentation and had procedural deficiencies, including the reported procurement of four laptops worth US$12,500 (PHP 700,000).²⁸ Another indication of dysfunctions with the government's pandemic response is purchasing personal protective equipment. Local producers with prior experience with government projects were eased out in favour of a minor, obscure, and new company called Pharmally Pharmaceutical Corporation, which managed to get a government contract worth US$143.8 million (PHP 8 billion).²⁹ Favouring local producers could have prevented job losses during the pandemic. Further senate hearings and investigations revealed that Pharmally has connections with the Duterte administration through the former chief of Procurement Service of the Department of Budget and Management, Lloyd Christopher Lao, and Duterte's former economic adviser, Chinese national Michael Yang.³⁰

In sum, the discussion indicates that the Philippines exhibited defeatism vis-à-vis China in four areas: its pursuit of an independent foreign policy, involvement in the BRI, joint exploration in the West Philippine Sea, and pandemic response. In all these instances, the Philippines displayed that it was willing to set aside its national interests in the West Philippine Sea and relegate the 2016 arbitration award aside in exchange for short-term benefits like support for a controversial drug war, infrastructure financing, and COVID-19 vaccines.

The following section discusses how these symptoms developed and their implications to the Philippines.

IMPLICATIONS OF DEFEATISM IN THE SOUTH CHINA SEA

The defeatism that the Philippines exhibited during the Duterte years is deeply rooted and engendered at the very least three narratives circulating and contributing to general public discourse in the country. The narratives that are presented here are culled from original research conducted by a team based at Arizona State University (ASU), the University of Arkansas at Little Rock (UALR), and De La Salle University (DLSU). Data collection was conducted by the UALR team and employed a computational method called "data crawling".[31] The method uses keywords drawn from expert workshops, which were then categorized into strings and matched against posts on social media platforms, including Twitter, YouTube, and blogs. The social media posts on the South China Sea that were examined were from 1 January 2016 to 31 July 2022. In total, the team gathered a total of 19,358 Twitter posts, 756 YouTube videos, and 163 blog posts. The collected data were converted to an Excel spreadsheet with sample numbers, IDs, titles, and descriptions.

The data were initially run through *NVivo* to group them into categories. The research team thereafter did a manual review of the grouped data and proceeded to code and annotate based on Y, N, or D. Y referred to data that met these three conditions: the data is relevant to the topic, the data has potential to influence an audience, the data is a narrative story. N was used to code data that did not meet these criteria. Meanwhile, D referred to exceptions to the Y criteria. The data were cross-checked by research team members and validated by subject-matter experts in another series of workshops to ensure the consistency of the coding process.

Based on the data collection and analysis, three narratives emerge that can explain the deeply rooted defeatism in Philippine foreign policy during the Duterte administration. The first narrative is entrapment, which pivots around the idea that the United States' actions in the region induce China to behave in ways it would have otherwise. The entrapment narrative is essentially anti-US and supports the idea that enemies surround China, which justifies why it protects and defends what it considers its rightful territories. Accordingly, the Philippines' alliance with the US will be detrimental to the former because it is being taken advantage of.

In this context, the Philippines' pivot to China is unsurprising as there had always been tension and frustration from a violent colonial history and America's "democratizing mission" to the Philippines.[32] Thus, the decision not to renew the American military bases in Clark and Subic in the early 1990s rode on anti-US rhetoric.[33] Likewise, the move was seen as an assertion of Filipino independence. This history set the stage for Duterte, who made it clear very early during his term that he was separating from the United States and reinvigorating relations with China. In one of his State of the Nation Addresses, he said, "I have nothing against America ... but if you put bases here [again], you will double the spectacle of a most destructive thing just like Manila during the Second World War – during the retaking of this city. ... [So if we put American bases] at this time, this will ensure [that] if war breaks out, because there would be atomic arsenals brought in, this will ensure the extinction of the Filipino race."[34] Others echo similar rhetoric in his administration. For example, a provincial governor objected to live-fire exercises between the Philippines and the US under the aegis of the 2022 Balikatan exercises—an annual drill between the two countries—because "we don't want to anger China".[35]

Data collected from social media posts show opposition to the live-fire drills of the Balikatan exercises. Most point out that military exercises are costly and should not be held at a time when the Philippines is slowly emerging from the pandemic. Some also highlight that closer military relations with the United States have never benefitted the Philippines, considering the two countries' colonial past. Furthermore, Tweets and YouTube videos converge on the risks for the Philippines if and when a Taiwan contingency takes place, particularly in light of the United States' inability to guarantee that it would offer aid to the Philippines if war were to break out.

Building on historical tangents accounts for Duterte's doubling down on setting the award aside and justifying China's incursion in the West Philippine Sea by arguing that the Philippines is caught in the crosshairs of a brewing US-China conflict. He said,

> China [is] building structures and military bases, I must admit it. But is it intended for us? You must be joking. It's not intended for us. ... It's really intended against those who the Chinese think would destroy them, and that is America. *Wala tayong kasali diyan.* (We're not a party to that fight.) Then why would I go there ... bring my navy, my soldiers, my police, and everything only to be slaughtered? I will not commit the lives of the Filipinos only to die unnecessarily. I will not go into a battle which I can never win.[36]

Here we see a different rhetoric than the bold, flag-planting, gunfight-or-fistfight claims of the Duterte campaign; instead, we see him convey fatalist (and isolationist) view on China by first casting aspersions on US intentions and then using the most extreme (war) outcome as the consequence of US presence in the Philippines.

Social media posts echo the former president's views and minimize the concerns about China's "creeping assertiveness". Duterte's supporters reiterate that China's military presence in the South China Sea is directed towards the United States, which holds China's maritime-dependent economy by the throat. In this instance, China cannot be expected to stand by and do nothing. Interestingly, the hype over China's assertiveness in the waters is blamed on the media. Accordingly, these posts are manipulated and funded by the US Central Intelligence Agency and oligarchs whose goal is to get contracts to drill for oil in the South China Sea. Under this narrative, cooperating with China is the best course of action for the Philippines to lessen the tensions in the waters.

Russia's invasion of Ukraine added fuel to the fire. Considering the administration's resigned attitude regarding the South China Sea, it is no wonder it announced its neutrality in the Ukraine crisis.[37] Saying that "it's not our battle to fight", Duterte was inclined to avoid any position to ensure the country would not be dragged into a war.[38] Even though the Philippines voted to support the UN General Assembly resolution that condemned the invasion, Duterte's neutrality makes sense, considering his plans early in his administration to acquire weapons from Russia, including aircraft and submarines. But when the United States advised the Philippines against purchasing Russian submarines, Duterte responded, "You sold us six helicopters. One or two or three crashed already. ... Is that the way you treat an ally, and you want us to stay with you for all times? Who are you to warn us?"[39] The US$249 million deal for Russian Mi-17 helicopters went through in November 2021, with an initial payment in January 2022.[40] It is against this context that the Philippines opted for a neutral policy, which earned the praise of Russia's ambassador to the Philippines.[41]

In the early days of the invasion of Ukraine, the knee-jerk reaction of Filipinos on social media was to be neutral, which was understandable considering the incompleteness of the country's military modernization. The spin, however, on social media is that Duterte was brave to announce neutrality because doing so precludes the Philippines from becoming a pawn of the West. Not taking sides is considered courageous and laudable in standing up against the West. The hashtag #neutralphilippines trended on Twitter as a call against being sacrificial lambs to the altar of great power rivalry and the interests of military-industrial complexes.

The entrapment narrative emphasizes that if China is perceived to have behaved assertively or aggressively, it is simply because circumstances force it. Implicitly, others—the United States, the Philippines, and the West—are at fault for placing China in untenable situations where it has no choice but to defend itself. This narrative complements the second storyline found in the study's data collection, that is, since all great powers misbehave and take advantage of others, China is the lesser evil because, unlike the United States, it has never been a colonial master. In this context, China is portrayed as a benign and friendly power, although it is often a victim of being misunderstood. Hence, countries like the Philippines are better off cooperating with China against the evil West. Implicit here is that the non-West must stand up against the West's unceasing and unfettered colonialism.

Social media posts categorized under the cooperation narrative promote friendly, diplomatic, and economic ties with China. References to culture, cuisine, tourism, student exchange, and educational visits underscore the value of people-to-people ties. Most of the posts were also authored by members of the Filipino-Chinese business community and advanced the gains that the Philippines could get from the BRI. Here, Duterte is projected as a wise and pragmatic statesman whose diplomatic skills brought the Philippines to an even keel with great powers.

Against this backdrop, it makes sense why the Philippines under Duterte displayed acquiescence towards and appeasement of China. Duterte went so far as to joke in public that the Philippines can be "a province of China".[42] A parallel rhetoric was in his State of the Nation Address in 2020:

> ... unless we are prepared to go to war, I would suggest that we better just call off and treat this, I said, with diplomatic endeavors. China is claiming [the South China Sea]. We are claiming it. China has the arms, we do not have it. So, it is simple as that. They are in possession of the property. ... So what can we do? We have to go to war and I cannot afford it. Maybe some other president can, but I cannot. *Inutil ako diyan, sabihin ko sa inyo.* (I'm useless when it comes to that, I'm telling you.) And I'm willing to admit it. *Talagang inutil ako diyan. Wala akong magawa.* (I'm really useless. I cannot do anything.)[43]

Finally, the third narrative that emerged from the data collection is *utang na loob* (debt of gratitude), which, like the narratives of entrapment and cooperation, can explain why the Philippines swung from being a staunch defender of international law concerning the South China Sea to undermining the foundational principles of a rules-based international order. *Utang na loob* is a Filipino concept of reciprocal obligations and behavioural expectations.[44] Considering the deep embeddedness of this trait in Filipinos, it makes sense to set it—and the resulting defeatism—as the price to pay for a tit-for-tat strategy. After all, a reinvigorated bilateral relationship with China translated to support for Duterte's war on drugs despite mounting criticisms from the United States, the European Union, and the International Criminal Court that found evidence of crimes against humanity being perpetrated in the country.[45] Aside from this, closer ties with China meant support for Duterte's flagship "Build, Build, Build" programme, to which China offered US$24 billion in investment pledges in 2016. However, the return on investment is lacking as Duterte ended his term in 2022.

The swirling threads of defeatism in the Philippines became fertile ground for information operations that propelled the restoration of the Marcos family into power. Ferdinand Marcos Sr. ruled the country from 1965 to 1986 in what is known and documented as one of the most violent periods in Philippine history. The 2022 electoral victory of the dictator's son, Ferdinand Marcos Jr., was not a surprise to many, given his consistently wide lead in pre-election surveys.[46] To others, this made little sense because Marcos Jr. was equally consistent in being absent during presidential debates. Numerous issues involved his candidacy, educational background, and estate tax liability.[47] What is clear is the vast information ecosystem on which the Marcos campaign relied and utilized for years before the 2022 elections. In particular, he succeeded in convincing many during the campaign that he would continue the foreign policy of Duterte, a position that amplified underlying anti-US sentiments in the country.[48] Marcos Jr. benefitted from coordinated amplification online, particularly of stories that depict the martial law years under Marcos Sr. as the "glory days" or the "golden age" of the country, through an extensive network of pages and groups on social media platforms like YouTube, Facebook, Twitter, and TikTok.[49] Besides historical revisionism, the information ecosystem exaggerated the Marcos family's success and vilified the opposition. This point is further expounded in Labiste's chapter in this volume, which discusses disinformation under the Duterte administration.[50]

The new battlefield is truly in the cyber sphere.[51] Knowledge production and narratives in social media inevitably shape foreign policy and international relations. The South China Sea disputes are a good example. As the Philippines proceeds with the modernization programme of its armed forces, there must be a corresponding transition in strategic thinking to emphasize deterrence, let alone making that posture credible against adversaries.[52] The National Defense Strategy is still built on the "minimum credible defence" concept as a response to hostile acts.[53] The prerequisites of deterrence—actions that need to be taken even before the emergence of hostilities—are still largely missing in Philippine discussions. One reason for this is that since the Cold War and especially during Marcos Sr.'s time, the Philippine military has been tasked to handle internal security operations, especially counter-insurgency operations. The assumption was that the alliance with the United States could handle external security. In this sense, the Philippines engaged in a classic buck-passing strategy insofar as its external security was concerned. Not only did this cement complacency on the part of the Philippines, but also made transitioning from internal defence to externally oriented deterrence more difficult, especially since the move will require calculations involving grey zone operations, such as China's maritime militia in the South China Sea and Chinese counter-narratives about the contested waters.

Another aspect of the South China Sea that online narratives can imperil is the Philippine national interest to decouple territorial disputes from Chinese development assistance. The entrenchment of the issue solely in the political and security realm implies that the choice for the Philippines is to either confront China militarily or befriend it in the hopes that it could be persuaded from further incursions in the West Philippine Sea. Online narratives depict the choice strictly as binary, but there are alternatives that the Philippines can pursue. First, the disputes can be framed as food security issues. The South China Sea contains 190 trillion cubic feet of natural gas and 11 billion barrels of oil.[54] It also contains rich fishing grounds of up to 27 per cent of the Philippines' commercial fisheries production.[55] China's unabated construction of artificial islands compounded the pressures of overfishing, clam extraction, dredging for constructing artificial reefs and other features, and hydrofracking. Thus, fisher folks' inability to access fishing grounds translates into higher market prices and uncertainty in regular provisions for their families and communities.

Second, the South China Sea can be reframed as an environmental issue. The waters contain diverse ecosystems ranging from 3,000 species of fish and 600 species of coral reef, mangrove, and seagrass, as well as turtles and seabirds that depend on the islands.[56] The destruction of the marine environment due to the construction of artificial islands disrupts the natural processes of the ecosystems. Furthermore, it robs coastal communities of the opportunity to rely on and replenish natural marine resources sustainably. Attention likewise needs to shift to the critical role of the blue economy, which is crucial to maritime safety and security. A vibrant blue economy hinges on sustainable coastal tourism, improved port infrastructure, and managed and regulated fishing. Coastal welfare is an important part of this equation because economic insecurity onshore usually translates to illicit maritime activities. Hence, improved maritime governance in fisheries—to begin with—can prevent coastal populations from turning to criminal networks and activities such as piracy incidents, armed robbery at sea, human smuggling, trafficking, slavery, and illicit trade of drugs and wildlife, among others. Likewise, better maritime governance can prevent people from resorting to illegal means to exploit marine resources.

CONCLUSION

Foreign policy defeatism as a political rhetoric in the Philippines has been expressed primarily through the Duterte administration's pivot to China policy. His administration's pursuit of a so-called independent foreign policy while overturning historic partnerships with the United States, its decision to join China's Belt and Road Initiative, hold joint explorations, and profusely express its gratitude to China during the COVID-19 pandemic are symptomatic of a deeply rooted defeatism that exacerbates the country's insecurity in the context of the South China Sea. Furthermore, these symptoms indicate powerful undercurrents in the general discourse in the Philippines, including narratives on entrapment, cooperation, and *utang na loob*. Defeatism as the key conceptual anchor of the way Duterte's foreign policy is communicated to the public has been so entrenched that it became fertile ground for the massive information campaign that propelled Marcos to win the 2022 election cycle. As the Philippines embarks on a new administration, there is all the more reason to carefully examine the extent to which vast information ecosystems can impact foreign policy.

A year into the Marcos presidency, it seems that the administration's pursuit of an independent foreign policy differs substantially from Duterte's. Whereas Duterte's definition was presupposed on a strict binary between the United States and China, Marcos exercises an independent foreign policy by diversifying the country's international relations. He has so far made fourteen foreign trips since taking office, including state visits (Indonesia, Singapore, China, Japan, and Malaysia), a working visit to the United States to attend the 77th Session of the United Nations General Assembly and again for an official visit for the US-ASEAN meetings, an unannounced visit to Singapore to watch the F1 race, summits (Cambodia, Thailand, Belgium, Switzerland, Indonesia), and as a guest of the United Kingdom to attend the coronation of King Charles III. While costly for a country still struggling to re-emerge from a pandemic, these trips reintroduce the Philippines to the international community and are, in many ways, an effort to distinguish the Marcos administration from Duterte's more insular orientation. The most substantial foreign policy gains that Marcos has done, however, is in the reinvigoration of the Philippines' alliance with the United States by identifying new sites under the EDCA.

The new locations prepare the country for potential contingencies as regards not only the South China Sea, but also Taiwan. Henceforth, the Philippines needs to be consistent in the exercise of its foreign policy so that it can minimize the oscillation from one great power to another. One way to avoid these shifts is to staunchly defend the country's national interest. Allies and partners come and go, but the national interest remains the same.

The cyber sphere remains active in the Philippines, but less so now than in the Duterte years. Still, influence operations continue to be rampant. At the national level, situational awareness is crucial. A prerequisite here is to understand that data—or information—is a strategic resource. As such, knowledge of the information ecosystem is necessary for agents of the government. Communicating with constituents is equally important, where information is disseminated proactively, credibly, and in a timely manner. Controlling the narrative is key here, and its impact can be magnified by public diplomacy efforts and coordination with partners in the private sector, academia, and the international community. At the societal level, the key to addressing misinformation and disinformation is to rebuild public trust in the authorities. Here, confidence-building measures can be conducted via media literacy programmes, responsible journalism, and investing in education. At the individual level, there are psychosocial means to defray the costs of parasocial relationships and narrow the cognitive dissonance that people experience as a result of heavy dependence on social media. It begs emphasizing that an online/offline distinction in one's personal life is helpful in today's world.

If left unchecked, the complications for the Philippines of information campaigns and influence operations can be critical as these can lead to intensified democratic erosion and further divisions in society. Likewise, they can diminish the clout and centrality on which ASEAN—the region's premier grouping—depends, especially if China continues its bold moves in the South China Sea and the negotiations on the Code of Conduct remain stalled. The global impact is not so much rooted in defeatism *per se* but in what defeatism engenders. The Philippines, in this instance, is the proverbial laboratory in terms of the power of online machinery to warp history, determine elections, and chart the future.

Notes

* Acknowledgments: The author is grateful for the invaluable research contributions and insights of Scott Ruston, Peggy-Jean Allin, and Jihyun Kang. This study was produced with a grant from the Office of Naval Research (ONR N00014-21-1-2121) under the Minerva Research Initiative of the United States Department of Defense. Any opinions, findings, conclusions, or recommendations expressed here are those of the author and do not necessarily reflect the views of the funding organization.

1. The World Bank, "Population, Total – Philippines", 2023, https://data.worldbank.org/indicator/SP.POP.TOTL?end=2021&locations=PH&start=1960&view=chart.
2. Simon Kemp, "Digital 2023: The Philippines", *Datareportal*, 9 February 2023, https://datareportal.com/reports/digital-2023-philippines.
3. Aim Sinpeng, Dimitar Gueorguiev, and Aries A. Arugay, "Strong Fans, Weak Campaigns: Social Media and Duterte in the 2016 Philippine Election", *Journal of East Asian Studies* 20 (2020): 353–74; Aries A. Arugay and Justin Keith A. Baquisal, "Mobilized and Polarized: Social Media and Disinformation Narratives in the 2022 Philippine Elections", *Pacific Affairs* 95, no. 3 (September 2022): 549–73.
4. "Duterte to Ride Jetski, Plant Flag in Spratlys and Challenge China: Suntukan o Barilan?" *Politiko*, 12 April 2016, https://politics.com.ph/duterte-to-ride-jetski-plant-flag-in-spratlys-and-challenge-china-suntukan-o-barilan/.
5. Aries Joseph Hegina, "Duterte: Kill Me If I Fail to Bust Crime, Corruption in 6 Months", *Inquirer.net*, 17 January 2016. https://newsinfo.inquirer.net/756194/duterte-kill-me-if-i-fail-to-bust-crime-corruption-in-6-months.
6. "Philippine President Duterte Curses Obama over Human Rights", *BBC*, 5 September 2016, https://www.bbc.com/news/world-asia-37274594.
7. Pichayada Promchertchoo, "'Enormous Machine Spreading Disinformation' Casts Shadow over Philippine Presidential Contest", *CNA*, 7 May 2022, https://www.channelnewsasia.com/asia/philippines-presidential-election-disinformation-mislead-voters-bongbong-leni-2667791.
8. Lowy Institute, "Asia Power Index 2023", https://power.lowyinstitute.org/countries/philippines/.
9. Sharon Seah, Joanne Lin, Melinda Martinus, Sithanonxay Suvannaphakdy, and Pham Thi Phuong Thao, *The State of Southeast Asia 2023 Survey Report* (Singapore: ISEAS – Yusof Ishak Institute, 2023), https://www.iseas.edu.sg/wp-content/uploads/2025/07/The-State-of-SEA-2023-Final-Digital-V4-09-Feb-2023.pdf.
10. Joyce Ann L. Rocamora, "DFA Tells China to Engage PH Based on Facts after Laser-Use Row", *Philippine News Agency*, 17 February 2023, https://www.pna.gov.ph/articles/1195467.

11. Vicente L. Rafael, *The Sovereign Trickster: Death and Laughter in the Age of Duterte* (Durham: Duke University Press, 2021).
12. Willard Cheng, "Duterte Heads Home from China with $24 Billion Deals", *ABS-CBN News*, 21 October 2016, https://news.abs-cbn.com/business/10/21/16/duterte-heads-home-from-china-with-24-billion-deals.
13. Enrico V. Gloria, "The Future of Duterte's Pivot to China: A Non-defeatist Approach", *Fulcrum*, 16 November 2021, https://fulcrum.sg/the-future-of-dutertes-pivot-to-china-a-non-defeatist-approach/.
14. Philippines Department of Tourism, "Tourism Demand Statistics", 2016–19, http://tourism.gov.ph/tourism_dem_sup_pub.aspx.
15. Alvin A. Camba, "Where Is China Money Going? Gambling, Real Estate, Tours, Big Cities Big Winners", Philippine Center for Investigative Journalism, 9 March 2019, https://pcij.org/article/3483/where-is-china-money-going-gambling-br-real-estate-tours-big-cities-big-winners.
16. Ralf Rivas, "In Numbers: Risks, Benefits of POGO Operations", *Rappler*, 19 October 2022, https://www.rappler.com/business/numbers-risks-benefits-philippine-offshore-gaming-operations/.
17. Zacarian Sarao, "Construction of Kaliwa Dam Pushed through Even without Permits – COA", *Inquirer.net*, 16 September 2021, https://newsinfo.inquirer.net/1488470/implementation-of-kaliwa-dam-project-pushed-through-even-without-permits-coa.
18. Geela Garcia, "China-Funded Water Project Meets Stiff Opposition in the Philippines", *China Dialogue*, 4 March 2021, https://chinadialogue.net/en/nature/china-funded-water-project-meets-stiff-opposition-in-the-philippines/.
19. Aaron Jed Rabena, "The Belt and Road Initiative and the Philippines' Post-Duterte China Challenge", *Fulcrum*, 25 March 2022, https://fulcrum.sg/the-belt-and-road-initiative-and-the-philippines-post-duterte-china-challenge/.
20. Miriam Grace A. Go, "Arroyo Gov't Pleasing China Since Day 1", *ABS-CBN News*, 14 March 2008, https://news.abs-cbn.com/special-report/03/14/08/policy-betrayal-first-three-parts.
21. "Philippine Court Voids Oil Exploration Pact Involving China", *Nikkei Asia*, 11 January 2023, https://asia.nikkei.com/Politics/International-relations/South-China-Sea/Philippine-court-voids-oil-exploration-pact-involving-China.
22. Maria Ela L. Atienza, Aries A. Arugay, Jean Encinas-Franco, Jan Robert R. Go, and Rogelio Alicor L. Panao, *Constitutional Performance Assessment in the Time of a Pandemic: The 1987 Constitution and the Philippines' COVID-19 Response* (Stockholm: International Institute for Democracy and Electoral Assistance and University of the Philippines Center for Integrative and Development Studies, 2020).
23. Sofia Tomacruz, "China to Donate More Coronavirus Testing Kits, Protective Equipment to PH", *Rappler*, 18 March 2020, https://www.rappler.com/nation/254993-china-donation-coronavirus-testing-kits-protective-

equipment/; Sofia Tomacruz, "12 Chinese Experts Tapped to Aid PH Coronavirus Response", *Rappler*, 2 April 2020, https://www.rappler.com/nation/256816-chinese-experts-tapped-aid-philippines-coronavirus-response/.
24. Sofia Tomacruz, "Duterte Thanks Xi Again during Coronavirus Briefing", *Rappler*, 14 April 2020, https://www.rappler.com/nation/257909-duterte-thanks-china-xi-again-coronavirus-briefing-april-13-2020/.
25. Lian Buan, "DOH Discards Some Inaccurate Virus Test Kits from China", *Rappler*, 28 March 2020, https://www.rappler.com/nation/256253-china-test-kits-discarded-poor-accuracy/.
26. Rebecca Ratcliffe, "Philippines and Indonesia Back Chinese Covid Jab despite Efficacy Doubts", *The Guardian*, 14 January 2021, https://www.theguardian.com/world/2021/jan/14/philippines-and-indonesia-back-chinese-covid-jab-despite-efficacy-doubts.
27. Reuters, "Philippines' Duterte Defends Purchase of Chinese COVID-19 Vaccine", 14 January 2021, https://www.reuters.com/world/china/philippines-duterte-defends-purchase-chinese-covid-19-vaccine-2021-01-13/.
28. Adrian Ayalin and Katrina Domingo, "COA Flags 'Deficiencies' in DOH Management of P67-B COVID Funds", *ABS-CBN News*, 11 August 2021, https://news.abs-cbn.com/news/08/11/21/coa-spots-deficiencies-in-handling-of-p67-b-covid-funds; Katrina Domingo, "After Backlash, DOH Halts Procurement of Laptops Worth P700,000", *ABS-CBN News*, 16 August 2021, https://news.abs-cbn.com/news/08/16/21/doh-halts-purchase-of-laptops-worth-p700000.
29. Lian Buan, "Pharmally Had P625,000 Capital before Bagging P8 Billion in COVID-19 Contracts", *Rappler*, 30 August 2021, https://www.rappler.com/newsbreak/in-depth/pharmally-pharmaceutical-corporation-capital-billion-covid-contracts.
30. Pia Ranada, "Biggest Pandemic Supplier Has Links to Ex-Duterte Adviser Michael Yang", *Rappler*, 28 August 2021, https://www.rappler.com/newsbreak/investigative/biggest-pandemic-supplier-has-links-to-ex-duterte-adviser-michael-yang; Sofia Tomacruz, "How the Duterte Gov't Shut Out Local PPE Producers during a Pandemic", *Rappler*, 6 September 2021, https://www.rappler.com/newsbreak/in-depth/how-duterte-government-shut-out-filipino-ppe-producers-during-pandemic; Sofia Tomacruz, "'Betrayal' of Filipinos: Senators Bare Cost of Gov't Preference for PPE Imports", *Rappler*, 8 September 2021, https://www.rappler.com/nation/betrayal-of-filipinos-senate-bares-cost-government-preferrence-ppe-imports.
31. Joseph Kready, Shishila Awung Shimray, Muhammad Nihal Hussain, and Nitin Agarwal, "YouTube Data Collection Using Parallel Processing", *2020 IEEE International Parallel and Distributed Processing Symposium Workshops (IPDPSW)* (2020): 1119–22.

32. Adele Webb, "He May Have Insulted Obama, but Duterte Held Up a Long-Hidden Looking Glass to the US", *The Conversation*, 9 September 2016, https://www.abc.net.au/news/2016-09-09/he-may-have-insulted-obama2c-but-duterte-held-up-a-long-hidden/7830872.
33. Charles P. Wallace, "Manila Senate Rejects US Pact", *Los Angeles Times*, 16 September 1991, https://www.latimes.com/archives/la-xpm-1991-09-16-mn-1690-story.html; Alfred W. McCoy, "Circles of Steel, Castles of Vanity: The Geopolitics of Military Bases on the South China Sea", *The Journal of Asian Studies* 75, no. 4 (2016): 975–1017.
34. Rodrigo Roa Duterte, "5th State of the Nation Address of the President of the Philippines to the Congress of the Philippines", Presidential Communications Operations Office, 27 July 2020, https://pcoo.gov.ph/wp-content/uploads/2020/07/20200727-5TH-State-of-the-Nation-Address-of-Rodrigo-Roa-Duterte-President-of-the-Philippines-to-the-Congress-of-the-Philippines.pdf.
35. Frances Mangosing, "Pro-China Governor Opposes PH-US Live-Fire Drills", *Inquirer.net*, 13 January 2022, https://newsinfo.inquirer.net/1539757/pro-china-gov-opposes-ph-us-live-fire-drills.
36. Rodrigo Roa Duterte, "Speech during the 10th Biennial National Convention and the 20th Founding Anniversary Celebration of the Chinese Filipino Business Club Inc.", Presidential Communications Operations Office, 19 February 2018, https://pcoo.gov.ph/wp-content/uploads/2018/02/PRRD-10th-Biennial-National-Convention-and-20th-Founding-Anniversary-Celebration-of-the-Chinese-Filipino-Business-Club-Inc.pdf.
37. Ruth Abbey Gita-Carlos, "Duterte Maintains 'Neutral' Stance on Russia-Ukraine Conflict", *Philippine News Agency*, 17 March 2022, https://www.pna.gov.ph/articles/1170053.
38. Sundy Mae Locus, "Duterte on Russia-Ukraine Conflict: Not Our Battle to Fight", *GMA News*, 17 March 2022, https://www.gmanetwork.com/news/topstories/nation/825429/duterte-on-russia-ukraine-conflict-not-our-battle-to-fight/story/.
39. Camille A. Aguinaldo, "Duterte Slams US for Warning against Buying Russian Submarines", *Business World*, 18 August 2018, https://www.bworldonline.com/the-nation/2018/08/18/181280/duterte-slams-us-for-warning-against-buying-russian-submarines/.
40. "Philippines to Proceed with Deal to Buy Russian Helicopters", *ABC News*, 9 March 2022, https://abcnews.go.com/International/wireStory/philippines-proceed-deal-buy-russian-helicopters-83337867.
41. Michaela del Callar, "Russian Envoy Praises Duterte Neutrality on Ukraine War", *GMA News Online*, 21 March 2022, https://www.gmanetwork.com/

news/topstories/nation/825772/russian-envoy-praises-duterte-neutrality-on-ukraine-war/story/.
42. Nestor Corrales, "Make PH a Province of China, Duterte Jokes in Front of Chinese Envoy", *Inquirer.net*, 19 February 2018, https://globalnation.inquirer.net/164413/rodrigo-duterte-jest-making-ph-chinese-province.
43. Duterte, "5th State of the Nation Address", 27 July 2020.
44. Charles Kaut, "Utang na loob: A System of Contractual Obligation among Tagalogs", *Southwestern Journal of Anthropology* 17, no. 3 (1961): 256–72; Vicente L. Rafael, *Contracting Colonialism: Translation and Christian Conversion in Tagalog Society under Early Spanish Rule* (Durham: Duke University Press, 1993).
45. *Insider*, "China: 'We Understand and Support' the Philippines' Drug War", 14 October 2016, https://www.businessinsider.com/afp-china-says-supports-philippines-duterte-drug-war-2016-10; International Criminal Court, "Report on Preliminary Examination Activities 2020", 14 December 2020, https://www.icc-cpi.int/itemsDocuments/2020-PE/2020-pe-report-eng.pdf.
46. Pulse Asia, "April 2022 National Survey on the May 2022 Elections", 2 May 2022, https://www.pulseasia.ph/april-2022-nationwide-survey-on-the-may-2022-elections/.
47. Jairo Bolledo, "Bello Urges Youth: 'Force Marcos Jr., Sara Duterte to Join Debates'", *Rappler*, 9 April 2022, https://www.rappler.com/nation/elections/walden-bello-youth-should-force-ferdinand-bongbong-marcos-jr-sara-duterte-join-debates/; Dwight de Leon, "Comelec's Prolonged Marcos Ruling Prompts Second Follow-Up from Petitioners", *Rappler*, 8 April 2022, https://www.rappler.com/nation/elections/comelec-prolonged-ruling-marcos-jr-cases-prompts-follow-up-petitioners/; Lian Buan, "Oxford: Bongbong Marcos' Special Diploma 'Not a Full Graduate Diploma'", *Rappler*, 27 October 2021, https://www.rappler.com/nation/elections/oxford-bongbong-marcos-special-diploma-not-full-graduate-diploma/; Lian Buan, "SC Record Shows Marcos Estate Tax Final in 1999, Unpaid until Now Says DOF", *Rappler*, 30 March 2022, https://www.rappler.com/nation/marcos-estate-tax-final-executory-1999-dof-unpaid/.
48. Aries A. Arugay, "Foreign Policy and Disinformation Narratives in the 2022 Philippine Election Campaign", *ISEAS Perspective*, no. 2022/59, 6 June 2022, https://www.iseas.edu.sg/articles-commentaries/iseas-perspective/2022-59-foreign-policy-disinformation-narratives-in-the-2022-philippine-election-campaign-by-aries-a-arugay/.
49. Gemma B. Mendoza, "Networked Propaganda: How the Marcoses Are Using Social Media to Reclaim Malacanang", *Rappler*, 20 November 2019, https://www.rappler.com/newsbreak/investigative/245290-marcos-networked-propaganda-social-media/.

50. Enrico Berdox, "Propaganda Web: Pro-Marcos Literature, Sites, and Online Disinformation Linked", Vera Files, 11 December 2020, https://verafiles.org/articles/propaganda-web-pro-marcos-literature-sites-and-online-disinf?fbclid=IwAR0KSUlLNyBksiFRnJqf-NyPOAM3PfjYij2MP0kAhATDtCiphefBCYDxUks.
51. Alan Robles and Raissa Robles, "The Manchurian Candidate: Why China's Interest in the Philippine Election Is under Scrutiny as Duterte Prepares to Leave Office", *South China Morning Post*, 20 November 2021, https://www.scmp.com/week-asia/politics/article/3156732/manchurian-candidate-concerns-rise-over-puppet-politicians; Shibani Mahtani and Regine Cabato, "Why Crafty Internet Trolls in the Philippines May Be Coming to a Website Near You", *The Washington Post*, 26 July 2019, https://www.washingtonpost.com/world/asia_pacific/why-crafty-internet-trolls-in-the-philippines-may-be-coming-to-a-website-near-you/2019/07/25/c5d42ee2-5c53-11e9-98d4-844088d135f2_story.html; Ronald U. Mendoza, Imelda Deinla, and Jurel Yap, "Philippines: Diagnosing the Infodemic", *The Interpreter*, 1 December 2021, https://www.lowyinstitute.org/the-interpreter/philippines-diagnosing-infodemic.
52. Erick Nielson C. Javier, "Rethinking the Philippines' Deterrence in the South China Sea", *The Diplomat*, 26 March 2022, https://thediplomat.com/2022/03/rethinking-the-philippines-deterrence-in-the-south-china-sea/.
53. Department of National Defense, Philippines, *National Defense Strategy 2018-2022*, https://www.dnd.gov.ph/FilesUploaded/Ckeditor/file/NDS_7_August_2019.pdf.
54. "South China Sea Energy Exploration and Development", *Asia Maritime Transparency Initiative*, 2022, https://amti.csis.org/south-china-sea-energy-exploration-and-development/#:~:text=The%20South%20China%20Sea%20holds,with%20much%20more%20potentially%20undiscovered.
55. Leilani Chavez, "Geopolitical Standoff in South China Sea Leads to Environmental Fallout", *Mongabay*, 12 August 2021, https://news.mongabay.com/2021/08/geopolitical-standoff-in-south-china-sea-leads-to-environmental-fallout/.
56. Pratnashree Basu, "In Deep Water: Current Threats to the Marine Ecology of the South China Sea", Issue Briefs and Special Reports, Observer Research Foundation, 8 March 2021, https://www.orfonline.org/research/in-deep-water-current-threats-to-the-marine-ecology-of-the-south-china-sea/#_edn1.

4

Course Correction from Over-Militarization: National Security from the Duterte to the Marcos Jr. Administration

Julio S. Amador III and Deryk Matthew Baladjay

> *President Rodrigo Duterte's administration was a monumental shift in Philippine domestic and international security policies. His controversial stances have significantly affected how many view the Philippine security policy landscape. These would not have been possible without the prevalence of retired military personnel in civilian positions and their basic disposition to further the president's reactive agenda. This shift paved the way for the election of Ferdinand "Bongbong" Marcos Jr. to the presidency in 2022, marking the return of the Marcos family to public life. But while President Marcos ran on many of his predecessor's platform, he has conducted himself in a manner distant from and, at times, contrary to that of his predecessor. Marcos Jr. used the success and popularity*

of his predecessor to catapult himself to the highest office with the base of his government platform improving upon the mistakes of the previous administration.

Keywords: Duterte, Marcos, 2022 elections, national security, civil-military relations

INTRODUCTION

President Ferdinand Marcos Jr. won 58 per cent of the vote in the 2022 presidential elections and his running mate, Sara Duterte, daughter of his predecessor, won 61 per cent.[1] This victory would not have been possible without the seismic shifts of President Rodrigo Duterte's policies. While many of Duterte's statements and actions during his term were controversial, he remained popular in the eyes of the public, garnering the highest approval ratings of any president since 1986. However, not everything the Duterte administration enacted remained well-received. The more consequential effects that have taken the public eye are the impacts of the previous administration's policies on the COVID-19 pandemic and China.

The Duterte administration will probably go down in history as one whose reputation is mixed. On the international stage, he turned the Philippines away from its longstanding ally, the United States and pivoted towards China, a rival claimant state in the South China Sea. President Duterte notably acted in a manner contrary to his predecessor, the late President Benigno Aquino III. This, in and of itself, is not a surprising development given the pendulum nature of Philippine foreign policy. What is noteworthy is Duterte's public calling out of historical grievances and negative personal experiences with the United States, contributing to his antagonistic view towards it. To further spurn the United States, Duterte turned to China, which has since 1995 been a frequent intruder in Philippine waters and, in recent years, has become a great power openly challenging the United States for regional primacy. He described this as the Philippines enacting an "independent" foreign policy and trying to balance relations. Sidestepping the external security threat of China for most of his term, President Duterte then shifted security focus internally—a marked about-face from the Aquino administration considering that tensions in the South China Sea have been unresolved since 2012. This resulted in three "wars" or local campaigns against drugs, terrorism, and the communist insurgency.[2]

Taken by surprise by the COVID-19 pandemic, President Duterte, in concert with the rest of the international community placed the country under a mandatory lockdown to stem the rise of infections. The severity of the epidemic was first underestimated in the Philippines. The Philippines' Department of Health (DOH) rejected the concept of mass testing at the early onset of the pandemic, and the country resorted to military and other security officials as the frontline force in curbing COVID-19 breakouts after failing to take preventative measures.[3] Jan Robert Go's chapter in this volume explains Duterte's militarized approach to COVID-19 in more detail. President Duterte often used force and military display to enforce the quarantine measures, resulting in the world's longest lockdown.[4] The lockdowns themselves were endorsed by the Inter-Agency Task Force for the Management of Emerging Infectious Diseases (IATF-EID), partially dominated by ex-military figures.[5]

The *Bayanihan* to Heal as One Act of 2020 was then promulgated by the Congress that simultaneously declared a nationwide health emergency in the country and granted President Duterte temporary special powers.[6] However, alongside its implementation, President Duterte started providing law enforcement bodies with "shoot to kill" orders directed towards quarantine violators which consequently garnered criticisms from lawmakers and human rights advocates.[7] Detainment threats towards protestors asking for government aid during the earlier period of the lockdown were also issued by the president. Despite all of these, at the peak of the pandemic in 2020, eight in ten Filipinos expressed approval for the Duterte administration's response to the pandemic.[8]

This chapter explores the policy divergences of the Duterte and the Marcos Jr. administrations about national security governance. Prominent national security themes under the Duterte administration will be explored, followed by a section on the blurring lines of civil-military relations. The chapter then explores how the Duterte administration's policy preferences reverberated even throughout the 2022 presidential elections and contributed to the then-candidacy of incumbent President Ferdinand Marcos Jr. This chapter argues, however, that Marcos Jr., having relied on the political capital of the Duterte administration, sought to revise, change, or update the national security policies of his predecessor. There are distinguishable observations in the comparisons between the Duterte and the Marcos Jr. administrations. Lastly, the chapter offers policy recommendations on key national security concerns.

THE DUTERTE ADMINISTRATION'S SECURITY POLICY IMPRINTS

As early as the campaign period, Duterte had his eyes set on internal security, calling out social ills and woes as matters to be dealt with draconian measures.[9] Duterte doubled down on language and policy concerning drugs and criminality, extremist fundamental terrorism, and political violence from the communist insurgency. Coming from Davao in Mindanao, Duterte not only amplified internal sentiments but also brought security concerns of Mindanao into national prominence.[10] He precisely ran on these platforms and saw the state security apparatus as the primary instrument in executing his national policies. The Duterte administration would lay out in its 2017 National Security Policy and its 2018 National Security Strategy a strong emphasis on public safety.[11]

War on Drugs and Criminality

The most (in)famous position of President Duterte was the securitization of the drug problem, arguing that it was from which other criminal acts stem from.[12] Based on a 2015 survey, the prevalence of drug usage among Filipinos aged 10 to 69 years old is 2.3 per cent, or an estimated 1.8 million users, which was higher than the 2012 and 2008 estimates.[13] This spurred his most well-known campaign promise to eliminate drugs and crime in "three to six months".[14] Whether or not he genuinely thought he could accomplish that within the established timeframe, Duterte was serious about undertaking an anti-drug campaign. He repeated his determination to tackle this problem in his inaugural speech[15] and in his first State of the Nation Address (SONA)[16].

Any good intentions to address this problem were immediately marred and undermined by rampant extrajudicial killings by vigilantes and accusations of state-sponsored executions. Within the president's first 100 days in office, more than 3,000 people were reported to have been killed (half by unidentified attackers and the other half in police operations).[17] By the end of his term, around 6,000 people were killed during official anti-drug operations.[18] The chapter in this volume by Bianca Franco discussed this issue extensively. The controversial war on drugs garnered widespread criticism from both within the Philippines and from the international community, such as the United Nations Human Rights Council[19] and the International Criminal Court (ICC).[20] The ICC's criticism prompted President Duterte's move to withdraw from the international body, which took effect in 2019.[21] Despite the controversies, the drug war was largely approved by the public at its apex in 2018.[22] The popularity continued until the end of his term in early 2022 with record-high approval ratings.[23] Duterte's drug war was a pivotal policy because of its geopolitical ramifications; Duterte lambasted statements of concern by the United States, European Union, and international bodies as political interference and also contributed partly to his pivot to China, which this chapter later discusses.

The impact of the anti-drug campaign continued long after his end of term. As of 26 January 2023, the ICC has authorized its prosecutor to resume the investigation in the country,[24] and more recently rejected a domestic court appeal against the resumption of the probe.[25] The Chamber stated that "the various domestic initiatives and proceedings, assessed collectively, do not amount to tangible, concrete and progressive investigative steps", which indicated that the ICC has declined the inadmissibility of the investigation from the Philippines. Given this verdict, the investigation will cover the alleged crimes committed from November 2011 to March 2019, covering the war on drugs campaign by President Duterte when he was Davao City's mayor until the early years of his presidency.[26] As a response to this, President Duterte asserted that the reported killings under his war on drugs campaign are based on his oath "to protect the [Filipino] people" when he assumed presidency (see Bianca Francos's chapter on political violence and the drug war).[27]

His justification has been then supported by some of his government allies from both the legislative[28] and the Justice Department[29] as they argue the state's supposed judicial capacity and independence in investigating the alleged crimes against humanity under the controversial campaign. Notable political personalities made justifications of President Duterte's war on drugs strategy and protected him from potential prosecution by the ICC.[30]

Anti-Terrorism Campaign

On 23 May 2017, a five-month-long siege of the Islamic City of Marawi in Lanao del Sur began. It started when a combined Philippine military and police force attempted to apprehend Isnilon Hapilon, an Abu Sayyaf leader and an Islamic State (IS)-affiliate. A firefight broke out in the afternoon, and Hapilon's forces in the city called on reinforcements from another IS-affiliated group—Maute.[31] The entirety of Mindanao was placed under martial law at the onset of the battle.[32] More than 200,000 residents in Marawi were forced to evacuate after the IS group took over the city.[33] By the end of the conflict, nearly a hundred civilians died,[34] about 168 government personnel and almost a thousand IS terrorists were killed. Among the estimated 127,000 people from the most affected area, none were able to return to their homes destroyed by the siege. Only short, accompanied visits by the military were done.

Duterte created Task Force *Bangon* (Rise) Marawi, "an inter-agency force for the recovery, reconstruction, and rehabilitation of the city of Marawi and other localities", through the Administrative Order No. 03. The task force is responsible for organizing and deploying a response team to accommodate needs of the affected families, conducting post-conflict needs assessment, facilitating and supervising the construction of the shelters for the displaced persons and restoration of public utilities, assisting their basic needs and providing an environment conducive to the revival of business and livelihood activities, and ensuring the restoration and maintenance of peace and order.[35] With this, rehabilitation and reconstruction was 75 per cent complete by the end of President Duterte's term[36] and is currently ongoing.

Martial law in Mindanao persisted after the Marawi Siege until the end of 2019. It was extended thrice by Congress to continue the anti-terrorism campaign requested by President Duterte as there seemed to be an unspecified rebellion in the region. Opposition politicians and private petitioners argued that there was no rebellion that could justify the president's request. Mindanao was under military rule for two years and seven months.[37] Upon its lifting, former Department of National Defense Secretary Delfin Lorenzana stated that there is already confidence among security officials that peace and order in Mindanao can be continuously maintained.[38] It was then reported that violent conflict was reduced by a 30 per cent drop from 2017 to 2018, with the regional crime rate in the SOCCSKSARGEN region dropping to 27.04 per cent in November 2019 from 36.64 per cent in 2017. However, incidents of extrajudicial killings persisted.[39]

Of the many pieces of legislation passed by the Duterte administration, none have been as controversial as the Republic Act No. 11479, also known as the Anti-Terrorism Act of 2020.[40] Much like the drug war, the Anti-Terrorism Act has been a subject of extensive criticism. The Human Rights Watch (HRW) called it a "human rights disaster in the making".[41] Within the Philippines, thirty-seven petitions have been filed against the law as of publication.[42] Opposed stances on the said law are primarily due to the tendency of some of its portions to violate basic rights and induce red-tagging (that is, harassing or persecuting individuals or groups for known or suspected communist activities), such as Section 29 that "allows law enforcers or military personnel to take custody of suspected terrorists for 14 days, extendible by another 10 days, before bringing them before judicial authorities".[43]

The United Nations Human Rights Committee also raised its concern on the possible legitimation of antagonism and red-tagging towards critics, human rights advocates, and journalists under the said law, as well as its implications on one's freedoms of speech and peaceful assembly.[44] Despite these concerns, the Supreme Court ultimately declared the law to be constitutional save for a couple of provisions in December 2021.[45] It only declared the unconstitutionality of two provisions, specifically the inclusion of "mass actions and similar exercise of civil and political rights" as one of the definitions of terrorism under Section 4 and the allowing of the Anti-Terrorism Council to grant requests from foreign agencies or bodies to designate individuals or groups as part of terrorist organizations under Section

25.⁴⁶ The Duterte administration paid lip service to combating terrorism by overly militarizing its securitization of the issue instead of focusing on social and economic development.⁴⁷

The Anti-Communist Insurgency Campaign

President Duterte initially announced a cease-fire with "leftist rebels", that is, the New People's Army (NPA) and the Communist Party of the Philippines (CPP) during his first SONA.⁴⁸ The cease-fire persisted until February 2017. During this time, peace talks were conducted in Oslo, Norway. Conflict resumed when the NPA-CPP accused the Duterte administration of failing to release all political prisoners and when the government cited NPA clashes with the military. Peace talks ultimately dissolved in November 2017.⁴⁹

In a shift in policy, President Duterte signed Executive Order No. 7 which formed the National Task Force to End Local Communist Armed Conflict (NTF-ELCAC), designed to implement a "whole-of-nation" approach to eradicate communist rebellion⁵⁰ and achieve a "sustainable and inclusive peace" through a multi-pronged approach to ensure there will be no reason for a communist group to call on vulnerable sectors and communities.⁵¹ President Duterte explained that the NTF-ELCAC addresses "root causes" of communist armed conflict and builds conflict-resilient communities.⁵² The focus on counterinsurgency was interesting because the Philippine military had for years—between the Arroyo and Aquino administrations from 2001 to 2016—argued that it had significantly diminished the combat strength of the NPA. But in contrast, in many of the subsequent pressers of NTF-ELCAC, it would defend its budget allocation and the military's internal security focus by emphasizing the threat of the communist insurgency.

In 2021, NTF-ELCAC was credited with designating the NPA-CPP as a terrorist organization, providing livelihood training to 194 *barangay*s, establishing more than 8,000 Barangay Health Stations, and many others.⁵³ In 2022, 822 *barangay*s reported benefitting from the task force's Barangay Development Program, at least 56 NPA guerrilla fronts dismantled, and neutralized 314 key members of the NPA on the ground.⁵⁴ NTF-ELCAC came under fire for accusations of red-tagging several groups in Philippine civil society and Congress. The same group was also previously called out for "posting fake quote-graphic on its social media channel and spreading false allegations" against ABS-CBN.[55] The outcry against the task force's actions led some in the legislature to move to defund it.[56] Additionally, the task force has failed to provide a complete accounting of its 2021–22 budget, leading to suspicions of "pork barrel".[57] However, in December 2022, the Congress' Bicameral Conference Committee decided to restore the PHP 10 billion budget initially allocated to NTF-ELCAC.[58] The task force was then reminded of its need to expedite the completion of its projects after a report showed its glacial progress in 2022, specifically having only accomplished 2 per cent of its projects with the remaining 98 per cent still under the pre-procurement or procurement stage.[59]

CIVIL-MILITARY RELATIONS AND GOVERNANCE

A staple of President Duterte's administration was the prevalence of retired military heads in senior civilian positions in the bureaucracy. President Duterte would repeatedly praise what he saw as the lack of debate and the non-confrontational attitude of the military when it came to directives.[60] His preference for military (and police) discipline compelled him to increase their take-home pay.[61] The various appointments to civilian positions were seen as means of facilitating coordination.[62] Duterte had appointed more than fifty key military appointments to high civilian positions[63] over the course of his six-year term (see Table 4.1 for a partial list), notably handing them ministerial portfolios not only in security affairs but also in local governance, the environment, human settlements and urban development, and social welfare.

With Duterte unabashedly being the law-and-order president, he also doubled salaries of military and uniformed personnel (MUP) a little after a year in office. This will become a major fiscal issue years down the line since retired personnel's pensions are indexed to salaries of active-duty personnel. Furthermore, MUP pension in the Philippines is mostly funded from public coffers, with security personnel not contributing to the fund—one of the most generous pension systems in the world. Many have warned that Duterte created an impending fiscal crisis leading to 2030 due to the populist move and also puts future chief executives in an awkward position where exercising fiscal

TABLE 4.1
Partial List of Retired Military Personnel Occupying Civilian Positions under Duterte

Government Agency	Appointment *Tenure*		
Department of the Interior and Local Government (DILG)	**Ret. Police Maj. Gen. Catalino Cuy** *April 2017–January 2018*	**Ret. Gen. Eduardo Año, AFP** *January 2018; November 2018–June 2022*	
Department of National Defense (DND)	**Ret. Major General Delfin Lorenzana, AFP** *June 2016–June 2022*		
Department of the Environment and Natural Resources (DENR)	**Ret. General Roy Cimatu, AFP** *May 2017–February 2022*		
National Security Council (NSC)	**Ret. General Hermogenes Esperon, AFP** *June 2016–June 2023*		
Department of Human Settlements and Urban Development (DHSUD)	Ret. Major General Eduardo del Rosario, AFP *January 2020–June 2022*		
Department of Information and Communications Technology (DICT)	**Ret. Brigadier General Eliseo M. Rio, Jr., AFP** *October 2017–June 2019*	Ret. Colonel Gregorio Honasan, PA *July 2019–October 2021*	
Department of Social Welfare and Development (DSWD)	Ret. Lieutenant General Rolando Joselito Bautista, AFP *October 2018–June 2022*		
Maritime Industry Authority (MARINA)	**Ret. General Rey Leonard Guerrero, AFP** *April 2018–October 2018*	**Ret. Vice Admiral Narciso A. Vingson, Jr., AFP** *October 2018–March 2020*	**Ret. Vice Admiral Robert Empedrad, PN** *March 2020–June 2022*

TABLE 4.1 (continued)

National Disaster Risk Reduction and Management Council (NDRRMC)	**Ret. Brigadier General Ricardo Jalad, PA** June 2016–June 2022
National Irrigation Administration	**Ret. General Ricardo Visaya, AFP** March 2017–June 2022
Philippine Coconut Authority	**Ret. General Benjamin Madrigal Jr., AFP** January 2020–June 2022
National Food Authority	**Ret. Major Jason Aquino, PA** December 2016–September 2018

Source: Collated by the authors.

prudence can only be done by taking away the benefits currently enjoyed by the Philippine military and police.

These developments play into the larger context of the Philippines' evolving democratic orientation with respect to its civil-military dynamics. This phenomenon, however, is not unique to the Philippines. As with any pseudo-democratic state, the relationship between the civilian and the military often blur as security apparatuses, such as the armed force, take on prominent roles in governance and public administration—a role usually reserved for the civil sector. But the military has long been a major actor in Southeast Asian history, often playing a significant role in nation-building and statecraft, political domination, and regime transitions.[64] Contemporary patterns have already been observed in Southeast Asia including Thailand, Malaysia, Singapore, Indonesia, and Myanmar.[65]

The Philippines is no different from the blurring of civil and military functions and actors. While its history with the armed forces points to similar development, the heavy reliance on security apparatuses in the context of a democratic regime became more pronounced under the leadership of President Duterte. The elevation of armed forces to public administration, and the convergence of national interests as interests of the armed forces, resulted in clashes between military-style leadership with democratic institutions and values.[66]

Two notable structural factors have contributed to the Philippines' recent militaristic disposition and securitization.[67] Firstly, civilian structures and functions have largely been militarized. Posts normally held by civilians, that is, departments and attached agencies, are held by retired military officials (refer to Table 4.1 again). The Armed Forces of the Philippines falls under the leadership of the Department of National Defense—a largely civilian body. Retired officials, however, find their way back to the government by accepting positions in the civilian bureaucracy.

Secondly, the Philippines' eroding democratic regime was instigated by Duterte's populist persona. President Duterte, having previously served as mayor of the city of Davao, had transformed national politics by consistently adopting a subnational mindset, bringing with him into the national domain the idiosyncrasies of running a city. This meant no room for debate and dialogue in the execution of national policies and that the president was to be at the centre of public affairs.

The benefits of having a government run by retired military officials depends on the context and nuance of military entrepreneurship, performativity, and legitimacy.[68] Drawing on their military training, uniformed personnel are known for their quick decision-making under extreme duress. Their strict adherence to hierarchy means public administration should be effective and top-down by default, following orders from a complex chain of command that views accountability as deference to someone with a higher rank. But military training may strictly be understood as resource management, and the need to adopt quick and responsive policies may also mean coming into headwinds with the rule of law, human rights, and democratic institutions in the process. A non-random elite survey of the Philippines' security and strategic sector found the military very supportive of appointing retired uniformed personnel to civilian government positions.[69] These only hints at the Duterte administration's growing reliance on utilizing the armed forces for both traditional and non-traditional security concerns.

INTERNAL SECURITY AMIDST THE 2022 PRESIDENTIAL ELECTION CAMPAIGN

Nearly two years after the COVID-19 pandemic's onset, President Marcos Jr. vowed an end to lockdowns.[70] Experts in different fields expressed their criticisms of the reliance on armed forces as a pandemic response.[71] The heavy dependence on military response and enforcing the lockdown has not produced commendable public health outcomes considering the slow testing, mounting fatality rates, and high positive cases.[72] Moreover, Duterte's militaristic response has failed to consider health and human security components, as well as science- and evidence-based approaches in dealing with the pandemic, as is discussed in Jan Robert Go's chapter in this volume.

The Marcos-Duterte ticket incorporated many of the Duterte administration's policies while simultaneously amending them to avoid repeating the same mistakes. The ticket supported the Anti-Terror Law and the NTF-ELCAC[73] and declared the need to defend the country's sovereignty against external actors, implying a desire to support the military and the coast guard, as well as recognizing the threat of China.[74]

Relations between the Duterte administration and China soured beginning 2020 on account of growing discontent with Chinese behaviour at seas. There were limited benefits gained from taking part in China's Belt and Road Initiative as investments failed to materialize,[75] with China expecting some *quid pro quo* in infrastructure contracts particularly the hiring of Chinese firms.[76] The intention was for China to assist in the "Build, Build, Build" infrastructure programme. Additionally, and most notably, Chinese incursions into Philippine territory did not cease. Unfortunately, open alignment with China did not result in a change to the status quo on the ground as the incidents only increased. In 2021 alone, vessels belonging to the Chinese maritime militia swarmed Julian Felipe Reef (Whitsun Reef)[77] and Chinese Coast Guard vessels fired water-cannons on Philippine vessels on their way to *Ayungin* Shoal (Second Thomas Shoal) for a resupply run.[78] As more of these incidents were reported, Filipino sentiments for sovereignty defence increased. The government faced growing pressure from various stakeholders (Filipino fishers, maritime domain experts, think tanks, and policymakers) to uphold a stronger stance and external defence posture.

Ultimately, the controversies and criticisms levied against the policies of the Duterte administration did not dissuade a majority of Filipino voters from choosing for their continuation.

FROM DUTERTE TO MARCOS: CONTINUITIES AND CHANGES

The popular policies and glaring setbacks of the Duterte administrations catapulted the Marcos administration to victory during the 2022 elections. Similarly, President Marcos inherited an overly militarized bureaucracy and has notably adjusted his predecessor's policies in security, government appointments and positions, and in foreign policy actions. In effect, the Marcos Jr. administration had to make sense of the leadership and governance norms internalized and executed by its predecessor.

Threats-based Securitization

The notable shift in security concerns was made during President Marcos's 2022 State of the Nation Address[79] when he declared that he "... will not preside over any process that will abandon even one square inch of territory of the Republic of the Philippines to any foreign power"—a strong policy pronouncement to begin his tenure and a marked departure from Duterte. While avoiding mentioning China by name, this signalled that his administration would reorient towards external actors who malign and impugn Philippine sovereign territory.

Thus, the internal security priorities developed during the Duterte administration were amended. First and foremost, the war on drugs, while praised for addressing a long-standing issue, would be restructured. The campaign going forward would officially focus on reduction, rehabilitation, and reintegration.[80] The Philippine National Police are reportedly emulating the whole-of-nation approach of NTF-ELCAC.[81] However, the Human Rights Watch states that there has been no significant difference under the administration and called for more substantive reforms.[82]

The same thinking was applied to the government's response to the COVID-19 pandemic. A re-evaluation in focus was given with the mask mandate lifted, the promise of no lockdowns, and the continuation of a vaccine campaign.[83] Sustained support for the campaigns of anti-communism and anti-terrorism remains in the new administration's agenda. One of the Marcos presidential campaign's promises was the assurance of funding for NTF-ELCAC.[84] Colonel Medel Aguilar, spokesperson for the Armed Forces of the Philippines (AFP), reaffirmed that the "defeat of threat groups", such as the communist rebels and terrorists, remains the most urgent task.[85] In this spirit, President Marcos has insisted on the AFP modernization to handle internal and external threats.[86]

Appointments: Towards Merit and Technocrats

President Marcos, prior to his official inauguration, announced a list of appointees. All eventually became part of his cabinet,[87] whereas some remain vacant. Civil-military relations have staggeringly blurred under the Duterte administration as key appointments were given to retired generals from the army and the police. This is not the case with the Marcos cabinet as key posts previously held by military personnel are now held by civilians with the experience and knowledge to steer departmental affairs, as shown in Table 4.2, as of writing.

TABLE 4.2
Cabinet Appointments of the Marcos and Duterte Administrations

Marcos Cabinet	Government Agency	Duterte Cabinet
Benjamin Abalos Jr. June 2022–Present	Department of the Interior and Local Government (DILG)	Ret. Gen. Eduardo Año, AFP January 2018; November 2018–June 2022
		Ret. Police Maj. Gen. Catalino Cuy April 2017–January 2018
Gilberto C. Teodoro Jr. June 2023–Present	Department of National Defense (DND)	Ret. Major General Delfin Lorenzana, AFP June 2016–June 2022
Ret. Gen. Carlito Galvez Jr., AFP January 2023–June 2023		
Ret. Gen. Jose Faustino Jr., AFP June 2022–January 2023		

TABLE 4.2 (continued)

Ma. Antonia Yulo-Loyzaga *July 2022–Present*	Department of the Environment and Natural Resources (DENR)	**Ret. General Roy Cimatu, AFP** *May 2017–February 2022*
Undersecretary (OIC) Ernesto D. Adobo Jr. *June 2022–July 2022*		
Ret. Gen. Eduardo Año, AFP *January 2023–Present*	National Security Council (NSC)	**Ret. General Hermogenes Esperon, AFP** *June 2016–2022*
Dr Clarita Carlos *July 2022–January 2023*		
Jose Rizalino L. Acuzar *July 2022–Present*	Department of Human Settlements and Urban Development (DHSUD)	**Ret. Major General Eduardo del Rosario, AFP** *January 2020–June 2022*
Undersecretary (OIC) Melissa Ardanas *July 2022–June 2022*		
Ivan John Enrile Uy *June 2022–Present*	Department of Information and Communications Technology (DICT)	**Ret. Colonel Gregorio Honasan, PA** *July 2019–October 2021*
		Ret. Brigadier General Eliseo M. Rio, Jr., AFP *October 2017–June 2019*
Rex Gatchalian *February 2023–Present*	Department of Social Welfare and Development (DSWD)	**Ret. Lieutenant General Rolando Joselito Bautista, AFP** *October 2018–June 2022*
Undersecretary (OIC) Eduardo Punay *December 2022–January 2023*		
Erwin Tulfo *June 2022–December 2022*		

TABLE 4.2 (continued)

Atty. Hernani N. Fabia June 2022–Present	Maritime Industry Authority (MARINA)	Ret. Vice Admiral Robert Empedrad, PN *March 2020–June 2022*
		Ret. Vice Admiral Narciso A. Vingson, Jr., AFP *October 2018–March 2020*
		Ret. General Rey Leonard Guerrero, AFP *April 2018–October 2018*
Engr. Eduardo G. Guillen *December 2022–Present*	National Irrigation Administration	Ret. General Ricardo Visaya, AFP *March 2017–June 2022*
Bernie F. Cruz *June 2022–Present*	Philippine Coconut Authority	Ret. General Benjamin Madrigal Jr., AFP *January 2020–June 2022*
Roderico R. Bioco *April 2023–Present* (As Administrator)	National Food Authority	Ret. Major Jason Aquino, PA *December 2016–September 2018*
Roderico R. Bioco *January 2023–April 2023* (As Acting Administrator)		
Atty. Judy Carol L. Dansal *June 2022–January 2023*		

Source: Collated by the authors.

The only notable appointee with a military background so far is Ret. General Eduardo Año as the new head of the National Security Council. In a stark contrast to his predecessor, only one key position in the civilian government is operated by an ex-military. The Department of National Defense now has a civilian secretary (minister)—the Philippines' first since 2010.

The New Normal: The World after COVID-19

There is now greater emphasis in opening the Philippine market in the context of the new normal. President Marcos has stated that he will appoint a health cabinet secretary once the pandemic situation stabilizes despite repeated calls to designate one.[88] He reasoned that the country could revive its economy and tourism industry when the DOH recovers from its "emergency stance". This became a major concern for the health sector considering his 100 days in position has already passed and yet he has not made any progress within the sector.[89] Yet, as mentioned previously, this situation was relatively welcomed in contrast to the previous administration's militarized approach.

Despite the vacant secretary position, DOH officer-in-charge (OIC) Maria Rosario Vergeire repeatedly gave assurances that the DOH is still fully functioning.[90] The DOH recommended the country to be lenient with border controls, reasoning that it "cannot be closed forever". Vergeire also stated that the longer it closes, the more it will affect people's health and livelihood.[91] Executive Order No. 7 was also issued by President Marcos detailing the voluntary wearing of masks indoors and outdoors, with the exception of health care facilities, medical transport vehicles, and public transportation. DOH asked the public to assess "individual risk" in spite of the relaxation of the mandatory face mask policy.[92]

The Philippine economy is still in the process of recovery from the pandemic's negative impact. With the recorded 8 per cent inflation rate in November 2022, the Marcos administration was looking into the areas that drove inflation and ways to lower the inflation rate.[93] During the 11th *Arangkada* Philippines Forum 2022 organized by the Joint Foreign Chambers (JFC), President Marcos mentioned that forming relationships with chambers of commerce will attract foreign direct investments. He also asked local and foreign business leaders to invest in "education and skills training, digitization of processes, research and development" to help the government in "transforming" the current economy.[94]

Due to the significant growth of e-commerce and digital economy during the pandemic, the Philippines' digital commerce environment should also be developed and transformed as it improves market access and expansion. This convinced President Marcos to issue an order to the Department of Information, Communications and Technology (DICT) to focus on the "need to digitalize the Philippines".[95] For the manufacturing sector, he emphasized the shift of focus to the development of local markets and its manufacturing capabilities. This is in the hopes that the manufacturing sector will be the driver of the country's economy in the years to come.[96]

Increase in International Visibility and Statecraft Performativity

President Duterte did not pay much attention to the strategic need for international posturing, perhaps due to a desire to attract foreign participation (mainly from China) into his ambitious infrastructure blitz by de-emphasizing territorial and geopolitical conflicts. In contrast, Marcos Jr. administration began recalibrating its visibility and posturing. Seven months after his inauguration, President Marcos has made eight official travels for the purpose of state visits and international conferences—a feat Duterte was not able to do. In an interview, he expressed that his travels signify "the visibility of the Philippines" in the international arena and it would be a big help in attracting investors and whipping up international support for the 2016 Arbitral Ruling.[97]

President Marcos recently went to Davos, Switzerland for the 2023 World Economic Forum (WEF) from 16 to 20 January 2023.[98] This trip favourably "positioned the Philippines" in the new global economy. According to the president, the country's participation in WEF is relevant in reintroducing itself to the international community considering that the forum is where "world leaders and executives of international companies" meet. His trip to Switzerland resulted in commitments from ten international companies to invest and expand their businesses in the country.[99] President Marcos's confidence in this endeavour was shown when, according to the Department of Finance Secretary Benjamin Diokno, he pitched the sovereign wealth fund as the country's financial portfolio despite not having been passed by the Senate.[100]

The Philippines' 2-plus-2 meeting with Washington on 11 April 2023 revitalized crucial aspects of the bilateral relations, including emphasis on the rules-based international order, modernization of the alliance, economic and environmental security, and advancing and developing new partnerships through minilaterals such as the Quad and AUKUS.[101] After six shaky years during Duterte's reactionary US policy, which Charmaine Misalucha-Willoughby's chapter discussed, Manila and Washington resumed security dialogues between their respective chief executives. The talks' agenda include the tension over the South China Sea and Taiwan. The bilateral relations between the Philippines and the United States have been around for seven decades and are tied together by its Mutual Defense Treaty and other agreements which allow the US troops to exercise its drills in the Philippines.[102]

While reconnecting ties with the United States, President Marcos is also strengthening economic ties with China, displaying a more calibrated attitude towards the economic giant. He visited Beijing on 4 January 2023 where he was able to bring home US$22 billion worth of investment pledges, in contrast to Duterte's US$24 billion which did not fully materialize.[103] He also signed fourteen bilateral agreements, including a deal regarding maritime issues.[104] Nevertheless, the Marcos administration maintains a careful eye towards Beijing as the country remains deeply enmeshed in maritime issues with China. During the visit, President Marcos brought up the "touchy issue" considering it was inevitable, but he did not expect any major resolution.[105] Aptly raised, the Marcos administration maintains the 2016 Arbitral Award as a core foreign policy element of its engagement with China, as President Marcos himself was cleverly quoted as saying: "We have no conflict claims with China. What we have is China making claims on our territory."

CONCLUSION

The discussion indicates a revival of the Philippines' international posturing and messaging, as it relates to Manila's national security priorities and outlook. All of these remains in stark contrast to the Duterte administration's securitized pandemic recovery and reactionary and brash conduct of foreign policy, resulting in an overall diminishing of the Philippines' international posturing and credibility. The Marcos administration uniquely positions the Philippines in a proactive manner seeking to recoup lost international footing, an unprecedented strategy not seen in the past administration. Notably, the Marcos administration is fixated on pump-priming the economy, facilitating post-pandemic recovery, and employing a clear hedging strategy that fluidly navigates the tense strategic competition between the two major regional powers.

This chapter offers several policy recommendations in the short-, medium-, and long-term. Some of these policies must be prompted by the national government at the soonest possible time, while others can serve as legacy legislations that will outlast the current administration.

1. Improving the procurement mechanisms for the modernization of the Armed Forces of the Philippines

The AFP's modernization is now entering its third and final years. This not only means an added list of military assets and materiel[106] but also means recouping time for assets from previous horizons that were left in the backburner.[107] There remain backlogs from Horizons 1 and 2 acquisitions as of this writing.[108] Delays in military acquisitions have long been attributed to the government's burgeoning procurement law ever since the first iteration of the modernization programme.[109] Because the modernization programme reflects the armed forces' perceptions of security outlook, the Philippines' procurement law needs to accommodate the fast pacing of strategic acquisition. President Marcos Jr. has assured that the modernization of AFP is on track.[110]

2. Implementing self-reliant defence measures

The government must understand that the more critical issue that needs addressing is developing a sustainable defence posture that is uniquely Filipino—a web of interconnected industries made by and for Filipinos from the top military brass, strategic thinkers, academe, research and innovation, and congruent critical defence industries. Manila has, for the longest time, leveraged its alliance with the United States and its partnerships with other like-minded countries to mitigate national security concerns. These are significant for the Philippines' grand strategy when it comes to securing its national interests at home and abroad. While the Philippines' alliances will play a huge role in boosting defence industries with strategic importance and much needed investments, overly relying on foreign powers to supplement national security needs is unsustainable and untenable.

3. Addressing the ballooning MUP Pension

Significant portion of the defence budget has gone to personnel pensions in recent history. This situation has to be remedied. National defence leadership must find ways to fund both the pension and its ambitions to expand and upscale.[111] Therefore, the defence budget must be diverted from pension expenditures. The national government is preparing to develop a "self-regenerating" plan to sustain pensions.[112]

4. Retired military officials and public administration

Occupying civilian posts and functions with retired military personnel have its benefits under unique circumstances, such as when the Philippines enter into wartime[113] scenarios. But until such time comes, posts should be left to the expertise and calibre of individuals well-versed in issues. Retired military officials carry with them rich experiences useful in the execution of national policies, but a number of years following their retirement must be prescribed before allowing them to serve in a government post, similar to the wording found in Section 18 of RA 11709 (sr. 2021) as amended by RA 11939,[114] prohibiting retired officials from immediately serving the post of the Secretary of National Defense within a year of their retirement.

5. Tenure of military officers serving in the AFP

The Duterte administration had initially implemented tenure security of military officers through RA 11709 and was improved upon by President Marcos Jr. through RA 11939.[115] These laws were efforts to institutionalize professionalism in the armed forces. Both the Department of National Defense and the AFP welcomed the revisions made on the tenure laws.[116]

6. Investing in research and development and pump-priming the defence industry sector

Research and development are crucial components to driving innovation and upskilling in national security initiatives. The Philippines boasts of agencies with exclusive focus on key aspects of national security such as the Departments of Science and Technology, National Defense, Trade and Industry, and Information and Communications Technology. But no overarching national policy has been forwarded to coordinate research and development efforts among these agencies. The national government must steer discussions and attention towards technologies that will impact the Philippines and direct these agencies, with fresh investment infusions, to conduct the necessary efforts. One important initiative in this front is the passage of a law on Special Defense Economic Zones (SpeDEZ), championed by select officials in both houses of Congress.[117] SpeDEZ are government lands to be developed by foreign investments that focus on defence industries utilizing domestic labour and resources. However, efforts from officials in this area remain scattered and stalled and have not been advanced in recent months.

7. Moving towards people-centric security policies

The common criticism raised against Duterte was his crass pursuit of internal stability, often at the expense of Filipino lives. As laid out in this chapter, the human security angle was left in the backburner; and even when the Duterte administration did manage to take this into account, it did so half-heartedly still to the detriment of Filipinos.[118] President Marcos has given his signal to continue the operations of the National Task Force to End Local Communist Armed Conflict (NTF-ELCAC),[119] but with an emphasis on peace, unity, and economic development as core principles.[120]

These policy recommendations are not new and have already been raised in previous administrations. The previous administration's fixation on internal security issues has derailed long-lasting policies that could have potentially shaped the Philippines' national posturing and have missed the rapidly closing window. The tendency to militarize governance and public administration was a pretence to resolving national security concerns. The same issues now face the Marcos Jr. administration and much like his predecessor, the window to enact meaningful national security reforms is fast closing.

Notes

1. ABS-CBN, "Halalan 2022 Philippine Election Results", https://halalanresults.abs-cbn.com (accessed 15 February 2023).
2. See Charmaine Misalucha-Willoughby, "From Entrepreneur to Saboteur: How the Philippines Won and Lost the South China Sea on Social Media", Chapter 3 of this volume.
3. Nyshka Chandran, "The Pandemic Has Given Armies in Southeast Asia a Boost", *Foreign Policy*, 15 June 2020, https://foreignpolicy.com/2020/06/15/coronavirus-pandemic-army-military-southeast-asia-boost-indonesia-philippines-jokowi-duterte-authoritarianism/ (accessed 17 January 2023).
4. Aie Balagtas See, "Rodrigo Duterte Is Using One of the World's Longest COVID-19 Lockdowns to Strengthen His Grip on the Philippines", *Time*, 15 March 2021, https://time.com/5945616/covid-philippines-pandemic-lockdown/ (accessed 17 January 2023).
5. Nikko Dizon, "Duterte and His Generals: A Shock and Awe Response to the Pandemic", *Rappler*, 31 July 2020, https://www.rappler.com/newsbreak/in-depth/duterte-shock-and-awe-coronavirus-pandemic-response-generals/ (accessed 17 January 2023).
6. Krissy Aguilar, "LOOK: Bayanihan to Heal as One Act Signed by Duterte", *Inquirer.net*, 25 March 2020, https://newsinfo.inquirer.net/1248107/look-bayanihan-to-heal-as-one-act-signed-by-duterte (accessed 24 March 2023).
7. Darryl Esguerra, "Palace: Duterte 'Shoot to Kill' Order Not a Crime, Allowed for 'Self-preservation'", *Inquirer.net*, 3 April 2020, https://newsinfo.inquirer.net/1253398/palace-says-duterte-shoot-to-kill-order-not-a-crime-violence-allowed-for-self-preservation (accessed 24 March 2023).
8. Darryl Esguerra, "Pulse Asia: 8 in 10 Filipinos Favor Duterte Admin's COVID-19 Response", *Inquirer.net*, 8 October 2020, https://newsinfo.inquirer.net/1345150/pulse-asia-8-in-10-filipinos-favor-duterte-admins-covid-19-response (accessed 17 January 2023).
9. Malcolm Cook, "Turning Back? Philippine Security Policy under Duterte", Lowy Institute, 24 June 2016, https://www.lowyinstitute.org/publications/turning-back-philippine-security-policy-under-duterte.

10. Christopher Ryan B. Maboloc, "Situating the Mindanao Agenda in the Radical Politics of President Duterte", *Iqra* 4 (2017): 3–24, https://www.researchgate.net/profile/Christopher-Ryan-Maboloc/publication/325466860_Situating_the_Mindanao_Agenda_in_the_Radical_Politics_of_President_Duterte/links/5b7dcc9b92851c1e1227ca82/Situating-the-Mindanao-Agenda-in-the-Radical-Politics-of-President-Duterte.pdf.
11. National Security Council, *2017-2022 National Security Policy for Change and Well-Being of the Filipino People*, https://nsc.gov.ph/attachments/article/NSP/NSP-2017-2022.pdf; National Security Council, *2018 National Security Strategy – Security and Development for Transformational Change and Well-Being of the Filipino People*, https://www.officialgazette.gov.ph/downloads/2018/08aug/20180802-national-security-strategy.pdf.
12. Ananda Devi Domingo-Almase, "The Case of the Philippine Drug War: When the State Securitizes an Existential Threat to Public Safety", Asia Research Institute-University of Nottingham, 1 June 2017, https://theasiadialogue.com/2017/06/01/the-case-of-the-philippine-drug-war-when-the-state-securitizes-an-existential-threat-to-public-safety/.
13. Jodesz Gavilan, "DDB: Philippines Has 1.8 Million Current Drug Users", *Rappler*, 19 September 2016, https://www.rappler.com/nation/146654-drug-use-survey-results-dangerous-drugs-board-philippines-2015/ (accessed 30 January 2023).
14. Ariel Paol Tejada, "Duterte Vows to End Criminality", *Philstar*, 20 February 2016, https://www.philstar.com/headlines/2016/02/20/1555349/duterte-vows-end-criminality-3-months (accessed 16 January 2023).
15. Official Gazette, "Inaugural Address of President Rodrigo Roa Duterte", 30 June 2016, https://www.officialgazette.gov.ph/2016/06/30/inaugural-address-of-president-rodrigo-roa-duterte-june-30-2016/ (accessed 16 January 2023).
16. Official Gazette, "First State of the Nation Address", 25 July 2016, https://www.officialgazette.gov.ph/2016/07/25/rodrigo-roa-duterte-first-state-of-the-nation-address-july-25-2016/ (accessed 16 January 2023).
17. Catherine S. Valente, "First 100 Days Yield Significant Accomplishments", *The Manila Times*, 8 October 2016, https://web.archive.org/web/20191205121827/https://www.manilatimes.net/2016/10/08/news/top-stories/first-100-days-yield-significant-accomplishments/290072/ (accessed 16 January 2023).
18. Argyll Cyrus Geducos, "Duterte Legacy: A Quick Look Back at Duterte's 6 Years", *Manila Bulletin*, 30 June 2022, https://mb.com.ph/2022/06/29/duterte-legacy-a-quick-look-back-at-dutertes-6-years/ (accessed 16 January 2023). Numbers have been disputed over the years and subjected to much debate.

19. Christine Avendaño, Jaymee Gamil, and Dona Pazzibugan, "38 Nations Ask PH: Stop Killings, Probe Abuses", *Philippine Daily Inquirer*, 24 June 2018, https://globalnation.inquirer.net/168095/38-nations-ask-ph-stop-killings-probe-abuses (accessed 16 January 2023).
20. Eimor P. Santos, "Int'l Criminal Court Chief Prosecutor Warns PH over Drug Killings", *CNN Philippines*, 14 October 2016, https://www.cnnphilippines.com/news/2016/10/14/Intl-Criminal-Court-chief-prosecutor-warns-PH-over-drug-killings.html_(accessed 16 January 2023).
21. "Republic of the Philippines", International Criminal Court, https://www.icc-cpi.int/philippines (accessed 16 January 2023).
22. Jelly Musico, "War on Drugs' Net Satisfaction Rating Remains 'Very Good': SWS", Philippine News Agency, 8 November 2018, https://www.pna.gov.ph/articles/1053323 (accessed 16 January 2023).
23. Azer Parrocha, "Duterte's End of Term High Rating 'Rarity' in PH Pres'l Politics", Philippine News Agency, 11 April 2022, https://www.pna.gov.ph/articles/1172012 (accessed 16 January 2023).
24. ICC-CPI, "ICC Pre-Trial Chamber I Authorises Prosecutor to Resume Investigation in the Philippines", International Criminal Court, 26 January 2023, https://www.icc-cpi.int/news/icc-pre-trial-chamber-i-authorises-prosecutor-resume-investigation-philippines (accessed 23 March 2023).
25. Kristel Limpot, Jelo Mantaring, and Anjo Alimario, "ICC to Continue Probe into Duterte's Drug War; Court Chamber Junks PH Appeal", *CNN Philippines*, 18 July 2023, https://www.cnnphilippines.com/news/2023/7/18/icc-to-continue-duterte-drug-war-probe.html (accessed 16 January 2023).
26. ICC-CPI, "ICC Pre-Trial Chamber".
27. Richa Noriega, "Duterte on ICC Probe: If I Have to Kill Those Who'd Want to Harm, So Be It", *GMA News Online*, accessed 31 January 2023, https://www.gmanetwork.com/news/topstories/nation/859245/duterte-on-icc-probe-if-i-have-to-kill-those-who-d-want-to-harm-so-be-it/story/ (accessed 23 March 2023).
28. Leonel Abasola, "Padilla Files Resolution Defending Former President Duterte", Philippine News Agency, 20 February 2023, https://www.pna.gov.ph/articles/1195640 (accessed 23 March 2023).
29. Ruth Abbey Gita-Carlos, "DOJ Tells ICC: We'll Settle Drug Issues on Our Own", Philippine News Agency, 28 January 2023, https://www.pna.gov.ph/articles/1193813 (accessed 23 March 2023).
30. Mainly Senator Robin Padilla, a popular actor-turned senator, and Senior Deputy Speaker (at the time, and former president) Gloria Macapagal-Arroyo.

31. Carmela Fonbuena, "How a Military Raid Triggered Marawi Attacks", *Rappler*, 29 May 2017, https://www.rappler.com/newsbreak/in-depth/171245-marawi-crisis-isis-plan-bautista/ (accessed 16 January 2023).
32. Agence France-Presse, "Martial Law in Mindanao: What We Know", *Inquirer.net*, 24 May 2017, https://newsinfo.inquirer.net/899173/martial-law-in-mindanao-what-we-know (accessed 16 January 2023).
33. Ted Regencia, "'A Failure': Marawi Verdict on Duterte Ahead of Annual Address", *Al Jazeera*, 22 July 2019, https://www.aljazeera.com/news/2019/7/22/a-failure-marawi-verdict-on-duterte-ahead-of-annual-address (accessed 23 March 2023).
34. *Gulf Times*, "Troops Kill Five Militants in Besieged Marawi City", 13 September 2017, https://www.gulf-times.com/story/563655/Troops-kill-five-militants-in-besieged-Marawi-city (accessed 16 January 2023); Carmela Fonbuena, "Gov't Death Toll in Marawi Siege Rises to 168", *Rappler*, 10 January 2018, https://www.rappler.com/nation/193307-government-forces-death-toll-marawi-siege-dna-test/ (accessed 16 January 2023); Victor Reyes, "12 Maute Stragglers Killed", *Malaya Business Insight*, 7 November 2017, https://web.archive.org/web/20181213131228/https://www.malaya.com.ph/business-news/news/12-maute-stragglers-killed (accessed 16 January 2023).
35. Official Gazette, Administrative Order No. 3, 28 June 2017, https://www.officialgazette.gov.ph/downloads/2017/06jun/20170628-AO-3-RRD.pdf (accessed 23 March 2023).
36. Elizabeth Marcelo, "Marawi Rehab 75% Complete", *Philippine Star*, 26 July 2021, https://www.philstar.com/nation/2021/07/26/2115159/marawi-rehab-75-complete.
37. Ian Nicolas Cigaral, "Martial Law in Mindanao Ends after 953 Days", *Philstar*, 1 January 2020, https://www.philstar.com/headlines/2020/01/01/1981218/martial-law-mindanao-ends-after-953-days/amp/ (accessed 24 March 2023); Antonio Montalvan II, "What Did Duterte's Martial Law Achieve in Mindanao?" *Al Jazeera*, 30 December 2019, https://www.aljazeera.com/amp/opinions/2019/12/30/what-did-dutertes-martial-law-achieve-in-mindanao (accessed 24 March 2023).
38. Cigaral, "Martial Law in Mindanao Ends after 953 Days".
39. Ryan Rosauro, "Martial Law in Mindanao: What Changed, What Didn't And—at What Cost", *Inquirer.net*, 2 January 2020, https://newsinfo.inquirer.net/1208251/martial-law-in-mindanao-what-changed-what-didnt-and-at-what-cost (accessed 16 January 2023).
40. Official Gazette, "RA 11479", 3 July 2020, https://www.officialgazette.gov.ph/2020/07/03/republic-act-no-11479/ (accessed 16 January 2023).

41. Human Rights Watch, "Philippines: New Anti-Terrorism Act Endangers Rights", 5 June 2020, https://www.hrw.org/news/2020/06/05/philippines-new-anti-terrorism-act-endangers-rights (accessed 16 January 2023).
42. Supreme Court of the Philippines, "Oral Arguments on the Anti-Terrorism Act of 2020", filmed 17 May 2021, https://sc.judiciary.gov.ph/oral-arguments/anti-terrorism-act/ (accessed 16 January 2023).
43. Kristine Patag, "SC Leaves Anti-Terrorism Act of 2020 Mostly Intact", *Philstar*, 9 December 2021, https://www.philstar.com/headlines/2021/12/09/2146795/sc-leaves-anti-terrorism-act-2020-mostly-intact (accessed 23 March 2023).
44. Mong Palatino, "UN Report Charts Human Rights Decline in the Philippines", *The Diplomat*, 11 November 2022, https://thediplomat.com/2022/11/un-report-charts-human-rights-decline-in-the-philippines/ (accessed 23 March 2023).
45. Rey Panaligan, "SC Declares Anti-Terrorism Act Constitutional except for 2 Provisions", *Manila Bulletin*, 9 December 2021, https://mb.com.ph/2021/12/09/sc-declares-anti-terrorism-act-constitutional-except-for-2-provisions-in-most-contested-law/ (accessed 16 January 2023).
46. Benjamin Pulta, "Anti-terror Law 'Constitutional': Supreme Court", Philippine News Agency, 9 December 2021, https://www.pna.gov.ph/articles/1162280#:~:text=The%20SC%20voted%2012%2D3,serious%20risk%20to%20public%20safety.%22 (accessed 24 March 2023).
47. Aries A. Arugay, Marc Batac, and Jordan Street, "An Explosive Cocktail – Counter-terrorism, Militarisation and Authoritarianism in the Philippines", Saferworld, June 2021, https://www.saferworld.org.uk/resources/publications/1351-an-explosive-cocktail-counter-terrorism-militarisation-and-authoritarianism-in-the-philippines (accessed 24 March 2023).
48. Official Gazette, "First State of the Nation Address".
49. RSJ, "TIMELINE: The Peace Talks between the Government and the CPP-NPA-NDF, 1986 - Present", *GMA News Online*, 24 November 2017, https://www.gmanetwork.com/news/topstories/specialreports/634324/timeline-the-peace-talks-between-the-government-and-the-cpp-npa-ndf-1986-present/story/ (accessed 16 January 2023).
50. Ruth Abbey Gita, "Duterte Creates Task Force to End Local Communist Armed Conflict", *SunStar*, 10 December 2018, https://www.sunstar.com.ph/article/1778056/Manila/Local-News/Duterte-creates-task-force-to-end-local-communist-armed-conflict (accessed 16 January 2023).
51. National Task Force to End Local Communist Armed Conflict, "About Us", https://www.ntfelcac.org/about (accessed 17 January 2023).

52. Lade Jean Kabagani, "NTF-ELCAC Addresses Root Causes of Communist Conflict: Duterte", *Philippine News Agency*, 26 July 2021, https://www.pna.gov.ph/articles/1148376 (accessed 17 January 2023).
53. Philippine News Agency, "NTF-ELCAC Sets Record Milestones vs. CPP-NDA-NDF", 23 July 2021, https://www.pna.gov.ph/articles/1148041 (accessed 17 January 2023).
54. Priam Nepomuceno, "NTF-ELCAC, Anti-Terrorism Act Crucial to PH Fight vs. Insurgency", *Philippine News Agency*, 30 May 2022, https://www.pna.gov.ph/articles/1175394.
55. Franco Luna, "More Raps Filed vs. NTF-ELCAC Execs over Red-Tagging, Fake News", *Philstar*, 7 December 2020, https://www.philstar.com/headlines/2020/12/07/2062096/more-raps-filed-vs-ntf-elcac-execs-over-red-tagging-fake-news (accessed 17 January 2023).
56. Vanne Elaine Terrazola, "'Waste of People's Money': Senators Want NTF-ELCAC Defunded over Red-Tagging Activities", *Manila Bulletin*, 22 April 2021, https://mb.com.ph/2021/04/22/waste-of-peoples-money-senators-want-ntf-elcac-defunded-over-red-tagging-activities/ (accessed 17 January 2023).
57. Melvin Gascon, "P10-Billion NTF-ELCAC 'Pork' Funds Flagged Anew", *Inquirer.net*, 7 October 2022, https://newsinfo.inquirer.net/1676484/p10-b-ntf-elcac-pork-funds-flagged-anew (accessed 17 January 2023).
58. Julie Aurelio, "NTF-Elcac Gets P10 Billion Back as Bicam Restores Fund Cuts", *Inquirer.net*, 6 December 2022, https://newsinfo.inquirer.net/1701751/ntf-elcac-gets-p10-billion-back-as-bicam-restores-fund-cuts (accessed 23 March 2023).
59. Daniza Fernandez, "NTF-Elcac Budget Restored to P10 Billion by Bicam", *Inquirer.net*, 5 December 2022, https://newsinfo.inquirer.net/1701375/ntf-elcac-budget-restored-to-p10-billion-by-bicam (accessed 23 March 2023).
60. Pia Ranada, "In 2018, Duterte Turns to Military for (Almost) Everything", *Rappler*, 12 December 2018, https://www.rappler.com/newsbreak/in-depth/218680-duterte-turns-to-philippine-military-yearend-2018/ (accessed 17 January 2023).
61. Ranada, "In 2018, Duterte Turns to Military for (Almost) Everything".
62. Gabriel Pabico Lalu, "Ex-military Chiefs at DND, NSC Facilitate Coordination - AFP SPOX", *Inquirer.net*, 16 January 2023, https://newsinfo.inquirer.net/1717055/fwd-afp-spox-says-having-ex-military-chiefs-at-dnd-nsc-good-for-coordination (accessed 17 January 2023).
63. Fe Zamora and Philip Tubeza, "Duterte Hires 59 Former AFP, PNP Men to Cabinet, Agencies", *Inquirer.net*, 27 June 2017, https://newsinfo.inquirer.net/908958/duterte-hires-59-former-afp-pnp-men-to-cabinet-agencies (accessed 17 January 2023).

64. Aurel Croissant, *Civil-Military Relations in Southeast Asia* (Cambridge: Cambridge University Press, 2018).
65. See relevant chapters in Alan Chong and Nicole Jenne, eds., *Asian Military Evolutions: Civil-Military Relations in Asia* (Bristol: Bristol University Press, 2023).
66. Aries A. Arugay, "The General's Gambit: The Military and Democratic Erosion in Duterte's Philippines", Heinrich Böll Stiftung Southeast Asia, 18 February 2021, https://th.boell.org/en/2021/02/18/generals-gambit-military-and-democratic-erosion-dutertes-philippines (accessed 17 January 2023).
67. Aries A. Arugay, "Militarizing Governance: Informal Civil-Military Relations and Democratic Erosion in the Philippines", in *Asian Military Evolutions: Civil-Military Relations in Asia*, edited by Alan Chong and Nicole Jenne (Bristol: Bristol University Press, 2023), pp. 68–89.
68. Henri J. Barkey, "Why Military Regimes Fail: The Perils of Transition", *Armed Forces & Society* 16, no. 2 (1990): 169–92. https://www.jstor.org/stable/45305829.
69. The security and strategic sector covers the academe, government (civilian and uniformed personnel), private sector, civil society and grassroots. The national security survey, however, was predominantly answered by military personnel (retired and active). See Julio S. Amador III, Aries A. Arugay, Deryk Matthew N. Baladjay, Justin Keith Baquisal, and Charmaine M. Willoughby, "National Security Survey 2022: Results and Findings", Amador Research Services, 24 May 2023, https://www.amadorresearchservices.com/publications/national-security-survey-2022%3A-results-%26-findings.
70. Jonas Alpasan, "Why Presidentiables' Stand on Terror Law Is an Election Issue", *Bulatlat*, 20 February 2022, https://www.bulatlat.com/2022/02/20/why-presidentiables-stand-on-terror-law-is-an-election-issue/ (accessed 17 January 2023).
71. Karl Hapal, "The Philippines' COVID-19 Response: Securitising the Pandemic and Disciplining the Pasaway", *Journal of Current Southeast Asian Affairs* 40, no. 2 (2021), https://journals.sagepub.com/doi/full/10.1177/1868103421994261 (accessed 5 July 2023).
72. Michael Yusingco and Angelika Pizarro, "The Militarized Response to the COVID-19 Pandemic in the Philippines: An Escalating Threat to Human Rights", *IACL-IADC Blog*, https://blog-iacl-aidc.org/2020-posts/2020/6/18/the-militarized-response-to-the-covid-19-pandemic-in-the-philippines-an-escalating-threat-to-human-rights (accessed 31 January 2023).
73. Alpasan, "Why Presidentiables' Stand on Terror Law Is an Election Issue".
74. Joseph Pedrajas, "PH Military Must Modernize, Respond to Eventualities – PBBM", *Manila Bulletin*, 9 November 2022, https://mb.com.ph/2022/11/08/

ph-military-must-modernize-respond-to-eventualities-pbbm/ (accessed 17 January 2023).

75. Jason Koutsoukis and Cecilia Yap, "China Hasn't Delivered on Its $24 Billion Philippines Promise", *Bloomberg*, 26 July 2018, https://www.bloomberg.com/news/articles/2018-07-25/china-s-24-billion-promise-to-duterte-still-hasn-t-materialized#xj4y7vzkg (accessed 17 January 2023).

76. Camille Elemia, "Duterte Aide: Marcos Administration Should Drop China-Backed Loans for Rail Projects", *BenarNews*, 20 July 2022, https://www.benarnews.org/english/news/philippine/projects-stalled-07202022141122.html (accessed 17 January 2023).

77. Sofia Tomacruz, "Timeline: China's Vessels Swarming Julian Felipe Reef, West PH Sea", *Rappler*, 30 April 2021, https://www.rappler.com/newsbreak/iq/timeline-china-vessels-julian-felipe-reef-west-philippine-sea-2021/ (accessed 17 January 2023).

78. Lucio Blanco Pitlo III, "The Second Thomas Shoal Incident and the Reset in Philippine-US Ties", *Asia Maritime Transparency Initiative*, 17 December 2021, https://amti.csis.org/the-second-thomas-shoal-incident-and-the-reset-in-philippine-u-s-ties/ (accessed 17 January 2023).

79. Official Gazette, "Ferdinand Marcos Jr's First State of the Nation Address", 25 July 2022, https://www.officialgazette.gov.ph/2021/07/26/ferdinand-r-marcos-jr-first-state-of-the-nation-address-july-25-2022/.

80. Chito Chavez, "PH Drug War Now Focuses on Remand Reduction, Rehab and Reintegration- PDEA", *Manila Bulletin*, 13 October 2022, https://mb.com.ph/2022/10/13/ph-drug-war-now-focuses-on-remand-reduction-rehab-and-reintegration-pdea/ (accessed 16 January 2023).

81. Beatrice Pinlac, "PNP Aims to Copy NTF-ELCAC's 'Holistic Approach' in War vs Drugs – Chief", *Inquirer.net*, 3 October 2022, https://newsinfo.inquirer.net/1674438/pnp-aims-to-copy-ntf-elcacs-holistic-approach-in-war-vs-drugs-chief (accessed 17 January 2023).

82. Human Rights Watch, "Philippines: No Letup in 'Drug War' under Marcos", 12 January 2023, https://www.hrw.org/news/2023/01/12/philippines-no-letup-drug-war-under-marcos (accessed 17 January 2023).

83. Cristina Eloisa Baclig, "From Duterte to Marcos: Covid Stays But Response Changes", *Inquirer.net*, 20 December 2022, https://newsinfo.inquirer.net/1707088/from-duterte-to-marcos-covid-stays-but-response-changes (accessed 17 January 2023).

84. Bernadette E. Tamayo, "Marcos Assures NTF-ELCAC of Funding", *The Manila Times*, 18 January 2022, https://www.manilatimes.net/2022/01/18/news/national/marcos-assures-ntf-elcac-of-funding/1829737 (accessed 17 January 2023).

85. Frances Mangosing, "AFP Chief: Ending Communist Threat Still Top Priority", *Inquirer.net*, 16 January 2023, https://newsinfo.inquirer.net/1716909/afp-chief-ending-communist-threat-still-top-priority (accessed 17 January 2023).
86. Pedrajas, "PH Military Must Modernize".
87. Martha Teodoro and Karol Ilagan, "Data: Bongbong Marcos' Appointees", Philippine Center for Investigative Journalism, 30 June 2022, https://pcij.org/data/366/data-bongbong-marcos-appointees (accessed 17 January 2023).
88. Cristina Eloisa Baclig, "Gov't Told: Permanent DOH Chief Needed Now, Not Later", *Inquirer.net*, 27 October 2022, https://newsinfo.inquirer.net/1685703/govt-told-permanent-doh-chief-needed-now-not-later (accessed 31 January 2023).
89. Bonz Magsambol, "Marcos' 100 Days: No Doh Secretary, Unpaid Health Workers' Benefits", *Rappler*, 8 October 2022, https://www.rappler.com/nation/marcos-100-days-no-doh-secretary-unpaid-health-workers-benefits/ (accessed 1 February 2023).
90. Ma. Teresa Montemayor, "Vacancy in Doh Chief Post Did Not Affect Services: Vergeire", Philippine News Agency, 28 October 2022, https://www.pna.gov.ph/articles/1187314 (accessed 1 February 2023).
91. Beatrice Pinlac, "No Need to Reimpose Tight Border Controls despite New Omicron Subvariants – DOH", *Inquirer.net*, 12 July 2022, https://newsinfo.inquirer.net/1626593/no-need-for-stricter-border-control-despite-new-omicron-subvariants-doh (accessed 1 February 2023).
92. John Eric Mendoza, "DOH Urges Public to Assess 'Individual Risk' as Easing of Indoor Mask Mandate Looms", *Inquirer.net*, 25 October 2022, https://newsinfo.inquirer.net/1684753/doh-urges-public-to-assess-individual-risk-as-easing-of-indoor-mask-mandate-looms (accessed 2 February 2023).
93. Azer Parrocha, "PH Economy on Track despite 'Out of Control' Inflation: Marcos", Philippine News Agency, 6 December 2022, https://www.pna.gov.ph/articles/1190237 (accessed 2 February 2023).
94. Ruth Abbey Gita-Carlos, "PBBM to Biz Community: PH Offers 'Endless Opportunities'", Philippine News Agency, 13 September 2023, https://www.pna.gov.ph/articles/1209820#:~:text=MANILA%20–%20President%20Ferdinand%20R.
95. Joe Zaldarriaga, "Marcos Administration to Ensure Economic Recovery", Philippine News Agency, 6 September 2022, https://www.pna.gov.ph/opinion/pieces/539-marcos-administration-to-ensure-economic-recovery (accessed 2 February 2023).
96. Parrocha, "PH Economy".

97. Kaycee Valmonte, "Marcos to Travel Abroad Less, but APEC in November Still a Priority", *Philstar.com*, 23 January 2023, https://www.philstar.com/headlines/2023/01/23/2239695/marcos-travel-abroad-less-apec-november-still-priority (accessed 2 February 2023).
98. Nestor Corrales, "Davos Will Be Marcos' 8th Foreign Trip in under 7 Months", *Inquirer.net*, 8 January 2023, https://globalnation.inquirer.net/209556/davos-will-be-marcos-8th-foreign-trip-in-under-7-months (accessed 2 February 2023).
99. Argyll Cyrus Geducos, "Marcos Wraps Up Davos Trip: 'We Have Positioned Ourselves Properly in Global Economy'", *Manila Bulletin*, 21 January 2023, https://mb.com.ph/2023/01/21/marcos-wraps-up-davos-trip-we-have-positioned-ourselves-properly-in-global-economy/ (accessed 2 February 2023).
100. Mong Palatino, "Marcos and the Philippines at Davos", *The Diplomat*, 30 January 2023, https://thediplomat.com/2023/01/marcos-and-the-philippines-at-davos/ (accessed 2 February 2023).
101. US Department of State, "Joint Statement of the U.S.-Philippines 2+2 Ministerial Dialogue", 11 April 2023, https://www.state.gov/joint-statement-of-the-u-s-philippines-22-ministerial-dialogue/.
102. "Philippines, US in Talks to Resume '2-plus-2 Meeting' as Relations Thaw", *The Straits Times*, https://www.straitstimes.com/asia/se-asia/philippines-us-in-talks-to-resume-2-plus-2-meeting-as-relations-thaw#:~:text=MANILA%20%2D%20The%20United%20States%20and,Rodrigo%20Duterte's%20anti%2DAmerican%20stance (accessed 31 January 2023).
103. Nyshka Chandran, "The Philippines' Pivot toward China Has Yet to Pay Off, as Manila Awaits Promised Funds", CNBC, 23 November 2018, https://www.cnbc.com/2018/11/23/chinese-investment-in-the-philippines.html (accessed 2 February 2023).
104. Agence France-Presse, "Philippines' Marcos Vows to 'Strengthen' China Ties on Beijing Trip", Voice of America, 4 January 2023, https://www.voanews.com/a/philippines-marcos-vows-to-strengthen-china-ties-on-beijing-trip/6903653.html (accessed 2 February 2023).
105. Jim Gomez, "Marcos Says Sea Feud Involving China Keeps Him Up at Night", *AP News*, 19 January 2023, https://apnews.com/article/philippines-government-ferdinand-marcos-jr-china-asia-f438cb484929d671f596122ae40b38c3 (accessed 2 February 2023).
106. Frances Mangosing, "AFP Submits Updated Wish List of Equipment to Marcos for Approval", *Philippine Daily Inquirer*, 19 May 2023, https://newsinfo.inquirer.net/1771212/afp-submits-updated-wish-list-of-equipment-to-marcos-for-approval (accessed 2 February 2023).

107. Frances Mangosing, "Military Modernization Program Stalled Again", *Philippine Daily Inquirer*, 12 August 2022, https://newsinfo.inquirer.net/1645329/military-modernization-program-stalled-again (accessed 2 February 2023).
108. Joviland Rita, "AFP Modernization's Horizon 1 80% Completed, Horizon 2 at 10% – Bacarro", *GMA News Online*, 6 September 2022, https://www.gmanetwork.com/news/topstories/nation/843907/afp-modernization-s-horizon-1-80-completed-horizon-2-at-10-bacarro/story/ (accessed 2 February 2023).
109. Julio S. Amador III, Deryk Matthew N. Baladjay, and Sheena Valenzuela, "Modernizing or Equalizing? Defence Budget and Military Modernization in the Philippines, 2010 – 2020", *Defence Studies* 22, no. 3 (2022): 299–326, https://www.tandfonline.com/doi/abs/10.1080/14702436.2022.2030713?journalCode=fdef20.
110. Helen Flores, "AFP Modernization on Track – Marcos", *Philstar*, 9 July 2023, https://www.philstar.com/headlines/2023/07/09/2279752/afp-modernization-track-marcos (accessed 25 July 2023).
111. Priam Nepomuceno, "DND Eyes Tapping 'Non-traditional Sources' for AFP Modernization", Philippine News Agency, 21 July 2023, https://www.pna.gov.ph/articles/1206086 (accessed 25 July 2023).
112. Argyll Cyrus Geducos, "Marcos: Talks Ongoing for 'Strategic' Pension for Uniformed Personnel", *Manila Bulletin*, 31 May 2023, https://mb.com.ph/2023/5/31/marcos-talks-ongoing-for-strategic-pension-for-uniformed-personnel (accessed 25 July 2023).
113. See Section 23 of the 1987 Philippine Constitution: Official Gazette, "The 1987 Constitution", https://www.officialgazette.gov.ph/constitutions/1987-constitution/.
114. Official Gazette, "Republic Act No. 11709: An Act Strengthening Professionalism and Promoting the Continuity of Policies and Modernization Initiatives in the Armed Forces of the Philippines, by Prescribing Fixed Terms for Key Officers Thereof, Increasing the Mandatory Retirement Age of Generals/Flag Officers, Providing for a More Effective Attrition System, and Providing Funds Therefor", https://www.officialgazette.gov.ph/downloads/2022/04apr/20220413-RA-11709-RRD.pdf.
115. Official Gazette, "Republic Act No. 11939: An Act Further Strengthening Professionalism and Promoting the Continuity of Policies and Modernization Initiatives in the Armed Forces of the Philippines, and Amending for This Purpose Republic Act No. 11709", https://www.officialgazette.gov.ph/downloads/2023/05may/20230517-RA-11939-FRM.pdf.
116. Frances Mangosing, "DND Wants Law on Fixed AFP Tenure Amended", *Philippine Daily Inquirer*, 7 December 2022, https://newsinfo.inquirer.

net/1702288/dnd-wants-law-on-fixed-afp-tenure-amended (accessed 25 July 2023).
117. See, for example, Senator Ralph Recto's version of SpeDEZ: https://legacy.senate.gov.ph/lisdata/3230229149!.pdf; Senator Ronald Dela Rosa's version of SpeDEZ: https://legacy.senate.gov.ph/lis/bill_res.aspx?congress=19&q=SBN-207; Representative Albert Garcia et al.'s version of SpeDEZ: https://hrep-website.s3.ap-southeast-1.amazonaws.com/legisdocs/third_19/HBT7764.pdf.
118. Alexis Romero, "Duterte Praises NTF-ELCAC, Says It Can Wipe Out Insurgency If Given Two More Years", *Philstar*, 7 June 2022, https://www.philstar.com/headlines/2022/06/07/2186723/duterte-praises-ntf-elcac-says-it-can-wipe-out-insurgency-if-given-two-more-years (accessed 25 July 2023); Alex Navallo, "Guevarra on NTF-ELCAC Red-Tagging: 'Don't Just Label, File Legal Action If You Have Evidence'", *ABS-CBN News*, 15 June 2022, https://news.abs-cbn.com/news/06/15/22/doj-chief-on-red-tagging-dont-just-label-file-legal-action?utm_campaign=2022-June15-Viber-promo-doj-chief-on-red-tagging-dont-just-label-file-legal-action-link-without-art-card&utm_source=viber&utm_medium=organic&utm_type=native&utm_content=text (accessed 25 July 2023).
119. Frencie Carreon, "Año: NTF-ELCAC Got Marcos' Order to Proceed with Campaign without Letup", *Rappler*, 11 May 2023, https://www.rappler.com/nation/eduardo-ano-says-ntf-elcac-got-marcos-jr-order-proceed-without-letup/ (accessed 25 July 2023).
120. Priam Nepomuceno, "PBBM Wants NTF-ELCAC Recalibrated; VP Now Body's Co-vice Chair", Philippine News Agency, 11 May 2023, https://www.pna.gov.ph/articles/1201245 (accessed 25 July 2023); Priam Nepomuceno, "NTF-ELCAC: Amnesty for Ex-rebels Proves Gov't Commitment to Peace", Philippine News Agency, 25 July 2023, https://www.pna.gov.ph/articles/1206340 (accessed 25 July 2023).

5

Duterte's Federalism and Constitutional Change Project: From Campaign Promise to Abandoned Reform

Maria Ela L. Atienza*

> *Charter change, more specifically, a shift from the current unitary to a federal form of government, was one of the promises of then Davao Mayor Rodrigo Duterte when he was campaigning for the presidency in 2016. However, midway into his administration, he abandoned the federalism proposal and instructed his administration and allies to focus instead on incremental amendments to the 1987 Constitution. But COVID-19 pandemic and other matters happened, and he left office without any amendment to the current constitution. Using diverse sources of information, this chapter looks into Duterte's federalism project and compares it with previous charter change initiatives. What factors led to its initial momentum but eventual failure? To connect with the current Marcos Jr. administration,*

the chapter also discusses the legacies or policy imprints left by the Duterte administration on the issue of constitutional change, federalism, and devolution in the Philippines.

Keywords: charter change; Duterte; federalism; Marcos Jr.; 1987 Constitution

INTRODUCTION

Rodrigo Duterte, a long-time mayor of Davao City in Mindanao, was not the first presidential candidate to advocate for federalism and changing the 1987 Philippine Constitution. However, he has advocated it with conviction even before formally running for president. Gloria Macapagal-Arroyo included this in her 2004 election platform with the prodding of pro-federalism advocates, and during her full presidential term created a Consultative Committee to propose constitutional changes; however, Arroyo's efforts failed for a number of reasons, including her unpopularity.[1] The report by Arroyo's Consultative Commission also did not advocate for federalism but only a shift to a parliamentary system. Earlier, various presidents after Corazon Aquino have also attempted to change specific aspects of the 1987 Constitution, including shifting to a parliamentary system and liberalizing the economy further to foreign ownership, but all these attempts failed as well. Duterte became the first Philippine president coming from Mindanao, the southern part of the Philippines, that has regularly supported federalism and where certain groups had harboured separatist ambitions. When Duterte made federalism one of the pledges of his campaign, there were renewed hopes from federalism advocates in the country that he could make this happen. Upon winning in 2016, he seemed to hit the ground running with this promise, but it took almost three years for a draft federal constitution to be finished. After the midterm elections in 2019, there was a sudden shift in his administration's approach to charter change, moving from "big bang" approach to incremental piecemeal reforms.

This chapter examines Duterte and his administration's attempts to change the 1987 Constitution—a product of People Power that toppled the Marcos dictatorship in 1986—and move towards federalism;

the obstacles encountered that led him to abandon his plans in the middle of his term and instead pursue incremental changes; and the fate of all these proposed amendments. How similar and/or different was this charter change proposal from that of his predecessors? What factors led to its initial momentum but eventual failure? To connect with the current Marcos Jr. administration, the chapter also looks into the legacies or policy imprints left by the Duterte administration on the issue of constitutional change, federalism, and devolution in the Philippines. Did charter change issues play a prominent role in the 2022 elections? What is the position of Marcos Jr. on federalism and charter change? What kind of support and/or resistance will his administration meet if he pushes for any form of charter change? In the concluding section, an initial assessment of the prospects for charter change under the Ferdinand Marcos Jr. administration will also be discussed. This chapter benefitted from scholarly materials, public documents related to federalism and charter change, online and media coverage, and the author's first-hand observations due to her own participation as one of the resource persons in various public fora discussing the issue, including committee hearings in both chambers of the Philippine Congress.

This chapter argues that while President Duterte officially made charter change in favour of federalism a key feature of his campaign and administration and he remained popular until the end of his term, he abandoned the federalism project midterm due to a number of reasons. These include his own lack of vision, leadership, and detailed instructions about the features of the federal constitution which led to the proposal losing momentum and strategic timing; his own cautious economic team who disagreed with charter change; the lack of public interest and support for charter change despite the president's popularity; and an unsupportive Congress despite the two Houses being packed by his so-called allies.

This chapter is divided into four parts. The first part discusses Duterte's promise of sweeping changes in the Constitution but the actual slow progress until the midterm. The second part discusses the aftermath of the 2019 midterm elections, including the presidential backtracking on a shift to federalism and the focus on incremental changes in the Constitution as well the new focus and issues that occupied Congress in the last three years of Duterte's administration.

The third part probes into the factors that contributed to abandoning Duterte's federalism plan despite the initial momentum. Finally, the last part concludes the discussion by answering the main questions of the chapter and also discusses the future of constitutional reform under the Marcos Jr. administration.

THE PROMISE OF SWEEPING CHANGES AND THE ACTUAL SLOW PACE OF ACTION

Under the 1987 Constitution, the Philippines established a presidential system and a unitary state with devolution of powers and responsibilities over some public services to local governments and allowed for the creation of two autonomous regions. Thus, the 1991 Local Government Code (Republic Act No. 7160) was passed and an Autonomous Region in Muslim Mindanao (ARMM) was created by law which established a functioning regional government when Duterte became president. As a presidential candidate in 2016, he promised to overhaul the constitution, including a shift to a federal system.[2] He repeatedly told the public during his campaign that nothing short of federalism can solve the problem of underdevelopment and conflict in Mindanao.

After assuming the presidency, Duterte promised a federal charter within one or two years. He immediately issued Executive Order No. 10 in December 2016 which created a twenty-five-person consultative committee to review the Constitution and propose changes. However, members of the committee were only appointed in 2018. After months of work, the Consultative Committee presented to the president the draft federal constitution, called the *Bayanihan*[3] Constitution, in July 2018. In his State of the Nation Address (SONA) later that month, President Duterte turned the draft chapter over to Congress for its approval.

Independent of the creation and progress of the Consultative Committee at the beginning of Duterte's term, the president's allies in Congress wasted no time filing legislative bills to revise or amend the 1987 Constitution. Various committee hearings and consultations in both Houses were conducted to discuss the advantages and disadvantages of shifting to a federal form of government. Offices of the executive branch were conducting their own fora and consultations about the pros and cons of federalism and information campaigns were being conducted to encourage people to support the shift to federalism even if details of the proposed shift and the specific type of federalism being advocated were not yet clear. Duterte allies and pro-federalism groups outside the government were also conducting their own fora and consultations around the country.

In his third SONA in July 2018, Duterte endorsed the *Bayanihan* Constitution drafted by the Consultative Committee. The draft federal charter retains the presidential system (unlike the parliamentary shift proposal of President Macapagal-Arroyo's team) and proposes a formal shift to a federal system with eighteen federated regions corresponding to the fifteen existing administrative regions, along with the Negros Island region (which was created by an executive order by President Benigno Aquino III in 2015 but later abolished by President Duterte through another executive order in August 2017), the Bangsamoro Region, and the Federated Region of the Cordilleras.[4] The basic federal structure would be insulated from future constitutional amendment or revision because the proposed charter prohibits the advocacy, demand, or support for the secession of any region from the envisioned Federal Republic. Article XXI of the draft charter also states that "The democratic and republican character of the government, its federal structure, its indissolubility and permanence shall not be subject to amendments or revisions."

The president also expressed confidence that Filipinos would back the shift to federalism in his 2018 SONA.[5] However, there were clear challenges and cautionary signs against his optimism. Nearly halfway into Duterte's term, the draft charter prepared by the Consultative Committee was not endorsed by the two Houses of Congress, nor by all cabinet ministers and agencies.[6] The president's economic team, in particular, raised a number of objections. In addition, the House of Representatives passed its own version of a draft federal constitution that removed many of the progressive provisions in the draft of the Consultative Committee. Without Senate interest and support, Congress failed to pass a draft federal constitution before the session closed in early 2019 and the midterm elections.

In November 2018, President Duterte established an Inter-Agency Task Force on Federalism and Constitutional Reform, with the Secretary of the Department of the Interior and Local Government (DILG) as chair, to rescue the reform drive.⁷ The task force's mandate was to host intergovernmental consultations, coordinate efforts towards garnering consensus, and make palatable changes to the draft of the Consultative Committee. It immediately began conducting consultations and proposing significant changes to the draft of the Consultative Committee as a basis to garner broad consensus. The May 2019 midterm elections saw Duterte-supported candidates winning a majority of the seats but with no clear indication that the push for charter change would be revived with renewed vigour.

THE AFTERMATH OF THE 2019 MIDTERM ELECTIONS

From Federalism to Enhanced Devolution and Regional Autonomy

With the overwhelming majority of both Houses of Congress filled with Duterte administration allies, there were some comments that charter change will push through after getting a fresh mandate during the midterm elections. However, in his fourth SONA, delivered in July 2019, President Duterte did not even mention charter change or federalism.⁸ At a press conference immediately afterwards, he indicated that a shift to federalism might not be feasible during his term, and that perhaps the focus should be on amendments that would, as he said, "change this nation". However, like most of his pronouncements on policy preferences, the president did not elaborate on what these specific amendments would be. He simply noted that his allies cannot agree yet on the suggested provisions and they should first discuss among themselves before presenting a final draft to the public.⁹ Duterte's allies said that what he really meant were provisions that would address corruption and huge economic disparities between regions.

After Duterte's backtracking on his federalism plans, in a forum on possible reforms in the 1987 Constitution organized in October 2019 by the DILG and the Development Academy of the Philippines, then DILG Undersecretary Jonathan Malaya noted that the Inter-Agency Task Force has not yet agreed on a new draft constitution.¹⁰ Nevertheless, according to him, broad consensus has emerged on certain constitutional reform proposals, which were presented to the House Committee on Constitutional Amendments upon the request of House Committee Chair Rufus Rodriguez during the Committee's hearings in September 2019.

Specifically, in the first package of proposed reforms agreed by the Inter-Agency Task Force and presented to the House Committee on Constitutional Amendments, there was a proposal to put in the constitution the 2019 Supreme Court decision (also known as Mandanas-Garcia ruling)[11] that mandates that shares of national income that would be given to local government units (LGUs) would not just be collections of the Bureau of Internal Revenue but all government agencies' collections. This ruling, according to proponents, would contribute to enhancing the financial autonomy and capacity of LGUs and takes effect in 2022.

Then Undersecretary Malaya also added that there was agreement that there should be a review of the 1991 Local Government Code's distribution of the internal revenue allotment (IRA) formula which currently favours cities that already have their own large revenues. The task force recommended that IRA allocation, now national tax allotment, should be based on need as well as certified performance, that is, those that are given the Seal of Good Local Governance for outstanding local governments based on certain standards.

Another proposed amendment to the Constitution would transform the current regional development councils into regional development authorities with their own budgets and the power to implement regional development plans, instead of their current mandate to merely provide recommendations. These proposals, according to the then Undersecretary, represent a move that reflects features of a future federal arrangement. There has also been agreement on the proposed amendments empowering Congress to authorize exceptions to restrictions on ownership in the economic provisions.

The then DILG Undersecretary also said that the Inter-Agency Task Force was, at the time he was speaking, working on the next package of constitutional reforms. This will comprise proposals to strengthen political parties, prevent turncoatism, and ban political dynasties. He admitted, though, that the anti-dynasty proposal is contentious, because many legislators are members of political dynasties, and there were still ongoing debates within the task force.

Malaya also noted that they have dropped the term *"chacha"*, the popular term used by many Filipinos to refer to charter change, in favour of a new label or brand for their constitutional reforms campaign. The new term or acronym is called CORE (for constitutional reform).[12] He admitted that the task force decided to focus on "surgical reforms" and a shift to a federal form is no longer the primary focus, considering the lack of agreement even among government agencies. However, in late 2019, he expressed confidence that a draft constitution would be ready by December 2019. He also said that federalism is still the long-term goal and that the reforms pursued at the time he was speaking will pave the way for that eventual change.

In the first two months of 2020, hearings of the House of Representatives Committee on Constitutional Amendments discussed the proposed constitutional amendments presented by the task force. However, COVID-19 struck hard and the Philippine government's efforts shifted to addressing the pandemic through declarations of limited emergency powers to address the crisis, passing of laws to support the healthcare system and the population heavily affected by the economic costs of the pandemic, and varying efforts to deal with the daily challenges presented by the pandemic. The task force initially attempted to gather support for their package of proposed reforms but both the DILG Secretary and the Chair of the House Committee said in 2020 that charter amendments would not be the priority due to the more pressing concerns of the COVID-19 pandemic.

In March 2022, President Duterte signed into law the consolidated bill allowing full foreign ownership in more public services like telecommunications and domestic shipping. At least, one of the proposals of the Inter-Agency Task Force became a law. However, the more political and governance-related proposals of the Inter-Agency Task Force still were not taken up even as COVID-19 restrictions later eased. Starting 2021, the country was already caught up in campaign and election frenzy for the 2022 national and local elections.

Congress: Focus on Reforming the Senate and Economic Liberalization

After the 2019 midterm elections, attempts for comprehensive constitutional reform largely subsided in Congress. Instead, efforts focused on piecemeal reform proposals. In particular, the Committee on Constitutional Amendments of the House of Representatives held public hearings in September 2019 on several proposals for constitutional amendments from members of the House. The Inter-Agency Task Force was invited to present their proposals as well.

In terms of institutional reforms, the main proposals from House Representatives contained separate bills and proposed resolutions filed by individual members related to changing the constituencies from which senators are currently selected in national, not regional, elections for a maximum of two six-year terms. The polls are staggered every third year so that half of the members face elections midway through the remaining senators' terms. An associated proposed amendment would reduce the term of the senators from six to four years and allow senators to run for three terms, rather than two, which would maintain the total twelve-year limit for individual senators.

Further proposals would also increase terms for the members of the House of Representatives from three years to four (or five). There was also a proposal to increase the term of elected local councils from three to four years. The House bills do not explicitly state the reasons for such proposed changes, but as can be recalled from the comments of Allan Peter Cayetano, who was House Speaker at that time, extending the term of House members to four or five years would be practical and make them more productive.[13] According to him, the current three-year term is not long enough to concentrate on legislative work as by the second half of the second year, legislators are already preparing for the next elections.

Most of the other proposals focused on further liberalizing economic provisions to achieve greater economic growth. The proposed amendments would allow Congress to establish exceptions to restrictions on who can partner with the state in relation to exploration, development, and utilization of natural resources, co-production, or joint ventures, all of which currently favour Filipino citizens. Furthermore, legislative exceptions would be permitted for restrictions that reserve certain economic activities to citizens of the country or corporations and associations with at least 60 per cent of capital owned by citizens. The proposed amendments would also create exceptions where the law may ease restrictions on using publicly owned land. Similar limitations on administrative control of educational institutions, which favour at least 60 per cent Filipino ownership or Filipino control and administration, would also be eased. The proposals would further allow Congress to create exceptions to the restricted access to ownership and management of the media and advertising sector. Current rules favour full Filipino ownership, and mandate only Filipino citizens, corporations, or associations with at least 70 per cent capital owned by Filipinos, to engage in the advertising industry and restrict participation of foreign investors in the governing body of entities in the advertising industry.

One last proposal would limit the need for Congressional approval for presidential appointments within the Armed Forces of the Philippines (AFP). Currently, such approval was required for all officers of the armed forces down to the rank of colonel or naval captain. The proposal would instead limit the need for Congressional approval to the AFP Chief-of-Staff and service commanders of the army, air force, and navy only. The reason stated by then Magdalo Party-List Representative Manuel Cabochan III in his proposed joint resolution is that the current appointment process has unfortunately led to the political polarization of the AFP as military officials chosen to be promoted are often forced to play politics and give in to the desires of politicians to ensure that their appointments or promotions will not be unduly blocked. The proposal aimed to insulate the AFP from partisan politics and political connections.

In terms of process, there was a proposed resolution in the House calling for members of Congress to convene as a Constituent Assembly, rather than the election of a separate constitutional convention to discuss and approve constitutional amendments. Under the proposed resolution authored by Representative Aurelio Gonzales Jr., it was not clear if the House and Senate would sit separately in considering and approving the proposed amendments. However, in the other bills and proposed joint resolutions, there was mention that each chamber would be voting separately on the proposed amendments. Voting of the two chambers in a constituent assembly had been a contentious issue in the previous Congress when then House Speaker Pantaleon Alvarez insisted that the two Houses of Congress should vote as one. However, when Alvarez was removed and replaced by Representative Gloria Macapagal-Arroyo, she and her allies agreed that in case Congress convenes as a constituent assembly, each House will be voting separately. This is a concession to the Senate, which has a much smaller number of members, whose votes would be discounted if the two Houses sat in a joint session.

Until at least February 2020, there were no proposed amendments discussed by the House Committee on Constitutional Amendments related to strengthening political parties, preventing turncoatism, and preventing or limiting political dynasties. Meanwhile, there appeared to be no urgent counterpart bills in the Senate seeking to change the Constitution. The lack of enthusiasm on the part of the Senate has been a pattern as well in previous administrations' attempts to change the charter and will be probed in the succeeding section. In early March 2020, before the country was placed in one of the longest lockdowns in the world due to the pandemic, the House of Representatives passed a bill allowing 100 per cent foreign ownership of public services, despite criticisms from opposition legislators that this was unconstitutional.

FACTORS CONTRIBUTING TO ABORTION OF THE FEDERALISM CAMPAIGN

Several factors prevented comprehensive constitutional change during the administration of President Duterte, especially a shift to federalism. Prominent were the lack of leadership and consensus within the administration and the president's allies about charter change, low public awareness and support, and the economic and fiscal costs of the transition, among other reasons. Furthermore, Duterte's allies in Congress were already preoccupied with the 2022 presidential elections and evaded the painstaking process of instituting changes in the charter.

Leadership Failure and Loss of Momentum

A key window of opportunity for constitutional change, the first half of the president's term, had lapsed. And with a second presidential term prohibited by law, an incumbent's influence often wanes in the second half of one's first and only term. Analysts have pointed to various difficulties in shifting to federalism, Duterte's flagship proposal, given the remaining limited time in his presidency. Duterte and his team lost momentum by failing to consolidate public and allies' support, leaving it to subordinates to deal with the direction and details of charter change campaigns, and push forward with the change during the first half of his presidency; thus, they instead focused on incremental changes during the second half.[14]

As Rood notes, Duterte was "not clear on details of what such a change in governance would entail".[15] He was not even clear about the model of federalism he wanted and showed unfamiliarity about which countries are actual federal states. He was drawn to many more pressing problems of the nation and his other major programmes, particularly the drug war. He did create a Consultative Committee early on in his first year in office but only appointed members eighteen months later in 2018. He would abandon the federalism project in the middle of his term after not getting legislative support for the draft charter and instead shifted to incremental changes. This abandonment of and lack of decisive leadership in a key project of his presidency, which he has strongly defended even before he ran for president, raises questions about his image as a "strong" man or leader.

The push for a new charter also lost momentum due to the passage of and approval in a two-part plebiscite of the Bangsamoro Organic Law in 2018 and 2019 that created a new and strengthened Bangsamoro Autonomous Region in Muslim Mindanao (BARMM). With many of the supporters of federalism from the South and the president himself highlighting that the reason for the shift to federalism is mainly to bring peace and development in Mindanao, the renewed attempt to create a stronger special autonomous region created a new alternative model through more asymmetrical devolution instead of full federalism for the entire country.

A Lukewarm Economic Team

Duterte's economic team, concerned with the cost of the proposed change, was lukewarm about the proposed charter, particularly the shift to federalism. Even before the president delivered his fourth SONA in 2019, his Central Bank Governor and former Department of Budget and Management Secretary, Benjamin Diokno, voiced his ambivalence (and that of the president's whole economic team) towards a shift to a federal form of government and its potentially negative impacts on the economy, especially in the second half of the administration's term.[16] He also noted that at that time, not all regions and localities were fiscally self-sustaining and ready for a sudden shift to a federal form, which would force them to rely more on local revenues.

Earlier in 2018, then Socioeconomic Planning Secretary Ernesto Pernia said that the country, especially the individual regions, were not yet ready for a full shift. For him, if done immediately, particularly during Duterte's term, a federal structure could destroy the country's fiscal health, lead to a deterioration in its investment-grade credit rating, and slow the infrastructure drive which is one of the hallmarks of the administration.[17] Then Finance Secretary Carlos Dominguez also informed senators in a hearing after the 2018 SONA that if not done correctly, the federalism shift can cause a "fiscal nightmare", pointing out that the draft constitution does not explicitly state who will pay the national debt and how will the national share of all income be distributed to the various departments, among other objections.[18]

Since Duterte was the first post-1986 president to strongly push for federalism, this factor of a president's economic team opposing federalism was not present in previous attempts at charter change as the latter mainly focused on shifting to a parliamentary system, changing some economic provisions, and/or extending terms of office.

Lacklustre Public Support

More importantly, there was low public awareness and poor public support for the reform initiatives, disputing proponents' claim that there was public clamour for change. Duterte enjoyed unprecedented high trust and confidence ratings until the end of his term, but these did not translate to high public support for the proposed charter change or shift to federalism, especially in 2018. Changes in the charter or the form of government did not figure in the top five national concerns in regular surveys conducted by Pulse Asia before the pandemic. The main concerns were with increasing workers' pay, controlling inflation, and reducing poverty.[19] In Pulse Asia's June 2018 survey on charter change (see Tables 5.1 and 5.2), 55 per cent of respondents said that they are aware of proposals to change the 1987 Constitution (higher than in 2016 with 41 per cent awareness), 18 per cent are "in favour of charter change now", while 67 per cent are not in favour of changing the constitution. Opposition to charter change now and in the future was more pronounced in June compared to March 2018. Worse, three out of four respondents (74 per cent) had "little / almost none / no knowledge at all" of the 1987 Constitution in June 2018, while most Filipinos (69 per cent) had "little / almost none / no knowledge at all" about the proposed federal system of government.[20] Social Weather Stations' survey from the first quarter of 2018 (see Tables 5.3 and 5.4 and Figures 5.1 and 5.2) corroborated these findings: one out of four respondents were aware of the federal system of government; 37 per cent supported it, 34 per cent were undecided, and 29 per cent opposed it.[21]

TABLE 5.1
Awareness of Proposals to Change the 1987 Philippine Constitution (2014–18)

AWARENESS OF PROPOSALS TO CHANGE THE 1987 CONSTITUTION
September 2014 to June 2018 / Philippines
(In Percent)

Base: Total Interviews

Now, let us talk about the Philippine Constitution.
Over the past few months, there have been proposals to change the Constitution.

Have you heard, read or watched anything about the proposals to change the 1987 Constitution before this or only now?		RP	LOCATION				CLASS		
			NCR	BL	VIS	MIN	ABC	D	E
Yes, before this	Jun '18	55	53	56	59	53	78	58	38
	Mar '18	49	52	56	34	47	60	51	35
	Jul '16	41	41	39	42	43	57	41	33
	Nov '14	60	67	64	38	65	67	61	51
	Sep '14	61	70	67	55	49	77	63	48
None, only now	Jun '18	45	47	44	41	47	22	42	62
	Mar '18	51	48	44	66	53	40	49	65
	Jul '16	59	59	61	58	57	43	59	67
	Nov '14	40	33	36	62	35	33	39	49
	Sep '14	39	30	33	45	51	23	37	52

MARCH AND JUNE 2018
NGAYON, PAG-USAPAN NAMAN NATIN ANG TUNGKOL SA KONSTITUSYON NG PILIPINAS. NITONG MGA NAKARAANG BUWAN, MAYROONG MGA PANUKALA NA AMYENDAHAN O BAGUHIN ANG KONSTITUSYON.
Q. May narinig, nabasa, o napanood na ba kayo tungkol sa mga panukalang baguhin ang Konstitusyon ng 1987 bago nito o ngayon lang?
JULY 2016 and NOVEMBER 2014
NITONG MGA NAKARAANG BUWAN, MAYROONG MGA PANUKALA NA AMYENDAHAN O BAGUHIN ANG KONSTITUSYON.
Q. May narinig, nabasa o napanood na ba kayo tungkol sa mga panukalang baguhin ang Konstitusyon bago nito o ngayon lang?
SEPTEMBER 2014
NITONG MGA NAKARAANG LINGGO, MAYROON MULING PANUKALA NA AMYENDAHAN O BAGUHIN ANG KONSTITUSYON. ISA SA MGA PANUKALANG ITO AY ANG PAGTANGGAL NG LIMITASYON SA ISANG TERMINO LAMANG PARA SA PRESIDENTE. KUNG MAIPASA ANG PANUKALANG PAGBABAGO SA KONSTITUSYON NA ITO, MAAARING TUMAKBO MULI ANG KASALUKUYANG PRESIDENTE PARA SA IKALAWANG TERMINO SA DARATING NA ELEKSYON NG 2016. BAGO ANG PANUKALANG ITO, ANG MGA LIDER NG KONGRESO AY UNA NANG ISINUSULONG NA AMYENDAHAN ANG MGA PROBISYON UKOL SA PAGLILIMITA SA MGA DAYUHAN NA MAG-MAY-ARI NG KORPORASYON AT IBA PANG ARI-ARIAN SA PILIPINAS.
Q. May narinig, nabasa o napanood na ba kayo tungkol sa mga panukalang baguhin ang Konstitusyon bago nito o ngayon lang?

Source: Pulse Asia, "June 2018 Nationwide Survey on Charter Change", 2018, http://pulseasia.ph/june-2018-nationwide-survey-on-charter-change/.

TABLE 5.2
Opinion on the Appropriateness to Amend the 1987 Philippine Constitution (2018)

WHETHER OR NOT IT IS APPROPRIATE TO AMEND THE
PRESENT PHILIPPINE CONSTITUTION AT THIS TIME
March and June 2018 / Philippines
(In Percent)

Base: Total Interviews

In your opinion, should the 1987 Constitution be amended or not amended *at this time*?		RP	LOCATION				CLASS		
			NCR	BL	VIS	MIN	ABC	D	E
YES, the Constitution SHOULD BE amended now	Jun '18	18	17	15	16	28	25	18	19
	Mar '18	23	34	18	23	24	23	21	28
	Change*	- 5	- 17	- 3	- 7	+ 4	- 2	- 3	- 9
NO, SHOULD NOT BE AMENDED NOW	Jun '18	67	63	70	74	60	68	68	62
	Mar '18	64	59	71	59	58	61	68	50
	Change*	+ 3	+ 4	- 1	+ 15	+ 2	+ 7	0	+ 12
NO, the Constitution SHOULD NOT BE amended now, but it may be amended sometime in the future	Jun '18	30	23	30	31	34	30	30	30
	Mar '18	32	29	33	31	33	36	34	21
	Change*	- 2	- 6	- 3	0	+ 1	- 6	- 4	+ 9
NO, the Constitution SHOULD NOT BE amended now nor any other time	Jun '18	37	40	40	43	26	38	38	32
	Mar '18	32	30	38	28	25	25	34	29
	Change*	+ 5	+10	+ 2	+15	+ 1	+ 13	+ 4	+ 3
Don't Know/Can't say	Jun '18	14	21	15	10	13	8	14	18
	Mar '18	13	7	11	18	18	15	11	22
	Change*	+ 1	+14	+4	- 8	- 5	- 7	+ 3	- 4

Note: *Change = Figures of June 2018 minus Figures of March 2018.
Q. Sa inyong palagay, dapat ba o hindi dapat baguhin ang Konstitusyon ng 1987 sa ngayon?

Source: Pulse Asia, "June 2018 Nationwide Survey on Charter Change", 2018, http://pulseasia.ph/june-2018-nationwide-survey-on-charter-change/.

TABLE 5.3
Knowledge of the 1987 Philippine Constitution (2018)

KNOWLEDGE OF THE 1987 CONSTITUTION
March and June 2018 / Philippines
(In Percent)

How would you describe the amount of knowledge you have regarding the 1987 Constitution of the Philippines? (Base: Total Interviews)	RP	LOCATION				CLASS		
		NCR	BAL LUZ	VIS	MIN	ABC	D	E
A great deal of knowledge								
June 2018	5	7	3	7	6	12	5	2
March 2018	4	4	5	2	2	9	3	3
Not a great deal, but a sufficient amount								
June 2018	21	10	25	26	18	34	22	15
March 2018	21	20	25	19	16	28	22	15
A little knowledge								
June 2018	43	48	40	48	41	36	43	43
March 2018	42	50	36	40	49	31	44	39
Almost none or no knowledge at all								
June 2018	31	34	33	20	35	18	30	40
March 2018	34	26	34	39	33	32	31	43

Question: Paano ninyo isasalarawan ang inyong kaalaman tungkol sa Konstitusyon ng 1987 ng Pilipinas?

Source: Pulse Asia, "June 2018 Nationwide Survey on Charter Change", 2018, http://pulseasia.ph/june-2018-nationwide-survey-on-charter-change/.

TABLE 5.4
Knowledge of the Proposed Federal System of Government (2018)

How would you describe the amount of knowledge you have regarding the proposed federal system of government?	RP	LOCATION				CLASS		
		NCR	BL	VIS	MIN	ABC	D	E
JUNE 2018 (Base: Total Interviews, 100%)								
GREAT DEAL - SUFFICIENT	31	23	26	37	40	46	32	21
A great deal of knowledge	8	8	7	11	9	13	8	7
Not a great deal, but a sufficient amount of knowledge	22	15	19	26	31	33	23	14
LITTLE - NO KNOWLEDGE	69	77	74	63	60	54	68	79
A little knowledge	43	55	41	42	38	35	42	49
Almost none or no knowledge at all	27	22	33	20	22	19	27	30
MARCH 2018 (Base: Total Interviews, 100%)								
GREAT DEAL - SUFFICIENT	29	38	21	38	32	36	29	25
A great deal of knowledge	7	18	7	4	1	4	8	4
Not a great deal, but a sufficient amount of knowledge	22	20	14	34	30	32	21	21
LITTLE - NO KNOWLEDGE	71	62	79	62	68	64	71	75
A little knowledge	43	45	45	41	41	50	42	44
Almost none or no knowledge at all	27	17	34	20	27	14	29	31

Q. Paano ninyo isasalarawan ang inyong kaalaman tungkol sa ipinapanukalang federal na sistema ng pamahalaan?
Note: Figures may not add up to 100% due to rounding off.

Source: Pulse Asia, "June 2018 Nationwide Survey on Charter Change", 2018, http://pulseasia.ph/june-2018-nationwide-survey-on-charter-change/.

FIGURE 5.1
Awareness of the Federal System of Government (March 2018)

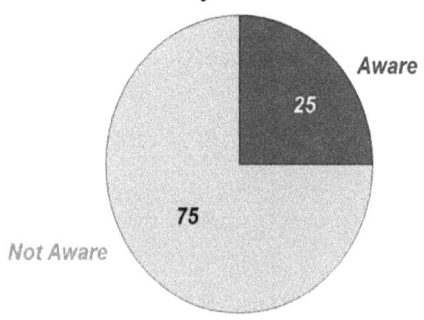

Note: Don't know responses are not shown.
Q116. Kung gagawing FEDERAL ang sistema ng gobyerno sa Pilipinas, magkakaroon ng mga bagong gobyernong lokal na mas mataas kaysa sa mga probinsya, ngunit mas mababa kaysa sa gobyernong pambansa. Dati na ba ninyong alam ito, o ngayon lang po ba?

Source: Social Weather Stations, "First Quarter 2018 Social Weather Survey: One of Four Pinoys Are Aware of the Federal System of Government; 37% Support It, 34% Are Undecided, and 29% Oppose It", 2018, https://www.sws.org.ph/swsmain/artcldisppage/?artcsyscode=ART-20180628003935.

FIGURE 5.2
Agreement or Disagreement on the Federal System of Government (March 2018)

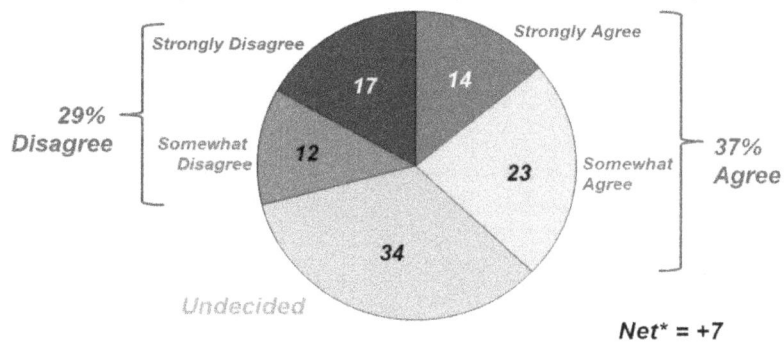

* Net figures (% Agree minus % Disagree) are correctly rounded.
Note: Don't know and No answer responses are not shown.
Q118. Kayo po ba ay sang-ayon o hindi sang-ayon dito sa FEDERAL na sistema ng gobyerno? (LUBOS NA SUMASANG-AYON, MEDYO SUMASANG-AYON, HINDI TIYAK KUNG SUMASANG-AYON O HINDI SUMASANG-AYON, MEDYO HINDI SUMASANG-AYON, o LUBOS NA HINDI SUMASANG-AYON)

Source: Social Weather Stations, "First Quarter 2018 Social Weather Survey: One of Four Pinoys Are Aware of the Federal System of Government; 37% Support It, 34% Are Undecided, and 29% Oppose It", 2018, https://www.sws.org.ph/swsmain/artcldisppage/?artcsyscode=ART-20180628003935.

Thus, even though Duterte remained very popular until the end of his term and initially pushed for federalism while Macapagal-Arroyo was very unpopular during hers and pushed for a parliamentary system, neither of their charter change initiatives were very popular. Rood highlighted survey results during Macapagal-Arroyo's attempts showing that moves to amend the 1987 Constitution were also not driven by popular demand.[22] This can extend to other charter change attempts, from President Fidel Ramos to President Duterte, where charter change and specifically federalism were unpopular with the general public. Why don't charter change efforts of succeeding administrations gain traction among the public? Perhaps, this can be explained by several factors. First, economic issues like inflation, employment, poverty, and salaries are the top concerns of Filipinos as evidenced by periodic surveys. Second, the average Filipino does not know much about the details of the 1987 Constitution and may be leaning towards conserving status quo. Third, there is a genuine lack of knowledge about forms and systems of government. Or perhaps, charter change initiatives since the 1990s have not started with genuine or comprehensive attempts to listen to people, increase their awareness of the current constitution, ask them what they think of the charter and its relevance to their day-to-day lives, and whether they think there are changes to be made.

As Ladia notes in his study of Duterte's rhetoric to convince the public to support the federalism shift, Duterte failed in this case because of the public's "lack of identification towards a common vision and a tradition of dissent against any amendment of the constitution".[23] This is not to discount the efforts of genuine federalism advocates (both individuals and groups), especially in increasing people's awareness of what federalism is and possible advantages. However, the federalism initiative was predominantly top-down, as in previous attempts. Public resources earmarked for public consultations and information initiatives were used instead to persuade people to support federalism immediately without much discussion. Influential pro-Duterte supporters also promoted federalism and charter change through social media without the use of empirical evidence and substantive and informed discussions—which was the common top-down characteristic of the pro-administration public campaign and disinformation that thrived under the Duterte administration to support its many programmes and actions and continue well into the new Marcos Jr. administration.

Questionable Congressional Support

The Philippines has a weak party system in which turncoatism (changing political party affiliation) is rampant. Most politicians gravitate to the president either by shifting allegiance to the latter's party or having their parties enter into an alliance or coalition with the president's party, particularly when they enjoy high trust ratings. However, Duterte's popularity and the overwhelming majority of members of both Houses of Congress swearing allegiance to him as part of the "super majority" were not enough to have the draft *Bayanihan* Constitution supported through Congress. Most politicians are concerned with protecting their own political interests. The weakness of Philippine political parties, the precariousness of political alliances supporting a sitting president, and the personalistic nature of politicians, coupled with the lack of sustained and focused leadership on the part of the president on the issue of the shift to federalism, contribute to Duterte's lack of full control of his allies in both Houses of Congress.

Former president and former House speaker Gloria Macapagal-Arroyo and her allies introduced their version of a new federal constitution in the House of Representatives. The House version removed many progressive aspects of the draft *Bayanihan* Constitution.[24] Notably, the House removed provisions on term limits of members of Congress, bans or limits on political dynasties, and reforms to strengthen political parties and make elections more representative and participatory. The House version proposed a presidential-federal set-up with the president and vice president elected together, for a maximum of two four-year terms instead of a single six-year term. Members of the bicameral Congress would be elected for a four-year term, and the two consecutive term limits for Senators and three consecutive term limits for House Representatives would be removed. The draft did not impose a specific number of regional states to be established. Instead, following a similar process in Spain, a state would be formed based on a petition addressed to Congress from a number of contiguous, compact, and adjacent local governments.

The House of Representatives passed their draft constitution overwhelmingly until the third reading, despite objections from critics and even members of the Consultative Committee. But the House bill lacked support in the Senate, with senators allied to Duterte saying there was simply no time to discuss it because of other priorities and approaching midterm elections in May 2019.[25] Arroyo's proposal had no counterpart in the Senate. No senator sponsored her proposal which already passed the House of Representatives. The Senate was stalled debating a resolution to establish separate Constituent Assemblies from the two Houses of Congress. Many senators, being nationally elected and fewer in number, as well as driven by clan and personal interests, loved to grandstand and take individual and popular stances on many issues like charter change publicly. Ironically, these factors could explain why the Senate, packed with so-called Duterte allies (unlike the Senate when Arroyo was still president), did not become Duterte's rubber stamp. As a result, a Congress composed of Duterte allies in both Houses failed to endorse any version of a federal constitution by the midterm elections of May 2019. As shown earlier, no further progress on federalism occurred in Congress after the midterm elections.

All concerns about charter change were overtaken in 2020 by COVID-19-related legislation as well as the posturing of individual legislators as the 2022 elections near.

CONCLUSIONS AND PROSPECTS OF CONSTITUTIONAL REFORM UNDER THE MARCOS JR. ADMINISTRATION

Given the unfolding of events since Duterte ran for the presidency, and until he departed the highest office of the country on 30 June 2022, promises of charter change and federalism with a short timeline have not been delivered. This is even though in contrast with Macapagal-Arroyo and other presidents who attempted to change the 1987 Constitution, Duterte made federalism the centrepiece of his presidential campaign and remained popular until the end of his term. But after thirty-seven years, the 1987 Constitution of the Philippines remains one of the few constitutions in the world without any successful amendments. Even the post-midterm shift towards incremental reform efforts was overtaken by efforts to combat the global pandemic and preparations for the 2022 elections.

In the end, the piecemeal proposals of the task force fell short of a fully-fledged federal arrangement. Nevertheless, some of the Inter-Agency Task Force's proposal had the potential to enhance levels of regional autonomy and could possibly address some of the perceived governance challenges the Philippines currently faces. The Marcos Jr. administration and Congress can pick up on these in current discussions. However, under Duterte's leadership, any genuine attempt to amend the charter was spoiled by rifts within his administration, the personal interests and ambitions of legislators allied to the president, the above-mentioned lack of public interest or support for a new charter, the COVID-19 pandemic, and the president's own fading commitment to federalism as he reached the end of his term. Duterte's COVID-19 response has been criticized by local government executives, civil society groups and scholars as top-down, executive-driven, and military-dominated at the expense of autonomy, increased national and local coordination, civil society participation, and human rights. Ironically, many aspects of his COVID-19 response were contrary to the goals of his federalism and charter change campaign at the beginning of his term.

At the end of Duterte's term, we can ask why a popular president's campaign and promise of charter change, particularly federalism, did not succeed? First, despite the president's strong advocacy of federalism and comprehensive charter change, he did not provide decisive leadership and clear directions about the details of this change and left it to others to do the job. This led to losing the time and strong momentum of the call to shift to federalism. Second, akin to the fate of earlier attempts to change the 1987 Constitution, the initiative was not publicly driven and had no widespread public support. Duterte, ever so popular, failed to convince his public due to top-down tactics.

Third, there are practical challenges facing the national economy, localities, and regions. Of course, federalism is supposed to encourage regions outside Metro Manila to develop more equitably but there are also practical considerations. If not properly managed and adequately prepared for these challenges, Duterte's economic managers were correct in exercising caution as a sudden shift may hurt rather than promote development initiatives at both national and local levels. At the same time, local governments are facing more challenges three decades since the devolution law was passed;[26] immediate federalism may further lead to more disparities in governance success and economic development. While the Supreme Court's Mandanas-Garcia ruling theoretically means more funds for local governments, the current sharing scheme of national government transfers to local governments is not yet equitable and commensurate to the devolved services they are now responsible for. At the same time, in 2021, Executive Order No. 138 was passed, mandating all local government units (LGUs) to perform all functions devolved to them starting in 2022. However, not all local governments have the capacity to manage resources judiciously, raise local funds, perform all devolved services, promote both economic development and people's participation, and deal with the continuing impact of the pandemic. The implementation of the order have been further delayed.

In addition, in terms of regional autonomy, the revamped special autonomous government in Muslim Mindanao is an ongoing experiment towards attaining genuine peace and economic development in the region. If the ongoing devolution process and regional autonomy will be supported to succeed in their original purposes, perhaps the federalism proposal can be revisited at a much later time, though the Local Government Code and the 1987 Constitution may be ripe for some incremental changes or fine-tuning to support these current processes.

Add to the above factors, of course, are the weak political parties and electoral system producing traditional politicians at local and national posts that look at charter review and policy reform changes with their vested interests in mind and not party programmes and interests. The fate of charter change in Congress during the Duterte administration showed that despite the president lobbying for federalism and the draft *Bayanihan* Constitution, his supposed "super majority" in both Houses did not follow his endorsement. This failure of Congress to deliver adds doubt to the "strong" and "dominant" leader image of Duterte.

Interestingly, Marcos Jr. who would win overwhelmingly as president ran under a party called *Partido Federal ng Pilipinas* (Federal Party of the Philippines). However, he never strongly emphasized shifting to federalism or changing the constitution in his campaign sorties around the country and through social media. Avoiding many public presidential debates and media interviews, he spent most of the campaign focusing on the very general theme of unity and the country rising again from the ravages of the pandemic. He did, however, say in one media interview during the campaign period that it would be difficult to talk about changing the charter because the people do not want that. He added in the same interview that people suspect that politicians merely want to extend their terms or cancel elections.[27] The candidate who campaigned for federalism was a Senate candidate who happened to be a popular action star and former convict who went on to top the senatorial race. However, charter change did not figure prominently in the 2022 campaigns and debates.

More than a year into the Marcos Jr. administration, charter change appeared not the priority of the new administration given the many problems it is facing now, though allies in Congress, particularly the House of Representatives, have started filing bills related to constitutional amendments. In a country now facing high inflation, unemployment, poor public health response to the pandemic, and divisiveness, fewer people would be interested in prioritizing and supporting federalism and charter change. Upon election into the presidency, Marcos Jr. did not mention charter change in his inaugural address and his first SONA in July 2022. Meanwhile, early in 2023, the House Committee on Constitutional Amendments under Congressman Rodriguez held a series of nationwide hearings and consultations regarding bills seeking to amend the constitution, focusing on further opening the economy to foreigners. Federalism should have been discussed more prominently. In February 2023, President Marcos said that charter change is not a priority. Nevertheless, after the House hearings, the House in March 2023 passed a bill detailing how to proceed with charter change through a constitutional convention composed of elected district representatives and appointed sectoral representatives. However, the Senate again presents a different story with only one senator, a former actor, heavily pushing for charter change, particularly federalism, while the rest said they should prioritize more urgent national issues.

In terms of public support, interestingly, a Pulse Asia survey conducted in March 2023 shows that 41 per cent of Filipinos back charter change (significantly higher than during the Duterte years), though 45 per cent preferred delaying change, but more than half of the respondents were opposed to specific proposed changes listed in the survey, such as term extension for elective officials and removing caps on foreign ownership of companies; worse, 76 per cent (higher than during the Duterte years) admitted they had little to no knowledge of the 1987 Constitution.[28] Despite higher approval for charter change, the survey results show that charter change still appears to be divisive and betrays the lack of proper information and massive public information campaigns and deliberations on the issue.

Interestingly, by the end of 2023, President Marcos said that he asked the two Houses of Congress to look into possible changes in economic provisions in the Constitution to attract more foreign investors to come. Then, early January 2024, it appears that certain groups plus members of the House of Representatives were convincing their constituents to sign a petition for people's initiative to make any amendment in the Constitution by Congress voting together and not by chamber voting separately. This led to an immediate response from the Senate, which accused House members of disrespecting the

Senate and immediately conducted an investigation into allegations of politicians enticing unsuspecting constituents to sign the petition in exchange of getting funds from social welfare programmes. In the midst of these public conflicts between the two chambers, leaders from both Houses pledged to focus only on possible amendments to economic provisions to entice more foreign investors to come in. However, it is still a question if they can do all these proposed amendments before people get focused again on preparing for the May 2025 midterm elections. In the midst of these squabbles inside the legislature, to date, the president has not decisively stepped in to discuss how he wants these amendments to push through and to put an end to the public word war between the members of both chambers. He and his allies are also distracted by the split of the "unity team" with the Dutertes, with the former president and his sons attacking the president openly and Duterte even threatening secession of Mindanao from the Philippines.

Thus, charter change under the early part of the Marcos Jr. administration lacks the executive-driven character of the Duterte and past administrations' attempts but also suffers from other similar challenges, namely a divided Congress with only one house more intent on changing the constitution; the lack of overwhelming public support, massive public consultations as well as grassroots' information campaigns; and an even bleaker post-COVID-19 economy and more divisive politics and society. Nevertheless, reformists both inside and outside Congress can focus on other institutional and political reforms that would strengthen political parties, make elections more competitive and open, make government institutions more capable and accountable, and build genuine people's participation.

One law that is ripe for amendments is the 1991 Local Government Code. Amendments can include reflecting the Mandanas-Garcia ruling as the basis for the computation of the national tax allotment (IRA) for local government units (LGUs) instead of just internal revenues, revising the allotment share formula to reflect the needs and performance of LGUs, operationalizing the process of selecting the three sectoral representatives in the local legislative councils, giving the regional development councils more power and responsibilities, among other reforms.[29] Local autonomy and devolution in both the regular LGUs as well as in the autonomous region in Muslim Mindanao can also benefit from laws strengthening political parties and making the electoral system more inclusive, competitive, and beneficial to different sectors of the society (see Calimbahin and Guia's chapter).

As mentioned repeatedly in this chapter, people's awareness of the Constitution as well as other laws and basic political information is important before there could be genuine discussions on the ground about whether there is a need to revise the 1987 Constitution or not. This is a task not only for government agencies and public officials but also for academe, civil society, media, and other stakeholders who are genuinely concerned about getting people involved in any effort to amend or revise the charter and other laws as well as in the larger political life of the nation.

Notes

* Acknowledgments: This chapter was partly drawn from previous work, namely two blog articles for ConstitutionNet of the International Institute for Democracy and Development (IDEA) in 2018 and 2019 and a short presentation in "Constitutionalism in Crisis? The Path Ahead for Southeast Asia, Asia in Review" Online Panel Discussion Series on Law and Politics in Southeast Asia, jointly organized by the Asian Governance Foundation; German-Southeast Asian Center of Excellence for Public Policy and Good Governance (CPG), Faculty of Law, Thammasat University; and Hanns Seidel Foundation, 16 December 2020.

1. Steven Rood, "Finding Federalism in the Philippines: Federalism — 'The Centerpiece of My Campaign'", in *From Aquino II to Duterte (2010–2018): Change, Continuity—and Rupture,* edited by Imelda Deinla and Björn Dressel (Singapore: ISEAS – Yusof Ishak Institute, 2019), pp. 65–72.
2. Miriam Coronel Ferrer, "Duterte's Philippines and the Push for Constitutional Shift towards Federalism", *ConstitutionNet*, 14 December 2016, https://constitutionnet.org/news/dutertes-philippines-and-push-constitutional-shift-towards-federalism.
3. *Bayanihan* is a Filipino word used to describe the spirit of community, unity and cooperation, coming from the root word *bayan*, which alternately can refer to town, community or nation.
4. Consultative Committee to Review the 1987 Constitution, "Bayanihan Federalism: Power to the People, Power to the Regions (Draft Constitution for a Strong, Indissoluble Republic)", 2018, https://constitutionnet.org/sites/default/files/2018-07/Draft%20Constitution%20as%20adopted%20by%20Consultative%20Committee%209%20July%202018.pdf.

5. Alexis Romero, "Duterte Confident Filipinos Will Back Federalism", *Philstar*, 24 July 2018, https://www.philstar.com/headlines/2018/07/24/1836351/duterte-confident-filipinos-will-back-federalism.
6. Maria Ela L. Atienza, "A Federal Constitution for the Philippines? A Reluctant Congress and an Unsupportive Public", *ConstitutionNet*, 21 August 2018, http://www.constitutionnet.org/news/federal-constitution-philippines-reluctant-congress-and-unsupportive-public.
7. Azer Parrocha, "PRRD Forms Inter-agency Task Force on Federalism", Philippine News Agency, 5 November 2018, https://www.pna.gov.ph/articles/1052907.
8. *ABS-CBN News*, "No Mention of Federalism, Charter Change in Duterte's 4th SONA", 22 July 2019, https://news.abs-cbn.com/news/07/22/19/no-mention-of-federalism-charter-change-in-dutertes-4th-sona; Camille Elemia, "No Charter Change, Federalism Push in Duterte's SONA 2019", *Rappler*, 22 July 2019, https://www.rappler.com/nation/236044-no-federalism-duterte-sona-2019-philippines/.
9. Catalina Ricci S. Madarang, "Duterte's Federalism Agenda: Another of Campaign Vows Off the Table", *Interaksyon*, 30 July 2019, https://interaksyon.philstar.com/politics-issues/2019/07/30/152630/duterte-federalism-shelved-campaign/.
10. Consuelo Marquez, "DILG Task Force on Constitutional Reforms on Federal Charter Still Ongoing", *Inquirer.net*, 3 October 2019, https://newsinfo.inquirer.net/1173108/dilg-task-force-on-constitutional-reforms-on-federal-charter-still-ongoing.
11. Edu Punay, "It's Final: Supreme Court Orders Higher IRA for LGUs", *Philstar*, 11 April 2019, https://www.philstar.com/headlines/2019/04/11/1909099/its-final-supreme-court-orders-higher-ira-lgus.
12. *Rappler*, "DILG Relaunches Push for Constitutional Reforms", 8 October 2019, https://www.rappler.com/nation/242006-dilg-calls-for-constitutional-reform-anew/.
13. *ABS-CBN News*, "'It's a Practical Thing': Cayetano Seeks Term Extension for Congressmen", 11 July 2019, https://news.abs-cbn.com/news/07/11/19/its-a-practical-thing-cayetano-seeks-term-extension-for-congressmen.
14. MJ Blancaflor, "Rody Unlikely to Fulfill Federalism, Chacha Promise", *Manila Standard*, 22 July 2019, https://www.manilastandard.net/spotlight/state-of-the-nation-address-2019/300358/rody-unlikely-to-fulfill-federalism-chacha-promise-analysts.html.
15. Rood, "Finding Federalism in the Philippines", p. 63.
16. Charmaine A. Tadalan, "BSP Chief Says Change to Constitution Now Would Be 'Disruptive' to Economy", *BusinessWorld*, 5 July 2019, https://

www.bworldonline.com/editors-picks/2019/07/05/240551/bsp-chief-says-change-to-constitution-now-would-be-disruptive-to-economy/.
17. Jose Bimbo F. Santos, "State Economic Managers Cautious on Federal System — Pernia", *BusinessWorld*, 16 July 2018, https://www.bworldonline.com/editors-picks/2018/07/16/173056/state-economic-managers-cautious-on-federal-system-pernia/.
18. Ian Nicolas Cigaral, "Economic Managers Warn of Federalism Rush's Fiscal Risks", *Philstar*, 7 August 2018, https://www.philstar.com/business/2018/08/07/1840488/economic-managers-warn-federalism-rushs-fiscal-risks.
19. Pulse Asia, "March 2018 Nationwide Survey on Urgent National Concerns and National Administration Performance Ratings on Selected Issues", 2018, https://www.pulseasia.ph/march-2018-nationwide-survey-on-urgent-national-concerns-and-national-administration-performance-ratings-on-selected-issues/.
20. Pulse Asia, "June 2018 Nationwide Survey on Charter Change", 2018, http://pulseasia.ph/june-2018-nationwide-survey-on-charter-change/.
21. Social Weather Stations, "First Quarter 2018 Social Weather Survey: One of Four Pinoys Are Aware of the Federal System of Government; 37% Support It, 34% Are Undecided, and 29% Oppose It", 28 June 2018, https://www.sws.org.ph/swsmain/artcldisppage/?artcsyscode=ART-20180628003935.
22. Rood, "Finding Federalism in the Philippines", pp. 68–71.
23. Charles Erize Ladia, "Contextualizing Duterte's Rhetoric: The Rhetorical Situation of President Rodrigo Duterte's Public Addresses on the Philippines' Federal Shift", *Humanities Diliman* 19, no. 1 (2022): 30.
24. *Rappler*, "Arroyo's Proposed Constitution Reaches House Plenary", 7 October 2018, https://www.rappler.com/nation/213759-house-committee-recommends-arroyo-draft-constitution-plenary/; Mara Cepeda, "Highlights of the House's Draft Federal Constitution", *Rappler*, 15 October 2018, https://www.rappler.com/newsbreak/iq/214307-highlights-house-representatives-draft-federal-constitution/.
25. Camille A. Aguinaldo, "Senate Says No Time for Charter Change", *BusinessWorld*, 5 December 2018, https://www.bworldonline.com/editors-picks/2018/12/05/202984/senate-says-no-time-for-charter-change/; Camille Elemia, "'Dead on Arrival': Senate Leaders Reject Arroyo's Draft Charter", *Rappler*, 9 October 2018, https://www.rappler.com/nation/213862-senate-leaders-reject-arroyo-draft-constitution/.
26. Maria Ela L. Atienza, "Local Matters in the 2022 Philippine Elections", *Fulcrum*, 29 April 2022, https://fulcrum.sg/local-matters-in-the-2022-philippine-elections/.

27. Neil Arwin Mercado, "Federal Gov't System Fits PH But Cha-cha 'Difficult' – Marcos Jr.", *Inquirer.net*, 25 January 2022, https://newsinfo.inquirer.net/1544985/federal-govt-system-fits-ph-but-cha-cha-difficult-marcos-jr.
28. Dwight De Leon, "41% of Filipinos Now Back Charter Change, Up By 10 Points from September 2022 – Survey", *Rappler*, 4 April 2023, https://www.rappler.com/nation/pulse-asia-survey-support-opposition-charter-change-march-2023/#:~:text=The%20pollster%2C%20which%20surveyed%201%2C200,survey%20conducted%20in%20September%202022.
29. Maria Ela L. Atienza and Jan Robert R. Go, *Assessing Local Governance and Autonomy in the Philippines: Three Decades of the 1991 Local Government Code* (Diliman, Quezon City: University of the Philippines, 2023), https://cids.up.edu.ph/download/assessing-local-governance-autonomy-philippines-three-decades-1991-local-government-code/.

6

Experiencing Grief: Duterte's Lethal Drug War and Its Widows

Bianca Ysabelle E. Franco

This chapter focuses on widowhood in the context of the Philippine war on drugs. It responds to the gap in the literature on how drug wars in general and specifically in the Philippines, adversely affect marginalized women. Data from in-depth interviews with drug war widows show that instead of receiving sympathies and support from society and the state, these women were stigmatized. Their husbands' brutal deaths are deemed "ungrievable" for having lived as drug offenders. With their grief disenfranchised, the widows suffered social isolation and a host of adversities in the aftermath of their husbands' deaths—all while dealing with the trauma from witnessing the violence or being in the periphery of where it occurred. It also cites reports indicating that the drug war continues under the presidency of Ferdinand Marcos Jr., indicating that the latter's administration stands to be tested on whether it wants to leave a legacy of justice or impunity.

Keywords: Duterte; war on drugs; widowhood; political violence; Marcos Jr.

INTRODUCTION

"For every *tokhang* victim, there is a woman wailing beside",[1] says human rights lawyer Neri Colmenares, an insight immortalized in media pictures depicting women cradling their husband's lifeless bodies. President Rodrigo Duterte launched a brutal campaign against illegal drugs in 2016, promising that drug suspects and other criminals would be killed. The campaign, led by the Philippine National Police (PNP), is officially called "Double Barrel". The "upper barrel" of the programme is called Project High-Value Target, aimed at high-level drug traffickers and syndicates. The "lower barrel" is Project *Tokhang*, which involves door-to-door visits of suspected drug personalities' homes to convince them to cease their illegal activities. These visits highlight *tokhang*, a play on the Visayan words for knock (*toktok*) and plead (*hangyo*).[2] In implementing *tokhang*, thousands of lives were lost in violent police operations, which the police claimed happened because the suspects resisted arrest or fought back (*nanlaban*). Most of these killings took place in urban poor communities; the sudden uptick in violence is historically unprecedented in the Philippines and has raised macro-political concerns about police impunity, the erosion of due process, and the militarization of political life. All these are inextricably linked to the state of Philippine democracy.

The Philippine Drug Enforcement Agency (PDEA) reports that 6,221 have died during anti-drug operations. Human rights groups, however, peg the number at around 30,000 casualties, including killings by unidentified assailants linked to the police.[3] These deaths have been popularly called in the Philippines as extrajudicial killings (EJKs), defined as slayings perpetrated by or encouraged by government officials without due process. The escalated killings in the drug war have prompted a response from the United Nations, including findings of reasonable basis by the International Criminal Court (ICC), to begin investigations.

Despite the killings, the drug war has been highly popular among Filipinos. In 2019, a public opinion survey found that 82 per cent of Filipinos were satisfied with the campaign against illegal drugs.[4] The most recent World Values Survey suggests that 95.4 per cent of Filipinos would not like to have drug addicts as neighbours.[5]

Many of the casualties of the drug war are men from low-income communities in Metro Manila. The other victims are the survivors who bear the brunt of their deaths. These include young widows who, while grieving the sudden deaths of their husbands, struggle to survive, raise their children, and overcome worsening poverty. Widowhood is understood as the loss of a spouse in the context of marriage.[6] However, in this chapter, the definition does not distinguish between legal marriage and cohabitation. The term "widow" refers to women who lost their male partners or husbands to drug-related violence, regardless of whether they were legally married. Reports state that these men were shot dead by police or by unidentified gunmen linked to law enforcement.[7]

This chapter has two objectives. First, it narrates the experiences of President Rodrigo Duterte's drug war widows, arguing that drug war widows experience a host of adversities because their spouses' deaths are deemed "ungrievable" by society and the state. Their slain husbands are vilified as immoral criminals who destroy the country. Second, it presents the widows' experiences of social isolation, bullying, and endless battles in the context of their grief and survival, reflecting the stigma surrounding the deaths. It contributes to earlier studies on Duterte's drug war.[8] Specifically, Vicente Rafael's "biopolitics of fear" also frames these narratives as he explained that the brutality itself tells "that someone is in charge, that authority works because there is fear, and therefore order".[9]

How are widowhood and grief constructed and experienced by young women in the context of the Philippine war on drugs? This chapter addresses this question through in-depth interviews with a total of ten drug war widows with the help of Project Taguyod,[10] a church-based non-government organization that provides financial assistance and livelihood for widows and mothers of drug war casualties in a city in Metro Manila. The in-depth interviews were conducted online in the context of the limitations brought upon by the COVID-19 pandemic. However, prior to the pandemic, I have already spent three years visiting and talking to drug-war survivors for various research projects.

Highlighting the experiences of drug war widows will glean insights on the possible policy and programme interventions that can be done to support them and eventually end the violent approach to illegal drug control. Finally, the chapter presents how Marcos Jr.'s entry in the political fray as presidential candidate and Sara Duterte's sliding down to the vice-presidency position limited the potential of the drug war as an electoral issue in the 2022 elections. It also shows that in the first few months of Marcos Jr.'s presidency, pronouncements of a different approach to addressing the illegal drugs problem have been made, all while NGO reports continue to indicate that the drug war killings continue.

EXPERIENCES OF WIDOWHOOD AND GRIEF

The experiences of widowhood and grief for women affected by the war on drugs are rife with brutality, social isolation, and endless battles. It started when their husbands were killed and linger to this day as the campaign against illegal drugs continues in their community and as they endure the stigma of being a drug war widow. These women experienced violence at the hands of armed men and witnessed their husbands fight for their lives in bloody alleys. But the violence does not end there. They continue to face endless battles after their husbands' deaths, including the struggles of burying their dead and having persistent confrontations with law enforcement officers. On top of this, they must bear the social isolation enforced by their community because of the circumstances of their partners' death.

They agonized over the brutality of the killings, became isolated in their communities, and endured many adversities. This chapter shows that for the widows of the war on drugs, their suffering is not only a result of the violence waged on their partners and families. These women must also pay the social and economic costs of being a widow of a suspected drug personality. The experiences of these widows depict the brutal deaths and suffering they encountered even as they compellingly resisted the narrative that their partners fought back (*nanlaban*). Most do not know the perpetrators and continue to live in a climate of fear. In dealing with their grief, they face social isolation due to the stigma from their communities who did not want to be associated with them. The widows also had to struggle with endless battles as they continued to deal with financial troubles, burying their partners, and the erasure of evidence marking the true cause of their partners' deaths. In many ways, the personal is ultimately political. The following vignettes narrate these stories in detail.

Brutal Deaths and Threats of Violence

Aida was a mother of three in her late twenties when her first live-in partner was killed in a buy-bust operation as a suspected drug courier. She met Raffy when they were kids and started dating as teenagers. They have lived in Barangay Pagbangon[11] their entire lives. One morning in December 2016, six months into the war on drugs, Aida heard an ambulance and police cars passing through their neighbourhood. She did not mind this at first, but then Aida's mother came knocking at her door saying her husband was the target of a police operation. Aida then connected the dots and realized the ambulance and police cars were for her partner. *"Hindi rin ako makapaniwala. Naniwala na lang po ako nung nakita ko na po doon sa baracks na tinutuluyan nila na nililinis na po yung mga dugo doon"* [I could not believe it at first. But then I saw the pools of blood getting mopped up at the barracks], Aida said as she recalled the events of that day. Her partner, Raffy, was staying at the local junk shop because he worked as a garbage collector. Aida could not believe what had happened to her partner because she was not there. Her recollection is based on what the neighbours told her and what was reported in the media:

> *Pinasok po sila ng pulis at doon sila binugbog sa loob ... binugbog daw po muna bago daw po sila pinatay ... Pinahirapan daw muna po sa loob ng baracks bago sila pinagbabaril ... nabalita po yun ... tatlong pinaghihinalaan na drug pusher daw po, patay sa operation kasi nanlaban daw po ... Buy bust daw po. Ang sabi, yung mga asawa daw po namin nagtitinda daw po. Eh hindi naman po yun totoo.*

[Their barracks were raided by the police, and they were beaten up before they were killed. Our neighbours said they were tortured before they were gunned down. It was all over the news: three suspected drug pushers were killed in a buy-bust operation because they resisted arrest and fought back. They said our husbands sold illegal drugs, but that's not true.]

Many of the widows I spoke to recall violent encounters with law enforcement, especially on the day their husbands were killed. Nene was only twenty-three when her partner and the father of her eldest son were shot in the face inside their home. She went out early in the morning to go door-to-door around their neighbourhood to sell clothes. This was her daily routine. Jimmy, a garbage collector, called in sick that day. Similar to Aida's experience, Nene was alerted to several police cars passing through their neighbourhood and going in the direction of the home she shared with Jimmy. She kept trying to go back home but was stopped by the police. She recalled this encounter with a police officer:

> *Sabi sa'kin ng pulis, 'Alam mo kanina ka pa, gusto mo ipasok kita sa van?' Ang ginawa ko, tinulak ko yung pintuan kasi sinaraduhan ako ng pinto. Tinulak ko kasi ipapasok ako sa van eh. Nanginginig ako sa takot.*
>
> [After pacing back and forth, the police stopped me and said, "Do you want me to put you inside the van?" I forcefully pushed the door open because I didn't want them to take me. I was trembling in fear.]

Later that day, she heard the police say someone fought back during the anti-drug operation and was killed. The person was suspected of selling drugs and possessing an illegal weapon. It was Jimmy. *"Hinagis daw po sa ambulansya ng barangay na parang baboy"* [He was thrown into the ambulance like a pig], Nene recalled. *"Pinasok daw po si Jimmy sa loob [ng bahay], kinaladkad palabas ... Binugbog siya, kinaladkad, tapos kinuryente pa daw po"* [They stormed into our house, beat Jimmy up, electrocuted him, and dragged him outside] was how neighbours and witnesses told Nene the story of Jimmy's death. Nene refuted the police's claims that Jimmy fought back because he was too sick to go to work that day. And according to Nene, the drugs and firearms found in their home were planted. When I asked her what was going through her mind during this time, she had one thing to say: "*Masakit po na pinatay nila nang walang kalaban-laban. Hindi sila naawa.*" [It's painful to think that Jimmy was helpless when they killed him. The killers were merciless.]

Resisting the "*Nanlaban*" Narrative

The "*nanlaban*" (fought back or resisted arrest) narrative is commonly cited by the Philippine government as the reason suspected drug personalities end up dead after a police operation. Police insist the suspects resisted arrest and fought back during the operation, justifying the killing. This narrative is adopted by local governments too. The *nanlaban* narrative rationalizes these deaths, implying that the loss of such a population (i.e., drug personalities) is necessary to protect the lives of the greater public. This is a manifestation of the ungrievability of death.[12] The precarious position drug personalities hold in society renders them dispensable as war targets means that even before they have already been recognized as unworthy of protection they are dismissed as collateral damage.

Lyn's partner, Crispin, was also helpless at the hands of police when he was killed. Lyn had just given birth when Crispin was gunned down after police raided a suspected drug den in their neighbourhood. Lyn disclosed that Crispin's livelihood involved selling illegal drugs, but unlike the "*nanlaban*" story, Crispin was on his knees, surrendering to the police when he was shot dead. "*Yung asawa ko daw po, sumusuko na daw po, nakaluhod na daw po, nakaposas*" [They told me my husband was already cuffed and, on his knees, surrendering], Lyn recalled how she received the news of Crispin's death. Several of Crispin's relatives were there that night and lived to tell Lyn this story:

> *Sabi na lang po sa'kin na nilagay na lang daw po sa body bag. Ang sakit nga po ng narinig ko dahil nilagay po nila sa body bag yung asawa ko, gumagalaw pa raw po tapos kinaladkad lang nila, parang ginawa nilang hayop.*
>
> [Onlookers told me that he was put in a body bag shortly after. It was so painful to hear the stories that he was still moving when they dragged him out of the drug den and put him in a body bag. They treated him like an animal.]

Lyn's partner was killed in a buy-bust operation, and her partner's parents were arrested that night for allegedly serving as drug protectors. After Crispin's death, Lyn was left as the sole caregiver of their seven children.

Unknown Perpetrators

I also had the privilege of speaking to widows whose husbands were killed by unknown gunmen. Nonetheless, they understand their husbands were killed in the government's campaign against illegal drugs. Marty's estranged husband and father of her three children was one of those killed with uncertain details. From Marty's point of view, her husband Ilong was killed because he was part of the *barangay*'s master list. *"Nasa master list siya kasi nag-voluntary surrender po siya"* [He was on the master list because he voluntarily surrendered to the *barangay*], Marty shared. These lists are also cited in other scholarly works about the war on drugs in the Philippines. These master lists or watch lists consist of suspected drug couriers and users who are called to the *barangay*s for interrogation.[13] Marty's husband Ilong was afraid he would get killed if he did not surrender to the *barangay* as a drug user, so he did. This is how Marty describes her husband's decision:

> *Diba pinautos ni Duterte na lahat ng mga adik daw tokhangin diba? Eh siyempre natakot siya kasi gumagamit siya ... nag-voluntary surrender siya para magamot siya ... para hindi na siya matokhang. Eh wala, yun pa rin.*
>
> [Duterte said all drug addicts must be killed, right? As a drug user, he was scared for his life so he surrendered to the *barangay* in an effort to avoid *tokhang*. But it still happened.]

Ilong spent two months in the community drug rehabilitation centre. Shortly after his stint in rehab, he was gunned down in his neighbourhood. According to Marty, nowadays, people in their community would rather not surrender to the *barangay* because *"kalimitan ng nag-voluntary surrender, natokhang"* [many of those who surrendered to the *barangay* were killed in *tokhang*]. Even though Marty did not witness her husband's killing, she insists the police were responsible. *"Halos lahat naman dito sa amin pulis ang yumari"* [Almost all the killings in our neighbourhood were done by police], Marty asserts. She knows this because she is familiar with her community. She said that during Ilong's wake, *"merong nag-aaligid-aligid na minsan naka-van, minsan naka-motor. Ang layo-layo lang pero alam mong hindi taga doon sa lugar namin"* [there were outsiders closely monitoring the area. They would come in vans or motorcycles. They were obviously not from here]. For other community members, however, violent incidents happen as a result of cheating among those involved in the illegal drugs trade. I spoke to Tess, the chief of the *purok* (area) leaders in Barangay Pagbangon. According to Tess, *purok* leaders are responsible for identifying drug users and peddlers in their area. *"Sila po ang nakakakilala ng mga tao sa area nila, sila po ang nakakakilala ng mga adik, mga nagbebenta"* [They are familiar with everyone in their assigned area. They know who the drug users and pushers are], she explained. Given this experience, Tess says drug peddlers in their community are killed when they are not able to remit their sales to their bosses. This is referred to as *"onsehan"* (betrayal). *"Hindi naman sila titirahin kung wala silang atraso"* [They will not be killed if they did not upset anyone], clarified Tess.

Regardless of the circumstances of the killing, the widows understand that their spouses were killed as part of the war on drugs. Tin's partner was killed by van-riding unidentified men. Tin's partner went out to pee in the middle of the night because their house did not have a toilet. Tin was awoken by continuous gunshots coming from the alley outside their house. This is how Tin recalled that night:

> *Nung nawala po yung putok ng baril, lumabas po ulit ako. Ayun po, nakita ko na po yung mister ko nakahandusay na po. Nagkatitigan pa po kami bago mag close eyes tapos biglang stuck up na lang yung mata. Ginigising ko pa po siya noon. Sumisigaw ako.*

[When the gunshots stopped, I went outside and I saw my husband's almost lifeless body sprawled along the alley. We looked each other in the eyes before they went blank. I was trying to wake him up. I was shouting.]

Tin's memory of that night is blurry because of the trauma she suffered after witnessing her partner lie in a pool of his own blood.

But she does recall seeing the perpetrators hop in a white van after they gunned down another man five houses down Tin's. Tin recognizes her partner's killing as part of the war on drugs because she was aware of his drug use. *"Wala po akong suspetsa kung sino [ang gumawa] pero ayun na po yung pagkakaintindi ko, nasama siya sa tokhang, nasama siya sa EJK nga po, sa sinasabing war on drugs po"* [I don't have any suspicion about who did it but from what I understand, his killing was part of *tokhang*, it was an incident of extrajudicial killing in the war on drugs], Tin said. When I asked Tin why she thinks her partner was killed, this is how she responded: *"Noong time na yun, nag-declare na ng war on drugs eh. Tapos sa iba't ibang lugar, talagang yung mga involved sa ganun yung mga pinapatay nila."* [During that time, the war on drugs was declared. Those involved in drugs were getting killed everywhere.]

Threats of Violence from Perpetrators

Inday, a mother of seven in her thirties, shares Tin's sentiments. *"Hinuhuli kahit na adik, kahit na sino-sino yung masasagasaan nila"* [They were arresting all drug addicts and anyone who went in their way], Inday recalled the months leading up to her husband's killing. This is why her husband, Jay, left Barangay Pagbangon, to avoid the violence. This, however, did not stop the police from storming into Inday's home while she was eight months pregnant to interrogate her about her husband's whereabouts. This is how she remembers the events:

> *Nagising na lang ako ... may hinahanap sila. Nagbabanta din po sila noon. Sabi nga po sa akin, magpasalamat nga po ako buntis ako, kung hindi, pinatay na rin po ako ... mga nakasibilyan po sila na mga pulis, may mga armalite po sila. Tsaka may kasama po silang DDS, kasagsagan po ng DDS noon, yung Duterte Death Squad ... hinahanap po nila yung asawa ko tapos yun, sabi nila, saan daw po yung asawa ko ... Sinabihan po ako, 'Sige, ituro mo kung saan yung asawa mo dahil papatayin namin.'*
>
> [I woke up to police officers searching our home. They were threatening us. They told me I should be thankful I was pregnant because they might have already killed me. The police were in plain clothes, but they had armalites. They were DDS, the Davao Death Squad. They were looking for my husband and they told me, "Tell us where he is because we're going to kill him."]

Inday was arrested that night after the police interrogated her. They accused her of violating Republic Act No. 9165 (Comprehensive Dangerous Drugs Act) even though they found no illegal drugs in her possession. This law punishes the sale, possession, and transportation of illegal drugs. The maximum punishment for violating this law is life imprisonment. Months later, while in detention, Inday saw her mother-in-law on the news. Inday's mother-in-law was interviewed because her son had been killed in a buy-bust operation. Inday was devastated. *"Lugmok ka na nga po dahil nasa kulungan ka tapos mababalitaan mo ba na ganun ang mangyayari sa asawa mo. Tapos napakasakit po yun"* [I was already devastated while in jail when I heard the news of what happened to my husband. That was so painful], said Inday.

Climate of Fear

Fearing for their safety is common among the widows I spoke to. Some were understandably hesitant to talk about the circumstances of their husbands' deaths. *"Confidential po kasi"* [It's confidential], said Gina, whose husband was a police asset. *"Naging hawak siya ng mga pulis. Siguro marami siyang alam nung time na yun. Gusto na niyang umalis ... Yung tinatawag nilang DDS na pulis. Davao Death Squad"* [He worked for the police. Maybe he knew too much and wanted to get out. He worked for what they call the Davao Death Squad] was all Gina was comfortable sharing. Comparably, Linda, whose husband was killed in an alley near their house, preferred not to talk about what happened. *"Ayoko kasi masyadong mag-iingay kasi baka marinig ako ng kapitbahay. Kasi dito sa paligid namin, mahirap na. Eh dito lang yun nangyari sa kabilang eskinita"* [I would rather not talk about it because the neighbours might overhear. It might cause trouble. Because it only happened in the nearby alley], said Linda. The reluctance to share the details of their husbands' deaths is reasonable given the current situation. Many of these women still live in fear because the violence continues in their community.

DISENFRANCHISED GRIEF

The suffering of these women and their families is prolonged because their husbands' deaths never achieved closure, as perpetrators were never held accountable. The notion of their husbands as "deserving victims" robbed them of empathy and condolences from their community.[14] As a result of disenfranchised grief, some of these widows choose to suffer in silence and isolation.

The brutality surrounding these deaths is a manifestation of ungrievability. These widows' late husbands and partners were identified as drug personalities, reifying their precariousness. Precarious lives are ungrievable lives—this is one of the scholar Judith Butler's most striking arguments. The state of being precarious is the "politically induced condition in which certain populations suffer from failing social and economic networks of support and become differentially exposed to injury, violence, and death."[15] Thus, precarity and grievability reinforce each other.

Grief is a social construct because societal factors shape the practice and experience of it. The drug war casualties, like those who died after police encounters and sex offenders, have been identified as deserving of their tragic fates.[16] The legitimacy of their grief is denied because of the presumed criminality of their loved ones.[17]

Social Isolation

The widows I spoke to suffered social isolation after their spouses' deaths. And this social isolation is more present among spouses because of the intimacy of their relationship with the suspected criminal.[18] Their neighbours and friends avoided them, their children were bullied in school, and the condolences were few. They felt as if nobody wanted to be associated with the wife of a suspected drug personality.

Immediately after Marty's husband was killed by unidentified gunmen, she was called to the principal's office of her children's school for the first time. "*Yun yung kauna-unahang araw na pinatawag ako sa eskwelahan. Yung aking anak daw po ay nakipag suntukan*" [It was the very first time I was called to his school because my son got into a brawl], Marty shared. When she asked her youngest child about what happened, he said,

> Kasi mama, sila kasi. Niloloko nila ako, sinasabihan nila ako buti nga daw natokhang si papa, adik daw kasi. Kaya yun ma, naasar ako sa kanila, inaway ko sila, nakipagsuntukan ako sa kanila.

[Because they were bullying me, telling me that papa was killed in *tokhang* because he was an addict. I was so annoyed I started a fight with them.]

Marty's youngest child had to stop school for a year after that incident because of the bullying he experienced from classmates. And during the wake of her husband, Ilong, only immediate family members were present. *"Walang nakikipaglamay kasi takot sila baka mamaya daw magkaroon ng gulo, pati sila madamay ... May pupuntang kaibigan, aalis agad"* [No one paid their condolences at the wake because they wanted to avoid trouble. They were afraid they would get implicated too. The friends who went to visit left right away], Marty disclosed. Marty understood why people avoided her husband's wake. She knew that people feared another violent encounter might ensue at the wake, so they would rather not pay their sympathies.

These fears are not unfounded, according to Linda. *"Kasi meron nang pangyayari dito sa amin na ganyan. May lamay, tungkol din sa ganyan yung nangyari. Merong nakipaglamay doon. Ngayon, doon tinira sa lamay"* [One time during a wake, one of the visitors was shot dead], she revealed. For this reason, she no longer questioned why she was left alone during her husband's two-week wake. *"Buong magdamag, ako lang mag-isa"* [I was alone all night long], Linda shared. But this was common among the families of women like her. *"Halos lahat ng pamilya [ng natokhang] ganyan, wala gaanong naglalamay dahil sa takot na baka pati sila madamay"* [Almost all the families of those killed in *tokhang* experienced that. No one wanted to pay their condolences at the wake because they were afraid to get implicated] is Linda's explanation. Mila had a similar experience too. A few houses from hers, a couple was killed inside their home. *"Konti lang po ang naglamay kasi nauna yung kapitbahay namin na binaril din sa loob ng bahay ... Siyempre po alam mo naman dito, maraming droga. Siyempre takot sila sa ganyan, makipaglamay"* [Only a few people went to the wake because our neighbours were also killed inside their home. Drugs are rampant in our neighbourhood, so people were too afraid], Mila explained.

I heard this notion of *damay* quite often among the widows. Tin, whose first partner was killed in a dark alley outside their house, said similar views. *"Sa takot nila, baka daw po bumalik madamay sila. Yun po ang laging nasa isip nila, baka mamaril ulit dito habang nakaburol"*

[They fear that the perpetrators might return and target them next. They think that someone will get killed again during the wake], Tin explained. Fear is so embedded in their community that these widows can rationalize the lack of support they receive. Girly shares these sentiments about the low turnout at her husband's wake. *"Natatakot [sila] pumunta sa bahay dahil ayaw nga po nilang madamay"* [They would rather not visit us because they don't want to get implicated in drugs], Girly said about her friends and neighbours. She also described the major difference she felt in how they treated her:

> *Ang laki ng pinagkaibahan. Kahit hindi nila sabihin sa akin, nararamdaman ko pa rin sa kanila yung nandun yung nag-aalinlangan sila, baka mamaya bigla akong barilin, madamay sila … nararamdaman ko pa rin sa sarili ko na ilag nga po sila nung panahon na yun.*

[Even if they didn't say anything, I felt the difference. They were doubtful. They were afraid that someone might shoot me and then target them next. I felt that they avoided me during that time.]

But Girly met this ostracism with understanding. *"Nauunawaan ko rin sila kasi siyempre may pamilya din naman sila na natatakot din po na mawalan sila ng pamilya, anak, o kaya asawa"* [I understand them because they are also afraid to lose their sons and husbands]. Inday had similar thoughts. *"Iniingatan din po kasi nila yung pamilya nila. Mahirap po kasing makialam noon mas lalo noong panahon ng war on drugs dahil takot po talaga yung mga tao noon"* [They are only protecting their families. People did not want to intervene during the height of the war on drugs out of fear], said Inday. She said even the gossipers were too afraid to lurk around.

On the other hand, some widows took offense to these kinds of interactions. Here is Lyn's recollection of the exchange with one neighbour:

> *May isa po akong na-encounter na sobrang nasaktan yung dibdib ko. Hindi ko ine-expect na sasabihin nila yun kasi ang sabi kasi, 'Buti nga yun namatay, buti yun binaril.' Dahil nga daw po nagbebenta, salot daw po. Parang ang sakit. Ang sakit po sa dibdib na marinig po yung ganun. Namatayan ka na nga sasabihan ka pa ng ganun.*

[I encountered one painful experience. Someone told me, "It's good that he got killed because he was a drug pusher, he was a pest." It was so painful to hear that. You had just lost someone and would hear that said about him.]

The stigma around drug personalities transfers to their families, especially their wives. Tin would hear the following utterances from people around her: "*Ay, bakit sumasama ka diyan? Asawa yan nung pinatay na adik.*" [Why are you hanging out with her? She's the wife of the addict who got killed.] Tin dismisses these remarks but admits they sting. "*Parang jinudge na nila na pati ako ganun*" [It's like they already made their judgment that I'm like my late partner who was involved in drugs], she lamented. Gina, who refused to share the specific details of her husband's killing, isolated herself because of encounters like these. After her husband's death, law enforcement frequented her home, interrogating her about his colleagues and acquaintances. These visits prompted gossip from Gina's neighbours. "*Kaya raw ako pinupuntahan ng pulis kasi nagbebenta raw ako ng drugs*" [They speculated that police often paid me visits because I'm a drug pusher], she complained. "*Kami na lang ang iiwas*" [So I would rather avoid them], Gina added. She said she would rather ignore these remarks and avoid her neighbours than engage with them.

One striking example of social isolation in the aftermath of the death is Aida's experience during her husband's wake. Like the other widows I spoke to, Aida struggled to pool the money to pay for the burial. Often, the *abuloy* (donation) from mourners helps raise funds. But since no one visits to pay their sympathy, the wake lingered for almost a month. The little *abuloy* Aida received came in the form of coins.

> *Yung mga sasakyan doon, yung mga tricyle, naghahagis po doon [ng abuloy] ... Ayaw nilang pumunta doon talaga, hinahagis na lang nila ... Sa maghapon, nakakaipon kami ng isang daan sa barya-barya lang.*
>
> [The cars and tricycles that would pass by would throw coins at us as a form of donation. They didn't want to pay a formal visit to the wake; instead, they tossed coins at us. At the end of each day, we gathered 100 pesos worth of coins.]

Aida's children would run after the vehicles that passed by chasing after the coins they tossed. "*Wala naman sa akin tumutulong noon*" [Nobody helped me back then], she lamented. "*Nung nalaman nila na ganun nga yung pagkamatay niya na natokhang, iwas po yung mga kapitbahay ko noon sa akin"* [When they found out that my partner was killed in *tokhang*, all my neighbours avoided me], Aida added. But like the other widows, Aida thinks this avoidance is reasonable. This is how Aida describes it:

> *Kasi po nung mga panahon na yun, talagang ang init po, kung sino-sino na lang po yung pinapatay. Hindi namin alam kung talagang drugs ba talaga yung dahilan nun or anong dahilan talaga. Kaya po yung mga tao, nagkakaroon po sila ng takot na baka pag dumikit ka doon sa tao na yun, baka pati ikaw madamay ka din.*
>
> [Because during that time, it was so intense. There were so many killings happening. We weren't sure if they were killed because of drugs or something else. That's why people feared that if they spent time with someone involved in drugs, they would get implicated too and become the following targets.]

Despite her understanding of the fear, the social isolation left Aida resentful.

> *Bago pa man po yun nangyari, marami naman po akong nakakausap doon, nakakakwentuhan, tapos po nung nangyari po yun sa kanya parang nasa ibang lugar kami. Yun po bang hindi man lang sila nagtatanong, hindi man lang sila nagsasalita ... Yung pakikiramay na yan, hindi ko yan naramdaman sa kahit sino.*
>
> [Before that happened to my partner, I would hang out with my neighbours and chitchat. But after the incident, it felt like we were in a different place. They didn't even ask me what happened. They just didn't speak to me. I didn't get sympathy from anyone.]

Aida felt the absence of support around her husband's death. She felt othered by her community (*"parang nasa ibang lugar kami"*) where she has lived her entire life. These are the consequences of these ungrievable deaths.

Endless Battles

In the aftermath of such violent deaths, the widows pick up the pieces and confront the challenges of the loss. Authors have studied the experiences of families of people who died after police contact and identified the endless battles these families endure in the aftermath of their loved ones' deaths.[19] These battles include silencing their grief from community members and law enforcement and the constant intrusion into their lives. These battles have led these families to pause their grief, prolonging the suffering. They cannot express their grief because they must face endless battles, leaving them helpless even years after. For the drug war widows I spoke to, these endless battles include the struggles of financing burial services and the relentless confrontations with law enforcement because of the continuation of the war on drugs in their community. These following vignettes describe the endless battles widows of the drug war endure.

Documentation and the erasure of evidence is another struggle for these women. The evidence on the killings of their spouses is falsified to deny the occurrence of the crime. For instance, in their desperation to raise funds for the burial of their loved one, Inday and her family had to write a formal statement indicating they will not press charges against the perpetrators. *"Gumagawa sila ng kasulatan na ganito, na hindi sila magsasampa ng kaso para matulungan lang sila sa pagpapalibing"* [They had to put in writing that they would not press charges against the perpetrators so that they could be given financial assistance], Inday shared. To make matters worse, when Inday was released from detention, she found issues with her late husband's death certificate. *"Dalawang death certificate ang lumabas. Yung hypertension ang ikinamatay niya at tsaka yung namatay din siya sa gunshot bullet"* [Two death certificates were produced. One said he died due to hypertension and the other indicated death due to a gunshot], Inday complained. Lyn had a similar experience. According to Lyn, the funeral parlor insisted on changing the cause of death from gunshot to stroke because otherwise they could not ask for help from the government. This is how Lyn remembers it:

> *Nagkaproblema rin po yung death certificate ng asawa ko kasi po ang sabi ng funeral [parlor], hindi daw po kami makakalapit ng anumang tulong sa gobyerno kapag namatay daw po yung asawa ko na pinatay dahil sa droga. Kaya pinalitan po nila yung cause of death ng asawa ko. Yung cause of death ng asawa ko ay stroke, yung funeral po ang [gumawa] nun kasi wala naman po kaming kakayanan magpa-autopsy.*
>
> [We encountered issues with my partner's death certificate because the funeral parlor said government agencies wouldn't help us if they found out he was killed because of drugs. So they changed the cause

of death. They put "stroke". The funeral parlor did this, and we couldn't complain because we couldn't afford an autopsy anyway.]

Local and international media have also covered these issues by documenting the killings of drug war casualties. Efforts to erase the evidence of wrongdoing against drug personalities crystallize the ungrievability of these deaths. After all, if these deaths occurred out of natural causes, then there is no crime to be acknowledged or perpetrators to be held accountable. As a result, the grief of left-behind families is disenfranchised when their loss is not recognized and their suffering is prolonged when years later the death is still conflicted.[20]

These widows must endure these endless battles because of their spouses' ungrievable deaths. The drug war casualties are not considered heroes but instead dismissed as collateral damage or denied altogether. This is the twisted logic that justifies the loss of lives—when violence is deemed necessary to protect the lives of the living. As a result, widows struggle to find support. Since their husbands' deaths are deemed justified and necessary to address the illegal drug problem, these widows suffer from worsened poverty and marginalization. They suffer the consequences of the stigma associated with drug personalities.

THE 2022 ELECTIONS AND MARCOSES' RETURN TO POWER

Unfortunately, the 2022 elections were not the best time to seek accountability from Duterte. The entry of Ferdinand Bongbong Marcos Jr. changed the entire ballgame. Initially, the talk was that Sara Duterte, Duterte's daughter and mayor of Davao City, will run for president. Everyone, and even Duterte himself was caught by surprise, and was even disappointed that his daughter ran with Marcos Jr. But Marcos Jr.'s candidacy meant that the drug war was not going to be a big issue in the elections as he had nothing to do with it. Sara Duterte, for her part, distanced herself from her father even prior to her run. During the campaign, she stated that she will pursue the "war on drugs with love"[21] and will emphasize to the police that the latter should observe fairness in enforcing the law. Other presidential candidates were one in saying that the killings must be stopped, and that due process must be observed.[22] When asked about the drug war during his interviews with friendly media during the campaign, Marcos Jr. responded that he will continue the programme but with a benign strategy. However, months into his administration, signs that the violent strategy is still implemented, have been documented by Project *Dahas*.[23]

In the five months of the Marcos Jr. administration, 152 were killed in drug operations.[24] Human Rights Watch's World Report 2023 conveyed the same situation. These numbers suggest that the killings continue despite the current administration's pronouncements that the focus will be on rehabilitation and partnership with the private sector.[25] Moreover, while it is true that the killings continue under the Marcos government, the media seem to be distracted by the different narrative pushed by Marcos Jr.'s nostalgia for his father's presidency, his frequent trips abroad, and high inflation rates at the beginning of his term. For this reason, there is a lack of an almost daily media monitoring of drug war deaths that characterized the early Duterte years, suggesting that the normalization of violence has led to accountability fatigue.

Meanwhile, the International Criminal Court (ICC), in March 2023, rejected the government's appeal to suspend its investigation of the drug war. The ICC announced that it will launch an investigation in February 2018. However, it had to stop in November 2021 due to the government's appeal to halt its investigation following the Philippines' bid to conduct its own. However, based on the ICC findings released on 26 January 2023, it ruled that the Philippine side has not exhausted all its means in reviewing the drug war and the extrajudicial killings, and the Office of the Solicitor General sought to reverse the ruling. After two weeks of appealing, the ICC announced its rejection and bid to continue the investigation.

With these developments, two things are in Marcos's cards: the extent to which he will cooperate or not with the ICC, and whether or not he will unilaterally make strong pronouncements against the continued killings relating to the drug war.

CONCLUSION AND RECOMMENDATIONS

This chapter describes the violence widows experienced during and after their spouses' killings. They agonized over the brutality of the killings, became isolated in their communities, and endured many adversities. This chapter shows that for the widows of the war on drugs, the suffering is not only a result of the violence. These women must also pay the social and economic costs of being a widow of a suspected drug personality. The experiences of these widows depict the tragic consequences of this war on drugs that vilified drug users and peddlers the Duterte administration thought deserved to die. Their narratives represent the hidden impact of a punitive approach to illegal drug control, pushing marginalized people further into the peripheries.

Meanwhile, current reports suggest that the killings continue despite pronouncements from the present administration that its approach is rehabilitative. The next moves of the Marcos Jr. administration would define how it wants its legacy to be remembered.

The following are recommendations that can be explored. At the level of policy, a systematic monitoring of drug war casualties should be developed in order to acknowledge the wrongdoings committed. Similar to what the Mexican government did after Felipe Calderon's term, widows and families of drug war casualties should be tracked and be paid the necessary compensation. Tracking and keeping a database of drug war casualties and their families is a concrete way to recognize them as victims. Further, a government initiative relieves the widows and their families of the burden of reporting the offense and filing cases against perpetrators. As the widows' narratives in this research show, fearing retaliation from the perpetrators is the main reason they are discouraged to file complaints. The compensation would also help alleviate the financial burden of losing their breadwinners.

Notes

1. Eloisa Lopez, "Women Fighting: Widows, Mothers of Drug War Casualties Come Together", *Rappler*, 10 March 2018, https://www.rappler.com/nation/197731-women-widows-mothers-fight-drug-war-killed/.
2. Diliman Information Office, "Salita ng Taon 2018", 26 October 2018, https://upd.edu.ph/salita-ng-taon-2018/.

3. Gabriel Pabico Lalu, "52 Out of 30,000 Deaths? Rights Group Disputes Gov't Claims of DOJ Drug War Probe", *Inquirer.net*, 20 November 2021, https://newsinfo.inquirer.net/1517512/52-out-of-30000-deaths-petitioner-in-icc-case-disputes-doj-probe-of-drug-war; Phil Robertson, "Another Spike in Philippines' 'Drug War' Deaths: Latest Data Shows Police Killings Rising amid Covid-19 Pandemic", Human Rights Watch, 28 September 2020, https://www.hrw.org/news/2020/09/28/another-spike-philippines-drug-war-deaths.
4. Social Weather Station, "Second Quarter 2019 Social Weather Survey: Net Satisfaction with Anti-illegal Drugs Campaign at 'Excellent' +70", 22 September 2019, http://www.sws.org.ph/swsmain/artcldisppage/?artcsyscode=ART-20190922154614.
5. Christian Haerpfer, Ronald Inglehart, Alejandro Moreno, Christian Welzel, Kseniya Kizilova, Jaime Diez-Medrano, Marta Lagos, Pippa Norris, Eduard Ponarin, and Bi Puranen, eds. 2022. *World Values Survey: Round Seven—Country-Pooled Datafile Version 3.0*. Madrid, Spain: JD Systems Institute and WVSA Secretariat. https://doi.org/10.14281/18241.16.
6. Felix M. Berardo, "Widowhood Status in the United States: Perspective on a Neglected Aspect of the Family", *The Family Coordinator* 17, no. 3 (1968): 191–203.
7. Juni Gonzales and Fernando Cabigao Jr., "War on Drugs: The Unheard Stories—'Oplan Tokhang, from Tagging to Killing", n.d., https://news.abs-cbn.com/war-on-drugs/part4.
8. Steffen Bo Jensen and Karl Hapal, *Communal Intimacy and the Violence of Politics: Understanding the War on Drugs in Bagong Silang, Philippines* (Ithaca: Cornell University Press, 2022), http://www.jstor.org/stable/10.7591/j.ctv1sfsf6c; Anna Braemer Warburg and Steffen Jensen, "Policing the War on Drugs and the Transformation of Urban Space", *Society and Space* 38, no. 3 (2018), https://www.societyandspace.org/journal-essays/policing-the-war-on-drugs-and-the-transformation-of-urban-space-in-manila; Wataru Kusaka, "Bandit Grabbed the State: Duterte's Moral Politics", *Philippine Sociological Review* 65 (2017): 49–75, http://www.jstor.org/stable/45014309.
9. Vicente L. Rafael, "Photography and the Biopolitics of Fear: Witnessing the Philippine Drug War", *Positions: Asia Critique* 28, no. 4 (2020): 905–33. https://doi.org/10.1215/10679847-8606621.
10. *Project Taguyod* is used throughout this chapter in lieu of the real name of the widows' organization to protect their identities.
11. Barangay Pagbangon is used in lieu of the real name of the widows' location for safety reasons.
12. Judith Butler, *Frames of War: When is Life Grievable?* (London: Verso, 2016).

13. Marielle Y. Marcaida, "Understanding the Narratives of Pateros Mothers' Resistance under the Philippine Drug War", *Philippine Political Science Journal* 42, no. 3 (2021): 238–65, https://doi.org/doi:10.1163/2165025X-bja10022; Warburg and Jensen, "Policing the War on Drugs and the Transformation of Urban Space".
14. David Baker, Dana Norris, and Veroniki Cherneva, "Disenfranchised Grief and Families' Experiences of Death after Police Contact in the United States", *Journal of Death and Dying* 83, no. 2 (2019): 239–56, https://doi.org/10.1177/0030222819846420.
15. Butler, *Frames of War*, p. 79.
16. Danielle J.S. Bailey, "A Life of Grief: An Exploration of Disenfranchised Grief in Sex Offender Significant Others", *American Journal of Criminal Justice* 43, no. 3 (2018): 641–67, https://doi.org/10.1007/s12103-017-9416-4; Baker, Norris, and Cherneva, "Disenfranchised Grief and Families' Experiences of Death", p. 249.
17. Baker, Norris, and Cherneva, "Disenfranchised Grief and Families' Experiences of Death".
18. Bailey, "A Life of Grief".
19. Baker, Norris, and Cherneva, "Disenfranchised Grief and Families' Experiences of Death", p. 249.
20. Bailey, "A Life of Grief"; Baker, Norris, and Cherneva, "Disenfranchised Grief and Families' Experiences of Death".
21. Rex Remito, "If She Wins, Sara Duterte Vows Fair Enforcement of War on Drugs and Crime", *CNN Philippines*, 22 February 2022, https://www.cnnphilippines.com/news/2022/2/22/Sara-Duterte-fair-enforcement-war-on-drugs-crime.html.
22. Jodesz Gavilan, "Presidential Bets Call for Due Process, End to Killings in Drug War", *Rappler*, 3 April 2022, https://www.rappler.com/nation/elections/presidential-candidates-responses-war-on-drugs-comelec-presidential-debate-2022/.
23. Project Dahas is implemented by the University of the Philippines' Third World Studies Center, with the aim to document and build a database of the killings related to the drug war.
24. Margaret Simons, "The Philippines Is Losing Its 'War on Drugs'", *Foreign Policy*, 11 January 2023, https://foreignpolicy.com/2023/01/11/philippines-drug-war-manila-marcos/.
25. Tirana Hassan, "Philippines Events of 2022", Human Rights Watch, n.d., https://www.hrw.org/world-report/2023/country-chapters/philippines.

7

Tsek.ph and the Media's Pushback against Digital Disinformation

Ma. Diosa Labiste

> *To counter various forms of election-related information, media organizations, academe, and civil society built* tsek.ph, *a collaborative fact-checking organization that played the watchdog role of holding politicians accountable for their campaign statements. This fact-checking initiative has won over academe, media, and civil society members to collaborate and verify information during the election campaign period. In the 2019 and 2022 elections, the more prominent forms of disinformation include false and misleading claims concerning the Marcos dictatorship, anti-communist witch-hunting, and hate speech. Online disinformation became the trademark and legacy of President Rodrigo Duterte's administration that deployed trolls, bloggers, and apologists to justify his controversial policies and amplify them through social media platforms. The extent of deception*

and the reception of such forms of disinformation could help explain the electoral victory of Ferdinand Marcos Jr. and Sara Duterte in the 2022 elections because disinformation not only worked to their advantage, the purveyors of false and misleading claims have succeeded in seeding false information among misinformed voters.

Keywords: social media; disinformation; fact-checking; *tsek.ph*; 2022 elections

INTRODUCTION

On his 78th birthday on 28 March 2023, the former president Rodrigo Duterte received a fawning compliment from his successor, President Ferdinand Marcos Jr. "Happy birthday to you, Mr. President. I now understand why sometimes, you would cuss when you were still president", said Marcos, the namesake and son of a former dictator.[1]

Many newspapers and partisan blog sites reported the greeting felicitously, as if never wanting to pass off the chance of driving traffic to their websites through feel-good news or turning Marcos's inadequacies to his gain. However, the online news site *Rappler* offered a context for Duterte's aggressive speech habit, which defined his six-year term as president and whose politics portends a Marcos comeback. I argue that Duterte's playbook of hate speech and disinformation left the country's democratic traditions frayed and made it easy for Marcos's historical revisionism—about his father's martial law, dictatorship, and plunder—to mislead voters in the May 2022 elections. Thanks to Duterte's endorsement of Marcos's authoritarian rule, Marcos Jr. was elected president on a disinformation platform seeking to rehabilitate the legacy of his father who was ousted by the 1986 People Power uprising.

Disinformation was defined by Claire Wardle and Hossein Derakhshan as false information that intends to deceive and cause harm.[2] Sometimes, disinformation is interchangeable with misinformation, but misinformation is considered as false information that was not intended to cause harm, which is a degree lower than disinformation. Misinformation may spread out of a journalist's carelessness like when breaking a news with unverified information, or anyone sharing a post without first vetting it. When fact-checkers examine a claim, they pay attention to the inaccuracy of misinformation and leave out the intention. Similarly, with disinformation, which refers to false information that is deliberately shared to cause harm, fact-checkers may not be able to find out the motive. However, regardless of the presence or absence of a motive, fact-checkers consider it their responsibility to challenge both forms of false information that could mislead, influence, and harm people.

In the 2019 and 2022 national elections in the Philippines, when a lot of lies circulated online, many media-based fact-checkers avoided correcting small errors and minor details and instead focused on information that affected the public more. Moreover, they chose claims where they could provide empirically proven facts and also establish a binary of truth or falsehood. This strategic decision demonstrates the fact-checkers' agency to debunk disinformation before it gains traction. However, information that occupies the blurry line between opinion and facts, like an underhanded compliment or backhanded pronouncement, can easily slip through. For example, claims that President Ferdinand Marcos is the greatest president ever and that his fourteen years of dictatorship was the golden age of the country,[3] are among such problematic claims that can easily influence the public. However, some fact-checkers have ignored them because of their pointlessness or irrelevance. It is that kind of erroneous information that resonated with Duterte's and Marcos's supporters amid polarization and distrust of the media and experts because such claims have a nostalgic pull.[4] It is also the kind of information that was cleverly deployed first by Duterte, and then by Marcos Jr., as part of their election playbook and information strategy of their administrations.

This chapter provides a review of the systematic digital disinformation and online hate in the Philippines during the Duterte administration and challenges under the early part of the Ferdinand Marcos Jr. presidency. It answers the question: what is the role of fact-checking in countering disinformation during the 2019 and 2022 elections in the Philippines? This chapter argues that the media was able to have some success in repelling disinformation and hate speech through fact-checking and similar endeavours. The first section revisits the beginnings of hate speech and disinformation, and their deployment against Duterte's enemies, including the media. The second section examines the naturalization of hate speech and disinformation, how they become potent in public discourse, their effects in the 2019 and 2022 elections, and flagged by fact-checkers with *tsek.ph* coalition. The third and last section discusses the limits and possibilities of fact-checking, given the depth and extent of the problem of disinformation and the public's disaffection towards the media. Overall, the chapter will provide an overview of disinformation and hate speech, and media's intervention through *tsek.ph* fact-checking initiative.

DUTERTE'S DISINFORMATION PLAYBOOK AND THE MEDIA

The Duterte administration (2016–22) was the subject of a good number of books as well as articles, films, and memes too many to mention here.[5] To a great degree, media platforms contributed to his immensely popularity and political novelty as a folksy and foul-mouthed president. The disproportionate media coverage of Duterte has normalized his actions to the extent that some journalists would say that he was joking whenever he cursed or said something off the cuff. Labelling Duterte's sexism and incivility as a joke would then justify the inclusion of cuss words and false claims in the news story to attract a larger audience.[6] However, this light treatment of Duterte's virulent statement also eroded the credibility of the media at the same time that it alienated some individuals and groups.[7]

When Duterte became president, scholars, and political pundits started calling him a "populist" president, his ideology as "populism",[8] and that he is riding the so-called populism wave which counts Trump and Bolsonaro among the kindred far right[9] leaders. A look back on the political commentary in news media in 2016, a few months after Duterte became president, showed that using the term "populism", was confined to select pieces, several of them from foreign media.[10] The inquiry about the term's validity was hardly news material for the country's media. There seemed to be a reluctance among reporters to call him populist, a loaded terminology that goes against journalism's avowed neutrality. Columnists and academics have no consensus on what type of populism Duterte has, whether it is destructive or transformative.[11] Meanwhile, Duterte was portrayed as *sui generis* in the news stories, with eye-catching visuals, quotes, and headlines.

Duterte's stance against his political enemies was reported as a narrative of political retribution. As what happened to his tirades against opposition senator Leila de Lima, who was detained for what were said to be trumped up drug charges, the news media willingly gave Duterte a platform where he can weaponize his quips against her that, while without basis, they were considered newsworthy. For example, in a he-said-she-said fashion, a story allowed Duterte to malign de Lima by calling her immoral, adulterous, and had used drug money to fund her election campaign, but the reporter did not verify Duterte's claims, let alone supply evidence for the damaging accusations included in the story.[12] The latter is an example of how the media could amplify the disinformation project of Duterte.

In 2021, Duterte's official spokesperson Harry Roque denied that the government imposed censorship because the media could still report and criticize the government.[13] If there was criticism against the press, it is the case of "bad journalism", said Roque. However, the National Union of Journalists of the Philippines called out Roque's hair-splitting tactic because censorship is not simply a gag order as it comes in many forms.[14] For example, the government is behind arresting and filing of charges against Maria Ressa, and community journalists Lady Ann Salem, Margarita Valle, and Frenchie Mae Cumpio. Moreover, 5,000 media workers lost their jobs when Congress did not renew ABS-CBN's franchise in 2020. Duterte's hostile attitude towards some journalists earned condemnation from media associations, both local and international.

If media freedom is an index of democracy, then the latter needs an examination. Under Duterte, democracy is a poor emanation of its ideals because irrational and unacceptable actions are derived from the enjoyment of freedom or democratic guarantees. Aurelien Mondon and Aaron Winter termed "reactionary democracy" the deployment of the concept of democracy for reactionary ends.[15] The descriptor "reactionary" turns democracy against itself because the sense of power held by the people, or *demos*, is invoked to promote reactionary ideas for certain political ends. Under a reactionary democracy, certain rights are still enjoyed, like voting, media reporting, and protesting, but these are limited, heavily monitored, and easily disrupted by repressive state apparatuses.[16]

A slightly similar concept, "counterrevolution" is offered by Walden Bello in his recent book *Counterrevolution: The Global Rise of the Far Right*.[17] The concept encompasses forms of authoritarian, right-wing and fascist politics. A classical strand of counterrevolutionary politics is a response to a revolutionary struggle against the ruling class. The other strand, which is relevant here, is the response to the whole political and ideological framework for change that is seen to disrupt the status quo and install justice. Duterte, as a counterrevolutionary according to Bello, targeted the liberal-democratic ideology and political system that failed to deliver on its promise of progress, equality, and security, which is encapsulated by the spirit of Edsa uprising.[18] Duterte did not offer a corrective to liberal democracy, instead he pursued an authoritarian agenda as shown by the outright repression of his perceived enemies and the suppression of independent and recalcitrant media.

The attacks on independent media are central to Duterte's populist authoritarianism and his disinformation project. When Duterte moved against those who criticized the drug war, including Senator Leila de Lima, Chief Justice Maria Lourdes and Catholic bishops, among others, he was enjoying high approval and trust ratings.[19] However, Duterte's controversial policies on drugs received unfavourable coverage from some mainstream news organizations, with some news organizations[20] and journalists earning reprisals.[21]

Throughout his term as president, Duterte has cursed in his statements, interviews, speeches, and public appearances, and this harmful speech acts disturbed journalists and their audience alike. The early response by the media and some media educators to Duterte's foul-mouthed language was mixed. A communicators' forum in November 2020 attended by journalists, educators, and Duterte's officials discussed Duterte's speaking style and rhetoric as if it were the sole issue. They said Duterte's manner of speaking was effective in two ways: first, it was intended for media who are after soundbites that would sell the news; second, the words, like "I will kill you", were intended to scare drug dealers and users targeted by Duterte's so-called war on drugs.[22] In the forum, Ernesto Abella, then Duterte's spokesperson, denied that there was a policy of using violent, abusive, and threatening language; it was just Duterte's way of getting attention.[23] Journalists and other professionals in the forum pointed out that Duterte's language is divisive, abusive, and filled with lies and hubris.[24]

In the field, journalists tended to just report the event, without analysis or hint of bias. If Duterte strayed from the topic, cursed, or refused to answer their questions squarely, reporters let him be. Those who appeared critical of Duterte were threatened with denial of access to presidential press briefings, which happened to news reporter Pia Ranada of *Rappler* in February 2018.[25] Ranada's case was considered by media watch groups, Reporters without Borders and the Center for Media Freedom and Responsibility (CMFR), as a violation of media freedom. The CMFR also reported a pattern of restrictions on local and foreign media, "which signal crackdown on the press".[26] Some harassment did not reach the attention of media organizations. Reporters who were threatened by trolls and spurious social media users simply turned off the public settings of their social media accounts to stop the vicious attacks from pro-Duterte trolls. Some of these reporters were writing about drug-related killings. With his contempt for independent journalism, Duterte emboldened his supporters to take adversarial position against news organizations on social media, using hateful language similar to Duterte's.

Duterte went after the established news organizations, such as ABS-CBN television network and Rappler, an independent online news site. The ABS-CBN was shut down after its franchise expired and was not renewed by the House of Representatives, an institution dominated by Duterte's allies. Duterte had several times said the network had to be closed down because it did not air his election advertisement in 2016. Moreover, he disliked its owners, which he calls oligarchs. Since 2018, Rappler has faced a number of cases over its ownership structure, tax payments, and cyber libel, in which one of the accused is its CEO, Maria Ressa, a 2021 Nobel Peace Prize laureate. Rappler had published critical reports about Duterte's drug war. In 2016, Rappler's three-part story, "Propaganda War: Weaponizing the Net",[27] is one of the early exposes of Duterte's disinformation machinery that "unleashed a flood of anger against Duterte's critics". The report mapped the network of disinformation for Duterte, from bots or automated accounts to trolls with anonymous accounts that were all connected to smaller groups of operators who direct the attacks against the targets. Being part of the network is profitable, especially for the top operators and those who have thousands of social followers who can leverage their influence and monetize their social media presence. Rappler's report also showed how the network took its cues from Duterte who was indifferent to the media in general, and hostile to the independent minded ones. This stance remained throughout the six years of Duterte's administration.

Duterte exploited Philippine media's existing problems and vulnerabilities: precarity of labour, declining readership and trust in news media, and the unconcealed political and commercial interests of media owners that their employees have to negotiate. These issues rendered news organizations and journalists open to government pressures at the same time that they divided media ranks. Within the media community, some journalists maintained a neutral stance, with little sympathy for their beleaguered colleagues. Other media organizations, including state-owned media, offered receptive and favourable coverage to Duterte's tirades and narratives and even attacked independent media organizations. They also provided Duterte with regular and unhampered access to their news platform where he drummed up support for his authoritarian policies.

As a result, journalists have to deal with conflicting motivations—either they toe the line set by owners and editors or lose their jobs by defending media freedom. Many of them had chosen the former as evidenced by the generally anodyne coverage of the government. For example, many reporters did not call out Duterte's inaccuracies and innuendoes in his statements that got into their stories, choosing instead to simply attribute the words to him, as if these were sacrosanct. This stance is not surprising but nonetheless disheartening. There are enough incentives to maintain media independence. Between 2016 and 2022, many international and local media award-giving bodies, from Pulitzer, Society of Publishers in Asia, to CMFR, have handed annual awards to recognize critical reporting and praised the resiliency of journalists covering the Duterte government. For example, Reuters' Clare Baldwin, Andrew R.C. Marshall, and Manuel Mogato won the 2018 Pulitzer Prize for reporting on the brutal killings in Duterte's drug war.[28] Photojournalists who won international awards for covering the drug war include Ezra Acayan[29] and Eloisa Lopez.[30] Aside from raising the social capital of the recipients, the media awards affirmed what good journalism is: one which raises a protest against the loss of lives and freedoms, as opposed to the business-as-usual kind of reporting common at that time.

Digital disinformation has indeed been among the factors in the withering of press freedom and increasing distrust in media. Fact-checkers and investigative journalism were attacked by trolls on social media, calling their corrupt and paid hacks, and their work as nothing but "fake news". After the Philippine Center for Investigative Journalism (PCIJ) released a story on Duterte's undeclared wealth, the centre experienced a volley of troll attacks. This came after Duterte suggested that the centre was bribed by the opposition to embarrass him and his family. A few weeks into the 2019 elections, Duterte's spokesperson bared an unsubstantiated illustration of a web of conspirators out to overthrow the government. Dubbed "matrix", it named lawyers and journalists as part of the so-called plot.[31] Its publication in *Manila Times*, a newspaper owned by Duterte's publicist, led to the resignation of its managing editor, Felipe Salvosa, who denounced the matrix story on Twitter shortly before stepping down.[32] Interestingly, among the groups named in the alleged plot were the PCIJ that released the story on Duterte's wealth,[33] and Rappler and Vera Files which were in the thick of fact-checking the 2019 elections.

The government's spurious claim that three media organizations were among the coup plotters is the best example of disinformation with the intent to immobilize independent news organizations and destroy their credibility. While establishing the claims' veracity is a waste of time, it was difficult for those accused to ignore them because they were being reproduced by state media, partisan bloggers, and their followers on social media with the effect of making it believable. Journalists had to mind their personal safety, secure their newsrooms, and hire lawyers, just in case. In the end, the purported destabilization plot showed how the state-sponsored disinformation operated—barefaced, and without a hint of accountability before its citizens for the damage it had caused.

Duterte's stance on news media and his use of digital disinformation should be seen as a negation of democratic imaginary. It comes with unnecessary attacks on freedom of the press as a way to affirm political control. In Paolo Gerbaudo's work, this type of political control is termed "control as command", which involves an authoritarian claim to power supported by the threat of violence.[34] Command control is not based on consensus and persuasion but through the use of the means of coercion. Acquiescence to such control could be termed media capture, defined by Romanian political scientist Alina Mangiu-Pippidi as a situation in which news media is controlled by the government or by vested interest bound with politics.[35] However, it does not mean that control is total because the concept can be applied in a non-coercive setting where self-censorship and restrained reporting occur to avoid flak and pressure. In this sense, captured news organizations range from surrendering editorial independence to furthering the interest of Duterte and his government to a degree of complicity by allowing news to be influenced by Duterte's communication agenda. Arguably, behind the concept of media capture are reactionary and counterrevolutionary ideologies that Bello said Duterte represented. These ideologies are reproduced discursively by the pro-Duterte media and uncritical news organizations through news stories, interviews, and other forms of media products and also through related content on social media channels. The latter enable the naturalization of these ideologies so that they appear to be serving everyone's interests, while their claims and narratives are presented to be believable and true. At this point, the connection between the concept of media capture and disinformation and hate speech can be established through the proliferation of false and leading information tracked down by journalists through fact-checking projects. Fact-checking is an attempt to outwit media capture.

FACT-CHECKING IN THE 2019 AND 2022 NATIONAL ELECTIONS

Fact-checking is part of journalism's tenet of verification, which is a process of determining the accuracy of an information, often called a "claim" by fact-checkers.[36] Fact-checking initiatives trace their roots in newsroom routines of verifying information before they are published (*ex-ante*). This internal fact-checking aims to make news organizations a trusted source of information. In the last decade, fact-checking initiatives are often standalone projects to counter digital disinformation in the time of post-truth politics. The latter is a phenomenon where there is an abundance and influence of false and misleading political claims. Not necessarily tied to the routine of newsrooms, fact-checking initiatives verify information after it is released or published (*ex-post*). Fact-checking is the heir to adversarial tradition of journalism which points out what is wrong and what is not true. It is also a mechanism for accountability.

In the Philippines, the Department of Journalism of the University of the Philippines Diliman pioneered the teaching of fact-checking while Vera Files was the first news organization to become signatory to the code of principles of the International Fact-Checking Network (IFCN) in 2017. Rappler also became a signatory that same year. The code binds fact-checkers to become professional, ethical, and accountable practitioners.

Fact-checking captured interest when fact-checkers and some media organizations organized the pioneering collaborative fact-checking for the 2019 and 2022 national elections. The push to make fact-checking large-scale in 2019 aimed to create an impact at a time when Duterte's disinformation machinery seemed unstoppable, and some sections of the press were cowed to indifference. Politicians with social media campaign strategies are aware of the fact that Filipinos are among the top social media users globally, spending an average of four hours and twelve minutes online as against the global average of two hours and sixteen minutes.[37] Expectedly, the platform of choice for disinformation spreaders was Facebook.[38]

The first time when social media was heavily used for campaign was in 2016 when Duterte ran for president and admitted having substantially spent for his online campaign.[39] Duterte's social media strategy employed a network of operators, tools, and bots, which turned his campaign around. The network was not limited to promoting Duterte but also used black campaign, which spread lies against his rivals and opposing parties. The 2019 midterm elections in the Philippines marked the second time that disinformation became part of the campaign toolbox of politicians inspired by the 2016 campaign of Duterte.

Disinformation in the 2019 Elections

Tsek.ph was launched in February 2019, four months before the midterm elections, as a collaborative fact-checking project between academe and media. The Department of Journalism of the University of the Philippines (UP) organized and coordinated the project. Two other universities and eleven media partners joined the coalition that received support from

UP and Facebook.⁴⁰ *Tsek.ph* spent three months verifying claims from candidates' statements, platforms, press interviews, news, and social media posts. The collaboration facilitated the sharing of information and verification techniques among fact-checkers. The spirit of advocacy prevailed that they considered their work as an intervention to prevent the spread of disinformation in the period leading to the May 2019 elections.

In its three months of operations, *tsek.ph* had 130 fact-checks, more than half of the claims came from information taken from Facebook and were given a rating like False, Misleading, Needs Context, and True. Sixty-one per cent of the claims were rated False, in which the information targeted opposition candidates but was favourable to those associated with Duterte. Only a fifth of fact-checked claims appeared as text while close to half of the information debunked as False were visuals. Fact-checkers worked on claims in visual forms such as infographics, pull-out quotations, photographs, and memes. The emergence of non-text disinformation items could be interpreted in two ways: first, disinformation adjusts to its medium or platform, and second, they appear to be the handiwork of organized propaganda networks. Many of the claims rated False were meant to mislead voters. Examples of these are statements that Senator Imee Marcos graduated from Princeton despite evidence to the contrary, and Bong Go's fan pages that distorted Senator Bam Aquino's food waste quotation.

Fact-checkers also verified the statements of opposition and independent candidates, but this was the weak spot in their work. Many such claims were rated as having incomplete data or incorrect numbers. Examples are "De Guzman, a labour candidate, out-of-school youth figure wrong" and "Samira Gutoc gets ARMM police figures wrong". With their reliance on government data which they considered as official, fact-checkers regarded the numbers given by independent candidates as inaccurate. However, fact-checkers overlooked that these candidates disputed government statistics as part of their critique, and they offered different numbers and frameworks of analysis. Moreover, unlike in the usual news story when reporters interview the source to clarify a contentious point or a quote, fact-checkers did not always contact the source.

Fact-checking had disrupted the usual style of election speeches and spectacles by holding politicians to account for their unverified and overblown claims. Some *tsek.ph* partners carried out live fact-checking during the widely watched debates. To avoid being fact-checked, politicians tended to be guarded, resorted to generalities, and refused to make specific claims that are likely to be verified. Some administration candidates for senator, like Cynthia Villar, skipped the high-pressured debates altogether or lessened their media appearances.[41] The politicians' cautious stance deprived voters of the chance to listen to substantial speeches of candidates.

Tsek.ph performed the watchdog role of the media, despite the limitations of fact-checking. It posed a challenge to a politics that does not submit to public scrutiny. It underscores the need for accurate and relevant information to create informed voters. While before, journalists covering the election were at the mercy of public relations and campaign machinery handlers, fact-checking became a way of answering back. Fact-checking broke away from the horse-race type of coverage and reverential reporting during election and made candidates answerable for their public statements. In effect, fact-checking casts a political role for journalists, even if they reluctantly admit it.

Red-baiting, also known as red-tagging, is the new type of disinformation identified by fact-checkers in the 2019 elections. It worked by labelling the opposition, independent candidates, and party-list organizations[42] as members, sympathizers, or supporters of the clandestine Communist Party of the Philippines. On the eve of the 2019 elections, Facebook accounts of the army and police were spreading lies that party-lists Bayan Muna, Anak Pawis, Alliance of Concerned Teachers, Gabriela, and Anakbayan were disqualified by the Commission of Election.[43] The fake announcement, which was debunked by fact-checkers, used the logo and the news bulletin format of ABS-CBN. Fact-checkers also debunked a claim by Duterte calling former congressman Erin Tañada an "insane senator", for defending communists in court. Tañada was never elected senator, although both his father and grandfather were. As to defending communists, it is well within his duty as a lawyer to do so.

Red-baiting is an example of state-sponsored disinformation but working non-state networks to discredit the opposition candidates and deliver votes to Duterte's allies. The 2019 midterm election came at a time when Duterte's popularity was secured, with the first quarter's satisfaction rating of "+66" per cent ("very good") across the country, and in all income levels, according to a Social Weather Stations survey.[44] Not one opposition candidate won the senatorial race while all pro-administration candidates who won were close allies of Duterte aside from having proven political bailiwicks or enormous wealth.

The question that occupied *tsek.ph* fact-checkers after the 2019 elections, just before they disbanded, was whether they were able to sufficiently warn and rally the public against election-related disinformation and falsehoods. One function of fact-checking is "prebunking", which entails warning and debunking false information before it gains traction. A related term is inoculation which, as the metaphor suggests, pre-emptively gives the public small doses of disinformation and tactics so that they could cultivate some kind of "mental antibodies".[45] By exposing the public to fact-checking, and disclosing the sources and methodology of verification, the public would be inoculated against the approaching falsehoods. However, studies are needed to establish a connection with fact-checks and voting behaviour in the context of Philippine elections. It turned out that disinformation techniques in the 2019 elections were a foretaste of a bigger crisis three years later.

COVID-19 AND DISINFORMATION

The intervening crisis of COVID-19 pandemic was favourable for disinformation spreaders who set their sights on the May 2022 elections. Disinformation did not ebb when work, and access to services and social interactions all shifted online during the lockdowns in 2020 and 2021. Fact-checkers from Vera Files[46] and Rappler[47] debunked vaccine misinformation mainly related to safety and efficacy of vaccines. Their fact-checks that examined pandemic-related claims which were false, erroneous, confusing, threatening, and entertaining somehow contributed to vaccine hesitancy.

There is a connection between pandemic disinformation and political disinformation. An unpublished study of COVID-19 fact-checking noted that a third of vaccine misinformation came from public figures of which 57 per cent are government officials, including Duterte.[48] The presence of the so-called social media influencers contributed to the proliferation of anti-vaccine narratives. The influencers' followers, which range from 100,000 to one million, were the targets of spurious claims, misleading use of studies and experts' knowledge, and pathological mistrust of the science of vaccines. One of the influencers included in the study was John Anthony Jaboya, popularly known as Sangkay Janjan, who had almost a million subscribers on his YouTube channel. Jaboya promoted cures and conspiracy theories on COVID-19, including the yarn that vaccines contain microchips from Bill Gates. In the 2022 elections, Jaboya was among the group of bloggers that attacked Vice President Robredo, opposition candidates, and news organizations. When Marcos Jr. won as president, Jaboya was given access to the president's office in Malacañang, along with other bloggers who make up the association, United Vloggers and Influencers of the Philippines.[49] The study also found that pro-Duterte social media influencers, among them RJ Nieto ("Thinking Pinoy") and Sass Sasot ("For the Motherland"), also contributed to vaccine misinformation. A number of their posts were directed at Robredo. During the 2022 elections, these bloggers supported the ticket of Marcos Jr. and Sara Duterte.

Another finding of the study is the preponderance of negative emotions such as fear and anger among the COVID-19 information debunked by fact-checkers. By examining the keywords and hashtags, it was found out that 63 per cent sought to instil fear and 19 per cent, anger, which includes cuss words and shaming targeted individuals or groups. These negative emotions that impugned people constitute hate speech.

A contested concept, "hate speech" has several meanings and legal interpretations. The Philippines has no specific laws on hate speech but relies on libel laws to deal with defamation. Hate speech in many national contexts, including in Asia, is understood as expressions that incite violence or prejudice against individuals or social groups. Some countries have laws on hate speech but in the Philippines, despite the dangers of hate speech spread over the Internet and proposed bills to curb it, no law has been passed so far. While hate speech online is not unlike those found offline, the manner in which it is amplified and distributed almost illimitably is a challenge to the media.

Duterte's speeches were the subject of another study that investigated how hate speech can be assessed not in the absence of legal recognition of its existence but as a form of political incivility and disinformation which could be both defined by their insufficiency. In political incivility, what is missing is the respect for personal freedoms and beliefs while in disinformation absent were factual and verifiable information. The analysis of Duterte's speeches in his first year as president showed that they contain lines, paragraphs and cuss words directed against the Catholic Church that can be considered as examples of hate speech. Hate speech, the study found out, are utterances that attack personal dignity, dehumanize groups, incite discrimination, advocate hostility, create a social wedge, and impute a crime.[50] The study found that top officials in his government were taking their cue from Duterte and also lambasted the religious leaders and the clergy. In addition, bloggers supporting Duterte, including Mocha Uson who was appointed assistant secretary of the Presidential Communications Operations Office in 2017 and had five million followers on Facebook, were amplifying his anti-Church polemic.

During the COVID-19 pandemic, among the targets of online attacks are then Vice President Leni Robredo and the *Kabataan* party-list representative Sarah Elago. Contempt against their politics is also a form of misogyny, which is not strictly woman-hating but a symptom of insecurity towards the power of women politicians. By attacking Robredo, the bloggers deflected criticisms for the government's bungled responses to the pandemic. The criticisms against Elago were meant to undermine the voices of young people, whose education was affected by the prolonged lockdowns, as well as discredit the politics that she represents. Since the pandemic years preceded the election in 2022, it appears that the larger goal of disinformation was to ensure the victory of Marcos Jr. and Sara Duterte among young voters.

Impostor content and misappropriated logos of government offices, international organizations like the World Health Organization (WHO) and the United Nations International Children's Emergency Fund (UNICEF), and the media like the *Philippine Daily Inquirer*, were common disinformation tactics.[51] The use of the term "disinfodemic", by Posetti and Bontcheva is applicable here because not only does it refer to lies but it also relies on anger, prejudices, cynicism, and polarization.[52] Disinfodemic is an update of the WHO's term infodemic, which refers to a surfeit of information including false or misleading information in digital and physical environments during a disease outbreak that it causes confusion and risk-taking behaviours which can harm health.[53] Disinfodemic is infodemic on steroids. Disinfodemic includes political disinformation which fosters distrust and negative impression on the targeted personalities, like Robredo, and also the fact-checkers who debunked conspiracy theories, vaccine misinformation, and related hoaxes. Michael Hameleers[54] termed this type of false information "populist disinformation", which he defines as the cultivation of division between people and the targeted elites through a discourse that sidesteps expert knowledge and verified evidence in favour of common sense and emotion-driven judgment.[55] Populist disinformation could lead to the creation of, what Hameleers calls, "uncivil communication sphere" where deliberation and rational exchanges are replaced by partisan and narrow political views.[56] A communication sphere is akin to the Habermasian public sphere,[57] which is a space where people discuss issues that are of interest to them with the goal of reaching understanding. The task of fact-checkers is to ensure that misinformation and false claims are corrected in that sphere, especially during election campaigns when candidates are communicating to the voters through news media and social media.

The COVID-19 pandemic had made it possible for fringe ideas, such as "anti-vaxxers" and peddlers of conspiracy theories, to take centre and challenge scientific data and studies and the experts. For example, homemade and bizarre cures were freely circulating on social media rather than statements of virologists and epidemiologists. In addition, the arresting military presence during the hard lockdown, and in the subsequent localized quarantines, conveyed a sense of coercion rather than reason in the government's response to the pandemic. Added to that was Duterte's "shoot to kill" order for those who will defy the lockdown, along with his other threatening statements.[58] With the public exposed to pandemic-related misinformation and disinformation, it was easy for partisan social media influencers to shift gear to digital disinformation for the May 2022 elections.

Often forgotten in the critique of COVID-19 disinformation is the role of major social media platforms like Facebook, Twitter, YouTube, Instagram, and even TikTok which allowed anti-vaccine and conspiracy theories to proliferate. The business model of social media platforms which allowed data mining of users' personal data that will be used for targeted advertising has not been closely scrutinized for accountability.[59] In addition, the platforms' opaque algorithms would allow the creation of echo chambers around cultural and political beliefs. In the end, the COVID-19 infodemic represented an elaborate manipulation of information. It combined state-sponsored disinformation, presence of disinformation intermediaries, predatory social media business model, and receptive social media users that have made it easy to spread propaganda and unscrupulous narratives.

DISINFORMATION IN THE 2022 ELECTIONS

The 2022 national election took place when pandemic restrictions were still in place.[60] For the elections, *tsek.ph* was revived and has thirty-four partners. While before the members came from academe and media, the rebooted *tsek.ph* included six civil society fact-checkers from multi-sectoral groups, NGOs, election-watch coalition, and historians' organization. Civil society fact-checkers brought into the coalition their advocacies which became the lens through which they analysed disinformation. There were twelve media organizations that joined the fact-checking coalition, and groups of student fact-checkers supervised by the faculty from the University of the Philippines and the University of Santo Tomas (see Table 7.1).

Compared with that in 2019, *tsek.ph* in 2022 has improved in terms of skills, resources, and reach. There were ten training sessions held for *tsek.ph* partners, including verification workshops, fact-checking historical distortions, ethical fact-checking, and digital hygiene. Whereas in 2019 only Facebook gave a grant, *tsek.ph* in 2022 enjoyed support from Google News Initiative, Rakuten Viber, Meedan, the Canadian embassy, and Meta/Facebook. The academic support was mainly from grants from the University of the Philippines.

Tsek.ph gained a steady growth of followers in social media channels such as TikTok and Instagram, in addition to the existing Facebook, Twitter, and YouTube whose views and interactions also grew substantially. For example, *tsek.ph* Facebook page started with only 500 followers in January 2022 but grew to more than 12,000 followers three months after the May 2022 elections. Its website's traffic increased tremendously. In January 2022, daily page views increased from 600 to 4,650 views in May, just before the election day. News organizations, like Vera Files, ABS-CBN, and Philstar, have their own social media followers that were exposed to their fact-checks, but they

TABLE 7.1
List of Tsek.ph Fact-Checking Partners

Media	Academe	Civil Society
ABS-CBN	Ateneo de Manila University Asian Center for Journalism	Akademiya at Bayan Kontra Disimpormasyon at Dayaan
Agence France Presses	Carlos Hilado Memorial State College	Barangay Hub
Baguio Chronicle	Letran University	e-Boto
DZUP 1602	Philippine Association for Media and Information Literacy	Fact Check Philippines
Fyt	Trinity University of Asia	IDEALS
Interaksyon	University of Santo Tomas	Kontra Daya
MindaNews	Xavier University	
Philippine Press Institute	University of the Philippines (UP) System	
Philstar Global	UP Baguio	
Press One	UP Cebu	
Probe	UP Los Banos	
Vera Files	UP Open University	
	UP Visayas	
	FactRakers (UP Diliman)	
	Fact Check Patrol (UP Diliman)	
	UP sa Halalan 2022 (UP Diliman)	

were not counted among *tsek.ph*'s audience. Civil society fact-checkers, like Fact-Check Philippines, enjoyed a sizable following. *Tsek.ph* was cited in more than ninety reports in local[61] and international media.[62]

Tsek.ph fact-checkers soon faced a backlash from online attacks of trolls, supporters, and politicians. A Duterte official, Lorraine Badoy, threatened to sue Vera Files for flagging disinformation in Facebook as a third-party fact-checker. Five media partners of *tsek.ph* were subjected to a distributive denial of service attacks, knocking their website offline.[63] Two leaders of civil society fact-checkers were tagged as communists, without basis, thus making them take security precautions.

In the run up to the 2022 elections, *tsek.ph* produced more than a thousand fact-checks, released eighteen weekly summaries and three in-depth analyses on fact-checks and disinformation trends throughout six months of operations. The in-depth analyses were published by news organizations and used as sources by the foreign press. *Tsek.ph* also released video fact-checks that racked up record views, likes, comments, and shares in six-digits. The success of video fact-checks encouraged other *tsek.ph* partners to start their own video fact-checks for social media. However, *tsek.ph* video fact-checks were late in the game. The combined Marcos and Duterte video content was entrenched on Facebook and YouTube channels and had an early start in TikTok. The videos were glorifying the Marcoses and were intended to mask the massive corruption, human rights violations, and unrestrained desire for power that the Marcos dictatorship was known for.

Tsek.ph termed the disinformation that sought to rehabilitate the Marcos "martial law fact-checks", to denote content that concerned martial law under Ferdinand Marcos, the 1986 People Power Uprising that ousted Marcos in 1986, and the comparison between the Marcos administration (1965–86) and President Corazon Aquino who succeeded Marcos. Disinformation that was subject to fact-checking was gathered through Facebook's CrowdTangle, which is a social media monitoring tool tracking public pages and groups on Facebook, Instagram, and WhatsApp. The most prominent social media post as disinformation was a claim that Marcos did not arrest his critics during martial law, which had 187 million views and 95,000 interactions such as comments and likes. The no-arrest statement was made by Marcos's former defence chief, Juan Ponce Enrile, in 2018, during an interview with Marcos Jr., who posted it on his Facebook page. However, it was reposted in September 2021, when Marcos Jr. declared his plan to run for president, and earned 40,000 views as of February 2022. The related claims fact-checkers debunked are the so-called Tallano gold and Maharlika kingdom, which are incredulous stories laced with conspiracy theories of Marcoses' wealth that their supporters spread on social media. Still another made-up story that gained traction was a claim that the older Marcos was a decorated World War II hero which was rated False by fact-checkers. The martial law fact-checks offered proof of the Marcoses' attempt to revamp their image in order to avoid accountability for ill-gotten wealth and human rights violations (see Table 7.2).

TABLE 7.2
Fact-Checked Claims on Martial Law and the Marcoses

CLAIM*	GROUPS THAT POSTED CLAIM	INTERACTIONS	VIEWS
Totoo o hindi? Wala raw inarestong mga kritiko si Ferdinand Marcos Sr. noong Martial Law	194	95,842	187,703,980
Tsek/Eks: Sabi sa isang FB page, 'kwentong kutsero' raw ang mga Martial Law victims, at maraming nagpalista para makakuha ng danyos na pera	514	162,279	89,191,861
Ferdinand Marcos Sr., pinahiram ng 3,500 toneladang ginto ang 170 na mga bansa?	265	159,070	28,136,885
Tootoo o hindi? Si Marcos Sr. raw ang nagdala sa Pilipinas sa 'modern world'?	2,177	722,409	25,501,287
Totoo o Hindi? Si Ferdinand Marcos Sr. raw ang 'most decorated war hero' sa Pilipinas noong World War II?	67	26,668	13,702,622
Totoo o Hindi? Walang kontraktwalisasyon noong pangulo si Ferdinand Marcos, Sr.?	457	385,789	6,847,072
Hindi namatay si Jose Rizal at nabuhay siya bilang si Fr. Jose Antonio Diaz na nakilala ni Ferdinand Marcos Sr.?	61	29,435	490,674
Swiss bank accounts ng diktador na si Marcos, ibinulsa ni Cory Aquino?	145	9,400	180,659
Totoo o Hindi? Mapayapa at maunlad ang Pilipinas noong panahon ng Batas Militar?	14	8,940	123,415
Tsek/Eks: Malaking karangalan daw sa mga Marcos ang pamimigay ng masustansyang Nutribun sa mga pampublikong paaralan noong dekada 70s	157	69,025	

*Title of fact check article listed here

Analyses of the *tsek.ph* fact-checks showed that Marcos Jr. benefitted from election-related disinformation because 94 per cent of them discredited opposition presidential candidate Robredo and her running name, Senator Francis Pangilinan. Inversely, nine in ten disinformation claims identified by fact-checkers favoured Marcos Jr. and his running mate, Sara Duterte. Marcos also racked up the greatest number of fake endorsements coming from beauty queens, celebrities, and world leaders. From the spread and tactics of the election-related disinformation, the Marcos's camp pulled out all the stops, as shown by the range of disinformation created, from the innocuous endorsement to virulent and malicious accusations against Robredo, her senatorial line-up, and even her daughters. *Tsek.ph* classified the targeted content as positive and negative messaging. What is even more significant is how supporters of the Marcos-Duterte tandem have succeeded in further boosting narratives in their favour through an increase in the volume of negative messages against Robredo.

Two weeks before the elections, 92 per cent of fact-checks about Marcos were false or misleading information but they were working in his favour. The proportion of debunked false claims praising Sara Duterte was even higher at 95 per cent. However, 96 per cent of disinformation targeting Robredo has negative tone. Pangilinan consistently received negative messaging among the fact-checked claims since November. Non-candidates like the Catholic Church and the Communist Party of the Philippines were also targets of negative messages. Negative messaging refers to claims that malign their targets while positive messaging denotes claims praising their targets. Both positive and negative messaging convey sentiments ranging from approval, support, contempt, and ridicule, to attempts to deny and justify wrongdoing. See Figure 7.1.

Disinformation had been without let-up towards the 2022 election. *Tsek.ph* termed the burst of disinformation "firehose of falsehood", as a strategy that uses a high number of channels and messages to distribute rapid and repetitive messages. As a result, fact-checkers encountered the same false claim even though these were previously fact-checked.

Another form of disinformation that intensified is red-baiting or red-tagging, which links opposition candidates with the clandestine Communist Party of the Philippines-New People's Army, even without basis. The red-baiting tactic painted Robredo and her line-up as being ideologically aligned with communist party considered as terrorist organization by the controversial 2020 Anti-terrorism Law. While obviously a form of disinformation, red-baiting appeared as conjectures and opinions, not statements of facts that can be easily verified by media fact-checkers. However, civil society fact-checkers were more consistent in debunking red-tagging because the accusations are not only false, but also a form of harmful speech that could harm a person's life and reputation.

The voting results did not favour those fighting election disinformation in the trenches. The Marcos Jr.-Sara Duterte tandem trounced the opposition slate, partly aided by the well-financed networked disinformation. The *tsek.ph* partners admitted that despite their effort, they could not rouse voters to renounce the purveyors of disinformation and politicians who benefitted from it. Even with the scale of the work within *tsek.ph* and with other fact-checking group, *FactsFirstPH* organized by Rappler, fact-checking is not enough to rebuild

FIGURE 7.1
Positive and Negative Fact-Checked Content/Messaging

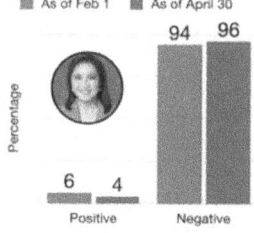

Type of messaging by candidate

LENI ROBREDO — As of Feb 1: Positive 6, Negative 94; As of April 30: Positive 4, Negative 96

FERDINAND MARCOS JR. — As of Feb 1: Positive 10, Negative 90; As of April 30: Positive 8, Negative 92

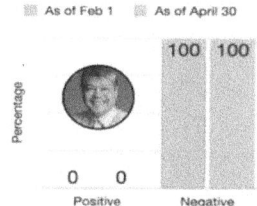
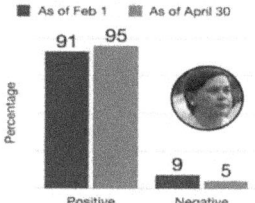

Type of messaging by candidate

FRANCIS PANGILINAN — As of Feb 1: Positive 0, Negative 100; As of April 30: Positive 0, Negative 100

SARA DUTERTE — As of Feb 1: Positive 9, Negative 91; As of April 30: Positive 5, Negative 95

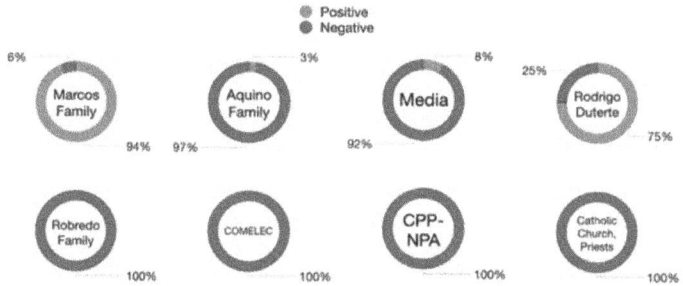

Type of messaging by non candidate

- Marcos Family: Positive 6%, Negative 94%
- Aquino Family: Positive 3%, Negative 97%
- Media: Positive 8%, Negative 92%
- Rodrigo Duterte: Positive 25%, Negative 75%
- Robredo Family: Negative 100%
- COMELEC: Negative 100%
- CPP-NPA: Negative 100%
- Catholic Church, Priests: Negative 100%

a frayed democracy. While the opposition started self-recrimination, fact-checkers have started talking about preparing for the midterm election in 2025. With machine learning technology (AI) on the rise, fact-checking will be more challenging. The next fact-checking venture would require both commitment and skill that fact-checkers displayed in the 2022 elections.

CONCLUSION AND LESSONS

Fact-checking started as a journalistic genre that challenges false and misleading statements of elected officials, politicians, and individuals with public standing. During elections in the Philippines, fact-checking became the media's intervention to prevent the spread of disinformation and misinformation that could affect voters' decisions. Trained to sift through claims and debunk lies, fact-checkers perform the role of expert sources by determining the validity of information. The practice of fact-checking embodies the media's role in democracy, which is to provide accurate and relevant information so that citizens can make informed decisions. Fact-checking in the 2019 and 2022 elections in the Philippines is a tool for accountability because it makes politicians more prudent and truthful in their public statements during election campaigns.

Fact-checking during elections has drawn in non-media organizations to join coalitions like *tsek.ph* which trains members, coordinates the fact-checking operation, and provides a website where fact-checked information is found. The predominance of disinformation and misinformation during the two-election cycles points to the crucial role of fact-checking during a highly partisan election period and beyond.

Fact-checking is indicative of the social crisis of information, and it is difficult to see how fact-checkers can fix it alone, without working with other groups. A concerted and sustained effort to keep in check disinformation is needed. The discussion above suggests a two-fold proposal that could be taken up by journalists, educators, civil society, and the government. First, citizens should consider fact-checking as a life skill, given the availability of tools and techniques. Second, news literacy should be introduced to basic education and adult learning to underscore the role of news media in the production of verified and accurate information.

News literacy is recognizing the value of news—accurate, verified, and accountable to the public. At its core, news is information that can be trusted. As citizens become more news literate, it is assumed that they will demand better channels of news and information that the media should provide. It is further assumed that in the process of honing their disinformation detecting skills, the media would be able to improve their product, circulation, and trustworthiness. As demonstrated in the fact-checking projects initiated by *tsek.ph*, news organizations can commit themselves to improving civic discourse by providing accurate and truthful information so that citizens can make informed choices. Advocacy fact-checkers who joined *tsek.ph* appreciated the fact-checking skills they learned from the media to empower their communities. Thus, broader opportunities for learning and partnerships should be explored. Perhaps the first and most feasible one is introducing fact-checking side by side news literacy, as a practice of citizenship. For promoting critical understanding and accountability, fact-checking and news literacy could become pillars of renewed democratic engagement.

Notes

1. Bea Cupin, "Marcos to Duterte: 'Naiintindihan ko na kung bakit napapamura ka'", *Rappler*, 29 March 2023.
2. Claire Wardle and Hossein Derakshan, "Information Disorder: Toward an Interdisciplinary Framework for Research and Policy Making", Council of Europe, 2017.
3. "WE love Ferdinand Marcos" Facebook Page, https://www.facebook.com/306664229500184/posts/marcos-erathe-golden-age-of-the-armed-forces-of-the-philippines-afp-marcos-era-1/1232569936909604/.
4. Floyd Whaley, "30 Years after Revolution, Some Filipinos Yearn for 'Golden Age' of Marcos", *The New York Times*, 23 February 2016.
5. Carolyn O. Arguillas, "In Six Years, at Least 30 books on Rodrigo Duterte as President", *MindaNews*, 17 July 2022, https://www.mindanews.com/booksmindanews/2022/07/in-six-years-at-least-30-books-on-rodrigo-duterte-as-president/.
6. Miriam Grace Go, "Sexism is President's Power Tool: Duterte Is Using Violent Language and Threats against Journalists, Rappler's News Editor Explains", *Index on Censorship* 48, no. 4 (2019): 33–35.

7. Joseph Parugganan, "Misogyny, Neoliberalism, and Despotism: Shoring Up Duterte's Anti-women Agenda", *Focus on the Global South*, 9 May 2019.
8. Aries A. Arugay, "When Populists Perform Foreign Policy: Duterte and the Asia-Pacific Regional Order", Stiftung Wissenschaft und Politik Working Paper, 2018.
9. Walden Bello, *Counter Revolution: The Global Rise of the Far Right (Agrarian Change and Peasant Studies)* (Manila: Ateneo de Manila University Press, 2019).
10. Adrian Chen, "When a Populist Demagogue Takes Power", *The New Yorker*, 14 November 2016, https://www.newyorker.com/magazine/2016/11/21/when-a-populist-demagogue-takes-power.
11. James Putzel, "Can Duterte 'Populism' Bring Lasting Peace, Development?" *Inquirer.net*, 28 August 2016; Bulent Kenes, "Rodrigo Roa Duterte: A Jingoist, Misogynist, Penal Populist", ECPS Leader Profiles, European Center for Populism Studies (ECPS), 17 September 2020.
12. Alex Ho, "Duterte Blasts de Lima: Immoral, Used Narco Money", *CNN Philippines*, 17 August 2016.
13. Press Briefing of Presidential Spokesperson Harry Roque, 11 October 2021, https://pco.gov.ph/press-briefing/press-briefing-of-presidential-spokesperson-harry-roque-223/.
14. National Union of Journalists of the Philippines, "[Statement] NUJP to Roque: Don't Deny Censorship on PH Press", 12 October 2021, https://nujp.org/statement-nujp-to-roque-dont-deny-censorship-on-ph-press/.
15. Aurelien Mondon and Aaron Winter, *Reactionary Democracy: How Racism and the Populist Far Right Became Mainstream* (London: Verso Books, 2020).
16. Mondon and Winter, *Reactionary Democracy*, pp. 75–79.
17. Bello, *Counter Revolution*.
18. Bello, *Counter Revolution*, p. 110.
19. Rie Takumi, "Duterte's Trust Ratings Remain at All-Time High in Q4 2017 — Pulse Asia", *GMA News Online*, 8 January 2018, https://www.gmanetwork.com/news/topstories/nation/638889/duterte-s-trust-ratings-remain-at-all-time-high-in-q4-2017-pulse-asia/story/.
20. James Griffiths, "She Exposed Duterte's Drug War in the Philippines. Now She Faces a Possible Prison Term", *CNN*, 2 December 2018, https://edition.cnn.com/2018/11/30/asia/maria-ressa-philippines-duterte-media-intl/index.html.
21. Ted Regencia, "Filipino Journalist Who Helped Probe Duterte's Drug War Shot Dead", *Aljazeera*, 9 December 2021, https://www.aljazeera.com/news/2021/12/9/filipino-journalist-who-investigated-duterte-drug-war-killed.
22. Mel Velarde, "Language Follows Strategy: Deciphering President Duterte's Rhetoric", in *Deconstruct to Understand: Why Duterte Talks His Way*, edited

by Crispin C. Maslog (Manila: Asia Media Information and Communication Center, 2017).
23. Ernesto Abella, "Spokesperson on Hi 'Pala-Away President", in *Deconstruct to Understand: Why Duterte Talks His Way*, edited by Crispin C. Maslog (Manila: Asia Media Information and Communication Center, 2017).
24. Crispin C. Maslog, ed., *Deconstruct to Understand: Why Duterte Talks His Way* (Manila: Asia Media Information and Communication Center, 2017), pp. 45–53.
25. Pia Ranada, "Duterte Himself Banned Rappler's Reporter from Malacanang Coverage", *Rappler*, 20 February 2018.
26. CMFR Staff, "Pattern of Restrictions Signals Crackdown on PH Press", Center for Media Freedom and Responsibility, 7 May 2018, https://cmfr-phil.org/press-freedom-protection/attacks-and-threats-against-the-media/pattern-of-restrictions-signal-crackdown-on-ph-press/.
27. Maria Ressa, "Propaganda War: Weaponizing the Internet", *Rappler*, 3 October 2016.
28. The Pulitzer Prizes, "The 2018 Pulitzer Prize Winner in International Reporting: Clare Baldwin, Andrew R.C. Marshall and Manuel Mogato of Reuters", 28 June 2017, https://www.pulitzer.org/winners/clare-baldwin-andrew-rc-marshall-and-manuel-mogato-reuters.
29. IAFOR Documentary Photography Award, "Grand Prize – Ezra Acayan: Duterte's War on Drugs Is Not Over", 9 October 2018. https://iaforphotoaward.org/grand-prize-ezra-acayan/.
30. *ABS-CBN News*, "Photojournalist Eloisa Lopez Wins Int'l Award for Courage in Drug War Coverage", 1 May 2019, https://news.abs-cbn.com/news/05/01/19/photojournalist-eloisa-lopez-wins-intl-award-for-courage-in-drug-war-coverage.
31. Azer Parrocha, "Palace Bares 'Oust Duterte' Matrix", Philippine News Agency, 22 April 2019.
32. CMFR Staff, "The Manila Times Editor Asked to Resign after Criticizing Ouster Plot Story", Center for Media Freedom and Responsibility, 29 April 2019, https://cmfr-phil.org/chronicle/the-manila-times-editor-asked-to-resign-after-criticizing-ouster-plot-story/.
33. Floreen Simon and Malou Mangahas, "Duterte, Sara, Paolo Mark Big Spikes in Wealth, Cash, While in Public Office", Philippine Center for Investigative Journalism, 4 April 2019, https://pcij.org/article/1472/duterte-sara-paolo-mark-big-spikes-br-in-wealth-cash-while-in-public-office.
34. Resource Center in Media Freedom in Europe, "Special Dossier: Media Capture: Toolkit for 21st Century Autocrats", 19 December 2019, https://www.rcmediafreedom.eu/Dossiers/Media-capture-Toolkit-for-21st-century-autocrats.

35. Paolo Gerbaudo, *The Great Recoil: Politics after Populism and Pandemic* (UK: Verso Books, 2021).
36. Bill Kovach and Tom Rosenstiel, *The Elements of Journalism: What News People Should Know and the Public Should Expect*, Revised and Updated 4th Edition (New York: Crown, 2021), pp. 100–103.
37. Gelo Gonzales, "Filipinos Spend Most Time Online, on Social Media Worldwide – Report", *Rappler*, 31 January 2019.
38. CNN Philippines Staff, "PH Takes Top Spot as Heaviest Internet Users Worldwide — Report", *CNN Philippines*, 1 February 2019, https://www.cnnphilippines.com/lifestyle/2019/02/01/2019-digital-hootsuite-we-are-social-internet-philippines-facebook.html.
39. Samantha Bradshaw and Philip N. Howard, "Troops, Trolls and Troublemakers: A Global Inventory of Social Media Manipulation", University of Oxford, Working Paper no. 12, February 2017.
40. Facebook gave funds in 2019 and supported several trainings.
41. Camille Elemia, "The Rise of Cynthia Villar: How Politics, Money, Networks Made Her No. 1", *Rappler*, 15 May 2019, https://www.rappler.com/newsbreak/in-depth/230633-how-politics-money-networks-made-cynthia-villar-number-1-senate-race-2019/.
42. The party-list system allows for the representation of marginalized sectors if they won a percentage of total votes cast for all party list organizations combined.
43. DZUP, "Accurate: PNP Distributes Publication Red-Tagging Partylists", *Tsek.ph*, 13 May 2019, https://2019.tsek.ph/article/accurate-pnp-distributes-publication-red-tagging-partylists.
44. Helen Flores, "SWS: Duterte Satisfaction Rating Up in First Quarter of 2019", *Philstar Global*, 11 April 2019, https://www.philstar.com/headlines/2019/04/11/1909113/sws-duterte-satisfaction-rating-first-quarter-2019.
45. Jon Rozeenbeek, Sander Van Den Linder, and Thomas Nygren, "Prebunking Interventions Based on 'Inoculation' Theory Can Reduce Susceptibility to Misinformation across Cultures", *Harvard Kennedy School Misinformation Review*, 3 February 2020.
46. Vera Files, "COVID-19 Watch", https://verafiles.org/section/covid-19-watch.
47. *Rappler*, "COVID-19 Fact Checks", https://www.rappler.com/topic/covid-19-fact-checks/.
48. Ma. Diosa Labiste and Yvonne Chua, "Vaccine Misinformation in the Philippines", 2022, unpublished study.
49. Gaby Baisas, "On YouTube, Vlogger Sangkay Janjan Gets Away with Lies and Hate", *Rappler*, 23 June 2022.

50. Yvonne T. Chua and Ma. Diosa Labiste, "Duterte's Polemic against the Catholic Church as Hate Speech", *Plaridel* 17, no. 1 (2020): 1–33.
51. Ma. Diosa Labiste and Yvonne T. Chua, "From Infodemic to Disinfodemic: A Typology of COVID-19 Disinformation Debunked by Fact-Checkers in the Philippines", *Filipinas: Journal of the Philippine Studies Association* 3 (2020): 7–32.
52. Julie Posetti and Kalina Bontcheva, *Disinfodemic: Deciphering COVID-19 Disinformation* (Paris: UNESCO, 2020).
53. World Health Organization, "Infodemic", n.d., https://www.who.int/health-topics/infodemic#tab=tab_1.
54. Michael Hameleers, *Populist Disinformation in Fragmented Information Settings* (UK: Routledge, 2022).
55. Hameleers, p. 132.
56. Hameleers, p. 133.
57. Jürgen Habermas, *The Structural Transformation of the Public Sphere: An Inquiry into a Category of Bourgeois Society* (UK: Polity Press, 1989).
58. Amnesty International, "Philippines: President Duterte Gives 'Shoot to Kill' Order amid Pandemic Response", 2 April 2020, https://www.amnesty.org/en/latest/news/2020/04/philippines-president-duterte-shoot-to-kill-order-pandemic/.
59. Gabriele Cosentino, *The Infodemic: Disinformation, Geopolitics and the Covid-19 Pandemic* (New York: Bloomsbury Publishing, 2023), p. 43.
60. Franco Luna, "Comelec Warns Candidates: COVID-19 Violations in Sorties Are Election Offenses", *Philstar.com*, 16 February 2022, https://www.philstar.com/headlines/2022/02/16/2161210/comelec-warns-candidates-covid-19-violations-sorties-are-election-offenses.
61. Janvic Mateo, "Fact-Checking Initiatives Gaining Ground in Philippines", *Philstar Global*, 12 February 2022, https://www.philstar.com/headlines/2022/02/12/2160272/fact-checking-initiatives-gaining-ground-philippines.
62. Regine Cabato and Shibani Mahtani, "How the Philippines' Brutal History Is Being Whitewashed for Voters", *Washington Post*, 12 April 2022, https://www.washingtonpost.com/world/2022/04/12/philippines-marcos-memory-election/.
63. Committee to Protect Journalist, "Three Philippine Media Outlets Face Latest in a String of Cyberattacks", 1 February 2022, https://cpj.org/2022/02/three-philippine-media-outlets-string-of-cyberattacks/.

8

A Quixotic Quest? Electoral and Political Reforms from Duterte to Marcos Jr.

Cleo Anne A. Calimbahin and Luie Tito F. Guia

> *This chapter discusses the state of electoral and party politics under the populist Duterte regime, the role it played in the 2022 elections, and the prospects under Marcos Jr. With previous electoral reforms not getting attention or traction, there is reason for cautious optimism under the new leadership of the Commission on Elections (COMELEC) under the Marcos Jr. administration. After the 2022 election, the electoral commission demonstrated openness for reform and dialogue with advocates for a more free, fair, and transparent election. The first section details the missed opportunities from 2016 to 2022 on the electoral and party reform front. The second section briefly illustrates how the election management body performed its administrative and adjudication duties in the 2022 national electoral contest, shaping the conduct and outcome of that election. The third*

section examines the promise of electoral and political party reforms under the Marcos Jr. administration.

Keywords: 2022 elections; Duterte; Marcos Jr.; electoral reform; COMELEC

INTRODUCTION: THE REFORM MOMENTUM AND MISSED OPPORTUNITIES

Elections in the Philippines are free but not necessarily fair or competitive. The rising number of dynastic families in Congress and across different positions in local government has led to categorizations of "obese", "fat", and "thin" dynasties.[1] The rising cost of election campaigns favours incumbents with access to the patronage that flows from national political elites down to significant local political players. In the 2022 elections, the ad campaign spending of individual candidates in mainstream media amounted to PHP 1 billion within forty-five days of the ninety-day campaign period.[2] Election, originally meant to provide a change in leadership, is a continuity tool in the Philippines.

Political families have such a grip on the Philippine political landscape that the country volleys from democracy-good governance nostalgia to authoritarian nostalgia. In 2010 with the election of Benigno Simeon "Noynoy" Aquino III (PNoy) to the presidency, the public pined for good governance, especially after the death of democracy icon Corazon Aquino. Filipino voters in 2010 successfully catapulted a reluctant presidential candidate Noynoy Aquino to Malacañang riding on the coattails of the passing of his democracy icon mother. The election of PNoy raised hopes that reforms, especially in the political and electoral arena, would accelerate. In 2022 with the election of Ferdinand Marcos Jr., there was authoritarian nostalgia for the authoritarian leadership of Marcos Sr. It was a triumphant return to Malacañang of the namesake of deposed President Ferdinand Marcos.

In 2010, under PNoy's administration, there were high expectations that it would usher in political and economic reforms. Coming from the heels of the corruption-ridden administration of Joseph Estrada and

Gloria Macapagal-Arroyo, Aquino III's presidency was seen as a turning point towards a more accountable and transparent government. The public witnessed the initial reluctance of PNoy to run for president in the 2010 elections. Voters, wary of corrupt public officials, interpreted this reluctance of PNoy as his indifference to power, on-brand with Cory Aquino's legacy of leadership.

PNoy's administration-initiated reforms included several election-related laws passed in rapid succession to improve the electoral process. One of these was the creation of exclusive precincts for persons with disabilities and senior citizens.[3] The law made the voting process accessible and convenient for sectors vulnerable to disenfranchisement. A law requiring qualified voters to submit their biometrics information as a registration requirement was passed on the same day.[4] The law should address the issue of multiple registrations, a persistent problem in Philippine elections. Three months later, on 27 May 2013, an amendment to the overseas absentee voting law was enacted.[5] This law streamlined overseas Filipinos' registration, voting, counting, and vote tabulation processes and authorized COMELEC to explore other technologies that can be adopted to improve voter turnout for many Filipinos working overseas.

In 2016, PNoy signed the *Sangguniang Kabataan* Reform Act of 2015 (SK Law).[6] This law is an amendment to the Local Government Code of 1991,[7] which provided for an elected youth council in every *barangay* or village in the country. The innovation includes an anti-political dynasty provision that prohibits candidates in the youth council if they have relatives, by two degrees, as incumbent national and local officials. The anti-dynasty provision in the SK Law is significant and even trail-blazing. Despite the clear mandate from the 1987 Philippine Constitution, Congress has failed to enact an anti-political dynasty law. That mandate is unfulfilled due to the strong resistance from a dynastic-filled Congress. The election for the village youth council is the only one with an anti-dynasty provision. The last election-related legislation Congress enacted under the PNoy presidency was the Election Service Reform Act or ESRA.[8] This law made public school teachers' role as members of the Electoral Board voluntary and fixed their compensation for electoral services. The old election law conscripts public school teachers to perform their election duty as election precinct managers. Failure to do so can amount to an election offense. During the administration of PNoy, the political environment appeared open to reform, and civil society groups lobbied and pushed these laws even with the support of the Commission on Elections (COMELEC)—a collaboration between state and society resulting in policy changes.

Despite the openness of the political environment and the tailwinds for change, there was apathy for significant reform measures on the political and electoral front. For one, the primary source of election laws remains an outdated Omnibus Election Code (OEC). The OEC was passed on 3 December 1985.[9] An apparent anomaly is that the OEC was enacted before the 1987 Constitution, which provides the design of the electoral system. Election law experts view the OEC as a law that distrusts COMELEC with its overly detailed prescription that deprives the COMELEC of flexibility to adjust appropriate procedural requirements in prevailing situations. There are several amendments already in place since 1985, among which are the Electoral Reforms Act of 1987,[10] the Initiative and Referendum Act of 1989,[11] the Synchronized Election Law in 1992,[12] the Continuing Voter Registration Act of 1996,[13] the Party-List System Law in 1996,[14] the Automated Election Laws in 1997 and 2007,[15] the Fair Election Act of 2001,[16] and the Overseas Voting Acts of 2003 and 2013.[17] However, the procedures for the candidacy and nomination process, political party registration, campaign finance, election offenses, and certain preparatory activities for voting remain sourced primarily from the OEC. Because the OEC is outdated, it accounts for the confusing process of political party registration and the nomination and substitution of candidates by political parties, among others. These are aspects of elections that are used with impunity by electoral contestants to game the system. Unless the OEC is updated, the problems from previous elections will persist in future elections.

A purportedly reformist president like PNoy failed to fulfil the promise of change that would even the political playing field. An area of electoral reform that advocates hoped the PNoy administration would shepherd is the law to strengthen and develop political parties. Some have argued that the lackadaisical attitude of PNoy to the political party reform bill was because he failed to see its relevance. PNoy may have downplayed the role of the political party that carried him to the presidency. Likely, he did not think it was the machine of the Liberal Party that handed over the presidency to him but the network of "campaign volunteers" outside his party. Again, on-brand for PNoy since his mother, Corazon Aquino, was catapulted by "people power" to Malacañang. Buoyed by confidence, allies of PNoy in Congress did not find the urgency to institute political party reform through legislation.[18] The Aquino administration and its allies in Congress became preoccupied with the impeachment of Chief Justice Renato Corona and the pork barrel scam involving senators. Electoral reform advocates were disappointed that an opportunity for a much-needed political party reform was lost.

2016–22: DUTERTE AND DEMOCRACY

The absence of a practical and effective statutory framework for political parties has increased political party fragmentation.[19] The weakness of the Philippine electoral process is a vulnerability that electoral contestants use to their advantage. Duterte showed this attitude towards formal institutions and democratic procedures. In the 2016 national elections, Rodrigo Duterte did not file his certificate of candidacy for the presidency within the period prescribed by COMELEC. Instead, he became a substitute for Martin Diño, a PDP-Laban party mate. It was Diño who initially filed the certificate of candidacy for the presidency.[20] COMELEC's rule on substitution, Section 77 of the Omnibus Election Code, allows candidates to be substituted for the latter's death, permanent incapacity, disqualification, and withdrawal of candidacy. Substitution of candidacy, under the law, applies only to political party members, and the substitute should come from the same party. There is no question that Diño was only a placeholder. There was a petition to declare Diño a nuisance candidate, claiming he had no real intention to run for president. Diño eventually withdrew his candidacy, paving the way for the candidacy of Duterte. A COMELEC division dismissed the petition because of the withdrawal but did not decide whether Diño was a nuisance candidate. With a substitution strategy at play, Duterte managed to be a presidential candidate, even if he failed to declare himself a candidate within the period allowed by the COMELEC.

Accounts from the former presidential adviser and now Senator Bong Go claim that it was his idea to have someone as a placeholder since he was confident that then Mayor Duterte would not make it in time to file the certificate of candidacy.[21] The ambivalence towards running for president displayed by Duterte projected what appeared to be reluctance. On the one hand, he was going around the country to drum up support for a federalist system but publicly denying he was making a bid for 2016 elections, declaring that "there was no ambition for me to aspire for the presidency. The country does not need me. I find no need for it."[22] Reminiscent of PNoy's initial disinclination to run for the highest office in the 2010 elections, in the case of Duterte, it was also evident that he and his supporters came well prepared for his 2016 presidential run. Duterte's campaign used an effective social media strategy that operated outside of the regulatory reach of COMELEC. Existing laws on campaigns, primarily the Fair Election Act of 2001, do not contain provisions on the use of social media and the Internet that can provide practical statutory guidance to enable effective administrative regulation.

Duterte campaigned and won the 2016 presidential election, promising a strong-willed presidency to address drugs, criminality, peace, and order. He presented himself as someone willing to confront elites and the establishment. Upon winning the presidency, Duterte enjoyed public support and made good on his promise of fighting crime with violence and illiberal rule. Duterte's violent populist rule included targeting critics and silencing any opposition. One of them is then incumbent Senator Leila De Lima. She was imprisoned and forced to perform her role as a legislator in a detention facility on questionable criminal charges. Franco's chapter (Chapter 12 of this volume) illustrated how gendered disinformation worked against Senator De Lima.

Duterte successfully delegitimized norms opposed to his approach, such as human rights and good governance. Accountability institutions in government and mainstream media were sidelined. Allies, or those with ties to Davao, had oversight functions. One result was a weakened demand for accountability. A climate of fear pervaded. Strong pushback was experienced by those who dared to oppose and criticize. The Duterte administration, or people with ties to him, filed cases against media companies and editors of various news outlets.

The franchise of ABS-CBN, the country's largest television network, was not renewed by Congress. Its broadcast reach is among Filipinos' primary sources of news and information. Duterte himself has publicly admitted he resented the network's refusal to accommodate his political advertisement during his campaign in the 2016 elections.[23] Duterte's runaway popularity, power, and influence were evident in the 2019 midterm elections. No opposition candidate won in the elections for twelve senatorial seats. Moreover, almost all Duterte-endorsed candidates for local government positions won.

On issues regarding political and electoral reform, Duterte campaigned to move for the adoption of a federal system of government. The existing charter provides for a unitary government structure in the Philippines. Among his populist tirades, Duterte repeated a narrative of the neglect of Mindanao and the provinces in favour of "imperial Manila". The elitism of Manila was the basis for his push for federalism.[24] Federalism promised representation and inclusivity. In truth, many of the country's economic elites come from Western Visayas and other provinces. Political elites come from across the country and have national-level roles. The House of Representatives has local, provincial, and regional elites. In recent elections, "provincial politicos have been consolidating among themselves and nominating one representative to deal with whoever becomes president as a single bloc, to have the most leverage for political survival".[25]

Duterte's charter change promise initially led many in the political and electoral reform community to participate in the federalism project. A number of those who supported the initiative for charter change were disappointed by the lack of interest shown by the PNoy administration to reform political parties, particularly for the political party-strengthening law. Duterte created a consultative committee to study an ideal form of federalism and draft the language of the constitutional revision for consideration by Congress. The idea was for Congress to use the draft when it puts together a constituent assembly and formally approve it.[26] Ignoring insinuations that their involvement in the federalism project amounted to being part of the administration's authoritarian trajectory, the advocates saw the federalism project as a rare opportunity for significant political reforms to gain traction. However, as things turned out, the federalism project faltered and halted, as Atienza's chapter in this volume showed.

Aside from the Duterte administration's failure to push for constitutional reforms, the political party strengthening bills, refiled by various legislators, continued to languish in the congressional committees. These bills suffered the same fate as those filed in previous congresses. Duterte's popularity and unchallenged political power could have been the most effective impetus for Congress to enact the law on political parties finally. Ironically, even the political party of Duterte, the Partido Demokratiko Pilipino-Lakas ng Bayan or PDP-Laban, did not utilize Duterte's substantial political clout to build a stronger political party. As a result, parties experienced more fragmentation by the end of Duterte's presidential term. Consistent with the history of political parties in the Philippines, PDP-Laban gained majority membership in the House of Representatives as soon as the 2016–19 Congress convened. However, the increase in membership did not necessarily make PDP-Laban a robust political party. Instead, PDP-Laban lost membership after the 2019 midterm election to parties like the National Unity Party (NUP) and the Lakas Christian Muslim Democrats (Lakas-CMD).[27] Duterte did not actively intervene as the party's titular head to calm the infighting among its members for the speakership.

Teehankee and Kasuya observed that Duterte eschewed patronage-based political party building in favour of what they call "populist mobilization", which is "a strategy to build a mass of supporters to gain and retain power with the minimum of institutional intervention".[28] Duterte did not see the need for a political party. However, the formation of political parties supporting the administration was encouraged, further reducing the institutionalization of political parties.[29] Part of Duterte's legacy for the lack of political party reform was creating an environment that allowed for "an anarchy of parties".[30]

The president's party, PDP-Laban, was divided into two warring factions between Senator Aquilino Pimentel III and Alfonso Cusi. The Commission on Elections recognized the Cusi faction in a party dispute. The Cusi faction is known to be more loyal to President Duterte. Effectively, the Pimentel faction was marginalized, notwithstanding that the founder of PDP-Laban was Aquilino Pimentel Jr., the father of incumbent Senator Aquilino Pimentel III. The irony, however, is that PDP-Laban, supposedly the strongest political party as the incumbent's party, did not have a presidential candidate in the 2022 elections. Consistent with his attitude towards institutions, Duterte shrugged off this matter: no intervention to unite the party happened. Moreover, party fragmentation is consistent with his strategy of playing off multiple players/interests against each other.[31]

The closest that the Duterte administration came to fulfilling Duterte's campaign promise of pushing for federalism is the passage of the Bangsamoro Organic Law or BOL.[32] The organic law came out on 27 July 2018. Ratified by a plurality of the votes cast in plebiscites held on 21 January 2019 and 6 February 2019, the law introduced a parliamentary form of government in the Muslim Mindanao region. The law also introduced a mixed system with an eighty-member parliament where half the members come from a proportional representation system. Forty per cent of its membership will be elected through a single-member district plurality from the thirty-two regional parliamentary districts, the boundaries of which will be determined by the Bangsamoro Transition Authority or BTA. The BTA performs the functions of the parliament before the first elected parliament convenes. The remaining 10 per cent of the seats are reserved for non-Moro indigenous people, settler communities, traditional leaders or elders, women, youth, and the *ulama*s. The BOL emphasizes that its primary goal is to develop genuine and principled political parties as the basis for its parliamentary governance. Therefore, it left the determination of the qualifications of political parties that will participate in BARMM parliamentary elections to the BTA through a Bangsamoro Electoral Code.[33] The laws and policies adopted in the BARMM are on top of the wish list of reforms that political party and electoral reform advocates have pushed for decades at the national level. While the success of the adopted reforms in the BARMM is yet to be realized pending its ground implementation, it can be asserted that the BARMM formula can be the blueprint for reforming politics at the national level both in substance and in process. Nevertheless, it is more likely that the benefits of the BARMM reforms to political party and electoral reforms are unintended.

Enough evidence shows further erosion of democratic values during the Duterte administration. Duterte did not push for meaningful political reform. Instead, he strengthened his hold on power and weakened any opposition and critics. He maintained his popularity by effectively managing the narrative that projects his populist personality. The colourful language and misogynistic remarks in official speeches and media interviews "endeared" him to the public. Many may have found the liberal democratic frame of past administrations too abstract. As a city mayor, Duterte projected an image of a leader with no qualms about employing forceful and violent methods to maintain order. Duterte's masterfully crafted messaging and his organization's skilful gaming of the rules solidified the narrative that he is the one the public identifies with among the presidential candidates. Democratic reform was not part of his campaign or agenda.[34]

Election-related legislation that Congress passed during the Duterte administration, apart from the BOL, includes three laws postponing the Barangay and *Sangguniang Kabataan* Elections (BSKE) scheduled for 31 October 2016, to the fourth Monday of October 2017. Incumbents were authorized to hold their position until then. The second was passed on 2 October 2017,[35] and postponed the BSKE scheduled on the fourth Monday of October 2017 to the 2nd Monday of May 2018. This law also authorized the incumbents to continue performing the functions of their office in a holdover capacity. The third postponement law relates to the scheduled first parliamentary election in the BARMM simultaneously with the 2022 national and local elections. As a result, a law was passed resetting said elections to 2025. Finally, one law passed in Congress increased the discounts on the cost of political advertisements in mass media. Other than this, Duterte only had those three election postponement laws.

The Duterte presidency also supported claims of electoral fraud alleged by then-losing vice-presidential candidate Ferdinand Marcos Jr. Marcos and his camp claimed widespread cheating in the 2016 elections in favour of Leonor "Leni" Robredo. Duterte occasionally made public statements referring to Marcos Jr. as vice president. Statements left doubt on the integrity of elections for many Marcos supporters. It is a narrative that helped Marcos appear relevant throughout the Duterte presidency and into the next election cycle. The claim was never proven and was discredited when the Presidential Electoral Tribunal ruled to dismiss the election protest of Marcos and even found that Robredo's lead over him was even more than the official tally. However, this no longer mattered. The cheating story arc was planted, supported by Marcos's allies, and effectively presented Marcos as an underdog. The biggest loser, however, was the credibility of the automated election system. It became the easy target, primarily due to the system's lack of transparency, and the COMELEC's apparent failure to fully explain its workings, and the technical glitches. With COMELEC unable to explain to a sceptical public, this played well on the narrative of Marcos being a victim of cheating. While there has never been any official investigation, nor is there proof that the results of the elections were fraudulent, the credibility of the automated election system was severely battered, increasing the call to abandon the optical scan system in favour of another system.

The electoral environment presented many novel challenges that impacted election integrity leading to the 2022 elections. Under Duterte, disinformation and misinformation persisted, primarily through social media. In addition, political parties are in disarray for lack of clear statutory and regulatory guidelines, strengthening the personality-based character of election contests. With the basic legal framework still the 1985 vintage OEC, the elections in 2022 were expected to experience many problems in previous elections, such as candidacy filing and substitution, campaign finance, election offenses, and accountability. Added to this are the continuing credibility issues of COMELEC and the election process it runs every election.

THE 2022 ELECTIONS ADMINISTRATION AND MANAGEMENT OF THE COMMISSION

The Commission on Elections is mandated to manage the electoral process in the Philippines. There is an expectation of autonomous organizational authority that can ensure a smooth transition of power through competitive, accessible, and fair elections. Over time, the autonomy and capacity of COMELEC, one of the oldest election commissions in the region, have been marred by allegations of complicity to power and politics.[36] The commission was discredited during the authoritarian regime of Ferdinand Marcos Sr. for running referendums and elections that were both partisan and favoured Marcos Sr.'s ruling party.[37] After the 1986 People Power Revolution, COMELEC was re-established as a constitutional commission. Empowered with a new set of commissioners appointed by Corazon Aquino, COMELEC recovered from its credibility issues even as it struggled to administer the manual elections efficiently.[38]

Designed with election administration and adjudication functions, the Philippines' COMELEC was considered, post-1986, as a model for other Southeast Asian countries looking to establish their election management bodies as part of the third wave of democratization in the 1990s. However, the commission continued to struggle with allegations of fraud well into multiple electoral cycles after 1986. Its institutional weakness was best revealed with the Hello Garci scandal of 2004 when then President Arroyo was caught on tape talking to COMELEC commissioner Virgilio Garcillano to pad her votes to assure her winning a margin of one million votes.[39] The Hello Garci scandal led to a serious credibility and legitimacy crisis not only for Arroyo but also for COMELEC and the electoral process. Together with the decision of the Supreme Court in January 2004 to nullify the contract COMELEC entered to automate the May 2004 elections on a national scale as required by law, the Hello Garci electoral fraud controversy triggered calls for urgent reforms in the electoral process. This circumstance fast-tracked an amendment to a 1997 law[40] allowing automated voting, counting, and voting tabulation.[41] The idea was that using an automated system would substantially reduce human intervention, which observers identified as the primary reason for the previous manual process's vulnerability to fraud. The 1997 law only allowed a paper-based optical mark reading counting process, but the 2007 amendment (Republic Act No. 9369) allowed COMELEC to use a paperless, direct recording electronic system. However, Congress passed the law only four months before the 2007 elections. As a result, COMELEC was constrained to employ a manual election process, the same process used in previous poll exercises, as there was not enough time to prepare. However, COMELEC was constrained to adopt automated elections in 2010 based on the prevailing view that it was the best way to prevent a repeat of the widely believed fraudulent 2004 and 2007 elections.

Another significant amendment in the 2007 law is the introduction of the crime of electoral sabotage, which penalizes offenders with up to life imprisonment for acts that would result in vote padding and shaving that will change the results of the elections or those which affect at least ten thousand votes.[42] Gloria Macapagal-Arroyo was indicted and detained for several years under said law concerning the 2007 elections. However, she was acquitted as the trial court did not see enough proof that she was involved in the alleged conspiracy to commit electoral sabotage.[43]

The decision to automate Philippine elections on a national scale starting in 2010 raised hope that it would minimize fraudulent practices in elections. However, the COMELEC at that time was, literally and figuratively, not wired to undertake such a massive information technology (IT) project. It needed the appropriate human resource skill and experience to implement an IT project nationwide as critical as organizing and managing nationwide elections. This COMELEC did not have.[44]

Nonetheless, the clamour to abandon the century-old manual voting, counting, and tabulation process was seen as urgent and imperative. Critics claimed that the automated election lacked safeguards against "electronic fraud". This claim persists. In addition, since 2010, there have been persistent calls to revert to the manual system or adopt a hybrid manual voting and electronic transmission of election results. Critics continue to assert the lack of transparency in the automated process. COMELEC, for its part, failed to respond to issues related to the automated election process adequately. As a result, problems cited by critics since 2010 continue to frame the current discourse against automated elections.

Nonetheless, the perspective that automation addressed election day problems led to reform advocacies in other areas. Advocates started looking at campaign finance regulation reforms, inclusive access to the electoral process, election dispute resolution, and legal framework reform—most civil society engagements before automation focused on being watchdogs on election day. COMELEC responded positively to this civil society reform initiative despite being constrained by the rigid legal framework that gives it little flexibility. It established the Campaign Finance Unit in 2011 to provide an office within the bureaucracy that exclusively focuses on campaign finance regulation. Previously, that function was just among the many responsibilities of the poll body's Law Department, the primary law enforcement unit of the agency. Special registration and voting procedures were adopted to make election processes more accessible to persons with disabilities and senior citizens, indigenous peoples, and persons deprived of liberties.[45] In addition, special voting arrangements for internally displaced persons or IDPs and incentives to increase women's participation in elections were examined. These innovations were limited in impact as they were essentially administrative adjustments that could not exceed the terms limited by existing election legislation. The primary source of election laws is still the 1985 OEC.[46] Most of the existing campaign finance laws are in the Code. The same Code still provides the procedure for determining the voting venues. While there are OEC amendments, the Code remains the guiding framework for implementing laws related to the election. Unfortunately, the importance of these reforms is overshadowed by the more controversial issues relating to so-called glitches in the automated election system processes, which tend to be highlighted more than the gains brought about by increased access to the electoral process and a more direct focus on campaign regulations.

Despite the antiquated legal framework in elections, gains are possible when COMELEC commissioners are open to innovations. This brings to the fore the importance of the appointments made by the president to the COMELEC. Under the Philippine constitution, the president appoints the COMELEC chairperson and the six commissioners.[47] The appointment to COMELEC is reviewed by the Commission on Appointment of Congress. The qualifications, vision, and work they will bring to COMELEC depend on the appointments. Once the chairperson and the commissioners are appointed, they are expected to be independent. Independence of action and being publicly perceived as independent become crucial in gaining public trust and credibility for the institution.

In 2017, then chairperson of COMELEC, Andres Bautista, resigned from his post[48] amidst the impeachment move by the House of Representatives against him.[49] The lower house at that time was known to toe the line for Duterte. There was speculation that Duterte's political allies may have engineered Bautista's resignation. The vacancies created by Bautista's resignation and those of the two commissioners whose terms expired in February 2018 were filled by the appointment of an incumbent justice of the Philippine Court of Appeals, Soccoro Inting, and of a COMELEC career official with a background in computer education, Marlon Casquejo. Their credentials are seemingly ideal for commissioners. An incumbent commissioner, Sheriff M. Abas, filled the vacant chairperson position. In turn, the vacant commissioner position left by Abas was filled by an undersecretary from the Department of Justice, Antonio T. Kho, Jr. Concerns were raised with the Duterte appointments as all of them are from Mindanao, a departure from the practice of appointing COMELEC commissioners to achieve geographical balance. Inting and Casquejo are from Davao City, where Duterte was a long-time mayor. The retirement of two commissioners in 2020 led to the appointment of Aime Ferolino-Ampoloquio and Reynaldo Bulay. Ampoloquio is a long-time COMELEC field officer from Davao, while Bulay was a City Prosecutor of Manila. These associations do not necessarily reflect each appointee's independence. The public perception was that Duterte was consolidating his hold on power even beyond his term.

Suspicions of partisan consideration also attended the appointments to COMELEC in previous administrations. COMELEC appointees are burdened with proving their independence through their decisions on controversial issues and election disputes. Duterte's appointments did not help build the desired impartial reputation of the commission. The perception was that the appointments were meant to strengthen Duterte's influence. These concerns were carried over to the holding of the 2022 elections. By that time and with the retirement of the chairperson, Abas, two commissioners, Rowena Guanzon and Antonio Kho, the chair and the six commissioners that oversaw the May 2022 elections were all Duterte appointees.

The contemporary electoral environment presents many novel challenges that impact election integrity. With elections still running under an antiquated legal framework, it is unresponsive to address current political practices. The role of social media influencers, the proliferation of disinformation and misinformation, and the use of hate and incendiary language in political discourse are expected to intensify and become more sophisticated.

COMELEC faced formidable challenges in organizing the critical 2022 presidential elections amidst the COVID-19 pandemic. It has never organized elections under the circumstances presented by the pandemic and the concomitant health restrictions. Philippine elections have a lot of in-person activities. Coming up with a novel and creative alternative to the old practices is a tremendous challenge to COMELEC. Election preparation demands clockwork precision in a three-year electoral cycle that was already challenging in pre-pandemic times. It was thus unimaginable how COMELEC, with all its institutional challenges, could prepare for the May 2022 elections. COMELEC had to focus on ensuring that the May 2022 elections are held by minimizing risk and adhering to health protocols.

Responding to these challenges includes adjustments in rules on voter registration to encourage newly qualified voters, specifically those who turned eighteen, to register in election offices in all the cities and municipalities of the country. In August 2020, COMELEC passed a resolution institutionalizing "health and safety standards under the new normal".[50] It also adopted a policy on dealing with local governments on mobility restrictions based on infection rate.[51] Regarding campaigns, the rules related to health protocols were incorporated into the appropriate regulations.[52] The special procedures requiring temperature checks were included in the General Instructions on Voting.[53] COMELEC's internal processes also had to contend with health protocols. It instituted special procedures for printing over 67 million ballots and for the operations in the storages assigned by COMELEC to test and deploy election documents, materials supplies, and vote counting machines nationwide. Considering the perceived weakness of COMELEC as an institution and the magnitude of the challenges posed by the pandemic, not a few had a pessimistic outlook of the conduct of the election. Generally, COMELEC overcame the challenges of holding elections under the pandemic conditions.

A few months before the 2022 elections, there were speculations about whom Duterte would endorse as a candidate. There were even speculations that he would run as vice president. With her high ratings in pre-election surveys, Duterte's daughter, Sara Duterte, initially decided to seek re-election as mayor of Davao City. The filing of certificates of candidacy was again not taken seriously, with the remedy of substitution still available as a political strategy. After withdrawing from being a candidate for mayor of Davao City, Sara Duterte later substituted someone virtually unknown and nominated by Lakas-CMD for vice-presidency to become a candidate for president. She became a member of Lakas-CMD at the last minute. It was unclear whether she left the party she founded, the Hugpong ng Pagbabago (Group for Change). It is important to note that nowhere have political parties performed their role of nominating candidates to simplify and clarify the choices that the people will make when they vote.

This confusing political circus is due to the lack of an adequate statutory framework to provide regulatory guidance and regulations to manage parties and candidates. The so-called tandems for president and vice president need not necessarily belong to the same party. The Partido Federal ng Pilipinas nominated Marcos Jr., while Lakas-CMD nominated Sara Duterte. Robredo chose not to run under the Liberal Party, which she chairs and instead ran independently. Her "running mate", Senator Francis Pangilinan, is with the Liberal Party. The senatorial candidates who campaigned under these two principal candidates came from different political parties. Even before election and Proclamation Day, the alliance is, at best, temporary. The rule on substituting candidates, which is supposed to be limited to members or nominees of political parties, does not prohibit persons who just became a party member a few minutes before the substitution to serve as a substitute. Political parties are entirely irrelevant and inconsequential in Philippine politics. COMELEC can display a level of administrative activism by interpreting the laws towards better regulation and enforcement.

On adjudicating disputes, the disqualification petition against candidate Marcos Jr. must be highlighted because of his previous conviction of non-filing income tax returns. The petitioner argued that this constituted valid grounds for his disqualification from continuing as a candidate. The legal issue is not as simple as it seems. The Supreme Court upheld the COMELEC decision and affirmed the dismissal of the petition. Before her retirement on 2 February 2022, then Commissioner Rowena Guanzon went public, accusing a fellow commissioner of delaying the release of the decision of the division of COMELEC. Under the constitution, all election cases go through one of two divisions of three members of COMELEC. The full commission recognizes the case only when reconsidering a division's decision is sought. Guanzon publicly released her position and vote on the Marcos case because she claimed that the commissioner assigned to write the majority opinion took too long and would not be released before her retirement. Guanzon was due for retirement in a matter of days. Her public statement increased concerns about the fairness and timeliness of the commissioners in deciding the Marcos case and raising issues of independence of the constitutional commission yet again.[54] This could have been avoided if controversial and high-impact cases were given ample time to seek review with the Supreme Court.

Critical in the 2022 election was the retirement of the sitting chair and two commissioners barely four months before election day. Commissioners Abas, Guanzon, and Kho completed their terms of office on 2 February 2022. With all the challenges cited above, a situation arose where newly appointed commissioners replaced commissioners who planned and prepared for the elections. Saideman Pangarungan was appointed chairman, while George Garcia and Aimee Torrefranca-Neri were appointed commissioners. Their appointments were in an *ad interim* capacity. Congress was in recess when the appointments were made. The appointments were effective immediately but would expire upon the next adjournment of Congress unless the Commission on Appointments confirmed them.

Pangarungan and Torrefranca-Neri are new to election administration. As far as Garcia is concerned, being an election litigator for decades, he is known to be familiar with COMELEC. Moreover, Garcia represented Marcos in the latter's election protest against Robredo in the 2016 vice-presidential race. As pointed out above, Marcos Jr. had continuously claimed that he was cheated out of victory by the failure of the automated election system used to count the votes correctly.

One notable issue of the 2022 elections was the refusal of Marcos Jr. to participate in the COMELEC-sponsored debates. Like his mother, Imelda Marcos, when she ran for president in 1992,[55] Marcos Jr. opted not to attend any debate that pits him with other candidates, including those organized by COMELEC.[56] Putting COMELEC in a bind, the election commission could not do anything when the major candidate refused to attend what should be a relevant public forum. While there is no law or regulation authorizing COMELEC to force a candidate to attend, the absence of one is seen as a failure of COMELEC to assert its authority as an election commission. Moreover, having all serious candidates participate in the presidential debate allows voters to be sufficiently informed about their candidates and differentiate one from the others.

CONCLUSION: THE PROMISE OF ELECTORAL AND PARTY REFORM FROM 2022 ONWARDS

Under the Marcos Jr. administration, there seems to be a semblance of openness to electoral reform. Stakeholders and some members of civil society were present in the by-invitation-only national election summit held from 10 to 13 March 2023. It was a "5-star affair" in a posh hotel that Senator Imee Marcos quipped that maybe COMELEC does not need an increase in its budget.[57] COMELEC Chair George Garcia presented the suitable optics and said the right words. However, he also quickly pointed out why some reform proposals were impossible. He mentioned that some reform proposals were outside the commission's powers. In that summit, Garcia reiterated that COMELEC wants to be transparent, including what others contest as the questionable electronic transmission of votes during the 2022 elections. Despite this, some civil society advocates and analysts remain sceptical that election reforms will occur.[58]

Upon the assumption to the office of Marcos Jr., several "recycled" bills from previous congresses relating to political and electoral reform were immediately filed. Most of them relate to political party strengthening and campaign finance. The highlight of these electoral reform bills is Senate Bill No. 179, which proposes a new Omnibus Election Code, replacing the 1985 code. Imee Marcos, the president's older sister, passed a version of this bill before the end of Duterte's term and was refiled in the new Congress. It is a compilation of legislative proposals that Congress has not yet passed. Imee Marcos herself said that the proposed Code is a working paper that would jumpstart discussion and deliberation of every portion of the bill—finally updating the legal framework of Philippine elections at a more comprehensive level. Notable in the bill, however, is the proposal to adopt what is called a hybrid election system for voting, counting, and vote tabulation. The proposal for a hybrid system is a reaction to the supposed non-transparent counting feature of the optical scan system used in Philippine national and local elections since 2010. Imee Marcos takes the position and shares her brother's belief that the automated election system stole the vice presidency from him. The central objective of the proposed New Omnibus Election Code is then to alter the automated election process. This is unfortunate because it distracts attention to other more substantial reforms, including political party strengthening, campaign finance, election justice, and more inclusive electoral access, especially for women.

The proposed Code also contains updates on campaign laws. There is a recognition of the need to regulate the use of the Internet, online and social media in campaigns. The Code will also update campaign finance rules and political party regulations. As a working draft formalized into a legislative bill, it facilitates a uniform analysis of the proposals for legal framework reform from a holistic perspective. However, historically, it is easier to pass proposals on a piecemeal basis than having the entire code pass. This happened to the 1993 Election Code proposed by COMELEC. The Code failed to pass, but some of its sections did. Also, electoral reform legislations are more likely to be passed before the midterm elections.

To date, observers find that the deliberation on the Code is not proceeding at a pace that ensures it will be deliberated in plenary from both houses before the members become occupied for the next election. Apart from the New Omnibus Election Code, the passage of the political party strengthening law is also on the table. The bill of former president and representative Gloria Macapagal-Arroyo is advantageous to her politically, mainly because the bill introduced a provision on limiting party switching. Her party, Lakas-CMD, is anticipated to be at the tragic end of party switching in the 2025 midterm election.

The appointments of Pangarungan and Torrefranca-Neri were no longer renewed by the new president, Marcos Jr. The new chair, George Garcia, is an experienced election litigator. This gives him familiarity with COMELEC as an organization. The COMELEC bureaucracy and Garcia's fellow election litigators generally welcome his appointment. However, there were also apprehensions about his having been the lawyer of Marcos Jr., and many other politicians whom many feared would take advantage of their relationship with him. In response to these concerns, Garcia committed to being independent and will recuse himself from participating in deliberations involving former clients.

Along with Garcia, Nelson Celis and Ferdinand Ernesto Maceda were appointed commissioners. Celis has been an IT professional and an academic in election technology advocacy since the early 2000s. He is, however, also a leading critic of the automated election system. He convened the Automated Election System Watch or AES Watch, a coalition of critics against the system since 2010. As a non-lawyer and an IT professional, many welcomed Celis's appointment—an opportunity to fill what is perceived as a gap in the necessary competency for COMELEC. Maceda, on the other hand, is a practising lawyer and comes from the academe.

COMELEC under Garcia has projected an openness to engage with the public and civil society groups involved in electoral reform advocacies. Garcia issued statements projecting a COMELEC willing to join electoral reform advocates in their push for the passage of laws updating the election legal framework. Moreover, this make it more responsive to current electoral practices and issues. Garcia publicly committed to undertaking internal reforms within COMELEC to make the institution more responsive to the public. The new chair is more available to interact regularly with the media, making the public understand better what COMELEC does between regular elections.

The National Election Summit was preceded by about sixty focus group discussions by various stakeholders and covering topics ranging from exploring alternative election technology, including blockchain, discussions on the concept of transparency in the use of technology, campaign finance regulation, and political party registration to voter education. The election summit was a public relations success, but it also raised expectations for better elections in future elections. Garcia is quick to address this and level expectations. He emphasized that for COMELEC to achieve its visions and plans, the legal framework must be updated, and the government must provide the necessary resources. The Garcia Commission's openness and public engagement initiative can gain allies to support its plans. This is an effective strategy not given sufficient emphasis by the previous administration in COMELEC. Civil society can exploit COMELEC's openness with hopeful but guarded optimism.

There is room to resolve the capacity and autonomy issues of the election commission. This includes revisiting electoral systems design and considering alternatives that will dissuade patronage politics while encouraging more programmatic politics. It will require administrative and legislative reform at this time, a constitutional reform sooner than later, and a constitutional amendment at the right time.

Some administrative reforms worth considering by the election commission include streamlining administrative and adjudication duties, an effective communication strategy that bolsters the credibility and legitimacy of the electoral process, and the institutionalization of inclusivity in election planning and preparation. It is essential to engage stakeholders in the process. Legislative reforms include the updating of the legal framework of Philippine elections. An updated Omnibus Election Code should address issues involving campaigns and campaign finance, use of state resources for campaigns, use of social media platforms in campaigns, and election dispute resolution, and provide election administrators the flexibility to adjust to new developments and contingencies. An update on laws can strengthen political parties, address accountability issues of incumbents running for public office and make elections genuinely competitive.

Constitutional reform can ensure that the appointments generate an independent commission. The appointment of commissioners can include a public vetting process; reform can do away with the requirement that most commissioners be lawyers and create a gender and geographical balance in the composition of commissioners. A constitutional amendment at the right time can look at the broader issue of election systems design. Maria Ela L. Atienza's chapter in this volume mentions that a constitutional amendment is unlikely soon. However, worth considering is the expansion of proportional representation in the legislature. At least half of the legislative seats, similar to the BARMM parliament, can be a model (50-40-10). It should include provisions for temporary quotas for women and reserve seats for sectoral/minority groups. This is one way to improve the chances of women and minorities in electoral success. However, as Encinas-

Franco in her chapter expounds, women and minorities have a long way to go to find an even playing field in the political arena. Another alternative model is to keep the bicameral legislature but with the Senate members elected by proportional representation and the House by single-member constituency. An election systems design can do away with the current split ticket of the president and vice president. The real test of the administration's and COMELEC's sincerity for reform will come a year before the midterm elections, where crucial decisions on important policy questions and direction can be made.

Notes

1. Ronald U. Mendoza, Leonardo Jaminola, and Jurel Yap, "From Fat to Obese: Political Dynasties after the 2019 Midterm Elections", Ateneo School of Government Working Paper Series, 19-013, September 2019, https://ssrn.com/abstract=3449201 or http://dx.doi.org/10.2139/ssrn.3449201.
2. PHP 1 billion = US$17.7 million at US$1 = PHP 56. Carmela Fonbuena, "2022 Candidates Run Over 20 Billion in Campaign Ads", Philippine Center for Investigative Journalism, 7 May 2022, https://www.rappler.com/nation/elections/2022-candidates-campaign-ads-spending/.
3. Republic Act No. 10366 [15 February 2013] entitled "An Act Authorizing the Commission on Elections to Establish Precincts Assigned to Accessible Polling Places Exclusively for Persons with Disabilities and Senior Citizens". A precinct is a geographical territory in a *barangay* (village) with at most two hundred registered voters as residents. The list of voters is organized by election precinct. A special precinct for persons with disability and senior citizens is a departure from the territorial groupings of registered voters.
4. Rep. Act No. 10367 [15 February 2013] entitled "An Act Providing for Mandatory Voter Registration".
5. Rep. Act No. 10590 [27 May 2013], otherwise known as the Overseas Voting Act of 2013. The law that it amended was Rep. Act No. 9189 [13 February 2003], otherwise known as the Overseas Absentee Voting Act of 2003.
6. Rep. Act No. 10742 [15 January 2016].
7. Rep. Act No. 7160 [1991].
8. Rep. Act No. 10756 [8 April 2016].
9. Batas Pambansa Blg. 881.
10. Rep. Act No. 6646.

11. Rep. Act No. 6735.
12. Rep. Act No. 7166.
13. Rep. Act No. 8189.
14. Rep. Act No. 7941.
15. Rep. Act Nos. 8436, 9369.
16. Rep. Act No. 9006.
17. Rep. Act Nos. 9189, 10590.
18. Jorge V. Tigno, "The Party is Dead! Long Live the Party! Reforming the Party System in the Philippines", Policy Studies for Political and Administrative Reform Series 1-04. (Diliman, Quezon City: University of the Philippines, Center for Integrative and Development Studies, 2023).
19. Yuko Kasuya and Julio C. Teehankee, "Duterte Presidency and the 2019 Midterm Election: An Anarchy of Parties?" *Philippine Political Science Journal* 41, nos. 1–2 (2020): 106–26, https://doi.org/10.1163/2165025X-BJA10007.
20. The form used by Diño for his certificate of candidacy indicates that it was actually for Mayor, but he filed it at the central office of COMELEC, which is where the certificates of candidacy of those running for national office should be filed.
21. Pia Ranada, "The Man They Call Bong Go", *Rappler*, 27 May 2016, https://www.rappler.com/newsbreak/in-depth/134361-christopher-bong-go-profile-rodrigo-duterte/.
22. Ben O. Tesiorna, "Duterte Won't Run for President: 'The Country Does Not Need Me'", *CNN Philippines*, 12 October 2015, https://www.cnnphilippines.com/news/2015/10/12/rodrido-duterte-presidency-2016-elections-wild-dream.html.
23. Ellen T. Tordesillas, "Bong Go Finds Another Reason for Duterte's Rage vs ABS-CBN", Vera Files, 26 February 2020, https://verafiles.org/articles/bong-go-finds-another-reason-dutertes-rage-vs-abs-cbn.
24. *Inquirer.net*, "Duterte Is Looking to Destroy 'Imperial Manila'", 28 June 2016, https://newsinfo.inquirer.net/792839/duterte-looking-to-destroy-imperial-manila.
25. Manuel L. Quezon III, "Barons Assembling", *Inquirer.net*, 24 November 2021, https://opinion.inquirer.net/146772/barons-assembling#ixzz7yRfPry3V.
26. See Phil. CONST. Article XVII.
27. Salvador Santino F. Regilme Jr., "Contested Spaces of Illiberal and Authoritarian Politics: Human Rights and Democracy in Crisis", *Political Geography* 89 (2021).
28. Kasuya and Teehankee, "Duterte Presidency and the 2019 Midterm Election".
29. Tigno, "The Party is Dead!"
30. Kasuya and Teehankee, "Duterte Presidency and the 2019 Midterm Election".

31. Pia Ranada, "4 Lessons about Rodrigo Duterte, the Boss", *Rappler*, 30 May 2016, https://www.rappler.com/newsbreak/in-depth/134759-rodrigo-duterte-boss-lessons-patmei-ruivivar/.
32. Rep. Act No. 11054.
33. Rep. Act No. 11054, Article VII, Section 7(a).
34. Yuko Kasuya and Cleo Anne A. Calimbahin, "Democratic Backsliding in the Philippines: Are Voters Becoming Illiberal?" *Asian Journal of Comparative Politics* (2022), https://doi.org/10.1177/20578911221136263.
35. Rep. Act No. 10952.
36. Cleo Calimbahin, "Exceeding (Low) Expectations: Autonomy, Bureaucratic Integrity, and Capacity in the 2010 Elections", *Philippine Political Science Journal* 32, no. 55 (2011): 103–26, https://doi.org/10.1080/01154451.2011.9723533.
37. International Observer Delegation, *A Path to Democratic Renewal: A Report on the February 7, 1986 Presidential Election in the Philippines* (A joint project of the National Democratic Institute and the National Republican Institute), USAID PN-ABK-494.
38. Cleo Calimbahin, "An Institution Reformed and Deformed: The Commission on Elections from Aquino to Arroyo" (Tokyo: Institute of Developing Economies, Japan External Trade Organization, 2009).
39. *Inquirer.net*, "What Went Before: 'I Am Sorry'", 30 November 2011, https://newsinfo.inquirer.net/102821/what-went-before-i-am-sorry.
40. Rep. Act No. 8436 [1997].
41. Rep. Act No. 9369 [2007].
42. See Section 42 of Rep. Act No. 9369.
43. Lian Buan, "Supreme Court 'Nipped in the Bud' Arroyo's Plunder Case – Morales", *Rappler*, 24 July 2018, https://www.rappler.com/nation/208078-sc-nipped-in-the-bud-gloria-arroyo-plunder-case/.
44. Luie Tito F. Guia, "Briefing Paper on Republic Act No. 9369 and the Automated Election System", IFES, Washington D.C., 31 March 2008, https://www.ifes.org/publications/briefing-paper-republic-act-no-9369-and-automated-election-system.
45. Luie Tito F. Guia, "Pandemic Elections: Can Senior Citizens, PWDs, IPs and PDL Vote in 2022?" PCIJ, Quezon City, 2021, https://pcij.org/article/6946/pandemic-elections-access-senior-citizens-people-with-disabilities-indigenous-people.
46. This law is known as Batas Pambansa Blg. 881 enacted in December 1985. It became law barely two months before the snap (unscheduled) presidential election in February 1986. Ferdinand Marcos called the holding of the elections amidst constant street protests against his twenty-year rule. The provisions of the election code are too detailed and specific that they

do not allow adequate room for administrative flexibility on the part of COMELEC to adapt to changing realities that affect elections. The reason for the rigidity of the provision of the Election Code is the lack of trust of the COMELEC capacity to run a free and fair process.

47. Article IX-C, Section 1 (2).
48. Chairperson Andres D. Bautista was appointed in 2015 for a term ending in 2022.
49. Bea Cupin, "House Impeaches Comelec Chairman Andres Bautista", *Rappler*, 11 October 2017, https://www.rappler.com/nation/184940-house-representatives-impeaches-comelec-chairman-andres-bautista/.
50. COMELEC Resolution No. 10674 [12 August 2020].
51. COMELEC Resolution No. 10718 [1 September 2021].
52. COMELEC Resolutions No. 10730 [17 November 2021], No. 10732 [24 November 2021], and No. 10769 [16 March 2022].
53. COMELEC Resolution No. 10763.
54. Cleo Calimbahin, "Reforming the Philippine Electoral Commission", *Fulcrum*, 15 March 2022, https://fulcrum.sg/reforming-the-philippine-electoral-commission/.
55. William Branigin, "Imelda Marcos Seeks Presidency of Philippines", *The Washington Post*, 8 January 1992, https://www.washingtonpost.com/archive/politics/1992/01/08/imelda-marcos-seeks-presidency-of-philippines/375d5609-60fa-47ff-8e9c-fdac2998625e/.
56. Angelica Demegillo, "Group Hits Marcos-Duterte's No-Show at Debates: Crucial for Public to Know Platforms", *CNN Philippines*, 19 March 2022, https://www.cnnphilippines.com/news/2022/3/19/ph-debate-union-bbm-duterte-debate-refusal.html.
57. *Rappler*, "LIVESTREAM: Comelec Holds Summit to Lay Out Election Reform Agenda", 8 March 2023, https://www.rappler.com/nation/video-comelec-mounts-election-summit-lay-out-reform-agenda/.
58. Segundo Eclar Romero, "Comelec's Burnt Offering", *Inquirer.net*, 4 April 2023, https://opinion.inquirer.net/162154/comelecs-burnt-offering.

9

The Changing Local Political Dynamics during the COVID-19 Pandemic: The Philippine Experience under Duterte (and Marcos Jr.)

Jan Robert R. Go

> *The global COVID-19 pandemic has exacerbated the centralizing tendencies of national governments. It has become an excuse for authoritarian leaders to exercise greater control over the subnational governments and impose measures limiting mobility and even political and economic activities. The Philippines under Duterte is a case in point. Duterte's presidency illustrates the failure of the three-decade-old decentralization framework in the country. The COVID-19 pandemic exposed the institutional flaws of decentralization in the Philippines and the local authority breakdown in favour of the president's domineering exercise of power. The pandemic has also*

played a crucial role in the 2022 Philippine national and local elections. After Duterte, President Ferdinand Marcos Jr. guaranteed less restrictive management of the pandemic and slowly lifted previously imposed policies one after another. However, challenges persist under the new administration: while a new health secretary has been appointed, tourism and economy remain favoured over public health, and there is no explicit support for local governments in managing the pandemic and improving the health sector. This chapter interrogates the dynamics of local governance during the pandemic under Duterte and the first year of Marcos Jr. It argues that the COVID-19 pandemic has changed national-local relations, but this is also due to the dominant leadership legacy of Duterte.

Keywords: COVID-19; local governance; Duterte; Marcos Jr.; decentralization

INTRODUCTION

About two months after the lockdown was implemented in Wuhan, China, the epicentre of the COVID-19 pandemic, the Philippine government decided to implement its version of restrictions beginning on 16 March 2020. Upon the recommendation of the Inter-Agency Task Force for the Management of Emerging Infectious Diseases (IATF-EID, commonly referred to as IATF), President Rodrigo Duterte ordered the closure of international borders,[1] restriction of mobility within the national capital and several provinces, and suspension of the public transportation system, among many other policies. Short of calling the entire response a "lockdown", the national government decided to use a supposedly lighter and less harmful term—"quarantine"—to avert strong opposition and resistance from the public and local officials.

Throughout the pandemic, the national government has periodically announced the extent of the quarantine measures to be applied in specific areas in the country—from general community quarantine (GCQ) to enhanced community quarantine (ECQ) to modified versions of GCQ and ECQ. The IATF has successfully created its own nomenclature system for the quarantines, which varies with every single iteration, resulting in confusion among the public and local officials. Absent a common understanding of these nationally imposed restrictions, the local governments are left to figure out the steps and specific strategies to control the further spread of the virus in their localities and manage social mobility and the local economy. While local governments were scrambling to implement the centre's directives, the national government enjoyed a wide range of powers, whether institutionally provided or politically constructed by power-bearers, namely the president and his underlings. This is symptomatic of the problems of the Philippine decentralized governance system.[2]

Undeniably, the global pandemic has exacerbated the centralizing tendencies of national governments. The restrictions imposed in Duterte's Philippines are no different from the strategies used by other national governments, regardless of their regime types. In authoritarian regimes like China, where it is expected to have strong central command power, centralization as a governance scheme might not appear as surprising.[3] However, in democracies or democratic-leaning states, the (re)concentration of power to the national executives became even more apparent.[4] In addition, although some states have been relatively lax in their strategies, others have employed militarized tactics in combating the challenges brought about by the pandemic.[5] Political leaders with combined authoritarian and populist characteristics, such as Duterte, took advantage of the situation to reveal their need for greater control and exercise of power. Indeed, the pandemic "reveals a national character under radical uncertainty".[6]

This chapter examines the dynamics of local governance in the Philippines during the COVID-19 pandemic. Its concern is not simply about the quality of the pandemic response.[7] Instead, it focuses on the processes involved in meeting the goals and desired outcomes of the said response.[8] In this case, the Philippines under Duterte is not examined through the results, that is, number of confirmed cases and deaths, vaccination rates, and so on, but on the process of the implementation, that is, Duterte's relations with the local governments and officials, (re)configuration of the institutional constraints, and use of power. These points are explored in the first part of the chapter. It argues that the pandemic exposed the institutional defects of decentralization in the Philippines and the breakdown of the local authority in favour of the president's almost absolute exercise of power. Undoubtedly, Duterte is at the front and centre of it all.

The second part briefly looks at the 2022 local elections which happened during the pandemic. It frames the discussion using this health crisis as the new context that could aggravate the existing political configurations at the local level. This would have implications, for example, in the outcome of the 2022 national elections, where Ferdinand Marcos Jr., son of dictator Marcos Sr., won as president and Sara Duterte, daughter of Rodrigo Duterte, as vice president. This part segues into the third part, which discusses the new administration's challenges.

Since his assumption in June 2022, Marcos Jr. guaranteed less restrictive management of the pandemic and slowly lifted previously imposed policies one after another. However, he earlier refused to appoint a health secretary and appointed one only a year after his election. His cabinet has focused mainly on the economy and tourism and less on health and pandemic concerns. Most importantly, in his first State of the Nation Address (SONA), Marcos Jr. has not explicitly supported local governments in managing the pandemic.[9] Practically, the pandemic has disappeared from the main priorities of the administration. This chapter focused on these aspects to understand the Philippines as it enters the post-pandemic era. It concluded with a summary of arguments and directions for future research.

LOCAL GOVERNANCE UNDER A CENTRALIZING PRESIDENT

Unlike other Philippine presidents, Duterte is presumed to have a better understanding of the local governments and the decentralization system of the country. After all, his entire political career before the presidency was spent at the local level. He is one of the longest-serving mayors in the post-EDSA People Power Philippines, having been Davao City's mayor since 1988.[10] He is also expected to grasp what the 1991 Local Government Code demanded fully, and the distinct realities faced at the grassroots level given his experience as a local official. As a lawyer and someone who has implemented many provisions of the Code for decades, Duterte would have seen the gaps in the current system that need rectification through amendments or policy recalibration. And yet, during his presidency, especially throughout its second half (2019–22), Duterte did not necessarily promote the interest of local governments.[11] Instead, he did the exact opposite.

Duterte became a centralizing president. He saw the local governments as subordinates who were simply tasked to follow the head of government. The Duterte administration's attitude towards local governments reflects the president's understanding and construction of his role and position as the country's leader. Extending this argument further, I contend that Duterte ran the country as if he was still running a city, where all units under his office are directly and totally subject to his executive oversight. Such leadership notions have shaped how the government treated and saw the local governments' place in the overall pandemic response. On the other end of this political relationship, local officials exhibited submission to the power and authority of the president with little or no resistance. Effectively, this dynamic has dampened the already struggling decentralization framework of the country, directly or otherwise.

Weakening Central-Local Relations

Before Duterte's presidency, central-local relations had already been riddled with conflicts and resistance. On the one hand, the national government does not want to let go of its local government control fully. It remains to be the centre of governance in the country—from the mere crafting of policies and programmes to the contentious distribution of resources to different subnational units. This demand for control allows the national government to act as a patron to its clients, the local governments. On the other hand, local governments enjoy significant autonomy in managing their affairs. Ranging from fully devolved functions to partly decentralized responsibilities, local governments have been more assertive in their positions and decisions through the years. The overlapping and frequently contradicting interests between the two levels of government make the progress of central-local relations a long-standing concern, regardless of who sits in Malacañang.

To illustrate, in 2018, the Philippine Supreme Court handed a significant ruling that would change the country's local political landscape. Known as the Mandanas-Garcia ruling, the Court's decision expanded the source of the local government's pool of funds to include other national revenues on top of the internal revenue collections. Thus, the local governments are supposed to receive a larger national tax allotment (NTA) instead of a smaller internal revenue allotment (IRA). This was deemed a victory for the local governments, which have been struggling with their financial resources and fighting for just distribution of revenues since late President Fidel V Ramos's time (1992–98).[12]

Unfortunately for the local governments, though, the Duterte administration interpreted this expansion of income sources as an expansion of local government functions. In 2021, Duterte issued an executive order seeking a full devolution of certain functions from the executive branch to the local governments. While this directive will be implemented after his presidency, Duterte demanded that local governments do more work since they now receive a larger share of the national government's funds.[13] However, the executive order's contents are not new. The 1991 Local Government Code already devolved some service delivery and administrative functions to the local governments. The problem exists in the implementation.[14] While the additional funds would augment the local coffers, they do not guarantee the effective and efficient delivery of services. A recent assessment showed that local governments have capacity and capability issues, making the quality of services unequal across units.[15] Instead of promoting the local governments, Duterte's order gave them more burden.

But more than the issue of increased funds and devolved functions, central-local relations have generally weakened under Duterte. Aside from the usual coordination problems, he was concerned with local governments following his orders. Thus, he recognized the autonomy of local governments to decide and implement policies when it was beneficial for him but ignored it when local governments began to challenge his position and authority.[16]

During the pandemic, local governments were at the political front lines of the response. While the national government provided the general framework for responding to the health crisis, local governments were tasked to design and implement context-specific strategies to ensure their residents were safe and protected from the virus.[17] For example, local governments were responsible for distributing financial assistance (or *ayuda*) from the national government. When these provisions were insufficient, local governments had to find ways to augment and provide additional support either in cash or in kind. In Mandaluyong City, officials sent vegetable baskets to residents through the *barangay*s on top of monetary assistance.

On other occasions, local governments, such as Pasig and Marikina city governments, had to step up their game and aggressively look for spaces to convert to make-shift hospitals and lying-in clinics to accommodate the patients. When the vaccines became available, local governments were also the first ones to set up a system to regulate and monitor the administration of vaccines to the public. Local governments in the national capital also developed their health monitoring applications and registration systems. These positive outcomes received a nod from Duterte, affirming his construction that local governments are his subordinates. After all, the success of the local governments is interpreted as the national government's success.

However, Duterte became sensitive, if not paranoid, when his subordinates started taking a different direction, or worse, bested his efforts. He extended the national government's strong arm when local officials took actions inconsistent with his idea of social order and administrative compliance. More importantly, Duterte used the "president card" when local officials were perceived to defy him. Ironically, Duterte promoted federalism but now wanted centralized control of local governments.[18]

Several cases illustrate this point. Pasig City requested to allow tricycles and pedicabs, local forms of public transportation, to operate limitedly for the use of medical professionals. Others like Valenzuela and Quezon City have permitted households to organize roving markets or community pantries to help the disadvantaged barter or acquire cheaper goods. This did not sit well with Duterte, the chief executive. In this sense, the innovations and initiatives by local governments—supposedly good results—were received as an affront to the presidency and the national government efforts.

In one of his late-night "Talk to the People" speeches, Duterte threatened to file administrative and possibly criminal cases against local officials who were not acting according to the national government's directives, some of which encroached upon decision-making functions that are properly in the purview of local governments as per the Local Government Code. He said, "There is only one republic here, the

Republic of the Philippines, and therefore, you should abide by the directives of the national government when it sets ... the directives ... for the good of the country."[19] This statement reveals Duterte's centralizing tendency as he harbours totalizing authority under the blanket of the national government and thereby disregarding local autonomy. As far as local governments are concerned, the pandemic was not meant to shrink their powers and functions. In fact, it allowed them greater leeway for manoeuvring. But for Duterte, the pandemic was the perfect opportunity to assert central dominance over local governments and officials—thanks to his popularity.[20]

Ideally, the relationship between the centre and the local should be balanced. If all politics is indeed local, then the centre must give its attention not only to improving the conditions at the local level but, more importantly, to ensuring the smooth relationship between the officials of national government agencies and the local governments. However, the status of this relationship was already one of love and hate, with a stronger focus on the latter. If anything, Duterte simply built upon the existing institutional configurations while bringing his personality into the equation.[21]

Taking Advantage of Decentralization's Institutional Flaws

As the national chief executive, Duterte has supervisory authority over local governments. The 1987 Constitution gives this authority to presidents to ensure that local actions are within the scope of their functions. While local governments enjoy autonomy under the 1991 Local Government Code, they cannot escape the national government's gaze. This broad institutional arrangement allows the president to inject their political interests into managing local affairs. This is short of saying that the decentralization framework implemented in the Philippines for more than three decades has loopholes that occupants of political offices, namely the president, have taken advantage to the detriment of the local governments.

Of course, it cannot be assumed that local governments are strictly autonomous from the national level. Local officials are part of wider networks at the national or provincial levels, whether in terms of political parties, at least by name, or other forms of political affiliation. Given this, Duterte or any president can always shepherd local officials to their bidding, taking advantage of state capacity's inherent weaknesses. This may not seem a force-induced arrangement as the local officials, on many occasions, are also willing to submit to the national patron for spoils.[22] This further complicates decentralization's institutional framework and exposes its cracks.

The first problem is the president's oversight power on local governments. From the beginning of his presidency, Duterte has co-opted the local governments and used them as instruments for his political agenda. Arguing that local governments are subject to the national government's regulation, the president instrumentalized local officials and the state apparatus in implementing the deadly war on drugs.[23] As Duterte's flagship programme, the war on drugs sought to clean the country from the use of illegal drugs, initially within three to six months but later stretched out to his full term. Some local government units became active participants in identifying and, whenever necessary, eliminating suspected drug pushers and users in their localities.[24] Practically, it was a manhunt operation that claimed thousands of innocent lives and affected hundreds of families.[25] The police force, which answers locally to the governors and mayors, was this war's prime movers.

While most local officials, such as those from Quezon City, Manila, and Caloocan, submitted to the full instrumentalization of their units, some resisted or modified their strategies. For example, in Valenzuela and Pampanga (north of Metro Manila), local chief executives turned to a more rational and compassionate method of implementing the war. It was a combination of active leadership on the part of the mayor and governor, ownership of the strategies of the residents, and resistance from external—that is, the national government, pressures which allowed the units to prevent the loss of lives that were seen in other localities. Interestingly, even Duterte's daughter Sara, then mayor of Davao City, also deviated from the national mandate on the war.

But the above cases are outliers. The norm is submission to the national government's will. Big cities and rich provinces can afford to stand against institutions, but smaller units and poorer areas have little or no choice. In addition, some local politicians, mainly from the political opposition, were subjected to public embarrassment and scrutiny by including them on a drug list or matrix.[26] They were accused as either backers or accessories to drug-related crimes. Without solid evidence, Duterte used his position as president to intimidate local officials into compliance.[27] In effect, for local officials, submission to national authority is not just by force; for some, it is the only option.

Under Duterte, local officials were also threatened with suspension for different reasons. The second concern, then, is the disciplinary power of the president over local governments and its weaponization, albeit rhetorical. Through the Department of Interior and Local Government (DILG), the president has issued warnings of suspension to several local officials for what he deems to be a violation of laws or, in some cases, out of pure whim. For example, to respond to the problematic traffic situation in Metro Manila, Duterte in 2019 said he would suspend local officials who would not clear out the streets. Traffic is a perennial problem in the national capital. Duterte promised to reduce travel time in EDSA, a major thoroughfare, within his first six months. This did not happen. Instead, he gave mayors forty-five days to remove blockages in all major roads through a memorandum circular. It was extended to sixty days after city mayors said the earlier instructions were unrealistic. No one was suspended under this circular.

Indeed, even if the power to suspend is well within the hands of the president, most of his proclamations were verbal. In 2017, Duterte made a statement denouncing corruption related to processing permits and official documents at the local level. He said, "If I see you making the public suffer or you allow corruption to thrive in your locality, then as mayor or governor, I will order the new secretary of the DILG, the chief of staff, General (Eduardo) Año, to investigate you ... I'll give you about three days to explain."[28] Duterte would be uttering the same threats to local officials three years later. With a sense of exasperation, he said, "I just want graft and corruption [to] be stopped, and the parties involved in that corruption be prosecuted, be the mayor, city council or *barangay* captain." He also criticized the courts for halting his suspension orders. These verbal threats, of course, remained as threats. Later, during the pandemic, Duterte suspended not the local officials but the investigations and ongoing proceedings against suspected corrupt local officials.

If these coercions and threats were possible before the pandemic, the situation worsened when the series of quarantines beginning in March 2020 was enforced. The Bayanihan to Heal as One Act, a legislative measure which seeks to address the pandemic, bestowed upon Duterte even more powers. The new law not only echoed the existing institutional frameworks, but also strengthened, if not made explicit, the president's authority to "ensure that all local governments act within the letter and spirit of and are cooperating fully with the directives and regulations of the national government" related to COVID-19 emergency.[29] Once again, this time with a congressional nod on the emboldened presidential power, Duterte assumed an intimidating position over the local governments.

But with all these new and old authorities, did Duterte really see the importance of local governments in providing health services at the local level? The third issue, and the last one I raise here, is the extent of responsibilities devolved to local governments. The health sector has already been devolved to local governments for thirty years.[30] Fortunately for Duterte, the existing problems in the health sector cannot be solely attributed to him. Unfortunately for the residents, they must always wait for national support for services, even during a pandemic—a dynamic that counters the very reason for decentralizing the government.

For one, the 1991 Local Government Code gave local governments responsibilities they could not realistically perform.[31] *Barangay* (or village) levels are expected to provide primary health care, while municipalities are tasked to ensure the availability of secondary health care. Cities and provinces with more financial and human resources are responsible for the tertiary level. However, health services are not necessarily part of the local priorities for many reasons.[32] Some mayors are not inclined towards health and focus more on tangible outputs such as infrastructure. Others relegate the management of health to their local health officers. Likewise, local health spending did not improve over the years, and dependence on the IRA remained high for many local governments. The Duterte administration's support for health was also far from desirable, despite the presence of a pandemic. National spending, arguably, has concentrated on military and defence support. And so, throughout the pandemic, the health sector was not in a healthy condition. In a way, the pressures brought by the increased number of confirmed cases pushed the health sector to its lowest. Local officials heavily relied on the national government to purchase health equipment, face masks, and protective gear. This becomes a trap for many local governments: they cannot fully assert institutional autonomy from the national government, even if they want to, because they are incapable.

While institutions were in place to constrain actors' behaviours, the actors' constructions of their positions are critical in the overall process and reveal a particular political dynamic. Decentralization in the Philippines is not perfect, and the laws need periodic review, assessment, and, if necessary, amendments. However, political leaders' personalities cannot be divorced from the institutions they serve. In the case of Duterte, the institutions were used to achieve his vision, whether for the realization of his drug war or to expand his disciplinary control over local officials. Conversely, the local officials saw it necessary to accept the executive and national government's dominance against asserting their local autonomy. Success was not even guaranteed on those occasions. In the long run, the services that could help the citizens during emergencies such as the pandemic suffered.

President Duterte's Almost Absolute Power

If Duterte indeed had authoritarian fantasies,[33] the COVID-19 pandemic gave him the platform to realize such fantasies further. The pre-pandemic Duterte presidency has been regarded as populist and authoritarian, hounded by human rights abuses.[34] He already has the makings of a dictatorial ruler. Apart from his drug war and threats to local governments, Duterte tinkered with his powers to experiment with authoritarianism. From 2017 to 2019, he imposed martial law in Mindanao, an extreme solution to control security, peace and order, and terrorist activity which began in the Maute group's siege of Marawi City. Whether the imposition of military rule has been successful or not, the move recentralized the management of local governments in Mindanao—from the provinces to the *barangays*—under the chief executive.[35]

But without implementing martial law in the entire Philippines, Duterte placed the country under his spell. Public opinion polls released by Social Weather Station (SWS) and Pulse Asia show that Duterte consistently received a positive reception from the Filipinos. His satisfaction and approval ratings have always been very good or excellent (see Figure 9.1). Duterte's official spokespersons, Harry Roque and Salvador Panelo, interpreted these positive numbers as a stamp of approval not only of Duterte's leadership but, more importantly, his method and governance strategies. The high ratings also indicated that the criticisms and opposition to Duterte's brand of politics—the so-called Dutertismo[36]—did not resonate with the majority.

There is an explanation behind the president's almost absolute power and the acquiescence of the local officials to Duterte's handling of local governments and understanding of local governance. Any local official who cares about their political career and ambition and does not necessarily have a solid political backing or foundation or wants to strengthen or re-establish their political hold of the local government would not go against a *very* popular president. Governors, mayors, and *barangay* captains benefitted from associating their actions with Duterte. During the 2019 midterm elections, for example, being a Duterte ally could mean an almost guaranteed re-election to their local offices. Some local officials have also adopted a Duterte-style of politicking, that is, using expletives, misogyny, and rash language.

In addition, Duterte's familiarity with local politics allowed him to recreate the local dynamics and transplant them to the national level. Formally or informally, the mayors are small authoritarians in their local territories. If labels are any indicator, his close allies and aides calling him "mayor" or "president mayor" affirms this construction. The mayor, as a personality, did not leave Duterte, despite his ascent to the highest office in the country. Instead, Duterte administered or manoeuvred government processes according to his practices as city mayor.

The chief executive's dominance became more apparent during the pandemic.[37] Whatever irregularities in the decentralization scheme continued, if not worsened, while several areas were placed under extensive quarantine measures. Local governments received orders from the top without the financial support to implement those orders. Duterte's threats also became commonplace in his weekly addresses. Less than a month into the quarantine, he ordered the police and the military to kill violators. "My orders are to the police and military, also village officials, that if there is trouble or the situation arises that people fight and your lives are on the line, shoot them dead."[38] He also commanded the local governments to punish those violating national government restrictions, or the so-called *pasaway* (disobedient).[39]

At the local level, this statement was interpreted in many ways. In Santa Cruz, Laguna, (south of Manila) five children were put inside a dog cage for violating the evening curfew. Two individuals were placed in a coffin in Cavite for the same offence. In several localities, groups of young LGBTQ residents were forced to kiss and dance and asked to strip naked or cut their hair as punishment. In Tacloban, a mother was imprisoned for allowing her children to play. The list goes on.

Despite all these issues, Duterte remained popular until the end of his term (see Figure 9.1). His pandemic response was also perceived as satisfactory. The public acknowledged several controversies, such as the face shield fiasco with Pharmally,[40] the Social Amelioration Program (SAP) subsidy distribution anomalies, or the incompetence of then Secretary of Health Francisco Duque, but Duterte was shielded from all these. Such unprecedented immunity gave Duterte a license to make policy proclamations, orders, and commands that tap into not only the former powers of the president but also the informal politics and residual powers of the office. More importantly, Duterte's exercise of his powers—his centralizing tendencies, exacerbated by weak state capacity—eclipsed the authority and autonomy of local governments in many respects.

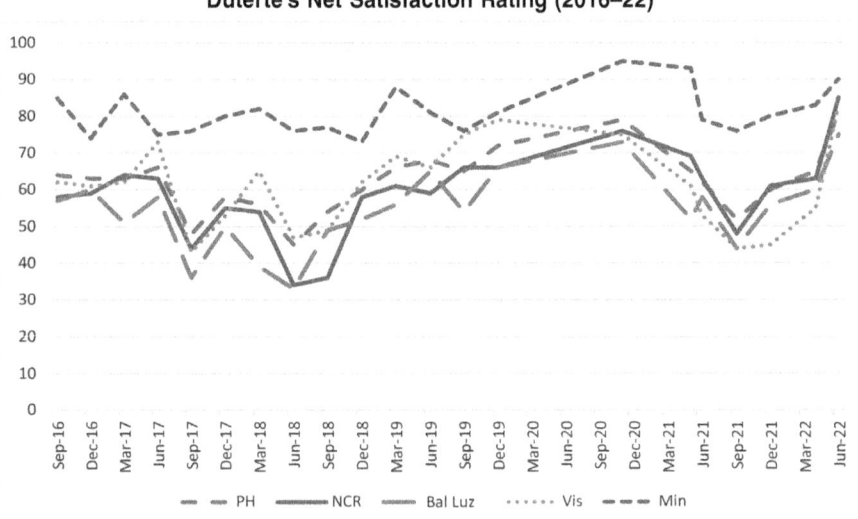

FIGURE 9.1
Duterte's Net Satisfaction Rating (2016–22)

Source: Social Weather Stations.

PANDEMIC AS A NEW CONTEXT OF LOCAL ELECTIONS

2022 is an election year in the Philippines. It is a critical election since almost all officials will be up for grabs—from the president, the members of Congress to the municipal officials. One of the challenges during the pandemic, then, is how the elections will be held amidst the restrictions. Several scenarios were floated, including the cancellation of elections altogether. This meant Duterte and the rest of the national and local officials would remain in power in a holdover capacity. As this idea did not sit well with many, primarily those with political ambitions, the suspension of the 2022 elections did not materialize.

In a way, the local elections served as a referendum on the quality and effectiveness of the pandemic strategies employed by local governments, as local officials became the front liners in designing their specific strategy based on the IATF-approved national framework. Incumbent governors and mayors, who were due for re-election, had to perform and be more visible online through social media and offline on the ground. Those ending their third term also needed to show up if they wanted their anointed successors to win. In effect, the local pandemic response became another criterion for choosing the candidate, on top of the usuals in Philippine local politics—name and fame, connections and networks, and money.[41]

If anything, the pandemic exacerbated the sorry state of Philippine local politics. In the pre-pandemic era, local politics and elections have always been marred by violence, coercion, and extensive vote buying, especially in rural communities. Controlling the electorate was more manageable during the pandemic. With the imposition of localized lockdown, officials can immobilize supporters and campaigns of electoral opponents while allowing free passes to their own factions and loyalists. In addition, political dynasties have their localities within the grasp of their hands by dispensing pandemic-related assistance to their constituencies, ensuring electoral victory.

As usual, the national races, particularly the presidency, overshadowed the attention on local political contests. Media coverage and social media discussions centred on Bongbong Marcos Jr. and Leni Robredo.[42] Despite the ongoing pandemic, campaign sorties became a show-of-force competition between the camps. The huge crowds at campaign events suggested that the public was more concerned now with the elections than the pandemic. However, the long-standing attempts to revise history and cleanse the image of the Marcoses, including the efforts of Duterte to valorize the Marcoses, proved to be a force more significant than the pandemic.[43] Despite her clear agenda of moving forward and recovering from the pandemic, Robredo lost by a large percentage to Marcos Jr.

More than the pandemic narratives and social media discussions, local politics played a significant role in the success of Marcos Jr.'s campaign. Many local politicians expressed their support for Marcos Jr. from the very beginning. In fact, it was clear to them what a Marcos Jr. presidency would be like—a continuation of their rule in their localities. Marcos Jr. does not seem to be one who will shake the system but rather let the system work on its own. For one, Marcos Jr. ran with Duterte's daughter Sara as his vice president, which solidified the backing for their ticket.[44] Thus, the overwhelming support of governors and mayors across the country meant Marcos Jr.'s candidacy would be carried. And with the pandemic as the new context for the elections, local officials have a sense of security that the voters remain under their close control.

MARCOS JR. BECOMES PRESIDENT

On 30 June 2022, Bongbong Marcos Jr. assumed the Philippine presidency. There is a noticeable departure from the ways of his predecessor, Duterte. The politics of informality under Duterte was replaced by Marcos Jr.'s restoration of the old political game rules. If Duterte constructed his position as a city mayor-turned-president with authoritarian fantasies, I argue that Marcos Jr. is far simpler, yet lacklustre. Based on his first six months as president, it seems he is a placeholder president without any active and conscious effort to redefine his office the way Duterte did. This is evident in the lack of clear policy directions on many aspects, including the pandemic and the absence of a well-defined agenda for local governments.

Interestingly, like Duterte, Marcos Jr. had experience at the local level. He served as vice governor and later governor of Ilocos Norte province for almost fifteen years. However, unlike Duterte,[45] he occupied a national position as a one-term senator. As a senator, he chaired the Senate Committee on Local Governments. Later, in several speeches delivered as president, Marcos Jr. claims his experience at the local level allowed him to understand the situation and contexts of those far from the direct reach of the national capital.[46] However, a closer inspection of his presidential agenda shows otherwise, with the lack of concrete programmes to help improve local governance. What follows, then, is a post-pandemic scenario that is "business as usual", which ought to preserve the status quo.

Pandemic as "Business as Usual"

In his first State of the Nation Address (SONA) less than a month into his presidency, Marcos Jr. said he was not inclined to continue the quarantine measures implemented during the Duterte administration. For him, lockdowns and other similar policies hurt the economy. The direction he wants to follow is the loosening of restrictions and a route back to normalcy. Many local governments followed this principle and implemented relaxed policies in their locality. One after another, local officials issued orders and ordinances that reverted the rules to pre-pandemic contexts. This would make sense, though, if the world has already completely overcome the pandemic. At that time, the number of cases remained high. While significant COVID-19 surges did not occur anymore, people still felt the effects of the pandemic.

Marcos Jr. was sending mixed messages with regard to the pandemic. On the one hand, he claims to give full attention to the pandemic and related issues, and minimizing the number of cases, in the long run, was the objective. On the other hand, his actions show the reverse. During the first year of his presidency, the Department of Health (DOH) did not get a full-time secretary among the executive departments. Dr Maria Rosario Vergiere, an undersecretary, served as the officer-in-charge of the department until the appointment of Dr Teodoro Herbosa as secretary in June 2023. Initially, Marcos Jr. refused to appoint a secretary and argued that DOH would only have a secretary once the pandemic ended, which is ironic given the pandemic is primarily a public health concern. Having a full-time DOH secretary at that time would have allowed the department to fully mobilize its resources and set its direction for the pandemic response and beyond.

On several occasions, the DOH has been bypassed by other executive departments in decisions regarding the pandemic. For example, despite the medical professionals' opposition, Marcos Jr. lifted the mask mandate nationwide.[47] In one press briefing, the Tourism Secretary announced that an executive order making mask-wearing optional would be released. In another instance, according to statements of economic managers, the government decided to remove the screening requirements when travelling domestically, notwithstanding the constant increase in the number of cases in the country. In fact, the DOH has not been as frequent in reporting COVID-19 cases. The sensible conclusion is that the Marcos Jr. administration no longer prioritizes the pandemic. The treatment of the pandemic under the new administration is that we are fully back to normal, even before the WHO officially "ended" the pandemic. In July 2023, Marcos Jr. finally lifted the national state of health emergency.

Under Marcos Jr., the government's priority is economic recovery. This priority is not without merits. During the lockdowns, many small- and medium-scale industries faced significant losses and had to close their businesses or lay off workers. Unemployment rates were high, while the inflation and foreign exchange rates rose to record levels. Many of the interventions by the government focus now on reducing the impact of these economic issues on businesses and the prices of commodities. However, focusing on economic recovery must be balanced with the prioritization of the health sector, whether there is a pandemic or not. After all, a healthy population would mean an economically viable population.

Silence on Reforms, Preserving the Status Quo

In the 19th Congress, there are renewed initiatives to amend the constitution, but these do not include further devolution to the local level, unlike the proposals during the Duterte administration. Likewise, Marcos Jr. has shut down the idea of charter change, including the federalism agenda, during his term. More importantly for local governments, Marcos Jr. has not explicitly taken a position on whether he intends to pursue extensive local government reforms.[48] The lack of clear policy direction has been an ongoing criticism of the Marcos Jr.

administration. Even during the presidential campaign, his platform of government was not well-defined. He skipped the debates and only granted interviews where he felt comfortable.

Such silence from the chief executive, then and now, indicates his preference to keep the status quo. Marcos Jr. benefitted from the support of the local elites during the 2022 elections, as argued above. Changing the rules of the game now is like betraying the very source of his electoral victory. Local political dynasties are arguably an essential asset to the Marcos Jr. presidency. As the national level takes care of the more significant issues, such as the sugar and onion crises, the families and clans in power ensure that the local narratives remain in favour of the Marcoses. Marcos Jr. sees this as a means to create stability—or "unity"—both at the national and local level, where Duterte tried to centralize control in his person and polarize the public. Clearly, the two presidents were using different playbooks.

Marcos Jr. is also a popular president. He received the highest number and percentage of votes for a presidential candidate in post-authoritarian Philippines. He received a 78 per cent approval rating for his first seven months in office.[49] Therefore, like in Duterte's case, local officials would most likely submit to the directives of the national level, particularly of the president. Resistance to a Marcos Jr. presidency is also less likely at this point. However, such acquiescence is not out of fear of an authoritarian leader but the political mandate that flows from his election. Whether he will maintain the support from local officials remains to be seen. That is why Marcos Jr. refrains from making too many changes and modifications that could hurt the interest of the local elites and officials. Equally important is that Sara Duterte is more popular and has a higher approval rating of 83 per cent. One can argue that Sara's prominence is a spillover from the older Duterte.

Thus, while the review of the thirty-two-year-old Local Government Code is long overdue,[50] a total overhaul or a systematic reform is probably unlikely under a Marcos Jr. presidency. Indeed, some provisions need to be amended considering recent local developments, changing political landscape, and jurisprudence. Delivering health, education, and other social services continues to burden many local governments, even with a revised national tax allocation scheme, especially in the context of a post-pandemic Philippines. But for political survival, Marcos Jr. remains silent on the reforms he intends to do, if any.

CONCLUSION

This chapter discussed the changing local political dynamics during the Duterte presidency and the first months of the Marcos Jr. administration. This analysis is situated within the context of the COVID-19 pandemic. While many of the observations on Philippine local politics remained the same, the leadership of Duterte and Marcos Jr undoubtedly shaped the national and local picture. Their approaches to the pandemic revealed the unqualified strength of the presidency as constructed by its occupants versus the gradual erosion of local autonomy.

Under Duterte, central-local relations did not significantly improve. Despite developments that could empower local governments, such as the Mandanas-Garcia ruling, the centre backpedalled and remanded more responsibilities to the local officials. Duterte, once a city mayor, used his position to control local governments and coerce their officials to his bidding—a consistent observation from the war on drugs to the pandemic response. With Duterte's almost absolute exercise of power, the cracks in the decentralization framework became more apparent. The extensive use of oversight and disciplinary power, bordering on intimidation, by the chief executive weakened and threatened the authority of local governments. During the pandemic, local autonomy was set aside in favour of the national government's strong arm.

As for Marcos Jr. administration, the pandemic as an issue was discarded and replaced by efforts to boost business and economic interests. Safeguards and restrictions were lifted, and the public was encouraged to go out and spend. Local governments responded to the new national framework and reopened their areas to tourists and businesses. Meanwhile, DOH, the lead agency in the pandemic response, had a full-time secretary only one year after Marcos Jr. began his term. Regarding local reforms, Marcos Jr. has been silent about his agenda and keeps the status quo to satisfy the local elites.

What lies ahead? The remaining years of Marcos Jr. administration would be important for local government reforms. Improving health and other service sectors is no longer an option but an imperative. Taking from the lessons learnt during the pandemic, efforts should be made at the national and local levels and equip the officials and the public should other crises come—whether health or environmental. The government needs to strengthen the capacity of the local governments in different governance aspects. For one, the Mandanas-Garcia ruling can enable greater fiscal decentralization. Amending provisions of the Local Government Code on fund utilization, creating a health sector funding source (like the Special Education Fund), redistributing powers and functions reflecting the realities on the ground are the first steps to achieving a more effective local governance.

Indeed, the centralizing strategies of Duterte, coupled with the weak state capacity, did not benefit the people in the long run, nor did Marcos Jr's tolerance of local elite capture. After all, the goal is about survival—to stay in power. But the public can constantly challenge the current local political dynamics, albeit complex. That is one step closer to meaningful reform at the local level.

Notes

1. This was done belatedly. Initially, the Philippine government hesitated to impose travel bans, especially for Chinese tourists. See Janine Peralta, "Duterte Not Keen on Banning Travel to China amid Coronavirus Scare", *CNN Philippines*, 29 January 2020, https://www.cnnphilippines.com/news/2020/1/29/duterte-on-china-travel-ban.html.
2. Perla E. Legaspi, "The Changing Role of Local Government under a Decentralised State: The Case of the Philippines", *Public Management Review* 3, no. 1 (2001): 131–39.
3. Kerry Brown and Ruby Congjiang Wang, "Politics and Science: The Case of China and the Coronavirus", *Asian Affairs* 51, no. 2 (2020): 247–64, https://doi.org/10.1080/03068374.2020.1752567. The same is true for antiliberal regimes in Eastern Europe, see Dorothee Bohle, Gergő Medve-Bálint, Vera Šćepanović, and Alen Toplišek, "Riding the Covid Waves: Authoritarian Socio-economic Responses of East Central Europe's Anti-liberal Governments", *East European Politics* 38, no. 4 (2022): 662–86, https://doi.org/10.1080/21599165.2022.2122044.
4. Joseph Ward and Bradley Ward, "From Brexit to COVID-19: The Johnson Government, Executive Centralisation and Authoritarian Populism", *Political Studies* (2022), https://doi.org/10.1177/00323217211063730.

5. Fawzia Gibson-Fall, "Military Responses to COVID-19: Emerging Trends in Global Civil-Military Engagements", *Review of International Studies* 47, no. 2 (2021): 155–70, https://doi.org/10.1017/S0260210521000048.
6. Michael R. Kenwick and Beth A. Simmons, "Pandemic Response as Border Politics", *International Organization* 74 (Supplement) (2020): E36–E58.
7. Argyrios Altiparmakis, Abel Bojar, Sylvain Brouard, Martial Foucault, Hanspeter Kriesi, and Richard Nadeau, "Pandemic Politics: Policy Evaluations of Government Responses to COVID-19", *West European Politics* (2021), https://doi.org/10.1080/01402382.2021.1930754.
8. Sarah Engler, Palmo Brunner, Romane Loviat, Tarik Abou-Chadi, Lucas Leemann, Andreas Glaser, and Daniel Kübler, "Democracy in Times of the Pandemic: Explaining the Variation of COVID-19 Policies across European Democracies", *West European Politics* (2021), https://doi.org/10.1080/01402382.2021.1900669; Stephen Thompson and Eric C. Ip, "COVID-19 Emergency Measures and the Impending Authoritarian Pandemic", *Journal of Law and the Biosciences* 7, no. 1 (2020), https://doi.org/10.1093/jlb/lsaa064.
9. Ferdinand Marcos Jr., "First State of the Nation Address", Official Gazette, 2021, https://www.officialgazette.gov.ph/2021/07/26/ferdinand-r-marcos-jr-first-state-of-the-nation-address-july-25-2022/.
10. Joseph Estrada was also a mayor from 1969 to 1986. While he also enjoys extensive local experience, the context and existing legal framework are not the same with that of Duterte.
11. One can argue that he proposed adopting federalism, and such a proposal is supposed to benefit the local governments. However, Duterte gave up on this agenda after the 2019 midterm elections. There was also no systematic review of the local government conditions that would necessitate such radical change.
12. Maria Ela L. Atienza and Jan Robert R. Go, "Assessing Local Governance and Autonomy in the Philippines: Three Decades of the 1991 Local Government Code", Discussion Paper Series 2023-05 (Quezon City: UP Centre for Integrative and Development Studies, 2023).
13. Paul D. Hutchcroft and Weena Gera, "Duterte's Tight Grip over Local Politicians: Can It Endure?" New Mandala, Research Brief, February 2021, https://www.newmandala.org/wp-content/uploads/2021/02/Central-Local-Relations-under-Duterte.pdf.
14. Jan Robert R. Go, "Decentralisation Experiences in the Philippines: Social Services Sectors and the Local Government Code of 1991", in *A Better Metro Manila? Towards Responsible Local Governance, Decentralization and Equitable Development*, edited by Teresa S. Encarnacion Tadem and Maria Ela L. Atienza (Singapore: Palgrave Macmillan, 2023), pp. 157–92.
15. Ibid.

16. Paul D. Hutchcroft and Weena Gera, "Strong-Arming, Weak Steering: Central-Local Relations in the Philippines in the Era of the Pandemic", *Philippine Political Science Journal* 43, no. 2 (2022): 123–67, https://doi.org/10.1163/2165025x-bja10037. They argued that the local autonomy rhetoric of Duterte is different from reality.
17. Athena Charanne R. Presto, "Mayors Are Keeping the Philippines Afloat as Duterte's COVID-19 Response Flails", *New Mandala*, 8 July 2020, https://www.newmandala.org/mayors-are-keeping-the-phillippines-afloat-as-dutertes-covid-19-response-flails/.
18. See Atienza, "Duterte's Federalism and Constitutional Change Project: From Campaign Promise to Abandoned Reform" (Chapter 5 of this volume).
19. Sofia Tomacruz, "'Stand Down': Duterte Orders LGUs to Follow IATF Orders on Luzon Lockdown", *Rappler*, 20 March 2020, https://www.rappler.com/nation/255214-duterte-orders-local-government-units-follow-orders-luzon-lockdown/.
20. Readers may take interest in Lasco's work on medical populism, using the cases of Duterte, Donald Trump of USA, and Jair Bolsonaro of Brazil. Gideon Lasco, "Medical Populism and the COVID-19 Pandemic", *Global Public Health* 15, no. 10 (2020): 1417–29, https://doi.org/10.1080/17441692.2020.1807581.
21. Michael I. Magcamit and Aries A. Arugay, "Rodrigo Duterte and the Making of a Populist Demigod: Part 1", *The Asia Dialogue*, 2017, https://theasiadialogue.com/2017/03/17/rodrigo-duterte-and-the-making-of-a-populist-demigod-part-1/.
22. Hutchcroft and Gera, "Duterte's Tight Grip over Local Politicians". They argued that Duterte held the local politicians through patronage and clientelism.
23. Peter Kreuzer, "Governors and Mayors in the Philippines: Resistance to or Support for Duterte's Deadly War on Drugs", PRIF Report 5 (Frankfurt am Main: Peace Research Institute and Leibniz-Institut Hessische Stiftung Friedens-und Konfliktforschung, 2020), https://nbnresolving.org/urn:nbn:de:0168-ssoar-71309-0.
24. Luke Lischin, "Duterte's Drug War: The Local Government Dimension", *The Diplomat*, 14 April 2018, https://thediplomat.com/2018/04/dutertes-drug-war-the-local-government-dimension; Kreuzer, "Governors and Mayors in the Philippines".
25. Lowell Bautista characterized this as a "tragic blood bath", see Lowell B. Bautista, "Duterte and His Quixotic War on Drugs", *Thinking ASEAN* 20 (2017): 2–5. See also Franco, "Experiencing Grief: Duterte's Lethal Drug War and Its Widows" (Chapter 6 of this volume).

26. Nestor Corrales, "Palace Confirms Existence of 'Oust-Duterte Plot'", *Inquirer.net*, 22 April 2019, https://newsinfo.inquirer.net/1109147/palace-confirms-existence-of-oust-duterte-plot.
27. Mark Thompson, "Brute Force Governance: Public Approval despite Policy Failure during the COVID-19 Pandemic in the Philippines", *Journal of Current Southeast Asian Affairs* 41, no. 3 (2022): 399–421, https://doi.org/10.1177/18681034221092453.
28. Alexis Romero, "Duterte Vows to Suspend Local Officials Allowing Corruption to Thrive", *Philstar.com*, 12 November 2017, https://www.philstar.com/headlines/2017/11/12/1758229/duterte-vows-suspend-local-officials-allowing-corruption-thrive.
29. Jorge Tigno, ed., "A Primer on Bayanihan to Heal as One Act of 2020", UP Department of Political Science, 2020, https://polisci.upd.edu.ph/resources/bayanihan-primer/.
30. Maria Ela L. Atienza, "The Politics of Health Devolution in the Philippines: Experiences of Municipalities in a Devolved Set-up", *Philippine Political Science Journal* 25, no. 48 (2004): 25–54, https://doi.org/10.1080/01154451.2004.9754256.
31. Go, "Decentralisation Experiences in the Philippines".
32. Jan Robert R. Go, "Health Services and Re-election in Philippine Municipalities", 한국정책학회 추계학술발표논문집 [Korean Association of Policy Studies Autumn Papers] 2016, UCI (KEPA): I410-ECN-0102-2017-350-000497083.
33. Nicole Curato, "Flirting with Authoritarian Fantasies? Rodrigo Duterte and the New Terms of Philippine Populism", *Journal of Contemporary Asia* 47, no. 1 (2017): 142–53, https://doi.org/10.1080/00472336.2016.1239751.
34. Several works refer to Duterte as populist. For example, the work of Paul Kenny and Ronald Holmes looked at the combination of Duterte's populism, authoritarian attitudes, and harsh notions of justice against the "penal populism" thesis. See Paul D. Kenny and Ronald Holmes, "A New Penal Populism? Rodrigo Duterte, Public Opinion, and the War on Drugs in the Philippines", *Journal of East Asian Studies* 20, no. 2 (2020): 187–205.
35. Eliseo F. Huesca Jr. and Margie D. Fiesta, "Everyday Voices in Marginal Places: Political Anxiety, Resistance, and Mass Support under Duterte's Martial Law", Working Paper No. 44, Institute of Asian Studies, Universiti Brunei Darussalam, 2018, https://ias.ubd.edu.bn/wp-content/uploads/2020/12/working_paper_series_44.pdf.
36. A special issue of the *Philippine Political Science Journal* (PPSJ) dealt with the notion of "Dutertismo". See Antonio P. Contreras, "Rodrigo Duterte as Ideology: Academic vs. Social Media Myths and Representations and

Their Implications to Political Order", *Philippine Political Science Journal* 41, no. 1–2 (2020): 48–72, https://doi.org/10.1163/2165025X-BJA10004.
37. Maria Ela L. Atienza, "The Philippines under Lockdown: Continuing Executive Dominance and an Unclear Pandemic Response", in *Routledge Handbook of Law and the COVID-19 Pandemic*, 1st ed., edited by Joelle Grogan and Alice Donald (London: Routledge, 2022), pp. 445–56, https://doi.org/10.4324/9781003211952.
38. AFP, "Duterte to Philippine Police: Shoot Dead Coronavirus Lockdown Troublemakers", *Gulf News*, 2 April 2020, https://gulfnews.com/world/asia/philippines/duterte-to-philippine-police-shoot-dead-coronavirus-lockdown-troublemakers-1.1585816367011.
39. Hapal has an extensive treatment of this label. Karl Hapal, "The Philippines' COVID-19 Response: Securitising the Pandemic and Disciplining the Pasaway", *Journal of Current Southeast Asian Affairs* 40, no. 2 (2021): 224–44, https://doi.org/10.1177/1868103421994261.
40. One of the controversies during the pandemic is the over-priced government purchase of face shields. See Mara Cepeda, "List: Everything You Need to Know about the Pharmally Pandemic Deals Scandal", *Rappler*, 17 December 2021, https://www.rappler.com/newsbreak/iq/list-everything-need-to-know-pharmally-covid-19-pandemic-deals-scandal/.
41. Julio C. Teehankee and Cleo Anne A. Calimbahin, eds., *Patronage Democracy in the Philippines: Clans, Clients, and Competition in Local Elections* (Quezon: Bughaw, 2022).
42. Maria Elize H. Mendoza, "Philippine Elections 2022: TikTok in Bongbong Marcos' Presidential Campaign", *Contemporary Southeast Asia* 44, no. 3 (2022): 389–95.
43. Dean Dulay, Allen Hicken, Anil Menon, and Ronald Holmes, "Continuity, History, and Identity: Why Bongbong Marcos Won the 2022 Philippine Presidential Election", *Pacific Affairs* 96, no. 1 (2023), https://doi.org/10.5509/202396185.
44. Mely Caballero-Anthony, "A Marcos Returns to Power in the Philippines", Brookings Institute, 13 May 2022, https://www.brookings.edu/blog/order-from-chaos/2022/05/13/a-marcos-returns-to-power-in-the-philippines/.
45. Duterte served as a member of the House of Representative for one term (1998–2001). His constituency is Davao City's first legislative district.
46. Presidential Communications Office, "Speech by President Ferdinand R. Marcos Jr. at the 2023 General Assembly of the League of Municipalities of the Philippines", 22 February 2023, https://pco.gov.ph/presidential-speech/speech-by-president-ferdinand-r-marcos-jr-at-the-2023-general-assembly-of-the-league-of-municipalities-of-the-philippines/.

47. Mask wearing carries symbolism and communicates political, social and cultural values. These were explored in Mathea Melissa Lim and Jesse Hession Grayman, "Humanitarian Objects for COVID-19: Face Masks and Shields in the Philippines", *Philippine Political Science Journal* 43, no. 2 (2022): 224–51, https://doi.org/10.1163/2165025x-bja10033.
48. Maria Ela L. Atienza, "The Prospects of Local Governance, Devolution, and Local Autonomy Under Marcos II", *Australian Outlook*, 12 January 2023, https://www.internationalaffairs.org.au/australianoutlook/the-prospects-of-local-governance-devolution-and-local-autonomy-under-marcos-ii/.
49. Gabriel Pabico Lalu, "Marcos, VP Duterte Get High Approval Ratings in Latest Pulse Asia Survey", *Inquirer.net*, 12 April 2023, https://newsinfo.inquirer.net/1755331/marcos-duterte-get-high-approval-ratings-in-latest-pulse-asia-survey.
50. Atienza and Go, "Assessing Local Governance and Autonomy in the Philippines".

10

An Unchanging Terrain? Environment and Climate Change in the Philippines from Duterte to Marcos, Jr.

Ruth R. Lusterio-Rico

> *When Rodrigo Duterte was elected as president of the Philippines in 2016, many promises of change were made, including those about the protection of the environment and making the country climate resilient. Duterte seemed quite serious, especially after delivering strong-worded speeches against mining companies and their destructive activities and choosing an environment advocate to head the Department of Environment and Natural Resources (DENR). However, after six years in power, the Duterte administration only managed to give the Filipino people empty promises accompanied by an artificial beach in the nation's national capital and a full reversal of his stance on mining. Despite this, the results of the 2022 presidential elections appear to have not been affected by the Duterte administration's poor performance in environmental protection and climate change*

as a landslide victory in the polls was achieved by the tandem of Ferdinand Marcos Jr. and Sara Duterte. This chapter aims to provide an analysis of the policy legacies of the Duterte administration in the area of environment and climate change. It narrates Duterte's pronouncements to protect the environment and the Filipino people and examines what had happened to these. As it became clear in the end that Duterte prioritized interests other than those that he promised to uphold, the chapter attempts to determine the prospects for policy change and identify some policy recommendations for the administration of Ferdinand Marcos Jr.

Keywords: environment; Duterte; climate change; Marcos Jr.; Philippines

INTRODUCTION

The Philippines may be considered as one of the richest countries in the world if wealth is measured by the diversity of life. The country is home to over a thousand species of land mammals, birds, reptiles, and amphibians. It is considered a "mega-diversity" rivalled by only a few countries in the world when it comes to the variety of ecosystems, species, and genetic resources. However, the Philippines is also a biodiversity hotspot as the destruction of important natural resources is experienced at an alarming rate. The major causes of such destruction are overexploitation, deforestation, land degradation, pollution, and climate change.[1]

The Philippines is likewise identified as one of the countries that are most vulnerable to the impacts of climate change.[2] Various areas of the country, especially large urban areas where a majority of the population reside, are affected by devastation caused by natural hazards. An average of twenty tropical cyclones enter the Philippine Area of Responsibility (PAR) every year.[3] These tropical cyclones affect both urban and rural areas throughout the country where the poor in both areas are most vulnerable. Aside from these, other major environmental challenges presently confront the Philippines. These include water scarcity, particularly in urban centres, waste management, air and water pollution, clean and renewable energy sources, and illegal and unregulated mining.

In the specific context of the Philippines, environmental protection, access to natural resources, and climate change mitigation and adaptation are determined by the policies adopted and implemented by the state. The Philippines, in fact, is one of the countries that has enacted several laws to address the protection of the environment, climate change, and disaster risk reduction and management. Since the 1990s, the Philippines has adopted the concept of sustainable development in its development strategy following the commitments made during the Earth Summit held in Rio de Janeiro, Brazil in 1992. The Philippine Council for Sustainable Development (PCSD) was created through Executive Order No. 15 signed by President Fidel V. Ramos on 1 September 1992. This Executive Order reiterates the mandate of the 1987 Constitution of the Republic of the Philippines that it is the state's policy to protect and advance "the right of the people to a balanced and healthful ecology".[4] Over the years, important pieces of environmental legislation have been enacted by the Philippine Congress. Among these are the Clean Air Act of 1999 (Republic Act 8749), the Ecological Solid Waste Management Act of 2000 (Republic Act 9003), and the Climate Change Act of 2009 (Republic Act 9729). While these laws were passed presumably with good intentions, much is still to be desired regarding their implementation.

The direct relationship between environmental issues and politics in the Philippines can be seen in the weak implementation of its environmental laws. Many Philippine environmentalists believe and have asserted that the environmental issue in the country is, more than anything else, an equity issue. While the state is viewed and considered as both steward and manager of the country's natural resources, the Philippine experience has shown that the state has been unable to properly balance the pursuit of economic development and the protection of the environment. The experiences of local communities adversely affected by development activities such as mining provide evidence of this.[5] Moreover, despite declarations from previous Philippine administrations that protecting the environment and people's lives are the top priorities, an effective response has thus far not been achieved.

It is in this context that this chapter aims to provide an analysis of the policy legacies of the Duterte administration in the area of environment and climate change. Such analysis, which is based on the overall environment and climate change policy adopted by Duterte, will hopefully provide a springboard for understanding the current Philippine administration's priorities and policy agenda. The first part of the chapter narrates how Duterte campaigned for the presidency and began his term with pronouncements that protecting the environment and the people's welfare would be the priority of his administration. How these pronouncements and the promises made turned out were reviewed in the next section. Two key issues—mining and climate resilience—are discussed to illustrate how Duterte failed in his pronouncements and promises as well as to show that the Duterte administration did not deviate from previous Philippine administrations in terms of dealing with these issues. The last part of the chapter attempts to identify some policy recommendations for the current Philippine administration under Ferdinand Marcos Jr. based on the policy "legacy" of Duterte and the declarations that the new president himself had made.

DUTERTE'S PROMISES TO THE ENVIRONMENT

Part of Rodrigo Duterte's populist rhetoric when he ran for the presidency in 2016 was a strong stance for environmental protection, a clean environment, food security, and sustainable development. He once claimed he would be a green president and promised to enforce all environmental laws to protect people's lives. Duterte also promised to eradicate poverty, ensure job security, protect those in the agricultural sector and the fisherfolk, and overall, exterminate crime, drugs, and corruption.[6] These were huge promises that appealed to voters. Hence, presidential candidate Duterte was initially viewed by many, including environmentalists, as an ally. There was much hope that Duterte would fulfil his promises.

When Duterte was elected president of the Philippines, his electoral victory was considered overwhelming as he managed to get almost 40 per cent of the votes.[7] Indeed, his assumption to the presidency was full of great expectations from the Filipino people. Perhaps, part of fulfilling a promise he made during the election campaign, Duterte named a high-profile advocate of environmental protection, Regina Paz Lopez, as head of the Department of Environment and Natural

Resources (DENR). The commitment of his administration to protect the environment to ensure that lives and livelihoods are preserved and to prioritize the people's welfare was declared in Duterte's first three State of the Nation Addresses (SONA).[8] Duterte stated in his first SONA that he and Lopez "share the same paradigm: the interest of the country must come first".[9] One of the most remembered promises made by Duterte was stopping the massive environmental destruction caused by large-scale mining. In his first SONA, the newly elected president stated that he was strongly opposed to large-scale mining, specifically because of the ill effects it has brought to communities, and emphasized that his administration adheres to a "human approach to development and governance". Duterte likewise directed the military to intensify its support against illegal mining and logging and emphasized that this is to be done for the people's interest because their welfare must come first.

In the same address to the nation, Duterte also instructed the DENR to review all permits granted to companies involved in activities that affect the environment, including mining companies, and to ensure their compliance to environmental laws. Permits are to be suspended or revoked if these companies are found to be non-compliant. Aside from the issues concerning mining, Duterte also mentioned specific projects such as transforming the Laguna Lake area into a "vibrant economic zone" that will showcase ecotourism and give "priority in its entitlements to poor fishermen". The new president also announced the final closure and rehabilitation of the Carmona Sanitary Landfill and the exploration of appropriate waste-to-energy facilities.[10] Considering the time he spent talking about environmental issues and concerns, one could assume that the new president—who was already known for his bluntness and use of strong words and obscenities without hesitation—was dead serious about solving the environmental crisis in the country.

A year later, in his second SONA, President Duterte reiterated his strong stance against destructive mining and once again stressed the protection of the environment and local communities. He instructed local government officials and employees to do their part in monitoring mining operations. He likewise called on Congress to immediately pass a law—the National Land Use Act (NLUA)—which would ensure the rational and sustainable use of land and physical resources, given the competing needs of food security, housing, businesses, and environmental conservation.[11]

For his third SONA delivered in 2018, Duterte emphasized the environmental issues that must be addressed. He reiterated his call for the approval of NLUA, which was pending in the Senate at that time. He likewise made a call for the rehabilitation of Boracay Island and the need to provide support for those who will be adversely affected by the closure of the island to tourists. He also called on Congress with urgency to enact a law that will create a Department of Disaster Management which aims to strengthen the country's capacity for resilience to natural disasters. In this speech, Duterte repeated his warning to mining companies to stop destructive activities and repair what has been mismanaged. The president declared that his "policy in the utilization of these resources is non-negotiable: the protection of the environment must be a top priority, and extracted resources must be used for the benefit of the Filipino people, not just a select few."[12] Once again, he called on government agencies and local government units to uphold the "concept of intergenerational responsibility in [the exploration] and utilization of our mineral wealth, the protection and preservation of our biodiversity, anchored on the right to a balanced and healthy ecology".

After his third address to the nation, the focus on environmental issues in Duterte's speeches was no longer evident. In his fourth year as president, his statements were more general, giving a warning to local government units and stakeholders of tourist destinations "to take extra steps in the enforcement of our laws and the protection of our environment."[13] He briefly mentioned the start of the rehabilitation of Manila Bay and reiterated the need to have a Department of Disaster Resilience (DDR) which was earlier mentioned in the 2018 SONA as Department of Disaster Management. The last two speeches delivered in 2020 and 2021 also did not give the same emphasis on environmental and climate change issues as the first three speeches he gave, perhaps, because the country was already under a health crisis due to the COVID-19 pandemic at the time. However, no significant achievements were reported elsewhere regarding the environmental issues he discussed in his previous speeches.

Apart from the SONA, Duterte used other venues such as forums, interviews, and a regular weekly programme through the government radio station, to talk about issues that he considered important. On many occasions, Duterte did not hesitate to talk against the United Nations because of its criticisms of the former's war on drugs strategy and human rights violations. During the presidential campaign and after his election, Duterte also openly criticized the Paris Agreement on climate change (or the United Nations Framework Convention on Climate Change) stating that climate conferences do not accomplish anything and are a waste of time and money.[14] It should be noted, however, that despite this expressed stance, Duterte signed the ratification of the Paris Agreement and has sent official Philippine delegations to the Conferences of Parties (COP) in 2018, 2019, and 2021 where the commitments made by the country were periodically confirmed. In terms of climate justice, Duterte had called on ASEAN states to cooperate and make progressive countries accountable for climate change and to uphold climate justice.[15] He had also made the same declaration about making those responsible for the climate crisis accountable on several occasions, particularly during international meetings. However, environmental advocates in the Philippines believe that such a declaration was merely lip service.[16]

WHAT HAPPENED TO DUTERTE'S PROMISES?

It is quite understandable for environmental non-government organizations (ENGOs) and advocates to have had huge expectations of President Duterte considering the declarations that the latter had made during his campaign and in the early years of his administration. Duterte's appointment of a well-known environmentalist and anti-mining advocate as Secretary of Environment and Natural Resources surprised some sectors, to say the least. There was, indeed, much hope for the late Secretary Lopez to address one of the most controversial and contentious issues in the country. As head of the government agency responsible for taking care of the country's natural resources, Lopez took a strong position against large-scale mining which she believed to be not only environmentally destructive but also adversely affected people's lives. Early in Lopez's stint as Environment and Natural

Resources Secretary, the Department undertook an audit of the mining industry which resulted in the closure of twenty-three metallic mines and the suspension of five others in the first quarter of 2017.[17]

However, in May 2017, Lopez failed to get the confirmation of her appointment by the Commission on Appointments (CA), a powerful constitutional body whose membership is confined to members of Congress. Lopez's confirmation as DENR Secretary was rejected after three confirmation hearings conducted by the twenty-four-member body. It was reported that Lopez was questioned on her policies and competence in heading the DENR.[18] The mining industry welcomed the rejection of Lopez's appointment while the ENGO sector lamented the lost opportunity for the Duterte administration. Lopez was replaced by former military general Roy Cimatu who was appointed by Duterte less than a week after the CA rejected Lopez's appointment. The CA overwhelmingly approved the appointment of Cimatu as Secretary of Environment and Natural Resources in October 2017.[19]

As far as the issue of mining is concerned, there was a complete turnaround from Duterte's campaign promise and policy declaration as the moratorium for new mining agreements and the ban on open-pit mining were lifted in 2021. President Duterte, on 14 April 2021, issued Executive Order No. 130 to lift a nine-year moratorium on granting new mining permits in the country. It is believed that such a move was made in the mining industry to help revive the country's economy because of the impact of the COVID-19 pandemic. The mining industry was expected to support the Duterte administration's infrastructure projects and generate employment. For his part, DENR Secretary Cimatu reversed the ban on open-pit mining issued by his predecessor.

Certainly, the president's complete turnaround from his erstwhile strong opposition of mining disgusted environmental groups. There have been reports that mining activities have actually continued despite the pandemic thus putting people's lives in danger and creating tension between local government units and mining companies. There have also been reports of displacement of indigenous people's groups and threats on environmental defenders who were considered communist insurgents.

Aside from strongly addressing the issues surrounding the extractive industry of mining, expectations were likewise high in the push that the Duterte administration would give to the enactment of significant legislation on environment and climate change. Although not mentioned in any of his SONA, two important environmental laws were actually passed by the Duterte administration. These were Republic Act (RA) 11038, or the Expanded Protected Areas Act, approved on 22 June 2018 and RA 11285, or the Energy Conservation and Efficiency Act, which was signed into law on 12 April 2019. RA 11038 amends RA 7586, or the National Integrated Protected Areas System (NIPAS) Act, which was enacted in 1992. The new law expands legislation for all protected areas and promotes biodiversity conservation. RA 11285 makes energy conservation and efficiency mandatory and imposes strict sanctions for non-compliance to regulations set by the Department of Energy.

However, the important law which Duterte had called on Congress to enact—the NLUA—failed to be enacted. In three consecutive SONAs he delivered from 2017 to 2019, Duterte talked about the significance of this legislative measure. But these repeated calls were not heard by Duterte's allies in the legislature. Before the end of his term, a resolution and nineteen similar bills related to national land use remained pending in the House of Representatives' Committee on Land Use.[20] The NLUA, which supposedly aims to ensure the sustainable and efficient use of the country's land and physical resources, also did not get support in the Senate. The proposed bill remained pending in the Senate Committee on Environment, Natural Resources, and Climate Change whose head belongs to a family that owns one of the leading property development companies in the country. As a president who had strong support in both Houses of Congress, Duterte's influence could have been used to enact this important law.

The creation of a Department of Disaster Resilience (DDR) is another initiative pushed by the Duterte administration that needed the support of Congress. For Duterte and his cabinet members, the DDR had to be established to have a government agency that will focus on natural hazards and climate change. In his 2018 SONA, Duterte stated that this Department will respond to the "prevailing 21st century conditions and be empowered to best deliver an enhanced disaster resiliency and quick disaster response". In response to Duterte's call, several bills were introduced in the Senate in 2019. In the House of Representatives, a consolidated bill (House Bill 5989) had been approved and transmitted to the Senate on 24 September 2020. However, none of these measures were approved before the end of Duterte's term. Some ENGOs believe that this particular solution of the Duterte administration is not really an appropriate one to deal with the impact of natural hazards and climate change.[21] Indeed, if making the country climate resilient was in the agenda, a concrete plan of action that needs legislative support could have been articulated at the onset.

Duterte's Populist Environmental Policy

For the officials of the Duterte administration, the clean-up of tourist destinations, particularly Boracay Island and Manila Bay, are the major achievements that "define President Duterte's legacy on environment and climate governance".[22] In at least two of his SONAs, Duterte mentioned the clean-up and rehabilitation of tourist destinations as the priority environmental programme of his administration. On 26 April 2018, Duterte ordered the closure of Boracay Island to tourists for six months to allow a clean-up and rehabilitation. He subsequently issued Executive Order No. 53 to create the Boracay Interagency Task Force whose main function is to coordinate the tasks assigned to each member agency and local government unit and ensure the enforcement of all applicable laws and regulations.

In the case of Manila Bay, its clean-up and rehabilitation were likewise ordered in 2019, with the DENR spearheading the implementation of the Manila Bay rehabilitation project. The initiative to clean-up and rehabilitate an important water resource in the country is indeed laudable. However, the rehabilitation of Manila Bay stirred a controversy in September 2020 due to the overlaying of crushed dolomite sand in the Manila Bay beach in an attempt to create an artificial beach with white sand. For the DENR, this was important for "beach nourishment". But public criticism focused on its potential environmental and health hazards. More importantly, the move was criticized for its cost especially since the country was in the middle of a health and economic crisis brought about by the COVID-19 pandemic at that time.[23]

From the time of his presidential campaign until he became the country's president, Duterte had harshly criticized the actions of the United Nations, including the climate change meetings attended by government officials. As president, he had been vocal about his position that the rich, industrialized countries should pay for the costs of climate change. He likewise declared his disapproval in signing the Paris Agreement. Despite this, however, Duterte was eventually convinced by his cabinet members to sign the Paris Agreement. In fact, the country's Nationally Determined Contribution (NDC) was even increased from the initial 70 per cent commitment by 2030 (made in the Paris meeting in 2015) to 75 per cent (made in 2021). It should be noted, however, that a very small percentage (2.71 per cent) of this commitment is unconditional. This means that this is the part of the commitment that is supported by nationally mobilized resources. A very big part of the commitment (or 72.29 per cent) is conditional, which means that it requires support from developed countries. Although the Paris Agreement has reaffirmed the obligations of developed countries, the Philippines, for its part, has not come up with a climate financing scheme. Moreover, the Philippines is still very much dependent on coal since it is the most cost-effective source of energy for the country. The irony here is that the burning of fossil fuel, such as coal, increases greenhouse gas emission.[24]

Duterte's Environmental Legacy

There was much promise for environmental protection at the beginning of the Duterte administration. But that was all it was. The tough talk was neither translated into a concrete plan nor actual action. It was evident that what Duterte pronounced was not consistent with what his administration had actually done. No significant accomplishments in environment and climate change were made after six years in office. Environmental advocates and defenders are of the view that what Duterte left behind are problems. For some, Duterte has left behind a Philippine environment in crisis. The Philippines has become an even more dangerous place for environmental defenders as their lives are threatened and their basic rights violated. Throughout the Duterte administration, big development projects that have adverse impact on the environment were not really stopped. Those who opposed these projects to defend communities and the environment were even tagged as communists. The global watchdog, Global Witness, reported that the number of environmental defenders killed increased dramatically with Duterte in power. In 2018, the Philippines became the country with the greatest number of killings of land and environmental defenders.[25] For environmental advocates, this is the most harrowing legacy of Rodrigo Duterte. The lack of attention given to environment and climate change issues shows that what was important for Duterte were his war against illegal drugs and against communism.

Obviously, Duterte only used the anti-mining, pro-environment, pro-people rhetoric to his advantage. The lifting of the moratorium on new mining permits through Duterte's Executive Order signalled the primacy of the economy over the protection of the environment and local communities under his leadership. His declaration of putting the people's welfare on top of his administration's priorities is also questionable as development and infrastructure projects that have had an adverse impact on communities, including the displacement of indigenous peoples, were pursued. Duterte also proved to be a president who would not rock the boat. Although he talked tough on issues concerning the environment, he did not really exert a strong push to get Regina Lopez's appointment as DENR Secretary confirmed or have the needed legislation (i.e., NLUA) passed. In the final analysis, Duterte did not really change anything as far as environment and climate change issues are concerned.

WHAT TO EXPECT UNDER THE MARCOS JR. PRESIDENCY

In May 2022, Ferdinand Romualdez Marcos Jr. overwhelmingly won the presidential election over his closest rival, former vice president Leonor "Leni" Robredo. Electoral success was achieved by Marcos despite providing little information about his stance on various social and political issues, including those on environment and climate change. Throughout his campaign and that of his running mate (Sara Duterte), the need for the country's unity was emphasized. Marcos also pledged to continue his predecessor's policies and programmes.

In his inaugural speech on 30 June 2022 when he was sworn in as president of the Philippines, Marcos said that his administration will prioritize climate change issues. In this speech, the new president recognized the significance and urgency of addressing climate issues and said that he will seek the help of partners to help the country find solutions.

Environmentalists, however, observed the clear absence of an environment and climate agenda in Marcos's first SONA which he delivered on 25 July 2022. There was no mention in this speech about plans or legislation needed to implement programmes for environmental protection and to address the critical climate change issues. For environmental advocates, this omission indicates the priority that the new administration gives to economic development over people's welfare and environmental protection. For his first SONA, although the new president discussed energy security and renewable energy, he actually focused on the economic and development plans of his administration and did not discuss the controversial issue of mining, biodiversity and ecosystem protection, and upholding people's well-being and human rights particularly in areas where big development projects are undertaken, among others.[26]

About two weeks into office, Marcos nominated Ma. Antonia Yulo-Loyzaga, an expert in disaster risk reduction and climate protection, to be Secretary of Environment and Natural Resources. Yulo-Loyzaga's appointment was eventually confirmed by the Commission on Appointments on 27 September 2022. Such an appointment was welcomed by some pro-environment groups with optimism and have called on the new secretary to come up with an "environment agenda grounded on the needs of the people, environment, and the planet".[27] When news of Yulo-Loyzaga's appointment came out, there was hardly any opposition expressed by environment and civil society groups. The new secretary's professional experience and her being known by civil society groups have perhaps contributed to this seeming positive reception of her assumption to this crucial position. Some environmental groups, however, made calls for Secretary Yulo-Loyzaga to act on issues left behind by the Duterte administration such as the reversal of policies pertaining to mining and to declare a moratorium on destructive projects such as the Kaliwa Dam project.[28] Based on this, it seems that environmental groups expected the new Environment Secretary to implement changes and depart from the policy decisions made during Duterte's time.

Thus far, however, there seems to be no indication that there will be a significant shift in the policies pertaining to environment and climate change under the Marcos administration. Like Duterte, Marcos has declared himself to be a protector of the country against the impact of climate change and natural disasters. What he has emphasized so far is the strengthening of the people's resilience in meeting the adverse effects of climate change. Moreover, the Marcos administration is pursuing the path taken by the previous administration when it comes to the revival of the mining industry. The current Philippine administration considers mining as one of the important industries that could propel the country towards economic recovery. Marcos has declared that he is for "sustainable mining" and has ordered the DENR to bolster the enforcement of mining regulations, to assist small miners, and to study existing mining laws for possible legislative proposals that can be submitted to Congress. Hence, it is "business as usual" as far as mining is concerned, with the promise that the environmental regulations will be enforced well and properly.[29]

With respect to climate justice, so far, only pronouncements have been made. No concrete actions have been taken yet as regards the promise to seek the help of partners to find solutions to the climate issues that continue to affect the country. President Marcos was represented by DENR Secretary Yulo-Loyzaga who also served as head of the Philippine delegation in the 27th Conference of Parties to the United Nations Framework Convention on Climate Change (COP27) held in Egypt in November 2022. On this occasion, the Philippines asserted its "call for bolder climate action and demand the delivery of what is due for the developing countries".[30] So far, the impact of such a call is not yet known.

Into his second year in office, Marcos declared in his second SONA that "(t)he economic agenda cannot and will not ever be incompatible with our climate change agenda. Climate change is now an important criterion in our integral national policies, in planning, decision-making, up to the implementation of programs".[31] Like his predecessor, Marcos Jr. has made policy declarations without mentioning any specifics. The role of people's participation in this "new system" was likewise mentioned, but again, there was no mention of any particular plan on how this will be achieved.

THE ROAD AHEAD: CONCLUSION AND PROSPECTS

Like Duterte, Marcos has declared his pro-environment stance. It may not be as strong as how Duterte had declared his position, but still, Marcos's pronouncement of environmental protection and climate change as top priorities of his administration has been recorded. What remains to be seen is how such a declaration of priorities will be put in action. Clearly, the role of environmental and civil society groups remains crucial. These groups are important to make sure that demands are expressed and that government actions are monitored. As pro-environment groups have seen the current head of the DENR as someone who knows the situation on the ground, they have to sustain their efforts in making sure that demands are heard. Environmental and civil society groups can also support the government by providing information about communities that are severely affected by disasters and severe weather occurrences. As mentioned above, although President Marcos recognizes the importance of the participation of various sectors in carrying out the climate change agenda, there are no specific details yet on how this will be done.

Definitely, a balance between economic growth and the protection of the environment and its resources must be achieved by the government under Marcos's leadership in order to uplift the well-being of the Filipino people. After all, the ones most affected by environment and climate change issues are the majority of the Filipinos who are poor. The important question, however, is if the current political leadership is strong enough to withstand the pressures brought about by competing elite interests. Needless to say, a change in perspective in looking at environment and climate change issues is required. At present, the critical issues being raised by environment and civil society groups appear to be disregarded. If this continues, it is very likely that the environment and climate change terrain will remain unchanged.

Concretely, in the short-term, the Marcos administration needs to look into mining's real impact on the country, specifically looking at the actual gains that are enjoyed by the people who live in the mining communities. At present, the idea of "sustainable mining" is being adopted by the government as the industry is seen as a huge source of revenue for the country. Moreover, it appears that the administration sees the mining issue as one that can be simply resolved by enforcing regulations. If the impact on local communities is neglected, the cost of the undertaking might outweigh the potential benefits. Apart from mining, the Marcos administration, through the DENR, must also look into and carefully study the impact of development and infrastructure projects on local peoples, especially the indigenous communities. The review of the implementation of mining and development projects need to be done in the short-term and has to be prioritized. Finally, the president's declarations on climate change being a priority and an integral part of planning, decision-making, and implementation have to be accompanied by a concrete plan of action. The plan of action must clearly articulate how local government units and citizens will be a part of such a plan. On the part of civil society groups, their advocacies should be sustained while engaging policy and decision-makers. Overall, what is required to address the critical environment and climate change issues is a change in perspective, that is, to view people's lives within their environment as the priority.

Notes

1. Shaira Panela, "The Philippines: Where 'Megadiversity' Meets Mega Deforestation", *Mongabay*, 31 July 2014, https://news.mongabay.com/2014/07/the-philippines-where-megadiversity-meets-mega-deforestation/.
2. United States Agency for International Development (USAID), "Climate Risk Profile: Philippines", 8 February 2017, https://www.climatelinks.org/resources/climate-risk-profile-philippines (accessed 8 April 2023).
3. Philippine Atmospheric, Geophysical, and Astronomical Services Administration (PAGASA), Department of Science and Technology, "Tropical Cyclone Information", https://bagong.pagasa.dost.gov.ph/climate/tropical-cyclone-information (accessed 8 April 2023).
4. Republic of the Philippines, Official Gazette, Executive Order Number 15, s. 1992, 1 September 1992. https://www.officialgazette.gov.ph/1992/09/01/executive-order-no-15-s-1992/ (accessed 8 April 2023).
5. See, for example, Ruth R. Lusterio-Rico, "Globalization and Local Communities: The Mining Experience in a Southern Luzon, Philippine Province", *Philippine Political Science Journal* 34, no. 1 (2013): 48–61.
6. *Inquirer.net*, "#INQBack: Rodrigo Duterte's Agenda during the 2016 Campaign", 29 June 2016, https://newsinfo.inquirer.net/790812/inqback-president-rodrigo-duterte-agenda-2016-elections-campaign (accessed 28 March 2023).

7. Aries Arugay, "The Philippines in 2016: The Electoral Earthquake and Its Aftershocks", in *Southeast Asia Affairs 2017*, edited by Daljit Singh and Malcolm Cook (Singapore: ISEAS – Yusof Ishak Institute, 2017), pp. 277–96.
8. The State of the Nation Address or SONA is delivered by the Philippine president on the fourth Monday of July every year. In this address, the chief executive reports to the nation the state of the country and gives the agenda of his or her administration for the year. The president likewise enjoins Congress to enact the necessary laws to implement the identified programmes for the country.
9. Rodrigo Duterte, State of the Nation Address, 25 July 2016.
10. Jee Y. Geronimo, "Duterte: 'Amend, Suspend, Revoke' Environmental Permits, If Needed", *Rappler*, 25 July 2016, https://www.rappler.com/nation/140877-duterte-sona-2016-environmental-permits/.
11. Rodrigo Duterte, State of the Nation Address, 24 July 2017.
12. Rodrigo Duterte, State of the Nation Address, 23 July 2018.
13. Rodrigo Duterte, State of the Nation Address, 22 July 2019.
14. Pia Ranada, "Duterte Slams Climate Change Conferences for Accomplishing Nothing", *Rappler*, 31 May 2019, https://www.rappler.com/nation/231941-duterte-slams-climate-change-conferences-accomplishing-nothing/ (accessed 8 April 2023).
15. Climate Change Commission, "CCC Supports President Duterte's Call for ASEAN Member States to Step Up and Uphold Climate Justice", Press Release, 19 June 2019, https://climate.gov.ph/news/116 (accessed 8 April 2023).
16. Greenpeace Philippines, "Duterte's Climate Action Call a Little Too Late", 19 April 2022, https://www.greenpeace.org/philippines/press/53128/greenpeace-dutertes-climate-action-call-a-little-too-late/ (accessed 8 April 2023).
17. Department of Environment and Natural Resources, "Lopez Orders Closure of 23 Metallic Mines", 2 February 2017, https://www.denr.gov.ph/index.php/news-events/press-releases/520-lopez-orders-closure-of-23-metallic-mines (accessed 8 April 2023).
18. Eimor P. Santos, "CA Rejects Gina Lopez Appointment as DENR Chief", *CNN Philippines*, 3 May 2017, https://www.cnnphilippines.com/news/2017/05/03/CA-rejects-gina-lopez-denr-secretary.html (accessed 8 April 2023).
19. Jee Y. Geronimo, "CA Confirms Roy Cimatu as Environment Secretary", *Rappler*, 4 October 2017, https://www.rappler.com/nation/183468-ca-confirms-roy-cimatu-appointment-denr/ (accessed 8 April 2023).

20. Blanch Ancla and Jean L. Raoet, "SONA 2020 Promise Tracker: Environment", Vera Files, 25 July 2021, https://verafiles.org/articles/sona-2020-promise-tracker-environment (accessed 8 April 2023).
21. John Leo C. Algo, "Years Later, Department of Disaster Resilience Still the Wrong Solution", *Rappler*, 5 March 2023, https://www.rappler.com/voices/thought-leaders/opinion-years-later-department-of-disaster-resilience-still-the-wrong-solution/.
22. Statement by Acting DENR Secretary Jim Sampulna, "Duterte Legacy: Paving the Road towards More Sustainable, Climate Resilient PH", 1 June 2022, https://www.denr.gov.ph/index.php/news-events/press-releases/4031-duterte-legacy-paving-the-road-towards-more-sustainable-climate-resilient-ph (accessed 26 March 2023).
23. Kristian Karlo Saguin, "Urban Populist Ecologies and Duterte's Politics of Discipline in Manila's Dolomite Beach", *Political Geography* 92 (2022), https://doi.org/10.1016/j.polgeo.2021.102553.
24. Will Smith, "Climates of Control: Violent Adaptation and Climate Change in the Philippines", *Political Geography* 99 (2022): 1–10.
25. Global Witness, "Philippines", https://www.globalwitness.org/en/all-countries-and-regions/philippines/ (accessed 7 April 2023).
26. Ferdinand R. Marcos, Jr., State of the Nation Address, 25 July 2022.
27. Aaron Recuenco, "Pro-environment Groups Back Appointment of New DENR Chief", *Manila Bulletin*, 13 July 2022, https://mb.com.ph/2022/07/13/pro-environment-groups-back-appointment-of-new-denr-chief/ (accessed 14 April 2023).
28. Kalikasan People's Network for the Environment (KPNE) Secretariat, "Press Statement: Greens Urge New DENR Secretary to Impose Moratorium on Destructive Projects", 13 July 2022, https://kalikasan.net/moratorium-destructive-projects (accessed 20 April 2023).
29. Ruth Lusterio-Rico, "Talk is Cheap: The 2022 Philippine Elections' Climate Implications", *Fulcrum*, 18 April 2022, https://fulcrum.sg/talk-is-cheap-the-2022-philippine-elections-climate-implications.
30. Statement of the Philippine Delegation to the 27th Session of the Conference of Parties of the United Nations Framework Convention on Climate Change (COP27), 5 November 2022, https://www.denr.gov.ph/index.php/news-events/press-releases/4591-statement-of-the-philippine-delegation-to-the-27th-session-of-the-conference-of-parties-of-the-united-nations-framework-convention-on-climate-change-cop27 (accessed 21 April 2023).
31. Ferdinand R. Marcos, Jr. State of the Nation Address, 24 July 2023.

11
Mitigating Risks, Fostering Resilience: Human Security and Disaster Response Policy from Duterte to Marcos Jr.

Cherry Ann Madriaga

> *The Philippines has long been accustomed to confronting natural hazards. It consistently ranked as one of the most at-risk countries globally, with the World Risk Report classifying it as the country with the highest disaster risk in the world for 2022. This chapter focuses on the governance aspect of disasters and how the Duterte administration (2016–22) prepared, managed, and responded to the calamities that faced the country. Specifically, it tackles the implementation of the Disaster Risk Reduction and Management Act, the management of the country's calamity fund following consecutive and overlapping disasters, and the planned creation of the Department of Disaster Resilience, among others. As the Philippines is besieged by yet another disaster, this chapter also examines the policies of the*

new administration, under President Ferdinand Marcos Jr., based on the recent pronouncements and actions in the early part of his administration.

Keywords: natural hazards; disaster response; Duterte; Marcos Jr.; Philippines

INTRODUCTION

The Philippines is no stranger to natural hazards. Because it sits on the typhoon belt, the country is visited by an average of twenty typhoons each year, exacerbating flooding issues rampant all over the country. Due to its location within the Pacific Ring of Fire, it also experiences frequent earthquakes and disastrous volcanic eruptions.

Based on data compiled by the Emergency Events Database (EM-DAT),[1] the Philippines suffered from an annual average of 14 extreme events and major calamities from 2016 to the first seven months of 2023. During this period, the country faced around 53 storms, 7 of which were categorized as super typhoons, 17 flooding events, 14 earthquakes, eruptions from Taal Volcano and Mayon Volcano, epidemics like measles and dengue, landslides, and certain technological disasters.

With the earth continuously warming and the environment constantly destroyed, the probability of these hazards recurring, accompanied by increasingly catastrophic impacts, remains high. According to the most recent assessment of the Intergovernmental Panel on Climate Change (IPCC), human-induced climate change will likely worsen the frequency and intensity of extreme weather phenomena.[2]

With the high risk and exposure to various natural hazards, including slow-onset calamities such as rising sea levels and drought, and human-induced calamities, the Philippines has consistently ranked as one of the countries most at risk worldwide. Over half of the Philippine population lives in the coastal areas, around 18 per cent live below the poverty threshold, and about one-quarter are employed in the agriculture sector, a sector vulnerable to extreme weather events.

However, it is important to note that while natural hazards pose inherent risks, they do not necessarily constitute a disaster by themselves. The occurrence of a disaster is contingent not only on hazard exposure but also on society's vulnerability and capacity to mitigate, all of which are worsened by numerous drivers of risk, which include rising poverty and inequality, slow economic growth, unfettered urbanization, poor governance, and weak political institutions, among others.[3, 4]

Based on the World Risk Report 2022,[5] the Philippines has the unfortunate distinction of being ranked as the most disaster-risk nation in the world, underscoring the pressing need to develop comprehensive policies and programmes to address the issues of disaster risk reduction and management in the Philippines.

Disasters come at exorbitant costs, and this can hamper poverty reduction programmes and sustainable economic growth. According to the Department of Finance (DOF), from 2010 to 2020, the Philippines incurred damages and losses equivalent to 0.33 per cent of its annual average Gross Domestic Product (GDP), mainly affecting the agriculture and infrastructure sectors.[6] But these reported numbers often only consider the direct effects, which may result in underestimating their impact, especially in terms of the socio-cultural, economic, and environmental effects. However, despite suffering from multitudes of disasters over the past decades and the passage of Republic Act No. 10121, known as the Philippine Disaster Risk Reduction and Management (DRRM) Act of 2010, disaster preparedness in the Philippines remains wanting.

This chapter focused on the governance aspect of disasters and how former president Rodrigo Duterte and his administration prepared, managed, and responded to the calamities that faced the country. Specifically, it tackled the implementation of the DRRM Act, the management of the country's calamity fund following consecutive and overlapping disasters, and the planned creation of the Department of Disaster Resilience. As the Philippines is besieged by yet another disaster, it also examined the policies the new administration, under President Ferdinand Marcos Jr., will implement based on his recent pronouncements and actions.

BEFORE DUTERTE: THE DRRM LAW AND SUPER TYPHOON HAIYAN

Republic Act No. 10121: A Shift from Response to Prevention

Before delving into the disaster policies under Duterte's leadership, it is important to discuss the DRRM Law, the legal framework under which the government's disaster policies operates, as well as the limitations of and criticisms against the law. RA No. 10121 was primarily enacted to strengthen the country's disaster risk reduction and management system, shifting the focus towards disaster prevention and mitigation, and preparedness programmes instead of merely concentrating on response, relief, and rehabilitation efforts. The law called for the establishment of a coordinating and monitoring body called the National Disaster Risk Reduction and Management Council (NDRRMC), the creation and implementation of the National Disaster Risk Reduction and Management Plan (NDRRMP), the mainstreaming of DRRM with national and local development plans, the strengthening of capacity for disaster preparedness especially at the local levels, and the appropriation of government funds and resources for DRRM.

The NDRRMP for 2011–29[7] captures the overall strategic plan for DRRM in the Philippines to guarantee the welfare and security of Filipinos. Its goal includes achieving sustainable development by promoting inclusive growth, enhancing the adaptive capacities of communities especially against disasters, increasing the resilience of vulnerable sectors, and improving disaster mitigation measures. The concerns highlighted in the NDRRMP are intricately related to the medium-term Philippine Development Plan (PDP) 2017–22 and long-term national development strategies (*Ambisyon Natin* 2040). Furthermore, the plan is also consistent with international conventions, including the Sendai Framework, and its forerunner, the Hyogo Framework for Action, and the United Nations' Sustainable Development Goals (UN SDG).

In 2017, the NDRRMC conducted a midterm review of the NDRRMP. Its goal was to evaluate the country's progress in achieving the goals and targets outlined in the plan while identifying areas that need further improvement. The review acknowledged the significant progress, particularly in coordination and efficiency, that the Philippines has achieved in its DRRM efforts. Some of these accomplishments also include establishing early warning systems, community-based DRR, and initiatives to enhance the capacity of stakeholders involved in DRRM.[8]

However, the law's implementation and its corresponding NDRRMP were being criticized. Although the principles of DRRM have been instrumental in promoting the passage of programmes and development plans that complement and support the law, there remains a disconnect between the NDRRMP and other government agencies' plans and programmes.[9] Additionally, local government units (LGUs) may face fiscal constraints in their efforts to comply with the law, which may impede their ability to hire personnel with knowledge and expertise in DRRM and procure the necessary equipment to monitor and respond to disasters.

To enhance the law's effectiveness, it was stipulated that a sunset review be conducted five years after its date of effectivity or as deemed necessary. However, no review transpired in 2015, and until now Congress has yet to undertake such an evaluation. Because of this, civil society organizations (CSOs) such as the Disaster Risk Reduction Network Philippines (DRRNetPhils)—a collective of more than fifty civil society organizations, non-governmental organizations (NGOs), the academic community, and disaster experts, and a member of the NDRRMC—and the Partners for Resilience (PfR) conducted a comprehensive evaluation of the law. Both the PfR and DRRNetPhils highlighted some challenges in the implementation of the law especially at the local level.[10] Moreover, research studies evaluating the development and implementation of the DRRM Law until the end of Aquino's administration demonstrated that more work needs to be done to address the gaps and weaknesses in the Philippines' disaster policy.[11]

Super Typhoon Haiyan and the 2016 National Elections

One of the biggest tests for the government's DRRM system and the Philippines at large occurred in November 2013, with the entry of Super Typhoon Haiyan, considered to be one of the strongest tropical cyclones in the world and the deadliest Philippine typhoon in recorded history. Haiyan struck the Visayas region, which was recovering from a previous earthquake a month prior, Southern Luzon, and Northern

Mindanao and destroyed municipalities and cities, with estimated damages amounting to approximately US$2.05 billion. The impacts of Haiyan led to the loss of thousands of lives, with over 6,000 deaths. However, unofficial estimates suggest that the death toll could be much higher at around 10,000, more than a thousand people remained missing, and approximately 29,000 individuals injured.[12]

Before Haiyan, Duterte was not yet a familiar face to most of the population. He made his presence known when he travelled to Tacloban City in Eastern Visayas to provide aid and support to the affected communities, crying as he witnessed the effects of this devastation.

Contrast this emotional and seemingly compassionate response with the Aquino III administration's supposedly apathetic attitude to the disaster. Criticisms poured in on Aquino and other government officials for their sluggish and insufficient response, leaving many affected areas in desperate need of aid and assistance.[13] There were also complaints about the lack of transparency and inefficient coordination among government agencies and NGOs involved in relief and recovery activities.[14] These criticisms, which Duterte leveraged as an argument to discredit his presidential opponent,[15] combined with the magnitude of the devastation caused by Haiyan, drove public discontent and apprehensions about the Philippines' disaster preparedness and ability to manage large-scale disasters effectively.

A few years after Haiyan and Duterte's election to the Philippines' top-most position, however, a shift in public sentiment, at least in online spaces, was apparent. The disapproval previously directed at the Aquino administration's response to disasters were also now being thrown at the Duterte administration, an indication that the weaknesses of the Philippines' DRRM system persist. As typhoons battered the country, hashtags of #NasaanAngPangulo (translated to Where Is the President) proliferated social media spaces.[16] Despite frustrations over the Duterte administration's response to COVID-19 on top of various disasters, nonetheless, Duterte's approval ratings remained high.[17]

DISASTER POLICY IN THE TIME OF DUTERTE (2016–22)

The Philippines suffered from numerous disasters during the term of Duterte. Based on EM-DAT data, 2020 and 2021 were among the Philippines' top ten most costly years in terms of total damages.

Table 11.1 depicts the most destructive incidents that have occurred in the Philippines since 2016. The data displayed indicates that even milder weather phenomena, such as tropical storms, have the capacity to inflict substantial damage to the country. For instance, during the last month of 2018, Tropical Depression Usman brought in torrential rainfall in the Visayas and Bicol region. Despite being categorized as a relatively weak storm, the downpour, and its associated disasters like flooding and landslides, resulted in damages and losses amounting to US$124 million, killing 182 individuals, and affecting more than a million people.

TABLE 11.1
Ranking of the Most Destructive Calamities in the Philippines (2016–23)

Year	Event Name Local Name (International Name)	Total Damages, Adjusted ('000 US$)
2021	Super Typhoon Odette (Rai)	988,518.00
2020	Super Typhoon Rolly (Goni)	569,108.00
2020	Typhoon Ulysses (Vamco)	476,052.00
2019	Tropical Storm Falcon (Danas)	432,061.00
2018	Super Typhoon Rosita (Yutu)	355,465.00
2022	M7.0 Luzon Earthquake	151,000.00
2016	Typhoon Nina (Nock-Ten)	126,400.00
2019	Typhoon Tisoy (Kammuri)	124,947.00
2018	Tropical Depression Usman	124,416.00
2021	Severe Tropical Storm Maring (Kompasu)	111,381.00
2018	Tropical Storm Henry (Son Tinh)	102,560.00
2020	Typhoon Quinta (Molave)	98,490.00
2017	Tropical Storm Urduja (Kai-Tak)	85,845.00
2020	Taal Volcano Eruption	74,631.00
2016	Super Typhoon Lawin (Haima)	61,809.00

Source: EM-DAT: The Emergency Events Database-Universite Catholique de Louvain (UCL) - CRED, D. Guha-Sapir - www.emdat.be, Brussels, Belgium.

Table 11.2 presents the disasters that have affected the largest number of individuals. Similar to the information displayed in Table 11.1, minor storms and even flooding events attributed to the southwest monsoon, locally known as "Habagat", can have devastating effects on

TABLE 11.2
Ranking of the Highest Number of Affected due to Calamities in the Philippines (2016–23)

Year	Event Name Local Name (International Name)	Total Affected	Total Deaths	Total Damages, Adjusted ('000 US$)
2021	Super Typhoon Odette (Rai)	10,608,996	457	988,518.00
2018	Typhoon Ompong (Mangkut)	3,800,138	84	37,333.00
2020	Super Typhoon Rolly (Goni)	3,356,394	31	569,108.00
2022	Severe Tropical Storm Paeng (Nalgae)	3,323,291	158	45,569.00
2019	Typhoon Ursula (Phanfone)	3,297,246	63	17,997.00
2019	Typhoon Tisoy (Kammuri)	2,647,558	4	124,947.00
2023	Super Typhoon Doksuri (Egay)	2,500,052	45	108,052.00
2022	Tropical Storm Agaton (Megi)	2,298,788	346	41,556.00
2018	Tropical Storm Henry (Son Tinh)	2,231,101	16	102,560.00
2023	Flood	2,000,011	51	
2016	Typhoon Nina (Nock-Ten)	1,893,404	24	126,400.00
2017	Tropical Storm Urduja (Kai-Tak)	1,861,328	91	85,845.00
2018	Tropical Storm Karding (Yagi)	1,709,511	5	22,144.00
2017	Flood	1,500,000	9	9,671.00
2016	Flood	1,300,000	19	

Source: EM-DAT: The Emergency Events Database-Universite Catholique de Louvain (UCL) - CRED, D. Guha-Sapir - www.emdat.be, Brussels, Belgium.

the population. Although these calamities may not result in substantial damages and losses, they do cause the deaths of hundreds of lives and displace millions of people. One example is Tropical Storm Megi, which struck the Philippines in April 2022. Despite its weak intensity, it was responsible for a high number of fatalities, second only to Super Typhoon Rai. This is due to associated disasters such as heavy rainfall, floods, and massive landslides that occurred in the regions of Davao and Northern Mindanao and the provinces of Leyte, Southern Leyte, Negros Occidental, and Iloilo.

Although 2017 and 2019 logged the highest number of extreme events and major disasters, as seen in Table 11.3, the highest number of deaths was recorded in 2019 due to the dengue and measles epidemic in various parts of the country. This was followed by 2018 owing to the two epidemics as well. For 2021 and 2022, the significant loss of life was due to the impacts of Super Typhoon Rai, Tropical Storm Megi, and Severe Tropical Storm Nalgae.

The Philippines has faced a range of man-made disasters in recent years as well, including the five-month-long siege in Marawi, Lanao del Sur in 2017. However, the data presented in the tables do not

TABLE 11.3
Total Damages and Losses from Major Disasters (2016–23)

Year	Number of Events	Total Damages, Adjusted ('000 US$)	Total Affected	Total Deaths
2016	15	225,671.00	5,543,812	89
2017	20	192,478.00	4,881,786	331
2018	12	663,976.00	9,694,321	842
2019	20	679,470.00	6,928,491	1,037
2020	10	1,259,079.00	6,116,533	216
2021	15	1,164,003.00	12,471,732	622
2022	14	307,471.00	7,921,738	627
2023	9	138,052.00	4,821,136	179

Source: EM-DAT: The Emergency Events Database-Universite Catholique de Louvain (UCL) - CRED, D. Guha-Sapir - www.emdat.be, Brussels, Belgium.

reflect the Marawi siege and the COVID-19 pandemic, which killed more than 66,000 people since the country caught its first positive case in 2020.[18]

As shown in the tables, the Duterte administration was confronted with a series of calamitous events, which underscored the need to solve the issues surrounding the DRRM Law and its accompanying policies. In one of his statements during the Philippine national election campaign in 2016, Duterte promised to establish "a single, permanent Emergency Response Department in charge of disaster preparedness, relief, and rehabilitation". And in his first State of Nation Address (SONA) in July 2017, he called for creating a Department of Disaster Resilience (DDR).[19] He reiterated this plea several times during his term.

Duterte was seen as someone who could get things done and sense the urgency of reforming disaster policies in the Philippines, a perception fostered by his style of governing and track record in Davao City, as well as his actions during Typhoon Haiyan. However, it became apparent during his term that there is a disparity between his pronouncements, actions, and actual priorities. The next sections assess certain aspects of the Duterte administration's disaster policies such as funding and resource allocation, the role of local government, the discontinuation of relevant programmes, and the potential shift to a new department.

Funding Disaster Programmes

Investing in and financing disaster preparedness measures, according to a United Nations Disaster Risk Reduction (UNDRR) disaster risk assessment report,[20] can decrease the need for post-disaster relief and maximize the efficiency of earmarked resources. That, aside from preserving the lives of people, the cost of disaster response can be cut down by about US$4–11 for every dollar spent in preparedness efforts.

From 2016 to 2022, an annual average of PHP 21 billion (US$450 million) was allocated in the General Appropriations Act for the NDRRMC Fund, which is equivalent to 0.6 per cent of the Philippines' total budget. The fund, also referred to as the calamity fund managed by the Department of Budget and Management (DBM), is a lump sum fund meant to provide financial support for DRRM programmes at all levels of government, from the national down to the *barangay*.

Following the DRRM Law, the calamity fund can be utilized for numerous disaster-related activities such as pre-disaster measures including assessment of hazards and risks and development of early warning systems. It can be used to finance disaster preparedness programmes like the acquisition of equipment, supplies, and materials for response and recovery, and organizing capacity-building activities. The fund is also spent for providing relief goods, emergency shelter, and medical assistance to communities and households affected by the calamities, launching search and rescue teams, and rebuilding and repairing essential services and infrastructure. Finally, it supports post-disaster recovery and rehabilitation measures including the repair and restoration of damaged infrastructure and facilities and extending support for people's livelihood.

The calamity fund is a supplementary source of funding for the quick response fund (QRF) of implementing government agencies. The QRF can be utilized to restore the conditions of communities affected by disasters as well as the repair of damaged infrastructure and buildings in a prompt manner. It is built in the annual budgets of these agencies and the calamity fund becomes available when their QRF balances fall below 50 per cent and upon approval of the NDRRMC and the president.

In the UNDRR report, as well as the Philippine Development Plan,[21] however, the assessment is that the Philippines focuses more on post-disaster spending rather than on mitigation and preparedness. This concern is not exclusive to the national level but is also evident in the allocation of the Local DRRM Fund. This strategy is not aligned with the principles advocated by the DRRM Law and has been a persistent issue during the Aquino and the Duterte administrations.

Table 11.4 states the calamity fund and percentage share relative to the budget for each year starting from 2016 to 2023. In 2016, the total budget allocated for the NDRRMC Fund was PHP 38.9 billion (US$854 million), equivalent to 1.3 per cent of the total budget. However, Congress slashed this by more than half, leaving the Duterte administration with a calamity fund of PHP 15.76 billion (US$331 million) for 2017 or about a mere 0.47 per cent of the country's total budget. The allotted amount was insufficient as the NDRRMC reported that by March of that year, a mere PHP 5.8 billion (US$122 million), or one-third of the total, was left to spend for the remaining nine months. According to the Philippine Atmospheric, Geophysical and Astronomical Services Administration (PAGASA), the months of July to October mark the peak of the typhoon season, during which about 70 per cent of all typhoons are formed. The council had to request for supplemental funds from Congress to finance the recovery efforts from disasters suffered during the previous year. Nevertheless, the allocated funds do not even fully account for the requirements needed to recover from the flooding in Mindanao and the earthquake in the Caraga region in February 2017.

TABLE 11.4
NDRRMC Budget and Total Philippine Budget (2016–23)

Year	NDRRMC Fund (in '000 US$)	Total Budget	Percentage of Total Budget
2016	854,569	65,949,033	1.30%
2017	331,859	70,541,167	0.47%
2018	388,889	74,742,063	0.52%
2019	379,795	69,540,448	0.55%
2020	386,175	79,165,862	0.49%
2021	403,063	90,810,157	0.44%
2022	406,091	102,002,030	0.40%
2023	376,285	96,696,035	0.39%

Notes: Used annual average US$-PHP exchange rates from their respective prior year does not include continuing appropriations from the previous years.
Source: Department of Budget and Management.

The fund was slightly raised for 2018 and 2019. In 2020, however, the calamity fund was cut again to PHP 16 billion (US$386 million), which raised concerns among stakeholders given the high possibility of hazards occurring more frequently and severely in the Philippines. Despite the incremental uptick in the funds, as shown in Table 11.4, the percentage share of the NDRRMF gets smaller and smaller every year. At the end of the Duterte administration, the NDRRMF accounts for only 0.4 per cent of the aggregate budget of the Philippines.

Sufficient funding is crucial in guaranteeing that the government can efficiently and effectively respond to disasters and implement DRRM programmes. Reduction in financial support diminishes the country's capacity to effectively mitigate and reduce disaster risks and impedes response and support towards communities heavily affected by disasters.

Aside fund allocation, the Duterte administration faced criticism for the slow disbursement of calamity funds.[22] While this problem is not unusual for any administration as it is a long-standing structural issue, it demonstrated how Duterte was unable to strongly advocate for securing additional financial resources that are meant to effectively address disasters. As mentioned earlier, the DBM is only able to release the NDRRMF after receiving endorsement from the NDRRMC followed by approval from the president. For example, in early 2020, after the Marawi siege, about PHP 406.5 million (US$8 million) meant for the rehabilitation of the city of Marawi lapsed and was returned to the national treasury due to the NDRRMC and the president's sluggish approval.[23] This is despite President Duterte's promise to rebuild the city immediately.

Local Governments and the Mandanas Ruling

RA No. 10121 highlighted the importance of LGUs, from *barangay* up to regional levels, as frontliners in disaster policy implementation. It provides local governments with the structural, financial, and institutional capacity to facilitate the development and administration of DRRM programmes in their own communities.

For LGUs, RA No. 10121 widened the scope of their responsibilities by mandating them to allocate a minimum of 5 per cent of their Internal Revenue Allotment (IRA), 30 per cent of which is set aside as a QRF, towards financing DRRM efforts. This allows LGUs to gain access to DRRM funds without the condition that a state of calamity is declared, a requirement that was needed in previous years. When there are any remaining DRRM funds, they can be used as a revolving fund for future DRRM efforts. The LGUs also possess some autonomy in utilizing the funds to assist other LGUs affected by disasters.

In 2018, the Supreme Court ruling in the Mandanas case resulted in an increase in the IRA share for LGUs. This encourages LGUs to further enhance the disaster preparedness and response initiatives in their communities.[24] However, the expansion of the IRA raised concerns about exacerbating the already unequal distribution of funds. Wealthier LGUs receive greater funding while financially disadvantaged LGUs lack the necessary resources to effectively carry out DRRM operations. The uneven distribution of resources has been a long-standing issue and was not resolved during the Duterte administration.

Additionally, given this fiscal autonomy and the issues with local government politics, disaster preparedness and response plans can be heavily reliant on what a politician wants to prioritize. There is also insufficient awareness among some LGUs, and varying levels of knowledge and insight of DRRM concepts among different LGUs. One reason for this is because LGUs lack the human resources with knowledge and skills to understand and create hazard and risk assessment, development plans incorporating DRRM, and post-disaster assessment reports. Slow disbursement of calamity funds to victims of disasters is another issue faced by LGUs. The Philippine Development Plan (2017–22)[25] notes that it would take months before people can access these funds because of LGUs' noncompliance with the established criteria and requirements of funding institutions.

Discontinuation of Project NOAH

One of the most significant achievements brought on by the DRRM Law is the establishment of early warning systems, particularly the creation and launch of Project NOAH (Nationwide Operational Assessment of Hazards) in 2012 under the Department of Science and Technology (DOST). One objective of the project was to provide timely and accurate information on weather and flood conditions across the country. This involves the installation of weather monitoring stations, the development of flood and landslide hazard maps, and the dissemination of information through various channels such as social media, text messages, and radio broadcasts. The NOAH project has been recognized in a UNDRR report[26] for enhancing the country's capacity to monitor and respond to natural hazards.

However, with the slashing of the NDRRMC Fund in 2017, the Duterte administration announced it was discontinuing the project effective 1 March 2017. Aside from the financial constraints, the government wanted to consolidate DRRM activities under a single agency, transferring Project NOAH's functions and resources to PAGASA.

This action elicited diverse reactions, with some arguing that the termination of the programme will possibly affect the progress of the country's DRRM efforts especially in developing early warning systems and hazard mapping, among other aspects. On the other hand, the government reasoned that the decision to discontinue the project was part of a larger initiative to rationalize and improve the effectiveness of DRRM initiatives. Additionally, they claimed that it allows for better coordination among different stakeholders and that the resources previously allocated to Project NOAH could be redirected to other areas where they could have a more significant impact on DRRM efforts.

Considering Project NOAH's crucial role in minimizing risks, promoting resilience, and informing the public, the University of the Philippines decided to adopt the programme and renamed it to the NOAH Centre. For the institution, it was important that the gains achieved during the project's implementation be continued not just by the centre but also by other government agencies, especially enhancing accessibility of DRRM initiatives for communities, specifically those in rural and marginalized areas.

Disasters on the Back of a Pandemic

On the afternoon of 12 January 2023, reports were flooding in about activities in one of the Philippines' most active volcanoes, the Taal volcano. When Taal volcano made an explosive eruption, the Philippine Institute of Volcanology and Seismology (PHIVOLCS) subsequently raised the Alert Level from 1 to 4. According to the final reports by the NDRRMC, a total of 736,802 individuals, or more than 190,000 families, were affected by the eruption in the regions of CALABARZON, Central Luzon, and the National Capital Region.[27] At least 135,000 people were displaced, infrastructure and essential utilities were damaged, and livelihoods such as farming, fishing, and tourism were disrupted.[28] The total cost of damages and losses reached US$74.6 million.[29]

The government was criticized for their response as it seemed as if they were not prepared for the eventuality of a volcanic eruption in the Philippines. Some of the concerns raised was the insufficient transportation to evacuate the residents and inadequate facilities in evacuation centres.[30] The appeal of the Department of the Interior and Local Government for donations was also widely blasted[31] as this incident exposed the insufficiency of the government's budget allocation for disaster response. Hence, showing the need for a more robust and sustainable source of funding to assist communities stricken by calamities.

Still reeling from the effects of Taal volcano's eruption, the Philippines then had to face an unknown virus, one that was rapidly spreading all over the world. The COVID-19 pandemic started wreaking havoc in the country as the first confirmed case was reported on 30 January 2020. In less than two months, the government announced a nationwide quarantine to minimize the spread of the virus. This action significantly disrupted people's lives and livelihood. But the complication did not stop there.

The Philippines experienced about ten major calamities during that year, most of which were storms with one considered as the most powerful tropical cyclone to ever make landfall as of October 2020. On 31 October 2020, Super Typhoon Goni made landfall in Bato, Catanduanes and left the Philippines a few days later with 31 casualties, more than 3.3 million people affected, and US$569.1 million worth of damages and losses.[32] Given the scope, the public expected the president to attend and head the high-level public briefings of government officials. Duterte, however, remained in Davao City but was supposedly closely monitoring the situation despite not being present.

Disaster response policies in relation to natural hazards were already in place as early as May 2020. The NDRRMC released Memorandum No. 54, series of 2020 on COVID-19 Preparedness Measures for Rainy Season in anticipation of rain and typhoons. In accordance with this memorandum, the NDRRMC member agencies and response clusters were recommended that they make decisions based on risk-informed practices through the utilization of scientific information about the potential hazards present in the country. Moreover, the Bayanihan to Heal as One Act has lifted the 30 per cent cap for the QRF, allowing LGUs to use the remaining 70 per cent allocated in the LDRRMF.

COVID-19 efforts, however, were hampered because of the super typhoon. For instance, the government was confronted with the challenge of evacuating thousands of people while also enforcing COVID-19 protocols, such as social distancing and hygiene measures, to protect both responders and evacuees from infection. In the provinces of Albay and Camarines Sur, existing evacuation centres like basketball courts and multi-purpose halls were already occupied by COVID-19 positive patients, making evacuation for those affected by the typhoon more difficult.

The Philippines was not offered any respite with the arrival of another super typhoon on 8 November 2020. Typhoon Vamco tracked the same trajectory as that of Typhoon Goni. This compendium of events is probably one of the most formidable challenges the Duterte administration has faced. The country had to contend not only with the aftermath of the typhoons but with the consequences of the pandemic as well.

A few days later, Duterte signed Executive Order No. 120, establishing the Build Back Better Task Force (BBBTF), aimed at rationalizing and accelerating post-disaster rehabilitation and recovery efforts in a "sustained and integrated manner with a clear unity of command". This Executive Order was intended to be an interim measure while waiting for the enactment of a new law that will create a DDR.

A New Cabinet Department

Despite the landmark status of RA No. 10121, large-scale disasters have revealed the weaknesses in the institutional frameworks of the Philippines. This problem underscores the need for a body with sufficient authority, mandate, and resources to manage and direct the DRRM efforts of LGUs and other stakeholders, at the same time, ensuring the streamlined implementation of DRRM policies throughout the country.

Domingo and Olaguera's research findings[33] suggest that the current structure of the NDRRMC, with its coordinating role and frequently overlapping functions with other government agencies, is not sufficient to effectively address DRRM issues as the Philippines is and will be suffering from more frequent and severe natural and man-made calamities. Therefore, they propose exploring alternative institutional arrangements, such as the establishment of a unified disaster management agency that oversees all aspects of DRRM.[34] Furthermore, they recommend that the NDRRMC leverage its regional and local partnerships to enhance its networks and institutional support.

During President Duterte's 2017 SONA, he urged the Congress to promptly draft legislation establishing a new department that will be responsive to the current and future conditions of the country and has the capacity to deliver better and prompt DRRM programmes. In response to the president's call, both the Senate and the House of Representatives, during the 17th and 18th Congress, introduced various legislative proposals that would establish the DDR.

The proposed creation of a new agency is aimed at consolidating all disaster-related concerns and functions in the country, emphasizing the adoption of a centralized DRRM system. Given this consolidation, the NDRRMC and the Climate Change Commission will be dissolved to pave the way for the newly established department. The proposed bills seek to restructure the current DRRM framework/system by entrusting the responsibility to this new national government agency. One of the goals of the creation of this department is to expedite post-disaster response and rehabilitation efforts.

However, opposition from some members of Congress arose due to apprehension about duplication of tasks already performed by other government agencies.[35] Additionally, according to then Senator Panfilo Lacson, a new department will require at least a billion pesos (US$20 million) to cover salaries, maintenance and operating expenses, and capital outlay.[36]

DRRNetPhils also expressed their reservations regarding the bills filed.[37] Specifically, they argued that the proposed legislation, instead of building upon the achievements of the current law made in the past years, would actually negate the achievements gained. The new law, according to the group, would also exclude CSOs from participating in discussions on climate and disaster-related matters.

One notable aspect of RA No. 10121 was the emphasis on community-based DRR (CBDRR), which is a comprehensive approach to mitigating and reducing risks posed by disasters wherein at-risk communities are empowered to take an active role in identifying, analysing, addressing, monitoring, and evaluating potential hazards and risks in order to reduce their vulnerabilities and enhance their capacities. It is, by design, participatory. This is intended to strengthen the community's resilience while reducing their vulnerabilities through their participation in the decision-making and implementation processes of DRRM activities.

A 2021 study by Domingo and Manejar,[38] proposed enhancing institutional mechanisms that promote the engagement and participation of various stakeholders, including CSOs, people's organizations, NGOs, church organizations, and other interest groups. This is consistent with the DRRNetPhils stance of strengthening community-based DRRM systems and councils, which should be used to reinforce participatory approaches in building resilience of various sectors of society, particularly those at the grassroots level. The group also recommended preserving local DRRM councils, which have established good practices under the DRRM Law, while also improving the oversight function of the Office of Civil Defense (OCD) and NDRRMC and clarifying the roles and responsibilities of government agencies. Ultimately, even though it was deemed as a priority measure by Duterte himself multiple times, the proposed pieces of legislation failed to pass.

NEW ADMINISTRATION, SAME OLD DISASTER POLICIES

The issues that remained unresolved during the Aquino administration spilled over to the Duterte administration as well as the new administration under President Ferdinand "Bongbong" Marcos, Jr. On 27 July 2022, a few days after his inauguration, Marcos Jr. expressed his intention to push for the approval of the proposed legislation that aims to create an agency specializing on DRRM—the Department of Disaster Resilience—in response to the challenges brought about by a warming planet. According to him, although the country has extensive experience in handling the aftermath of typhoons and earthquakes, the situation at present requires a dedicated department with expertise in managing the risks and impacts of climate-related disasters.

But just a day later, Marcos Jr. rejected the creation of a new department and instead echoed Senator Imee Marcos's statement that the proposed agency would instead be placed under the Office of the

President (OP). He argued that this strategy is better than creating a separate department that would entail a considerable budget for the salaries of officers. Another advantage of this is that it would streamline the national response process by removing the need to go through multiple agencies and chains of command. Again, echoing Senator Marcos, Marcos Jr. said that this body can be developed using the United States' Federal Emergency Management Agency (FEMA)—an agency whose job is to coordinate disaster aid and response—as a model.

Following this pronouncement, a bill proposing the establishment of the said agency was filed by Senator Marcos and supported by House of Representatives Speaker Martin Romualdez. At its core, the two proposals share a similar objective, that is to centralize the structure of the NDRRMC rather than simply having a coordinating role. However, there is distinction between the two, with the latter proposal eliminating the potential costs of establishing a separate department given that this body will fall under the scope of the OP. Furthermore, being under the OP's purview would ensure a quicker and more effective chain of command and control and improve communication and coordination among government agencies.

A few months after he floated the idea of an agency under the OP, Marcos Jr. was on a flight surveying the destruction brought about by Severe Tropical Storm Nalgae in the Maguindanao province in Mindanao. He attributed the extensive damages, amounting to US$45.6 million,[39] and the impact on more than three million people, especially the farmers, fisherfolk, and low-income households, to rampant deforestation, poor flood control, and insufficient planning. He expressed that the government could have done better, pushing for an examination of the area's flood-control infrastructure network and river systems. It remains to be seen, however, if the "Build Better More" Program will include infrastructure projects that will build resilience for future disasters.

In February 2023, the Philippines was once again faced with a major calamity, one that was not natural. On 28 February 2023, an oil tanker named MT Princess Empress carrying 800,000 litres of industrial fuel oil capsized and sank in the waters off Oriental Mindoro due to engine failure. According to the NDRRMC,[40] as of June 2023, the oil spill has affected more than 200,000 people coming from the CALABARZON, MIMAROPA, and Western Visayas regions. At least 200 individuals reported that they have suffered from health issues such as dermatitis, stomachache, aggravated asthma, and emphysema/chest pain, dizziness, abdominal pain, fever, coughs and colds, ingestion, as well as inhalation, among others. It has damaged the livelihood of more than 27,000 fisherfolks who depend on the sea for their food and livelihood. This paralyzed the livelihood of local farmers and tour operators as well as affecting over 60 tourist sites.

Like other disasters, the effects of the oil spill will most likely be felt for a long time. The Marine Science Institute (MSI) at the University of the Philippines has cautioned that the oil slick could threaten about 36,000 hectares of significant marine ecosystems—20,000 hectares of this are coral reefs, 9,900 hectares of mangrove, and 6,000 hectares of seagrass.[41] Moreover, there are reports[42] saying that the oil spill may have already contaminated the Verde Island Passage, a candidate for the UNESCO World Heritage Site and an ecosystem renowned for having one of the richest and most diverse marine ecosystems in the world.

Despite the occurrence of previous large oil spills in the Philippines, the response to the current environmental disaster has been slow. On 14 March 2023, the Philippine Senate initiated an investigation to see the sufficiency and efficiency of the government's response. During the hearing, the senators raised concerns about MT *Princess Empress'* seaworthiness, who is tasked to clean up, and how agencies are coordinating with each other to control the oil spill. Environmental and legal groups raised questions about the lack of transparency regarding the DRRM efforts, and why the details only emerged during the Senate hearing.[43] The sluggish response to another disaster once again exposed the weaknesses of the Philippines' DRRM system.

To expedite the implementation of disaster preparedness and response plans, Marcos Jr. signed Executive Order No. 24 on 30 April 2023 to create the Disaster Response and Crisis Management Task Force (DRCMTF). The primary mandate of the task force is to supervise and coordinate disaster planning, as well as monitor and evaluate disaster preparedness and response plans, with the objective of having a "clear command unity in government efforts".

However, questions arose with this announcement due to concerns about potential duplications with the existing functions of the NDRRMC. The establishment of the task force appears to contrast with Marcos Jr.'s goal of streamlining government structures and functions. But according to the administration, the DRCMTF would be specifically responsible for addressing the immediate effects of calamities, while the NDRRMC will be dedicated to developing long-term policies on disaster prevention, mitigation, and recovery. Additionally, the DRCMTF is meant to serve as a "transition mechanism" until a disaster-related agency is constituted.

The creation of the task force seems to be inducing the country's legislators to prioritize the creation of this specialized body. However, Marcos Jr., as of this writing, still has not designated a chairperson and vice chairperson that will lead the task force. Since its announcement, the Philippines has been struck by four storms, two of which were categorized as super typhoons, and the Mayon Volcano eruption.

CONCLUSION

According to the IPCC's sixth synthesis report, the rise in global temperatures resulted in more frequent and extreme weather events. Climate models are also predicting that a strong or super El Niño will occur in the latter months of 2023 and lasting until early 2024. This phenomenon raises the likelihood of experiencing not just below-normal rainfall but also above-normal rainfall, particularly during the southwest monsoon season. All these events will have devastating consequences to the economy, the environment, and society globally, including and especially the Philippines.

It is imperative for the Philippines, as one of the most at-risk countries in the world due to its high exposure to various hazards, such as typhoons or droughts, to prioritize the implementation of comprehensive policies and programmes aimed at mitigating and preparing for disasters, thereby reducing the vulnerability of its population.

Notwithstanding the ambitious legislation laid out more than a decade ago, for the country to attain disaster resilience, the government needs to evaluate the DRRM Law and significantly overhaul the current setup of the NDRRMC. Streamlining the procedures and eliminating redundancies and the complexities of going through multiple agencies and chains of command are crucial to improve the efficiency and effectiveness of DRRM efforts.

Duterte has repeatedly stated the need to establish a new agency to replace the NDRRMC, one that will centralize its structure and functions and provide an authority over disaster-related policies and programmes. Marcos Jr. also expressed the need to create a body under the OP that will be modelled after the FEMA. What the president should understand, however, is that no matter what agency or organization is created, this will not solve the country's problems in DRRM if the underlying issues left unresolved by his predecessors remain. The new agency may improve the organizational structure and chain of command as well as promote consistency in disaster policies but other issues must be given attention too. Issues such as inefficient coordination and communication among stakeholders, lack of adequate manpower and funds, insufficient capacity, and the top-down structure in implementing policies, among others, were not resolved during the Duterte administration.

DRRM policies must be mainstreamed and integrated in national and local development plans especially towards social protection, poverty reduction, capacity building, resilient infrastructure investment, and sustainable resource management. It also requires a multifaceted and multisectoral approach, involving the participation of all the stakeholders —from the government to CSOs and grassroots organizations to the vulnerable population. Good governance and institution building are vital as well in all aspects of DRRM.

As mentioned, the enactment of the DRRM Law in 2010 was a positive step forward in contributing to a more disaster resilient and sustainable future. However, solving DRRM problems and mitigating the effects of climate change needs more than just legislative measures. Addressing them requires an inclusive, participatory, and genuine whole-of-nation approach. If not, the country will always be playing catch up at the expense of the well-being and livelihood of Filipinos.

Notes

1. For a disaster to be incorporated in the EM-DAT database (www.emdat.be/database), it should fit at least one of these criteria: reports that ten or more people are killed, 100 or more are affected, state of emergency is declared, call is made for international assistance.
2. Hoesung Lee and José Romero, eds., "2023: Summary for Policymakers", in *Climate Change 2023: Synthesis Report*, Contribution of Working Groups I, II and III to the Sixth Assessment Report of the Intergovernmental Panel on Climate Change (Geneva, Switzerland: Intergovernmental Panel on Climate Change, 2023), pp. 1–34, https://www.ipcc.ch/report/ar6/syr/downloads/report/IPCC_AR6_SYR_SPM.pdf.
3. United Nations Office for Disaster Risk Reduction, "Sendai Framework for Disaster Risk Reduction 2015–2030", 2015, https://www.undrr.org/quick/11409.
4. Omar-Dario Cardona, Maarten K. van Aalst, Jörn Birkmann, Maureen Fordham, Glenn McGregor, Rosa Perez, Roger S. Pulwarty, E. Lisa F. Schipper, and Bach Tan Sinh, "Determinants of Risk: Exposure and Vulnerability", in *Managing the Risks of Extreme Events and Disasters to Advance Climate Change Adaptation*, A Special Report of Working Groups I and II of the Intergovernmental Panel on Climate Change (IPCC), edited by Christopher B. Field, Vicente Barros, Thomas F. Stocker, Qin Dahe, David Jon Dokken, Kristie L. Ebi, Michael D. Mastrandrea, Katharine J. Mach, Gian-Kasper Plattner, Simon K. Allen, Melinda Tignor, and Pauline M. Midgley (Geneva, Switzerland: Intergovernmental Panel on Climate Change, 2012), pp. 65–108, https://www.ipcc.ch/site/assets/uploads/2018/03/SREX-Chap2_FINAL-1.pdf.
5. "World Risk Report 2022", 2021, https://reliefweb.int/report/world/worldriskreport-2022-focus-digitalization.
6. Department of Finance, "Climate-Related Hazards Led to US$10-B Losses for Low-Carbon Emission PHL over 10-Year Period", 2 November 2021, https://www.dof.gov.ph/climate-related-hazards-led-to-us10-b-losses-for-low-carbon-emission-phl-over-10-year-period/.
7. National Disaster Risk Reduction and Management Council, "National Disaster Risk Reduction and Management Plan 2011-2028", 2011, https://www.adrc.asia/documents/dm_information/Philippines_NDRRM_Plan_2011-2028.pdf.
8. Sonny N. Domingo and Ma. Divina C. Olaguera, "Have We Institutionalized DRRM in the Philippines?" Policy Notes No. 2017-12 (Quezon City: Philippine Institute for Development Studies, 2017).
9. Ibid.

10. Partners for Resilience, "Before Sunset: Partners for Resilience Inputs to RA10121 Sunset Review", 10 October 2020, https://resilientphilippines.com/wp-content/uploads/publications/Before%20Sunset%20-%20PFR%20Inputs%20to%20RA10121%20sunset%20review.pdf.
11. Domingo and Olaguera, "Have We Institutionalised DRRM in the Philippines?"
12. National Disaster Risk Reduction and Management Council, "NDRRMC Situation Report on the Effects of Typhoon Yolanda", 22 January 2014, https://www.officialgazette.gov.ph/2014/01/22/ndrrmc-situation-report-on-the-effects-of-typhoon-yolanda-january-22-2014-600-a-m/.
13. Rosemarie Francisco, "Analysis: Hero to Zero? Philippine President Feels Typhoon Backlash", Reuters, 15 November 2013, https://www.reuters.com/article/us-philippines-typhoon-aquino-analysis-idUSBRE9AE07U20131115.
14. World Bank, "Philippines Lessons Learned from Yolanda: An Assessment of the Post-Yolanda Short- and Medium-Term Recovery and Rehabilitation Interventions of the Government", 2017, https://openknowledge.worldbank.org/handle/10986/28540.
15. Pia Ranada, "Duterte-Cayetano's Promise of Change for Haiyan's Ground Zero", *Rappler*, 15 March 2016, https://www.rappler.com/nation/elections/125932-duterte-cayetano-in-tacloban-promises-change-haiyan-ground-zero/.
16. Consuelo Marquez, "#NasaanAngPangulo Trends on Twitter as Duterte Skips Super Typhoon Briefing", *Inquirer.net*, 1 November 2020, https://newsinfo.inquirer.net/1354976/nasaan-ang-pangulo-bicol-trends-on-twitter-amid-supertyphoon-rolly.
17. Camille Elemia, "EXPLAINER: Duterte's High Ratings despite Poor COVID-19 Response", *Rappler*, 5 October 2020, https://www.rappler.com/newsbreak/explainers/explainers-reasons-duterte-high-ratings-poor-covid-19-response/.
18. "COVID-19 Dashboard", https://www.covid19.gov.ph/.
19. Rodrigo Roa Duterte, Second State of the National Address, 24 July 2017, https://www.officialgazette.gov.ph/2017/07/24/rodrigo-roa-duterte-second-state-of-the-nation-address-july-24-2017/.
20. United Nations Office for Disaster Risk Reduction, "2019 Global Assessment Report on Disaster Risk Reduction", 2019, https://www.undrr.org/publication/global-assessment-report-disaster-risk-reduction-2019.
21. National Economic Development Authority, "Philippine Development Plan 2017-2022", 2017, https://pdp.neda.gov.ph/philippine-development-plan-2017-2022/.
22. Michael Beltran, "Duterte's Sluggish Typhoon Rai Recovery Spending", *The Diplomat*, 31 December 2021, https://thediplomat.com/2021/12/dutertes-sluggish-typhoon-rai-recovery-spending/.

23. Ben O. de Vera, "P406M in Marawi Funds for 2018 Expire", *Philippine Daily Inquirer*, 27 January 2020, https://newsinfo.inquirer.net/1219861/p406m-in-marawi-funds-for-2018-expire.
24. United Nations Development Program, "Decentralisation, Digitalization, and Development: Strengthening Local Governance for Crisis Response, Recovery, Resilience, and the Sustainable Development Goals", 2022, https://www.undp.org/sites/g/files/zskgke326/files/2022-11/MANDANAS%20Report%202022_FINAL%20FINAL%20FILE_High%20Quality_NOV%2030.pdf.
25. National Economic Development Authority, "Philippine Development Plan 2017-2022".
26. United Nations Office for Disaster Risk Reduction, "Disaster Risk Reduction in the Philippines Status Report 2019", 2019, https://www.unisdr.org/files/68265_682308philippinesdrmstatusreport.pdf.
27. National Disaster Risk Reduction and Management Council, "NDRRMC Situational Report No. 87 re: Taal Volcano Eruption", 6 March 2020, http://www.ndrrmc.gov.ph/attachments/article/4007/Sitrep_No_87_re_Taal_Volcano_Eruption_as_of_06March2020_8AM.pdf.
28. National Disaster Risk Reduction and Management Council, "NDRRMC Situational Report No. 85 re: Taal Volcano Eruption", 28 February 2020, http://ndrrmc.gov.ph/attachments/article/4007/SitRep_No_85_re_Taal_Volcano_Eruption_issued_on_28Feb2020_5PM.pdf.
29. EM-DAT: The Emergency Events Database-Universite Catholique de Louvain (UCL) - CRED, D. Guha-Sapir, www.emdat.be.
30. Franco Luna, "'Heartbreaking' Situation for 'Under-Reported' Evacuees — Humanitarian Group", *Philstar.com*, 20 January 2020, https://www.philstar.com/headlines/2020/01/15/1985061/heartbreaking-situation-under-reported-evacuees-humanitarian-group.
31. Jeline Malasig, "Where is the Calamity Fund? Filipinos Question Eduardo Año's Appeal for Donations to the Public amid Taal Disaster", *Interaksyon*, 15 January 2020, https://interaksyon.philstar.com/politics-issues/2020/01/15/160303/calamity-fund-filipinos-question-eduardo-anos-appeal-donations-taal-volcano/.
32. EM-DAT: The Emergency Events Database-Universite Catholique de Louvain (UCL).
33. Domingo and Olaguera, "Have We Institutionalised DRRM in the Philippines?"
34. Sunny N. Domingo, "Institutional Issues on Disaster Risk Reduction and Management", Discussion Paper Series No. 2017-50 (Quezon City: Philippine Institute for Development Studies, 2017).

35. Butch Fernandez, "New Disaster Department Costly, Needless–Senators", *BusinessMirror*, 3 November 2020, https://businessmirror.com.ph/2020/11/02/new-disaster-department-costly-needless-senators/.
36. Ibid.
37. DRRNetPhils, "DRRNetPhils Position Paper on Proposed Department of Resilience", 22 February 2023, https://drrnetphils.org/2023/02/22/drrnetphils-position-paper-on-proposed-department-of-resilience/.
38. Sonny Domingo and Arvie Joy Manejar, "Policy, Institutional, and Expenditure Review of Bottom-Up Approach Disaster Risk Reduction and Management", Discussion Paper No. 2021-03 (Quezon City: Philippine Institute for Development Studies, 2021).
39. EM-DAT: The Emergency Events Database-Universite Catholique de Louvain (UCL).
40. National Disaster Risk Reduction and Management Council, SitRep No. 112 for the Effects of Oil Spill in CALABARZON, MIMAROPA, and Region IV, 29 June 2023, https://monitoring-dashboard.ndrrmc.gov.ph/assets/uploads/situations/SitRep_No__112_for_the_Effects_of_Oil_Spill_in_CALABARZON_MIMAROPA_and_Region_VI.pdf.
41. University of the Philippines Marine Science Institute, "Bulletin #02: Oil Spill Trajectory Model and Satellite Imagery Shows Oil Slick Trajectory and Affected Areas", 4 March 2023, https://www.msi.upd.edu.ph/News/content/Update-2-Mindoro-Oil-Spill.
42. University of the Philippines Marine Science Institute, "Bulletin #10: Oil Spill Trajectory Model Forecasts That Spill Will Flow through the Verde Island Passage for the Rest of the Week", 22 March 2023, https://www.msi.upd.edu.ph/News/content/Update-10-MTPE-Oil-Spill.
43. Greenpeace Philippines, "Communities, Various Groups Call for Transparency, Urgency amid Oil Spill's Worsening Impacts", 9 March 2023, https://www.greenpeace.org/philippines/press/56519/communities-various-groups-call-for-transparency-urgency-amid-oil-spills-worsening-impacts/.

12

Understanding Gendered Disinformation in the Philippines and Its Implications to Women in Politics

Jean Encinas-Franco

This chapter discusses the contours of gendered disinformation in the time of Duterte and beyond. Several cases of persecuted female politicians targeted by President Rodrigo Duterte demonstrated the extent and consequences of gendered disinformation in the Philippines. Media accounts, reports, and studies have already shown the country's rampancy of disinformation or so-called fake news. Some have even referred to the Philippines as a "petri dish" for this phenomenon. However, few have focused on how much such disinformation have been utilized to reify stereotypes of men and women with sexist narratives, therefore discrediting female politicians and their presence in formal politics. Such narratives rely on the following tropes, as this chapter finds: "immoral women, untrustworthy leaders", "bad mother", "incompetent manager", and "criminal partners, emotional women". More importantly, these accounts discourage women from entering political office, undermine democracy and the bid for more women in public positions. Drawing on the cases of former senator Leila de Lima and former vice president Leni Robredo, this chapter contributes to the emerging empirical armoury of gendered disinformation practices in the Philippines. It concludes by identifying critical policy interventions that may prevent gendered disinformation and create a safe space for women in the political sphere.

Keywords: misogyny; disinformation; gendered disinformation; Duterte; women in politics

INTRODUCTION

Disinformation has been a defining feature of nearly every country's political terrain in the past decade. It has become an important tool in quelling dissent and silencing opponents by a new batch of autocrats worldwide, prompting some to call it digital authoritarianism. Indeed, democratic backsliding, a phenomenon that Aurel Croissant and Larry Diamond argue "has emerged as a conspicuous global challenge",[1] is often discussed with disinformation. The advent of new information and communication technologies, while arguably providing a more cost-effective political space, has also become an arena for polarization, deceit, lies, and disinformation. In other words, fact-based information, an important ingredient of democratic discourse, is quickly becoming endangered.

While recognizing that it is not easy to define disinformation both at conceptual[2] and policy levels,[3] this chapter understands this phenomenon as a deliberate and organized attempt by individuals, groups, and even government entities to disseminate falsehoods against a person to benefit from the harm such information will inflict on the victims. The operative words in this definition are that these are "organized" and "deliberate" activities geared towards harming people. Labiste's chapter[4] differentiates between deliberate attempts and those done without malice and intent, which some authors label as misinformation.

In the Philippines, disinformation (used interchangeably in this chapter with the term, "fake news") was first discussed in the context of the 2016 elections, when social media was thought to have immensely contributed to President Rodrigo Duterte's victory. According to their story, the cash-strapped campaign has reportedly used social media to cost-effectively manage candidate Duterte's image and disseminate his message. Interestingly, Duterte admitted that he used troll farms[5] to be elected, thereby catapulting him to prominence from being a mayor, hardly known nationwide before his candidacy, to president. Aided by avid grassroots supporters, these troll farms went on a propaganda spree and defended Duterte via online harassments and threats during the 2016 elections and to his presidency.[6] Duterte's victory via social media was so phenomenal that by the 2019 and 2022 elections, organized online trolls became a fairly common feature in explaining electoral strategies in the Philippines. Such a strategy makes efficient sense in a country dubbed in 2018 as "patient zero" in online disinformation, by Katie Harbath, Facebook's Global Politics and Government Outreach Director.[7] According to reports, Filipinos' susceptibility to disinformation is heightened by their high Internet and social media use, which stood at 76.01 million and 92.05 million, respectively, in January 2022.[8]

Nonetheless, except for a few reports, and despite the prominence of disinformation tactics for the past several years, gendered disinformation, referring to "a subset of online gendered abuse that uses false or misleading gender and sex-based narratives against women, often with some degree of coordination, aimed at deterring women from participating in the public sphere", has not been a subject of focused inquiry in the Philippines.[9] Gendered disinformation combines three defining characteristics of online disinformation: falsity, malign intent, and coordination.[10] It is "diverse and can comprise misogynist comments that reinforce gendered stereotypes, the sexualisation and diffusion of graphic content, online harassment including threats of violence, and even cyber-attacks".[11]

A comprehensive report on the discourses surrounding the 2022 elections identifies "gendering as a legitimation strategy".[12] According to this report, online information about candidates pertain to dominant gender roles and norms, indicating that candidates subscribe to traditional beliefs about men and women in their key campaign statements to reinforce their claim to the presidency. However, this argument was not made in the context of disinformation but of public discourse in general during the elections. Meanwhile, reports pointing to disinformation during the 2022 elections as a "weapon of mass destruction"[13] and "cybermisogyny"[14] are noteworthy given that they already indicate its gendered nature. However, while media, academic, and policy discourses have focused on fake news, its gendered dimension has not been thoroughly discussed. Moreover, the societal context in which this happens and how it delegitimizes women in politics have not been explained. Such is unfortunate given that female politicians and non-binary individuals are specifically targeted based on sexist, misogynist terms and society's double standard of morality. Not recognizing and naming this as such makes it difficult to think of policies to address them. The absence of research and policy recognition also wrongly implies that online disinformation is waged uniformly against men and women. One factor explaining this lack of attention may be that electoral rules, laws, and politics are considered gender-neutral—an unsurprising situation given that Filipino women gained the right to vote only in 1937. Therefore, making gendered disinformation's impact visible is important as it helps us understand how men and women experience political life differently. Simply put, it is a key step towards naming and addressing it via a set of statutes and programmes, and hopefully, prevent it from harming individual women and non-binary politicians and what they represent in the public sphere.

Addressing gendered disinformation is important for democracy for many reasons. Women's suffrage has been a long-fought battle anywhere in the world. More than a century since suffrage was first granted, women occupy 26.5 per cent[15] of parliaments worldwide, indicating that the international standard of at least 30 per cent representation is still elusive. In 2022, the World Economic Forum estimated that closing the gender gap on the political front will take 155 years—the political empowerment gender gap is a key component of the Global Gender Gap Index.[16] While electoral systems, beliefs, and masculinist electoral rules have been pointed out as reasons for the gender gap, gendered disinformation is another factor that can broaden this disparity, making it even more difficult for women to enter formal politics. Specifically in the Philippines, only 20 per cent of candidates in the 2019 and 2022 elections were women, suggesting that urgent policy responses must be initiated to address this gap,[17] there is a compelling reason to highlight its presence and implications in Philippine politics, to add a Global South dimension to cases that are arguably coming from Euro-centric and North American perspectives.

This chapter explores the concept of gendered disinformation, what it does, and why it threatens democracy. It draws from two female politicians victimized by fake news: former senator Leila de Lima and former vice president Leni Robredo. In unpacking the nature of gendered disinformation and how it delegitimizes women's important role in politics, the chapter argues that fake news harms women politicians in ways different from their counterparts in the opposite sex. In its most pernicious form, it can potentially lead to physical harm and can further discourage women from entering politics and/ or silence their views in the longer term. It is a clear and present danger to any democracy.

While recognizing that non-binary individuals and members of the LGBTIQA are also subjected to gendered disinformation, the chapter is limited to these female politicians. Because the de Lima and Robredo cases are considered high profile and received wide media attention, they were publicized to the extent that its implications can be better studied and examined. Robredo and de Lima represent female politicians who have vocalized their criticisms against authoritarian and violent tendencies of a head of state, such as Duterte. Instead of listening, Duterte and his administration punished the two by maligning their personhood via gendered disinformation. Also in this chapter, the term "politics" refers to electoral politics, but it also recognizes that women outside the formal political sphere have been victims of gendered disinformation such as those working as journalists, civil society leaders, and members of the academe. While fake news has been omnipresent since 2016, the chapter limits itself to a few illustrative cases and does not in any way cover all the false narratives that surrounded de Lima and Robredo.

The following discussion is organized in six sections. First, it provides the journey of Filipino women in claiming their space in politics, locating the context in which Robredo and de Lima can be found. The section is followed by a brief overview of Duterte's hypermasculine leadership style and rhetoric. Third, the two politicians' backgrounds and the false narratives hurled at them are presented. The section analysing how such false narratives undermine their personhood and official positions, thereby unravelling the insidious ways gendered disinformation can delegitimize women in politics even as it legitimates the fake accusations thrown at them, follows. The fifth section discusses initial developments on disinformation in the advent of President Ferdinand Marcos Jr.'s administration. Finally, it concludes with a set of recommendations and ways forward.

FILIPINO WOMEN IN POLITICS, MISOGYNY AND DISINFORMATION

It is important to highlight that the rightful claim to political space by women, like her counterparts in the rest of the world, has been long and fraught with challenges. Long before the grant of suffrage and the advent of Spanish and American rule, historians described Filipino women as quite active in the public sphere. They were already leaders in their communities, thus giving credence to accounts of a more egalitarian society in the precolonial period. In a sense, this also means that their presence during this period indicates that they were hardly the docile and homebound women they were depicted by anti-suffragists in the 1935 Constitutional Convention. Eventually, the government of the Philippine Commonwealth granted women the right to vote in 1937. Interestingly, this was long before the United States, the supposed bastion of democracy and under whose tutelage Filipinos were supposed to have learned about democracy, granted suffrage to African American women.[18] It was a long and uphill battle led by suffragists from prominent elite Filipino families. Since then, women were steadily represented in the country's political life. The first woman in the House of Representatives was elected in 1939, while in the Senate, she was elected in 1947.

Ferdinand Marcos Sr.'s dictatorship in the 1970s until the mid-1980s would forever change women's political role. The women's movement that contributed to the anti-Marcos struggle was able to advocate several provisions in the post-Marcos constitution. Among others, a key provision in the 1987 Constitution, stating that "the State recognizes the role of women in nation-building, and shall ensure the fundamental equality before the law of women and men", paved the way for several landmark laws on women's rights that Filipino women currently enjoy.[19] However, the aggregate total of women in politics at all levels of government is still low. For instance, after the 2022 synchronized elections, women comprise 27 per cent of parliament, and only 23 per cent of all national and local elective positions in the country.[20] Surprisingly, data on candidacy, the most important indicator of women's inclusion in politics, is where the gap between men and women is even more alarming. Data from the Commission on Elections show that in 2010, only 16.7 per cent of candidates were women; in 2022, it increased to 20.6 per cent.[21] The small number of women entering politics should still be a cause for concern.

An argument made against the increasing number of Filipino women in politics is that most are members of political families, a dysfunction of the country's political system in which political parties hardly matter. The idea is that when women come from dynastic families, their interests are often suspected to be highly influenced by their clans. However, a recent study[22] indicates that some women from political families with progressive backgrounds and experience have supported gender equality policies and programmes, implying that there are a few serious legislators from dynastic families. There might be a need to conduct more research on this area.

While indeed, there have been two women presidents (also from dynastic families), which some regard as remarkable, given that other advanced democracies have not had any, their entry to political office was contentious. Corazon Cojuangco Aquino, the widow of Senator Benigno Aquino, an erstwhile anti-Marcos politician, was catapulted to power at the height of a People Power Uprising in 1986. Though she stood against Marcos Sr. in the snap elections, the dictator was proclaimed the winner amidst accusations of massive fraud. In 2001, Gloria Macapagal Arroyo came to power after Joseph Estrada's ouster in the aftermath of a stalled impeachment trial. It took a Supreme Court decision to legally install Arroyo as president. In 2004, she ran and won the presidency, but to this day, her victory is marred with doubts considering that she publicly apologized for calling an election commissioner to pad her votes. Once again, the Supreme Court decided unanimously in favour of Arroyo, on the electoral protest made by Fernando Poe, Jr., Arroyo's opponent in the 2004 elections. In other words, it is difficult to prove that the two women presidents' assumption to power indicated that Filipinos were ready for a woman head of state.

Meanwhile, research shows several structural and institutional barriers to women's participation in formal politics. Those that have been identified are the first-past-the-post electoral system, masculinist electoral and parliamentary rules, and the prevalence of traditional roles and norms on women's place in society.[23] While these are important gaps that need to be urgently addressed, the threat posed by gendered disinformation will further hinder women's political opportunities.

DUTERTE'S HYPERMASCULINE IMAGE AND RHETORIC

Gendered disinformation is a more recent phenomenon although there have been publicized sexist remarks against women politicians in the past. Arguably, this was not as potent as today, given the limitations of previous forms of communication and technology. In the 1986 snap elections between Ferdinand Marcos Sr. and Corazon Cojuangco Aquino, for instance, the strategy was to portray Aquino as "dumb" because of her inexperience in politics and her being a mere homemaker. A political advertisement mimicking Aquino's voice was disseminated via radio and television to reinforce this claim. It not only portrayed her as incapable of addressing the country's problems, but also put her in contrast with Marcos Sr.'s masculinist authority coupled with his long political experience. During the presidency of Joseph Ejercito Estrada, a former actor and known womanizer, he sometimes made sexist remarks, earning the ire of women's groups. The actor-turned-politician President Joseph Estrada has publicly confessed to having several women in his life. According to Vicente Rafael, even Presidents Manuel Quezon and Ferdinand Marcos Sr. were also strongmen but projected a "sense of respectability to hide from view the more brutal practices of their government".[24] However, no one had been as notorious as President Rodrigo Duterte whose rape "jokes", sexual innuendos, and wet kiss of a Filipino woman (in front of the presidential seal), made headlines worldwide.[25] He was likened to Donald Trump and Jair Bolsonaro who cultivated a cult-following with their unabashed machismo and populist leadership style. His remark that the presidency is not a job for women[26] has never before been publicly made by any president.

Duterte was a mayor of Davao City in Mindanao for nearly forty years. He would jump from one position to another, to skirt the constitutional ban on term limits. He was known for having eased crimes that the city was widely known for before he became mayor. Duterte was not nationally prominent but in late 2015, just before he surprised everyone with his candidacy for president, he was vocal against the *tanim-bala* (bullet-planting) incidents that angered overseas Filipinos whose travels were delayed when they were accosted at Manila's airports.[27] He not only volunteered to be their lawyer, but also made statements wanting to kill the perpetrators, thereby putting him in stark contrast with then President Benigno Aquino's administration which was widely perceived to have downplayed the issue.[28] When he finally announced his candidacy, his hypermasculine rhetoric in the bullet-planting cases, foregrounded his misogynist, sexist language and behaviour during the campaign, the highlight of which was the rape joke made towards a dead Australian missionary, who herself was raped and killed. When he finally won, despite the remarks, misogyny became his trademark. Women's groups had to monitor his speeches to account for his sexist language.[29]

Duterte's vulgarity and sexism are far different. Such sexism endeared him to his political base, further propelling his macho image and made the perception of his "decisiveness" believable. Arguably, this may have helped legitimize his notorious drug war and helped him achieve the highest trust and approval rating at the end of his term, compared to his predecessors. Though it might be difficult to come to terms with this, in a country touted to be a frontrunner in terms of the number of laws protecting women's rights. Moreover, the country's Safe Spaces Act, a law protecting individuals from gender-based sexual harassment in streets, workplaces, online, and educational institutions and all public spaces, was even signed by

Duterte. But there is a plausible explanation for this. The 2017–22 World Values Survey[30] results indicate that more than 50 per cent of Filipinos think men are better leaders than women. In the same survey, nearly 80 per cent of Filipinos believe that when jobs are scarce, men have more right to a job than women. Meanwhile the United Nations Development Program's Gender Social Norms Index (GSNI) finds that in the Philippines, 99.5 per cent of the population has biases against women. In comparison, 75.5 per cent have biases against women as leaders and men and women having the same rights as important for democracy.[31] Therefore, this data suggests that norms about women's role in society and the public sphere are still in progress in the Philippines. For this reason, it is not farfetched to suggest that Duterte's language, though many find vulgar, made sense to his constituents and a sector of Philippine society.

Buoyed by Duterte's victory as the "social media" president, the Duterte administration hired influencers and vloggers to pump prime his messages while maligning mainstream media, particularly those critical of him and his war on drugs.[32] In a congressional budget hearing, his then head of communications was questioned over the number of contractual employees the office proposed to hire.[33] The suspicion was these were online trolls that the government planned to hire to amplify Duterte's machinery. Instances of disinformation and misinformation were also flagged by fact-checkers and traced to Duterte's key communication officials suggesting that state-sponsored falsities are becoming the norm. This is aside from Duterte's off-the-cuff remarks in his public speeches that have also been subjected to fact-checking and were verified to be untrue.

This chapter argues that Duterte's leadership style and his administration's sponsorship of disinformation foregrounded Marcos Jr.'s candidacy and prepared and normalized for Filipinos the manufactured idea of a macho and "decisive" leader who "delivers". In the following section, this chapter demonstrates how Duterte's style, assisted by state-run trolls and so-called influencers, paved and smoothened the way for Marcos Jr. By relentlessly maligning Robredo and detaining de Lima on what is believed to be trumped-up drug cases, Duterte made possible Marcos Jr.'s virtual hypermasculine[34] campaign anchored on authoritarian nostalgia.

ROBREDO, DE LIMA, AND GENDERED DISINFORMATION

False "Leaks" and Leni Gerona Robredo

Robredo's entry into the political fray resulted from the death of her husband, who was a long-time mayor of Naga City. Jesse Robredo was credited for transforming and modernizing the city located in the Bicol Peninsula in Southern Luzon. Leni Robredo, a human rights lawyer with a background in economics, won the third district seat in her hometown a year after her husband died. For three years, she would actively legislate policies on anti-corruption measures, people's participation in governance, and the bill seeking a law on freedom of information. She also served as vice chair of important committees in the House of Representatives. She actively worked for the approval of a law paving the way for tax incentives management and transparency, among others, either as the principal author or a co-author.

In 2016, she ran as a vice presidential candidate to Mar Roxas, the Liberal Party's standard bearer for that election period. She was not only a reluctant candidate, but her candidacy was considered an uphill climb, mainly because she was relatively unknown outside her congressional district. Eventually, she won by more than two hundred thousand votes against Marcos Jr., who ran with Miriam Defensor-Santiago of the People's Reform Party. Marcos Jr., who ran as an independent, challenged Robredo's victory but the case was overtaken by his presidential candidacy in the 2022 elections.

As vice president, Robredo was twice invited to join the Duterte cabinet as Housing Secretary and co-chair of Duterte's anti-drug body. However, her suggestions and recommendations were deemed as criticisms and for this reason,[35] her position became untenable for an administration sensitive to any form of dissent. Duterte fired her from the anti-drug council when she asked for a copy of high-value targets—information that Duterte's camp deemed classified and which they feared Robredo would provide the United Nations. Overall, the Duterte administration did not work with her. Instead, Robredo relied on volunteer groups and her small budget to implement small projects nationwide. In her six years as vice president, Robredo was subjected to relentless sexist remarks[36] from Duterte, from his public admission to ogling her legs to ranting about her not being fit to be president and lying about her supposed lack of contribution to the Typhoon Ulysses's response in 2020. When Robredo started criticizing the drug war, Duterte's troll machinery disseminated fake news dubbed as the Naga Leaks/Leni Leaks. Naga Leaks told a story about Robredo's husband Jesse, who was allegedly corrupt and was a drug lord.[37] For its part, Leni Leaks concocted a story using emails that purportedly involved Robredo in a plot to overthrow Duterte, which his presidential communications secretary further amplified.[38]

But among the most sexist disinformation against Robredo were her alleged affairs, abortion, and boyfriends which she vehemently denied. Not to mention the one using a fake photo of a leftist (a New People's Army member in other accounts) who supposedly married Robredo when she was fifteen years old.[39] These false accounts were further amplified by palace vloggers and influencers who disseminated them in their various social media handles, thereby taking a life of its own and taken as "truth" by Duterte supporters. According to polling data from the Social Weather Station, in September 2016, Robredo's net satisfaction rating was +49 which is translated to "good", but it dropped to +1 by a few months before the presidential elections in 2022,[40] thereby weakening Robredo's chances for higher political office. Her initial reluctance to run in the 2022 elections may have to do with this.

Meanwhile, Marcos Jr. benefitted from Robredo's already low satisfaction ratings. Suddenly, previous false stories about Robredo and her husband were revived and made even more popular by a troll army which Marcos Jr. admitted in jest he hired.[41] Along with the false nostalgia associated with Marcos Jr.'s campaign, Robredo was portrayed as "dumb"[42] in spliced and edited videos of her speeches. At the same time, Robredo's daughter was a subject of a fake sex video,[43] prompting the Robredo camp to seek the assistance of the National Bureau of Investigation. According to *tsek.ph*, a fact-checking initiative, Robredo was the biggest target of negative disinformation, while Marcos Jr. was the biggest beneficiary of fake news supportive of him and his candidacy. Robredo lost to Marcos Jr. in the 2022 elections.[44]

Lies, Sex Tapes, and Leila de Lima

Leila de Lima served as Philippine Senator from 2016 to 2022. A bar topnotcher and a human rights lawyer, she made her way to elective politics as former chair of the Commission on Human Rights (CHR) during the Gloria Macapagal Arroyo administration. In the CHR, she worked on investigating the notorious Davao Death Squad[45] that became prominent when Duterte was mayor. She was then appointed as Justice Secretary by President Benigno Aquino in 2010. When she won as senator in 2016, she chaired the Committee on Justice and Human Rights where she investigated Duterte's drug war and its extra-judicial killings. When the Senate hearings gained wide public attention, Duterte supporters in the Senate managed to oust de Lima as chair of the committee. Subsequently, several charges were filed against de Lima based on accusations that she coddled jailed drug lords allowing them to continue their business while in detention in exchange for election funds. Her driver, whom de Lima admitted as her former lover, was allegedly her bag man, who does the illegal drug trade with imprisoned drug lords.[46]

During these charges, the House of Representatives, majority of which are Duterte supporters, initiated hearings on the de Lima issue. A sex video purporting to be of de Lima and her driver became the focus of public hearings and garnered wide public attention. The legislators' (most of them men) insistence to have it played during the hearing, along with their sexual innuendo-laden questions, became the talk of the town.[47] While de Lima admitted to her relationship with the driver, she vehemently denied that it was her on the video. As early as 2014, the head of the Whistleblowers' Association of the Philippines, who had a falling out with de Lima when she was Justice Secretary, threatened to expose the fake sex video. However, in 2016 the footage suddenly gained traction and was amplified by Facebook and YouTube accounts supporting Duterte.

Since 2017, de Lima has been detained based on what some believe are trumped-up charges to punish her for investigating the drug war and the Davao Death Squad. In 2017 and 2018, Amnesty International, the international human rights group, recognized her as one of the women human rights defenders.[48] The European Union and other members of parliament in other countries have severely criticized de Lima's detention and arrest. She ran and lost in the 2022 senatorial elections. Also in 2022, witnesses against de Lima recanted their statements, stating that the police coerced them into accusing her. In January 2023, the woman who was reportedly the source of de Lima's fake sex video asked forgiveness from de Lima and said that she was just used as a tool by the past administration to bolster the charges against her.[49] Finally, in May 2023, de Lima was acquitted of two of the three charges against her.[50] Six months after, she was finally released on bail.[51]

The following themes explore the typology of narratives present in the gendered disinformation hurled at both women.

"Immoral" Women, "Untrustworthy" Leaders

In almost all societies, women are held to a different standard than men, often associated with their socially ascribed roles as mothers and caretakers. Because they are supposed to carry and nurture the next generation, they must remain "pure". In the deliberations over the right to suffrage in the 1935 Constitution, anti-suffragists argued that women must remain in the private sphere and not concern themselves with public affairs, so as not to be tainted by dirty politics and not neglect their children and the household.[52] Therefore, de Lima's affair and Robredo's fake affair were meant to portray them as "immoral" women that risked transgressing Filipino society's moral code. In the only country without a law on divorce, marriage and family are considered sacred, with constitutional safeguards ensuring their role as important institutions in Philippine society. However, when it comes to marital infidelity, a double standard exists in which there is more shame for women committing it compared to men. Married male politicians (i.e., President Rodrigo Duterte and President Joseph Ejercito Estrada) can publicly admit siring children from many women and still win; however, their female counterparts are punished, and slut shamed. The country's legal framework sanctions this double standard. Under Philippine criminal laws, adultery (women) and concubinage (men) are crimes involving infidelity. Women accused of adultery have higher penalties compared to men accused of concubinage.

With this context, it is easy to see why the fake news about Robredo's affairs and de Lima's admission of her affair with the driver would negatively resonate with Filipinos. De Lima's statement on a televised interview that her affair was part of "the frailties of a woman"[53] did not help her cause precisely because the fake sex video had already painted her as "sex-hungry" enough to have an affair with her married driver, way below her level. In all, Robredo's fake affair and de Lima's fake video suggests that because they are "immoral" women, they are untrustworthy as leaders who lack control over their basic instincts. Duterte used this trope in these words: "What is really sad for this country, here is a woman posturing [herself] to be a crusader for good government. But because she could not stop her immorality—well, to De Lima's credit she is legally annulled like me and is a bachelorette—but her sex escapades led her to commit several serious violations of law."[54] Therefore, "immoral" women's actions and pronouncements should not be taken seriously. In other words, they should not be entrusted with governing. Never mind that Duterte himself admitted to having girlfriends, is not married to his partner, and has admitted to harassing their domestic worker.[55] In responding to the de Lima-led Senate investigations on the war on drugs, Duterte stated that the senator has a "propensity for sex" and "is not only screwing her driver, she is screwing the nation".[56] As "immoral" women, it became easy for Robredo and de Lima to be targeted with further fake accusations. The cracks in the solid foundation of what it takes to be a "decent" Filipino woman has already been made.

"Bad" Mother, "Incompetent" Manager

This trope is closely related to the one discussed above. Compared to men, women are traditionally associated with the family and children. Sociologist Belen Medina emphasized that "the responsibility for homemaking still falls in the hands of the wife".[57] For this reason, statutes and programmes are made with the customary phrase "women and children", suggesting that the latter's welfare is the former's sole responsibility. While this does not, in any way, take away the benefit of policies advocating for women and children as a sector, it also strips men of their responsibility towards their children. At the same time, it also makes men invisible and less likely to be blamed, whenever transgressions are committed in the name of the family.

A case in point is the "homewrecker" accusations against Robredo and de Lima, which largely puts the blame on them and invisibilizes the men who should also be held accountable. This narrative implies that "homewreckers" are not competent to take charge of the nation's children and families.

In the same vein, the target of fake sex video of Robredo's daughter was not the daughter but Robredo herself. During the campaign and throughout her vice presidency, the Robredo daughters were depicted as achievers and normal middle-class children. The sisters were also widely present in campaign sorties and media interviews, adding a sense of normalcy and relatability to Robredo's public image. In essence, the fake video attempted to depict candidate Robredo as a "bad" mother with a "slut" for a daughter. As mentioned earlier, because of women's traditional caretaking roles, mothers are always at the centre of society's moral judgment, not men. Therefore, accusing women of being "bad" mothers has arguably more weight than labelling men as "bad" fathers. For a female politician, this implies that if one cannot control and discipline her family, particularly her children, it suggests that she will do poorly as a manager of the nation's affairs. If she lacks control, then she will not perform well.

"Criminal" Partners, Emotional Women

When women commit supposed criminal acts, it is often portrayed that it is a result of her emotional ties to someone, thereby downplaying their agency.[58] Therefore, the company they keep, especially men, such as husbands, brothers, and boyfriends are put under societal radar whenever crimes are committed by women. The false narratives about Robredo marrying a rebel (member of the New Peoples' Army) when she was fifteen, and who was killed by dictator Ferdinand Marcos Sr.'s soldiers, is an example. By highlighting this, it then makes the claim that Robredo and the opposition she led are destabilizing the government, believable. Even more, her criticism against the Marcoses is framed under this fake news for emotional reasons and not as a matter of principle against the dictatorship. In other words, that she was supposed to be emotionally related to a leftist makes her criticisms of the government suspect, less objective, and illegitimate.

This then dilutes her entire position as the opposition with the highest government rank and strengthens the government's red tagging of opposition politicians. It will be recalled that in 2017, Duterte supporters floated the idea of making her liable for treason when she criticized the government's war on drugs in a video presentation that she made for the United Nations Commission on Narcotic Drugs Annual Meeting.[59]

Meanwhile, de Lima's admission that she was in a relationship with her driver was the important link to the illegal drug trade that the senator was accused of. Supposedly, the driver received payoffs meant for de Lima's 2016 elections, as stated above. At the same time, having a relationship with a man way below her economic and professional background made it easy to accuse her of corruption and bribery.

In other words, by supposedly cohabiting with "criminal" men as the above narratives suggest, de Lima and Robredo acted "illegally". Under this interpretation, women are supposed to be weak and emotional, who can be controlled by unscrupulous individuals. It will also be recalled that Duterte has been known for public statements stating that women are not fit for political office because they are "emotional".[60] As such, because de Lima and Robredo are emotionally "weak" and can be influenced by their supposed partners, they can hardly handle public office without committing treason, corruption, or any crime. The "criminal" partners, emotional women trope, therefore, disqualifies women from public office. Their decisions are not autonomous but a result of their emotional ties to men.

MARCOS JR. AND "VIRTUAL HYPERMASCULINITY"

As stated in this chapter, Duterte paved the way for Marcos Jr.'s candidacy and eventual victory. Arguably, Duterte's unabashed sexism resonated with Filipinos' latent gender biases. Robredo and de Lima, as discussed above, were at the receiving end of this. However, Maria Tanyag[61] rightfully pointed this out but she argues that unlike Duterte, Marcos Jr.'s gendered appeal is harnessed online, which she labels as "virtual hypermasculinity". Indeed, even as Marcos Jr. also admitted[62] to using trolls during the elections, a different information ecosystem permeates his supporters—one in which he is valorized as a competent and strong leader even if reports[63] contradict this. According to Tanyag, "his version relies on augmenting reality and cultivating a virtual presence on online platforms".[64] Nonetheless, Marcos Jr. does not only borrow from Duterte's playbook albeit in an online version, but he also largely still relies on authoritarian nostalgia from his father's administration, characterized by strongman rule. It remains to be seen how this virtual promotion will play out in years moving forward, and to what extent this will be used to criticize Marcos Jr.'s opponents. Marcos Jr. is arguably not Duterte, nor is he even close to his father's persona in rhetoric and style. But this is precisely why there is reason to believe that disinformation will continue under his administration. His administration's ability to manage his popularity and continue to revive the family name via false authoritarian nostalgia will be part of Marcos Jr.'s political currency in the next five years.

CONCLUSION AND RECOMMENDATIONS

This chapter presented the contours of gendered disinformation in the Philippine context via the cases of Robredo and de Lima. The political and historical context of women's participation in Philippine politics shows how women have fought for their rightful place in the public sphere. While the battle is far from over, the advent of gendered disinformation threatens to lose some of the gains. Robredo and de Lima dared to criticize Duterte and were silenced via false narratives that tapped into Filipino norms and beliefs about the role of men and women in society. On Robredo's part, her loss to Marcos Jr. was already foregrounded by the relentless fake news that started when she assumed the vice presidency.

Disinformation in general is difficult to address given the ever-changing nature of technology. Governments keeping up with their regulatory framework are in a quandary given that freedom of speech is a sacredly guarded liberty in democracies. As such, manoeuvring policy formulation that does not hamper this freedom makes regulation difficult, contentious, and always a work in progress. Moreover, the current potential of artificial intelligence and its evolution in the coming years is a cause of concern. Given what it can do in its present form, there is reason to be concerned about its future incarnation.

With the discussion above, moves to address gendered disinformation and all its forms, are steps in the right direction. Other countries are beginning to undertake mapping of gendered disinformation's possibilities and how it can best be addressed in the policy terrain. Obviously, because of its complexities, there is no one-size-fits-all solution. It may have to be a combination of policies, incentives, and programmes. Consensus on policy direction must be geared towards the roots of gendered disinformation. Social norms undermining women and sexual minorities' status, especially in the public sphere, must be addressed so that gendered disinformation does not have a solid foundation to stand on. Transforming deeply ingrained gender biases is difficult and requires a long-term approach, but it is an investment worth taking on. Meanwhile, the country's electoral laws, particularly the Omnibus Election Code, must be reviewed to align the statute to current technological developments. For as long as the laws are not updated, difficulty in prosecuting perpetrators and those that employ them will always rear its ugly head. Along with this, a gender analysis of the Code and all directives of the COMELEC is also imperative. Other electoral reforms needed are amendments to the Fair Election Law which needs to be updated in the age of social media and gendered disinformation. Punishing perpetrators of violence against women (disinformation included) will also help address the small number of women entering politics. Finally, political parties, the COMELEC, and electoral reform advocates must partner with women's groups, vloggers, influencers, and the social media industry, to agree on steps to prevent online harm to women in politics.

Notes

1. Aurel Croissant and Larry Diamond, "Introduction: Reflections on Democratic Backsliding in Asia", *Global Asia* 15, no. 1 (2020): 8, https://www.globalasia.org/v15no1/cover/introduction-reflections-on-democratic-backsliding-in-asia_aurel-croissantlarry-diamond.
2. Gavin Wilde, "The Problem with Defining 'Disinformation'", Carnegie Endowment for International Peace, 10 November 2022, https://carnegieendowment.org/2022/11/10/problem-with-defining-disinformation-pub-88385.

3. Ronan O. Fathaigh, Natalie Helberger, and Naomi Appelman, "The Perils of Legally Defining Disinformation", *Internet Policy Review* 10, no. 4 (2021), https://www.ivir.nl/publicaties/download/InternetPolicyReview_2021.pdf.
4. Ma. Diosa Labiste, "Tsek.ph and the Media's Pushback against Digital Disinformation", Chapter 7 of this volume.
5. John Paolo Bencito, "Duterte Admits Paying Trolls for 2016 Elections", *Manila Standard*, 26 July 2017, https://manilastandard.net/news/national/242853/duterte-admits-paying-trolls-for-2016-elections.html.
6. Aim Sinpeng, Dimitar Gueorguiev, and Aries A. Arugay, "Strong Fans, Weak Campaigns: Social Media and Duterte in the 2016 Philippine Election", *Journal of East Asian Studies* 20, no. 3 (2020): 353–74.
7. Pam Pastor, "PH, 'Patient Zero' in Fake News Epidemic Can Learn From Finland", *Global Nation Inquirer*, 19 June 2022, https://globalnation.inquirer.net/204626/ph-patient-zero-in-fake-news-epidemic-can-learn-from-finland.
8. Simon Kemp, "Digital 2022: The Philippines", *Data Reportal*, 15 February 2022, https://datareportal.com/reports/digital-2022-philippines?rq=Philippines.
9. Nina Jankowicz, Jillian Hunchak, Alexandara Pavliuc, Celia Davies, Shannon Pierson, and Zoe Kaufmann, "Malign Creativity: How Gender, Sex, and Lies Are Weaponized against Women Online" (Wahington, D.C.: Wilson Center, January 2021), p. 8., https://www.wilsoncenter.org/publication/malign-creativity-how-gender-sex-and-lies-are-weaponized-against-women-online.
10. Ibid.
11. Rita Jonusaite, Maria Jovanna Sessa, Kristina Wilfore, and Lucina di Meco, "Gender-Based Disinformation: Theory, Examples, and Need for Regulation", *EU Disinfo Lab*, 12 October 2022, p. 3, https://www.disinfo.eu/wp-content/uploads/2022/10/20221012_TechnicalDocumentGBD-2.pdf.
12. Jon Benedik A. Bunquin, Fatima Gaw, Julienne Thesa Y. Baldo-Cubelo, Fernando DlC Paragas, and Ma. Rosel S. San Pascual, "Digital Public Pulse: 2022 Philippines General Election", Philippine Media Monitoring Laboratory, College of Mass Communication, University of the Philippines, 2022, pp. 170–74.
13. Justin Muyot, "Weapons of Mass Destruction: Harnessing the Appeals of Sex Scandals against Political Opposition", FEU Public Policy Center, 7 June 2022, https://publicpolicy.feu.org.ph/article-series/weapons-of-mass-distraction-harnessing-the-appeal-of-sex-scandals-against-political-opposition/.
14. Elizabeth L. Enriquez, "Cybermisogyny and Human Rights", *Daily Guardian*, 12 May 2022, https://www.dailyguardian.com.ph/cybermisogyny-and-human-rights/.
15. Inter-Parliamentary Union, "Global and Regional Averages of Women in National Parliaments", 1 January 2023, https://data.ipu.org/women-averages?month=1&year=2023.

16. World Economic Forum, "Global Gender Gap Report", July 2022, p. 6, https://www3.weforum.org/docs/WEF_GGGR_2022.pdf.
17. James B. Jimenez and Teresita L. Cadiben-Villena, "Preserving Honest, Orderly, and Safe Election System in the Philippines: A Trend Analysis of Selected Election Statistics", n.d., https://psa.gov.ph/sites/default/files/kmcd/Preserving%20Honest%2C%20Orderly%2C%20and%20Safe%20Election%20System_.pdf.
18. Although suffrage for women in the United States was granted in 1920, it was not until the 1965 Civil Rights Act that African American women were allowed to vote without facing local regulatory discrimination, harassment, etc.
19. Jean Encinas-Franco, "Filipino Women's Substantive Representation in Electoral Politics", in *Substantive Representation of Women in Asian Parliaments*, edited by Devin K. Joshi and Christian Echle (London: Routledge, 2022), p. 140; Jean Encinas-Franco and Elma Laguna, "Overcoming Barriers to Filipino Women's Political Representation", UP-CIDS Discussion Paper Series 2023-01 (Quezon City: University of the Philippines, 2023), p. 9, https://cids.up.edu.ph/wp-content/uploads/2023/01/Barriers-to-Filipino-Womens-Political-Participation.pdf.
20. Philippine Statistics Authority, "Fact Sheet on Women and Men in the Philippines", 25 April 2023, https://psa.gov.ph/gender-stat/wmf/7.%20Public%20Life.
21. George Erwin M. Garcia and Selva Ramachandran, "Beyond a Glance: Digitalization and Enhanced Data Governance for Women's Political Participation in the Philippines", United Nations Development Program Philippines, 6 March 2023, https://www.undp.org/philippines/blog/beyond-glance-digitalization-and-enhanced-data-governance-womens-political-participation-philippines.
22. Encinas-Franco, "Filipino Women's Substantive Representation in Electoral Politics", p. 146; Encinas-Franco and Laguna, "Overcoming Barriers to Filipino Women's Political Representation".
23. Encinas-Franco and Laguna, "Overcoming Barriers to Filipino Women's Political Representation".
24. Vicente L. Rafael, *The Sovereign Trickster* (Durham: Duke University Press, 2022), p. 83.
25. Jean Encinas-Franco, "The Presidential Kiss: Duterte's Gendered Populism, Hypermasculinity, and Filipino Migrants", *NORMA* 17, no. 2 (2022): 107–23, https://doi.org/10.1080/18902138.2022.2026107.
26. Karen Lema, "Philippines' Duterte Says Presidency No Job for a Woman", Reuters, 14 January 2021, https://www.reuters.com/article/us-philippines-duterte-idUSKBN29J21U.

27. Encinas-Franco, "The Presidential Kiss".
28. Ibid.
29. Teresita Quintos-Deles, *Women Under Siege: Manifestations of Populism and Its Impact on Gender Equality in the Philippines* (Quezon City: ICITEGov, 2020), https://incitegov.org.ph/includes/publications/Populism%20&%20Gender%20[April2021].pdf, p. 8.
30. C. Haerpfer, R. Inglehart, A. Moreno, C. Welzel, K. Kizilova, J. Diez-Medrano, P. M. Lagos, E. Norris, Ponarin, and B. Puranen, eds., *World Values Survey: Round Seven - Country-Pooled Datafile Version 5.0* (Madrid, Spain and Vienna, Austria: JD Systems Institute and WVSA Secretariat, 2022), pp. 205, 213, https://doi.org/10.14281/18241.20.
31. UNDP (United Nations Development Programme), "2023 Gender Social Norms Index (GSNI) – Breaking Down Gender Biases: Shifting Social Norms Towards Gender Equality", June 2023, https://hdr.undp.org/content/2023-gender-social-norms-index-gsni#/indicies/GSNI.
32. Natashya Gutierrez, "State-Sponsored Hate: The Rise of the Pro-Duterte Bloggers", *Rappler*, 18 August 2017, https://www.rappler.com/newsbreak/in-depth/178709-duterte-die-hard-supporters-bloggers-propaganda-pcoo/.
33. Elmor Santos, "Senators Seek Records of 1,479 PCOO Workers Suspected to Be Trolls", *CNN Philippines*, 16 September 2021, https://www.cnnphilippines.com/news/2021/9/16/pcoo-contract-of-service-employees-trolls.html.
34. Maria Tanyag, "Marcos Jr. and the Dangers of Hypermasculinity", *Fulcrum*, 4 April 2023, https://fulcrum.sg/marcos-jr-and-the-dangers-of-virtual-hypermasculinity/.
35. Michelle Abad, "Robredo's Access to High-Value Target List 'Unnecessary' – Barbers", *Rappler*, 22 November 2019, https://www.rappler.com/nation/245553-dangerous-drugs-committee-robredo-access-high-value-target-list-unnecessary/.
36. *GMA News Online*, "Gabriela: Duterte's Remarks about Robredo 'Perpetuate Sexist Bullying'", 9 November 2016, https://www.gmanetwork.com/news/topstories/nation/588218/gabriela-duterte-s-remarks-about-robredo-perpetuate-sexist-bullying/story/.
37. Helen Flores and Janvic Mateo, "NagaLeaks Released; Leni Slams 'Lies'", *PhilStar Online*, 4 March 2017, https://www.philstar.com/headlines/2017/03/04/1676623/nagaleaks-released-leni-slams-lies.
38. Pia Ranada, "'LeniLeaks'? Cabinet Has 'More Important Matters' to Discuss – Esperon", *Rappler*, 9 January 2017, https://www.rappler.com/nation/157803-leni-leaks-cabinet-meeting-esperon/.
39. Vera Files, "Vera Files Fact Check: Wedding Pic Does Not Show Robredo and 'First Spouse'", 5 April 2022, https://verafiles.org/articles/vera-files-fact-check-wedding-pic-does-not-show-robredo-and.

40. Janvic Mateo, "SWS Releases Final Satisfaction Ratings of Robredo, Sotto", *PhilStar Global*, 5 October 2022, https://www.philstar.com/headlines/2022/10/05/2214358/sws-releases-final-satisfaction-ratings-robredo-sotto#:~:text=The%20former%20vice%20president%20started,her%20bid%20for%20the%20presidency.
41. Alan Robles, "Marcos Admits to Using 'Troll Army' in Polls Push", *South China Morning Post*, 14 June 2022, https://www.pressreader.com/china/south-china-morning-post-6150/20220614/281840057325122.
42. Vera Files, "Vera Files Fact Check: Misleading Video Portrays Robredo as Dumb", 21 November 2021, https://verafiles.org/articles/vera-files-fact-check-misleading-video-portrays-robredo-dumb.
43. Betheena Unite, "Spread of Fake Sex Video of Robredo's Eldest Daughter Is Now 'Backfiring'— Pangilinan", *Manila Bulletin*, 13 April 2022, https://mb.com.ph/2022/04/13/spread-of-fake-sex-video-of-robredos-eldest-daughter-is-now-backfiring-pangilinan.
44. Pola Rubio, "Robredo Biggest Fake News Victim: Fact-Check Group", *Tsek.ph*, 3 February 2022, https://www.tsek.ph/robredo-biggest-fake-news-victim-fact-check-group/.
45. Antonio J. Montalvan II, "Why Leila de Lima Was Marked for Assassination", Vera Files, 10 May 2023, https://verafiles.org/articles/why-leila-de-lima-was-marked-for-assassination.
46. *The Philippine Star*, "Senator's Lover-Driver Collected Drug Money", 18 August 2016, https://www.philstar.com/headlines/2016/08/18/1614683/senators-lover-driver-collected-drug-money.
47. Marc Jayson Cayabyab, "Alvarez: No Violation of Law in Showing Alleged De Lima Sex Video", *Inquirer.net*, 29 September 2016, https://newsinfo.inquirer.net/820394/alvarez-no-violation-of-law-in-showing-alleged-de-lima-sex-video.
48. Gaea Katreena Cabico, "De Lima Hailed as Most Distinguished Filipino Rights Defender", *Philippine Star Global*, 29 May 2018, https://www.philstar.com/headlines/2018/05/29/1819721/de-lima-hailed-most-distinguished-filipino-rights-defender.
49. Joahna Lei Casilao, "Sandra Cam: I Was Used as a Tool for the Imprisonment of Leila De Lima", *GMA Integrated News*, 18 January 2023, https://www.gmanetwork.com/news/topstories/nation/857841/sandra-cam-i-was-used-as-a-tool-for-the-imprisonment-of-leila-de-lima/story/.
50. Emmanuel Tupas, "De Lima Acquitted in 2nd Drug Case", *Philippine Star Global*, 13 May 2023, https://www.philstar.com/headlines/2023/05/13/2265957/de-lima-acquitted-2nd-drug-case.
51. Nillicent Bautistat, "De Lima Freed on Bail", *Philippine Star Global*, 14 November 2023, https://www.philstar.com/headlines/2023/11/14/2311242/de-lima-freed-bail.

52. Rhodalyn Wani-Obias, "The Debate on Women's Suffrage in the Philippines", *UP sa Halalan*, 13 July 2013, https://halalan.up.edu.ph/the-debate-on-womens-suffrage-in-the-philippines/.
53. *CNN Philippines*, "De Lima: Respect My Privacy", 15 November 2016, https://www.cnnphilippines.com/news/2016/11/15/de-lima-on-past-relationship-with-dayan.html.
54. Leila B. Salaverria, "Duterte: De Lima's 'Sexcapades' Led Her to Crime, Drug Pay-Offs", *Inquirer.net*, 24 August 2016, https://newsinfo.inquirer.net/809371/duterte-de-limas-sexcapades-led-her-to-crime-drug-pay-offs.
55. *Rappler*, "Duterte 'Confesses' He Molested Their Maid as a Teen", 13 December 2018, https://www.rappler.com/newsbreak/inside-track/219935-duterte-teen-molested-maid/.
56. Alexis Romero, "De Lima Screwing Not Only Her Driver But Also the Nation", *The PhilStar Global*, 23 September 2016, https://www.philstar.com/headlines/2016/09/23/1626562/de-lima-screwing-not-only-her-driver-also-nation.
57. Belen Medina, *The Filipino Family* (Quezon City: University of the Philippines Press, 2005).
58. Carol Gentry, "Women as Agents of Violence", 2017, https://doi.org/10.1093/acrefore/9780190846626.013.61.
59. Patty Pasion, "Robredo Only Stated Facts in UN Video, Says Spokesperson", *Rappler*, 17 March 2017, https://www.rappler.com/nation/164461-leni-robredo-reaction-criticism-un-video-message/.
60. Erin Cunningham, "Philippine Leader Rodrigo Duterte Says Women Are Not Fit to Be President", *The Washington Post*, 15 January 2021, https://www.washingtonpost.com/world/asia_pacific/philippine-duterte-woman-president/2021/01/15/47f1125e-5703-11eb-acc5-92d2819a1ccb_story.html.
61. Tanyag, "Marcos Jr. and the Dangers of Virual Hypermasculinity".
62. Alan Robles, "Marcos' 'Confessions': Philippine President-Elect Admits to 'Trolls', Needing Guidance – and Doing It for His Parents", *South China Morning Post*, 14 June 2022, https://www.scmp.com/week-asia/politics/article/3181416/marcos-confessions-philippines-president-elect-admits-trolls.
63. Dwight de Leon, "'Insensitive, Callous': Marcos Criticized over 'Luxurious' Singapore Grand Prix Trip", 3 October 2022, https://www.rappler.com/nation/lawmakers-reactions-marcos-jr-singapore-grand-prix-trip-october-2022/.
64. Tanyag, "Marcos Jr. and the Dangers of Virtual Hypermasculinity".

13

(Dis)continuities and Disruptions in Labour Migration Governance: The Philippines from the Duterte to the Marcos Jr. Administration

Bubbles Beverly Asor and Rizza Kaye Cases

> *Under what conditions do gradual and punctuated events maintain or disrupt and alter existing "regimes of governing practices"? To what extent do (un)anticipated turning points bring about (dis)continuities in migration governance? Within migration studies, some scholars tend to subscribe to such assumptions of dramatic shifts altering the migration landscape. However, what might be overlooked by these assertions are the enduring and self-perpetuating characteristics of the migration process. Considered to be one of the largest labour-exporting economies and a model for other labour sending countries, the Philippines developed a highly "institutionalized labour-export*

process" and interdependent government and non-government actors that manage and facilitate overseas deployment of Filipino workers. This chapter explored the persistence and (dis)continuities of regimes of governing practices that not only manage and regulate but also produce "highly desired" and "deployable" migrant workers from the Philippines. This is despite and amidst sociopolitical transitions and disruptions at the national and global levels. In particular, this chapter examined to what extent episodic events—global pandemic and leadership transition from Duterte to Marcos Jr.—shape and are shaped by migration governance.

Keywords: migration governance, institutional reproduction, crisis, critical junctures, Philippines labour migration

INTRODUCTION

The Philippines has long been regarded as one of the major sources of migrants across the globe. In 1997, the Commission on Filipinos Overseas (CFO) estimated the number of Filipinos residing and working abroad at 6,974,065 in 193 countries, and in 2007, there were 7,754,263 Filipinos overseas or almost 9 per cent of the total Filipino population. This aggregate which includes permanent, temporary, and irregular migrants, and sea-based workers consistently increased to 10,238,614 in 2013.[1] Consequently, the Philippines has become one of the most significant origin countries. In the World Migration Reports of the International Organisation of Migration (IOM) from 2000 to 2022, the Philippines was placed between 4th and 9th in the largest sources of migrants in the world.[2] It has also been positioned as a major remittance-recipient country together with China, India, and Mexico (ibid.). The Philippines has continuously been the recipient of one of the largest shares of remittance from US$5.4 billion in 1995 to US$13.7 billion in 2005 and US$29.8 billion in 2015. Prior to the COVID-19 pandemic, the remittances received by the Philippines peaked at US$33.47 billion. In 2020, both the personal remittances and cash remittances[3] had a slight drop to US$33.19 billion from US$33.47 billion and to US$29.90 billion from US$30.13 billion, respectively (ibid.).[4] There was a small dip in the remittance inflow between January and October 2020 at

–0.9 per cent compared to the same period in 2019. However, in 2021 and 2022, personal remittances peaked again at US$34.89 billion and US$36.13 billion.

This development is, in fact, unsurprising contrary to the worrying prognosis that crises such as the global pandemic would lead to remittance slump and "large-scale" retrenchment and repatriation of migrant workers because of their precarious positions during crises and disruptive times.[5] These spurious suppositions and swift conclusions have overlooked three important undercurrents: (1) there is a higher ratio of migrants in major migration corridors that are well established and institutionalized, hence these migrants are more likely to have more resources and capital to deal with migration disruptions; (2) the labour and employment niche where most migrant workers are embedded in is considered to be "essential", which continue to function and operate despite disruptions and crises; and (3) remittances tend to be countercyclical as migrants send large amount of money to their dependents in the origin country during crises with the assumption that migrant households may need more resources.[6]

The impact of crises on remittance inflow to home countries both at the micro and macro levels is but one of the many areas of the intricate migration-crisis dynamics. During crises or "exceptional events", common wisdom presupposes that most migrants are the first to be fired from their already precarious jobs in the host society, hence they are constrained and compelled to return to their home countries which leads to "large-scale deportations, repatriations, and contract interruptions and disruptions of labour migration patterns" and "state-induced immobility".[7] Both home and host societies are believed to institute protectionist and restrictive migration policies primarily because of the economic crises triggering unemployment and dismal labour market conditions engendered by the COVID-19 pandemic. Xiang et al. posit the COVID-19 pandemic led to what they term as "shock mobilities", which are "migratory routines that are radically and abruptly reconfigured in response to acute disruptions".[8] They involve both sudden surges and stoppages of movement as manifested in varied forms including panicked emergency flights from epicentres, mass repatriations, lockdowns, and quarantines imposed by the state as a "dramatic" response to the crisis not only to "enhance power and curtail freedoms", but also to generate a "new" geopolitical (re) order. This implies that a crisis such as the COVID-19 pandemic may have led to or paved the way for institutional change, institutional genesis, and other subsequent institutional developments stemming from critical junctures given that both sending and receiving states are afforded a political opportunity to "enact new plans and realize new ideas by embedding them in the institutions they establish". Crises and external shocks are debated whether they cause restrictive or liberalizing migration policy change.

However, on a note of caution, existing literature on crisis-migration nexus interrogate this "simplistic" migration-crisis link, especially in terms of crisis-induced changes in migration policy and institutional configurations related to migration dynamics.[9] They reveal that some changes can be observed initially during the time of crisis, yet the causal link between the crisis and changes in migration policies cannot be fully established. To comprehend the migration-crisis nexus, it is imperative to delineate first what the change is and what the scope, reach, breadth, process, and cause of the change is. In a similar vein, if crisis is treated as a critical juncture vis-à-vis institutional genesis (or continuity) in migration dynamics, what is "critical" in the phenomenon, moment, episode, or event at hand to overcome the contingency problem,[10] the likelihood of spuriousness[11] and/or premature prognosis of causality given that the impact of the crisis may still be cascading into various realms of society. Therefore, not all ostensibly dramatic disruptions no matter how significant may not subsequently spearhead social transformations and institutional changes. Continuity and institutional reproduction are part of the enduring pattern of social institutions and social processes, in this case, the enduring and self-perpetuating characteristics of the migration process.[12]

This chapter analyses the migration-crisis dynamics in a migrant-sending society like the Philippines, which is one of the largest labour-exporting economies and a model for other labour-sending countries. The Philippines has developed a highly "institutionalized labour-export process" and a "symbiotic" relationship between government and non-government actors that manage and facilitate the overseas deployment of Filipino workers.[13] In this chapter, we explore the persistence and (dis)continuities of regimes of governing practices that not only manage and regulate but also produce "highly desired" and "deployable" migrant workers from the Philippines despite and amidst sociopolitical transitions and disruptions at the national and global levels. In particular, we examine to what extent episodic events—global pandemic and leadership transition from President Rodrigo Duterte to Ferdinand Marcos Jr.—shape and are shaped by migration governance. This question is salient especially during the period when media and popular discourses anticipated the "radical" impact of the global pandemic and leadership transition on the Philippine policy on sending migrants for labour export. The COVID-19 pandemic led to initial and temporary (en)forced immobilities of migrants while the campaign promises of Duterte and Marcos Jr. to the Filipino migrants and the massive support of overseas Filipinos to both presidents were assumed to produce an increase in return migration because the Philippines would be "better" under both administrations. Was the establishment of the Department of Migrant Workers a product of these assumed "radical" changes or further institutionalization and persistence of existing migration policy? What is the impact of these periods of changes on the migration flow of Filipino migrants and Philippine migration policies? Did it lead to some institutional innovations (i.e., policy changes on "banning" some migrants based on occupation) in terms of managing migration, especially the exit and "deployment" of Filipino migrants, particularly the stoppage of outflow of migrant workers and/or return migration? Or did it lead to continuity and strengthening of existing migration policies, such as the labour export policy in place? To what extent do these two significant episodic events constitute a critical juncture, a "negative case of critical juncture",[14] a failed critical juncture,[15] or institutional continuity?

To address these questions and contribute to the debate between institutional reproduction and institutional change during times of upheaval, this chapter focuses on the persistence and continuity of institutional arrangements, especially in the migration process. It does not mean we overlook the significance and consequences of crises such as the COVID-19 pandemic especially to individual migrants and migrant households. However, this chapter underscores the entanglement of continuity and change, and that crisis-induced changes in migration flow and migration policies are usually initiated prior to the crises. The "exceptional events" such as health crisis, economic crisis, financial meltdown, natural catastrophes, and even recurring leadership transitions are utilized by various actors—state and non-state—as additional justification for any changes in migration policies and migration dynamics but not the primary cause of institutional changes.[16] We first present the theoretical underpinning of the chapter to address our main question: to what extent do "exceptional events", such as health pandemic and political leadership transition, produce institutional innovation or reproduction, particularly in relation to migration policies? The subsequent sections discuss the findings and analysis where we presented empirical pieces of evidence for our main argument.

CRITICAL (DIS)JUNCTURES, MIGRATION GOVERNANCE, AND "PERIOD OF UPHEAVAL"

Crises such as the COVID-19 pandemic were projected to cause significant changes in the migration flow and migration policies. Migration research done during and about the pandemic and its impact on migration flow presented that mobility restrictions were implemented which have altered "the relationship between outmigration and return, between mobility and stoppage, between migrants in sending and receiving communities".[17] Previous works on crisis-migration nexus also revealed that restrictive and protectionist migration policies took effect in the aftermath of the 2008 global financial crisis. Both exogenous and endogenous shocks concomitant with economic crisis were deemed to push states to "make migration more difficult, protect native workers, employ more measures to increase return migration and clamp down on irregular migrants".[18] Other scholars identified the COVID-19 pandemic as an opportunity for states to further implement bordering strategies and securitize migration and mobility.[19]

Crisis and migration are correlated concepts and realities, but they are not always causally related. When migration scholars presuppose that crises engender the "end of the age of migration"[20] given the "significant alterations to the timing, duration, intensity, and relations among existing movements" and that most of the alterations are due to "routinized state powers" in response to the "exceptional disruptions", it is crucial to primarily ascertain whether the crises initiated and induced the migration policy reforms, hence institutional genesis transpires or those changes would have ensued nonetheless.[21] In this regard, caution is necessitated to "avoid endogenous or exogenous events being randomly chosen as sweeping explanations for migration and integration policy reforms". Although crises correlate with changes in migration flow, it is problematic to find empirical confirmations of migration policy shifts and "radical" changes in migration governance as a direct outcome of crises. Post-crisis changes in migration dynamics are often based on "policy programs and ideas that were initiated long before the crisis even began".[22] For example, the COVID-19 pandemic was utilized by both migrant-receiving and migrant-sending states to instigate restrictive changes in migration governance and to justify a protectionist attitude towards migration.[23] Given the "exceptional character of the COVID-19 emergency"[24] with such dramatic magnitude in terms of extant, reach, and intensity, the global health crisis could have presented itself as a turning point, a tipping point, or a critical juncture defined as a key moment which transpires "during relatively compressed periods of major change in which new institutions are established, or previously relatively stable institutions are reformed or replaced with new approaches".[25] Yet, the reforms and changes in migration governance in the aftermath of the COVID-19 pandemic can be located within the understanding of institutional reproduction (continuity and persistence of the "status quo") rather than institutional genesis that would usher in "new" configurations, rules, logics, norms, and procedures that would (re)structure and (re)organize migration flows and migration behaviour.

This question on the causal link between crisis and migration policy shift remains to be unsettled in the same way that migration scholars wrestle with establishing the heuristic value of the crisis idiom to explain both the continuities and changes occurring within the process of migration and to expound the role of crisis in the making of migration regimes. The notion of crisis has been so encompassing and pervasive that it is alluded to as an "important way of thinking about some forms of contemporary social change" and has the potential for alternative possibilities.[26] In relation to the COVID-19 pandemic, the crisis was defined by Walby as "an event that has the potential to cause a large detrimental change to the social system and in which there is a lack of proportionality between cause and consequence".[27] This definition emphasizes the temporality of the historic event and dramatic moment, yet its consequences are massively greater than the event in scale and intensity. Consequently, Lupton and Willis are quick to describe the current global society as a "COVID society", whereby no area and realm of human life was untouched and unmarked by the global pandemic, although the account of the crisis's impact may still be partial and unfolding.[28]

To avoid making sweeping generalizations and conjectures about "exceptional events" with corresponding greater "exceptional consequences", it is imperative to establish that crises are often asymmetric, uneven, and heterogeneous when it comes to their *usage*, *nature*, and *impact*. In terms of the usage of crisis metaphor, there are two strands. The first is the imminent perspective on crisis and crisis-resolution, which posits that the crisis is not a permanent state. There is a need to explain the origins of the crisis and the conditions for its resolution by using the existing accounts of the resources of social organizations to institutionalize "cleavages" and reconfigure relationships under stress. The second perspective is the transcendental perspective which constructs crisis vis-à-vis "utopian politics calling for thorough going change in the social totality", yet social change may "not be rooted in observable social trends".[29] The essence and nature of a crisis may also diverge according to three variables: (1) the trigger for the crisis may be exogenous or endogenous. Exogenous shocks often engender institutional genesis or the displacement of established policies, practices, and institutions; while endogenous shocks often lead to incremental change or continuity of institutions. (2) The intensity and scale of a crisis is not equal and uniform even if the crisis is depicted as global. (3) Responses to crisis vary according to the existing discretion of policymakers. In terms of impact and crisis response, some countries have differing experiences, resources, and interpretations of what the crisis is and what to do with it. Walby[30] elaborated on four main types of the impact of crisis on society:

> first, a crisis may be recuperated, so that the possibility of significant or permanent change is not fulfilled; second, a crisis may intensify an existing set of social relations, that is, it may accelerate a trajectory of development; third, a crisis may lead to transformation of the societal system from one form to another; and, fourth, a crisis may lead to catastrophe and the ending of that form of society. A connecting concept is that of cascade, which includes a temporal element. It may appear at one moment in time as if one of these impacts is what has

happened; however, whether a crisis that might appear to be absorbed will cascade into adjacent institutional domains may not be known at the time of study.

TOWARDS INSTITUTIONAL INNOVATION? CRITICAL MOMENTS AND ITS IMPACT ON PHILIPPINE MIGRATION POLICY

This perspective of crisis when located within institutional analysis pertains to institutional flux or critical junctures, which are brief but dramatic key moments that poignantly punctuate a relatively long period of stability. Notwithstanding the brevity and swiftness of the key moment, its consequences "are both substantively important and endure over time, placing institutional arrangements on paths or trajectories, which are then very difficult to alter".[31] The swift "exceptional" moment, such as the COVID-19 pandemic albeit still unfolding in terms of its "significant, swift and encompassing" change and effects, may be regarded as a case of critical juncture given that it created a favourable climate for and moment of openness to discredit and replace old norms, beliefs, procedures, and organizations. Applying this argument to a migration policy shift, the COVID-19 pandemic could have been utilized by states to make some radical changes in their migration management regimes, such as the total deployment ban of healthcare workers to resolve the medical brain drain in the case of the Philippines.

The Duterte administration initially banned the deployment of newly hired Filipino medical workers by halting the issuance of the Overseas Employment Contracts (OEC) at the height of the pandemic in April 2020, but the travel ban was lifted in November 2020 on condition of setting an annual deployment quota of 5,000 nurses. By December 2021, around 7,000 newly hired Filipino nurses were deployed to various countries and by September 2022, the new administration under Marcos Jr. announced that the deployment quota would be further increased from the current quota of 7,500 newly hired nurses. This "moment of openness" for a shift in migration policy that was not seized and required considerable discretion can be regarded as a "missed critical juncture", but both the administrations of Duterte and Marcos Jr. have also exercised their political agency and choice that "appears deeply embedded in antecedent conditions".[32] Nurse and labour migration are "non-discretionary forms of migration that states are not free to regulate" in case the Philippines wishes to reduce or ban migrant labour deployment.[33] By non-discretionary migration, these are the forms of migration that migrant-sending states permit to leave their country and which migrant-receiving states accept into their countries as a consequence of recognition of rights (i.e., right to seek employment anywhere, right to travel, and mobility) and other international agreements (i.e., bilateral agreement, multilateral agreement, etc.).

The Philippines has one of the most highly institutionalized labour export policies in the world that was instigated by the Marcos Sr. administration in 1974 to respond to the mounting labour demand in the Gulf countries during the oil price crisis in the 1970s and to resolve the increasing unemployment and inflation rate at the domestic level. The former was the exogenous shock that caused the radical institutional configurations of the labour export policy, which led towards taking a particular institutional path and which caused significant impact on the subsequent path-dependent development of Philippine labour export policy. Three government agencies were created to regulate and manage migration flow—the Overseas Employment Development Board (OEDB), the National Seamen's Board (NSB), and the Bureau of Employment Services (BES). In 1982, there was an organizational restructuring by merging the three agencies into two units—the Philippine Overseas Employment Administration (POEA) and the Overseas Workers Welfare Administration (OWWA).

From 1986 up to the present, the Philippine state proactively incorporated labour export into the "national project" of development. Gradual unfolding changes or the "cumulative small moments" such as (1) the *bagong bayani* (modern-day hero) discourse first introduced by President Corazon Aquino to describe the utilitarian-nationalistic contribution that Filipino migrants play in the economic development of the country in 1988; (2) the institutionalization of the Migrant Workers and Overseas Filipinos Act of 1995, which reconstructed the national image of the Filipino migrants as "humans" and "citizens" with rights, protection, and entitlements after the controversial execution of Flor Contemplacion in Singapore; (3) the passage of the Overseas Absentee

Voting Act of 2003, which has given Filipino migrants direct access to political participation; and (4) institutionalization of centralized organizational structure, such as the One-Stop Service Center for Overseas Filipino Workers (OSSCO), a site where migrants could access all government services needed.

These policy and institutional developments culminated in the creation of the Department of Migrant Workers in February 2022. This government agency is mandated not only to implement an "effective" welfare and protection programme to benefit Filipino migrant workers in every migration phase, from application for overseas work to return migration, but also to produce "good workers" for the expansive labour market.[34] Rather than focusing on aggressive marketing strategies to deploy migrant labour, the Philippine states institutionalized a labour export policy that will serve as a comprehensive migration governance not only to produce "globally competitive workers" aligned with the demand and needs of migrant-receiving societies, but also to provide protection for Filipino workers during unexpected emergencies and crises. In this case, the migrant-receiving societies have lower costs, fewer responsibilities, and are not a burden on their integration and welfare system.

The Philippine migration management system's high level of institutional stability has been substantiated, especially during exceptional events such as the COVID-19 pandemic. Rather than the crisis as a poignant "moment of openness" for reversibility or introduction of new interpretive frames and alternative configurations such as immobility, non-migration, or "exodus of return migration" due to the global pandemic, the COVID-19 pandemic was another litmus test for the Philippine state[35] to gauge its own effectiveness and efficiency to provide safety nets for Filipino migrant workers in terms of relocation, disease prevention, repatriation and "readiness" for return migration at the end of the contract period or during emergency. This is not a COVID-19 pandemic-induced migration programme, but a culmination of incremental small events that the Philippine state has already encountered before such as the wars in Iraq, upheaval in Lebanon, or SARS epidemic in Hong Kong, and how the existing migration programmes were implemented to respond to these emergencies. In the next section, we further interrogate institutional reproduction over institutional genesis during "exceptional events" such as the COVID-19 pandemic and historic moments—leadership transitions of two "controversial" Philippine presidents—Rodrigo Duterte and Ferdinand Marcos Jr.

TOWARDS FURTHER INSTITUTIONALIZATION: THE ESTABLISHMENT OF THE DEPARTMENT OF MIGRANT WORKERS (DMW)

Fulfilling one of his presidential campaign promises in 2016, Rodrigo R. Duterte signed into law Republic Act No. 11641, known as the Department of Migrant Workers (DMW) Act on 30 December 2021.[36] It can be recalled that in a presidential town hall debate on 24 April 2016, Duterte first mentioned his proposal of creating one department "to take care of the OFW [Overseas Filipino Worker]".[37] In his previous State of the Nation Addresses (SONAs), Duterte reiterated the same proposal by asking the Congress to pass the bill that would create a department "that shall focus on and quickly respond to their [OFWs'] problems and concerns"[38] and "[focused] solely on addressing the concerns of Filipinos abroad and their families".[39] During the day of his last SONA,[40] on 26 July 2021, Congress passed the bill creating the DMW.

In his first SONA in 2022, Duterte's successor, Ferdinand Marcos Jr., dedicated considerable time discussing overseas labour migration and the newly created DMW. He thanked the legislators, and most especially Duterte, for passing the law "that created this new home[41] for our OFWs" (Ferdinand R. Marcos Jr., First State of the Nation Address, 25 July 2022). Indeed, such pronouncements signal that the new administration will continue and build on what has been started by the previous administration when it comes to migration governance. After all, all administrations had to deal—in one way or another—with overseas labour employment given that it is a staple feature of Philippine society in the past decades. In fact, as what can be considered as coming full circle, the start of the institutionalization process of managing overseas employment and deployment can be traced back to the enactment of the Philippine Labour Code by the administration of Marcos Sr. in 1974. As previously discussed, engagements of subsequent administrations with managing labour migration as a response to both domestic and international events contributed to further institutionalization of the governance and management of the Philippine state of labour migration.

Thus, the creation of the DMW can be seen as a culmination of decades-long engagement of the Philippine state with the contours of overseas employment. Primarily, the DMW Act consolidated various government agencies under one department dedicated to migration management and governance (RA 11641, Sec. 5):

> The Department shall absorb all the powers, functions and mandate of the POEA and all the entities enumerated in the preceding section, and shall be the primary agency under the Executive Branch of the government tasked to protect the rights and promote the welfare of OFWs, regardless of status and of the means of entry into the country of destination.

These merged agencies include (1) the Philippine Overseas Employment Administration (POEA), (2) the Office of the Undersecretary for Migrant Workers' Affairs (OUMWA),[42] (3) all Philippine Overseas Labour Offices (POLO),[43] (4) International Labour Affairs Bureau (ILAB),[44] (5) National Reintegration Center for OFWs (NRCO),[45] (6) National Maritime Polytechnic (NMP),[46] and (7) Office of the Social Welfare Attaché (OSWA).[47,48] Building on the infrastructure of the POEA, the DMW expands its functions beyond licensing, regulating, and monitoring the recruitment and deployment of Overseas Filipino Workers. It can be noted that the POEA, which provides the backbone for the DMW, was anchored on regulation of overseas employment and protection of OFWs' welfare and rights as outlined in its powers and functions in Executive Order No. 247, s. 1987.[49] While the newly constituted department continues to perform the licensing and adjudication functions and the promotion and protection of OFWs, it has been given the mandate to take over the decision-making and policy formulation functions concerning overseas labour migration. The creation of a dedicated department for overseas employment is important for migration governance for a number of things that go beyond mere consolidation and merging of agencies. For one, overseas employment becomes a separate and distinct matter from the general issues and concerns of (domestic) labour and employment. This signals a formal recognition of labour migration as a national issue and concern. Apart from the objective of effectively and efficiently responding to the needs of OFWs (and their families), this also means being able to craft and propose policies and programmes specifically for the needs, logic, and dynamics of labour migration and shape the trajectory of Philippine migration governance. This emphasis on policymaking can be observed in the stated powers and functions of the DMW listed in its Implementing Rules and Regulations (IRR of RA 11641) and in the Act itself (Sec. 6a):

> Formulate, recommend, and implement national policies, plans, programs, and guidelines that will ensure the protection of OFWs, including their safe, orderly and regular migration, the promotion of their interests, the timely and effective resolution of their problems and concerns, and their effective reintegration to Philippine society.

As explained by the current DMW Assistant Secretary for Land-Based Concerns and Chief of Staff Jerome Alcantara when asked why this is the time to have a dedicated department for migrant workers, apart from the "sheer volume" of those they are serving and the need for rapid response, there is a need for them to have "a seat at the table in terms of policy and decision making". And when asked if such a "seat" was not there before, he explained:

> Because it is diluted with DOLE [Department of Labour and Employment]. For a country that relies so much on remittances, and a country that sends a lot of people, both documented and undocumented, we need something like that. And then perhaps the realization that this is really our future.

Currently undergoing transition, Assistant Secretary Alcantara also discussed the need to fill in the gap for data gathering and analysis that could feed into policy and decision-making, while also filling in the necessary human capital and infrastructure for the DMW to fully fulfil all its functions. For instance, training for the staff is essential, especially as the department needs to coordinate and work closely with the Department of Foreign Affairs (DFA) in negotiating bilateral agreements concerning labour migration. As the DMW takes over the functions of the Philippine Foreign Service Posts related to OFWs through the Migrant Workers Office (MWO), the department has to also operate overseas by absorbing previous responsibilities of the DFA, which means learning the legal aspect of the operation as well as building and fostering connections and ties with local authorities in the countries of destination to ensure that the welfare and interests of OFWs can be protected and promoted. Indeed, as Assistant Secretary Alcantara mentioned, the transition period has been challenging as there is a need to balance building the department and introducing reforms while also continuing and maintaining the services of the agencies that have been subsumed or transferred to DMW. This also means balancing continuity and change not only in terms of organizational and institutional processes and goals, but also in terms of the people within the department.

A closer look into the functions and powers of the department and its organizational structure, one can say that further institutionalizing the governance and management of Philippine labour migration through the creation of the DMW means fully embracing the complexities of migration governance. As a "labour-sending country", the Philippines has been considered to have a highly institutionalized labour-export process and interdependent government and non-government actors which manage and facilitate overseas deployment of Filipino workers.[50] But as previously discussed, with the creation of DMW, migration governance has shifted beyond regulation and facilitation of recruitment and deployment of workers overseas to managing every phase of the migration process—from pre-migration to adjustment and integration and eventually to return and reintegration. Such consideration is anchored on the "Full-Cycle National Reintegration Program", which has a prominent place in the Act creating the DMW (Sec. 17) and the department's IRR (Sec. 36):

> The Department shall develop and implement a full-cycle and comprehensive national reintegration program for both documented and undocumented OFWs, which shall be embedded in all stages of migration for work beginning from pre-deployment, on-site during employment, and upon return, whether voluntary or involuntary. The reintegration program shall cover the different dimensions of support needed by the OFW such as economic, social, psychosocial, gender-responsive, and cultural, including skills certification and recognition of equivalency for effective employment services, and shall ensure

contribution to national development through investments and transfer of technology from skilled or professional OFWs. The reintegration program shall include promoting access to social protection instruments and financial services, and reintegration of survivors of VAW and trafficking in persons.

The embeddedness of "reintegration" in every phase of the migration process is a significant dimension of the country's current governance and management of overseas employment and has been formally institutionalized in the Act creating DMW. This focus, along with other shifts in the "regimes of governing practices", is expected to mirror changing dynamics of (international) migration as what refer to as the "central duality of migration governance".[51] In other words, "understanding governance sheds light on the specific forms and processes of migration, and that understanding migration sheds light on specific forms and processes of governance". Following Carmel et al., we argue that "[t]he iteration of governing practices over time produces and reproduces certain forms of rules and institutions that acquire a taken-for-granted character". However, these are always subject to the social actions of various actors who participate, willingly or unwillingly, in such practices. The DMW as a newly established ministry mandated to implement the governing practices, rules, and norms related to Philippine migration policy will eventually and gradually acquire this "enduring" character. Academic output and research on Philippine international migration may contribute to the further institutionalization of DMW as academic research could contribute to legitimizing a state agency dedicated to migration practices and policies. But at the same time, DMW as a "centralized" source of migration data will benefit academic and empirical work, including policymaking related to overseas employment policy.

CONCLUSION

This chapter problematized the causal link between crisis and migration policy shift that some scholars have strongly put forward using the COVID-19 pandemic as an empirical case. We argued that any migration policy change, such as decreasing or increasing admission quotas, stoppage of hiring and deployment of certain migration categories, and repatriations due to unemployment, are not primarily prompted by the crisis itself. Rather the changes (e.g., restrictive or more open migration policy programmes) that may have surfaced during and after the crisis or critical transitions were built upon policy programmes, philosophical assumptions, or positions that were already in existence prior to the crisis.

Policy shifts and changes in policy outcomes were due to long-term processes. Often, crises and transitions are utilized by various social actors to instigate changes or to justify their respective agenda. In the case of the impact of crisis and critical transitions on migration policy in the Philippines, the external shocks did not produce critical junctures for radical policy change. Rather, endogenous processes and developments, such as further institutionalization of migration agencies, produce gradual and incremental changes. This chapter contributed to the discussion of institutional reproduction and continuity during upheaval and transitions in the Philippines.

Notes

1. In 2013, the Commission on Filipinos Overseas (CFO) released the last stock estimate of Filipinos overseas. According to CFO, the agency would be relying on the data provided by the Department of Foreign Affairs to "ensure policy coherence". See https://cfo.gov.ph/statistics-2/.
2. International Organisation for Migration, *World Migration Report 2020* (Geneva: International Organisation for Migration, 2022), https://publications.iom.int/books/world-migration-report-2022.
3. The Bangko Sentral ng Pilipinas (Central Bank of the Philippines) categorized remittances into cash remittances and personal remittances. The former refer to cash sent by land-based and sea-based workers through the banking system, while the latter refer to cash sent through banks and informal channels as well as remittances in kind. According to the Bangko Sentral ng Pilipinas, personal remittances are computed as the sum of net compensation of employees, personal transfers and capital transfers. See https://www.bsp.gov.ph/Media_And_Research/Media%20Releases/2023_07/news-07172023a1.aspx
4. https://www.bsp.gov.ph/SitePages/Statistics/External.aspx?TabId=8.
5. World Bank, "World Bank Predicts Sharpest Decline of Remittances in Recent History", Press Release No: 2020/175/SPJ, 22 April 2020, https://www.worldbank.org/en/news/press-release/2020/04/22/world-bank-predicts-sharpest-decline-of-remittances-in-recent-history.

6. International Organisation for Migration, "COVID-19 Analytical Snapshot #66: International Remittances Update", 2021, https://www.iom.int/sites/g/files/tmzbdl486/files/documents/covid-19_analytical_snapshot_66_international_remittances_update.pdf.
7. Karen Anne S. Liao, "Infrastructuring Repatriation: The Philippine Sending State and the Return of Migrant Workers Caught in Disruptions", *International Migration*, 9 June 2023, https://doi.org/10.1111/imig.13155; Yasmin Y. Ortiga and Karen Anne S. Liao, "When a Pandemic Disrupts the Export of People", *Research Collection School of Social Sciences* 3578 (Singapore: Singapore Management University, 2021).
8. Biao Xiang, William L. Allen, Shahram Khosravi, Hélène Neveu Kringelbach, Yasmin Y. Ortiga, Karen Anne S. Liao, Jorge E. Cuéllar, Lamea Momen, Priya Deshingkar, and Mukta Naik, "Shock Mobilities during Moments of Acute Uncertainty", *Geopolitics* 28, no. 4 (2023): 1632–57.
9. Anna Lindley, "Exploring Crisis and Migration: Concepts and Issues", in *Crisis and Migration: Critical Perspectives*, edited by Anna Lindley (London and New York: Routledge, 2014), pp. 1–23; Sonia Gsir, Jean-Michel Lafleur, and Mikolaj Stanek, "Migration Policy Reforms in the Context of Economic and Political Crises: The Case of Belgium", *Journal of Ethnic and Migration Studies* (2016): 1651–69, https://doi.org/10.1080/1369183X.2016.1162352; Christof Roos and Natascha Zaun, "The Global Economic Crisis as a Critical Juncture? The Crisis's Impact on Migration Movements and Policies in Europe and the U.S.", *Journal of Ethnic and Migration Studies* 42, no. 10 (2016): 1579–89, https://doi.org/10.1080/1369183X.2016.1162351.
10. John Hogan, "Remoulding the Critical Junctures Approach", *Canadian Journal of Political Science* 39, no. 3 (2006): 657–79.
11. Roos and Zaun, "The Global Economic Crisis as a Critical Juncture?"
12. James Mahoney and Kathleen Thelen, "A Theory of Gradual Institutional Change", in *Explaining Institutional Change: Ambiguity, Agency and Power*, edited by James Mahoney and Kathleen Thelen (New York: Cambridge University Press, 2010), pp. 1–37; Jael Goldsmith Weil, "Using Critical Junctures to Explain Continuity: The Case of State Milk in Neoliberal Chile", *Bulletin of Latin American Research* 36, no. 1 (2017): 52–67.
13. Anna Romina Guevarra, *Marketing Dreams, Manufacturing Heroes: The Transnational Labor Brokering of Filipino Workers* (New Jersey: Rutgers University Press, 2009).
14. Theda Skocpol, *States and Social Revolutions: A Comparative Analysis of France, Russia, and China* (Cambridge and New York: Cambridge University Press, 1979).

15. James Mahoney, *The Legacies of Liberalism: Path Dependence and Political Regimes in Central America* (Baltimore and London: The John Hopkins University Press, 2001).
16. Roos and Zaun, "The Global Economic Crisis as a Critical Juncture?"
17. Xiang et al., "Shock Mobilities during Moments of Acute Uncertainty".
18. Gsir, Lafleur, and Stanek, "Migration Policy Reforms in the Context of Economic and Political Crises".
19. Christian Kaunert, Sarah Leonard, and Ori Wertman, "Securitization of COVID-19 as a Security Norm: WHO Norm Entrepreneurship and Norm Cascading", *Social Sciences* 11, no. 7 (2022), http://dx.doi.org/10.3390/socsci11070266; Maria Koinova, Franck Düvell, Foteini Kalantzi, Sara de Jong, Christian Kaunert, and Marianne H. Marchand, "International Politics of Migration in Times of 'Crisis' and beyond the COVID-19 Pandemic", *Migration Studies* 11, no. 1 (March 2023): 242–57, https://doi.org/10.1093/migration/mnac039; Nicola Montagna, "Quarantine Ships as Spaces of Bordering: The Securitization of Migration Policy in Italy during the COVID-19 Pandemic", *International Migration Review* (2023), https://doi.org/10.1177/01979183231154560; Noor J. ten Have, Kassandra J. Jimenez, Jonas Attilus, Maria B. Livaudais, and Brittney S. Mengistu, "COVID-19 and Protracted Displacement: A Scoping Review of Migration Policies in Mexico and Central America", *Journal of International Migration and Integration* (2023): 1–29, advance online publication, https://doi.org/10.1007/s12134-023-01040-w.
20. Alan Gamlen, *Migration and Mobility after the 2020 Pandemic: The End of an Age?* (Geneva: International Organization for Migration, 2020), https://publications.iom.int/system/files/pdf/migration-_and-mobility.pdf.
21. Gsir, Lafleur, and Stanek, "Migration Policy Reforms in the Context of Economic and Political Crises"; Xiang et al., "Shock Mobilities during Moments of Acute Uncertainty".
22. Roos and Zaun, "The Global Economic Crisis as a Critical Juncture?"
23. Terence M. Garrett and Arthur J. Sementelli, "COVID-19, Asylum Seekers, and Migrants on the Mexico-U.S. Border: Creating States of Exception", *Political Policy* (2022), https://doi.org/10.1111/polp.12484.
24. Marie McAuliffe and Anna Triandafyllidou, "Report Overview: Technological, Geopolitical and Environmental Transformations Shaping Our Migration and Mobility Futures", in *World Migration Report 2022*, edited by Marie McAuliffe and Anna Triandafyllidou (Geneva: International Organization for Migration (IOM), 2021).
25. Andre Sorensen, "Taking Critical Junctures Seriously: Theory and Method for Causal Analysis of Rapid Institutional Change", *Planning Perspectives* 38, no. 5 (2022): 929–47.

26. Sylvia Walby, "Crisis and Society: Developing the Theory of Crisis in the Context of COVID-19", *Global Discourse* 12, no. 3–4 (2022): 498–516, https://doi.org/10.1332/ 204378921X16348228772103; Janet Roitman, *Anti-crisis* (Durham: Duke University Press, 2014).
27. Walby, "Crisis and Society"; Weil, "Using Critical Junctures to Explain Continuity".
28. Deborah Lupton and Karen Willis, *The COVID-19 Crisis: Social Science Perspectives* (London and New York: Routledge, 2021).
29. R. J. Holton, "The Idea of Crisis in Modern Society", *British Journal of Sociology* 38, no. 4 (1987): 502–20.
30. Walby, "Crisis and Society".
31. Paul Pierson, *Politics in Time: History, Institutions and Social Analysis* (New Jersey: Princeton University Press, 2004).
32. Ruth B. Collier, and David Collier, *Shaping the Political Arena: Critical Junctures, the Labor Movement, and Regime Dynamics in Latin America* (Princeton: Princeton University Press, 1991).
33. Roos and Zaun, "The Global Economic Crisis as a Critical Juncture?"
34. International Organisation for Migration, *World Migration Report 2005: Costs and Benefits of International Migration* (Geneva: International Organisation for Migration, 2005), https://publications.iom.int/books/world-migration-report-2005-costs-and-benefits-international-migration.
35. See Chapter 9 of this volume for a discussion of the COVID-19 policies of the Duterte administration.
36. Sofia Tomacruz, "Duterte Picks Abdullah Mamao to Lead New Department of Migrant Workers", *Rappler*, 9 March 2022, https://www.rappler.com/nation/overseas-filipinos/duterte-picks-abdullah-mamao-lead-department-migrant-workers/; Pia Ranada, "Duterte Proposes OFW Department", *Rappler*, 24 April 2016, https://www.rappler.com/nation/elections/130639-rodrigo-duterte-proposes-ofw-department/.
37. *Inquirer.net*, "READ: Complete Transcript of Final Presidential Debate", 26 April 2016, https://newsinfo.inquirer.net/781485/read-complete-transcript-of-final-presidential-debate.
38. Rodrigo Roa Duterte, First State of the Nation Address, 25 July 2016, https://www.officialgazette.gov.ph/2016/07/25/rodrigo-roa-duterte-first-state-of-the-nation-address-july-25-2016/.
39. Rodrigo Roa Duterte, Fifth State of the Nation Address, 27 July 2020, https://www.officialgazette.gov.ph/2020/07/27/rodrigo-roa-duterte-fifth-state-of-the-nation-address-july-27-2020/.

40. In his sixth and last SONA, Duterte reiterated the same call to the Congress "to pass legislation to establish a single agency that shall focus on and respond quickly to the needs and concerns of our OFWs"; Rodrigo Roa Duterte, Sixth State of the Nation Address, 26 July 2021, https://www.officialgazette.gov.ph/2021/07/26/rodrigo-roa-duterte-sixth-state-of-the-nation-address-july-26-2021/.
41. Referring to the "slogan" of the department: "Ang tahanan ng OFW" [translated as "The home of OFW"].
42. Previously under the Department of Foreign Affairs (DFA).
43. Previously under the Department of Labor and Employment (DOLE).
44. Ibid.
45. Previously under the Overseas Workers Welfare Administration (OWWA).
46. Previously under the Department of Labor and Employment (DOLE).
47. Previously under the Department of Social Welfare and Development (DSWD).
48. Republic Act No. 11641 – Department of Migrant Workers (DMW) Act, https://www.officialgazette.gov.ph/20,21/12/30/republic-act-no-11641/.
49. Known as the Reorganization Act of the Philippine Overseas Employment Administration; "Executive Order No. 247, s. 1987", 24 July 1987, https://www.officialgazette.gov.ph/1987/07/24/executive-order-no-247-s-1987/.
50. Anna R. Guevarra, *Marketing Dreams, Manufacturing Heroes: The Transnational Labor Brokering of Filipino Workers* (New Jersey: Rutgers University Press, 2009).
51. Emma Carmel, ed., *Governance Analysis: Critical Enquiry at the Intersection of Politics, Policy and Society* (Cheltenham: Edward Elgar Publishing, 2019); Emma Carmel, Katharina Lenner, and Regine Paul, "The Governance and Politics of Migration: A Conceptual-Analytical Map", in *Handbook on the Governance and Politics of Migration*, edited by Emma Carmel, Katharina Lenner, and Regine Paul, pp. 1–23 (Cheltenham: Edward Elgar Publishing, 2021).

Index

A

Abas, Sheriff M., 217, 220
Abella, Ernesto, 176
ABS-CBN
  disinformation and, 91–92, 175, 177–78, 209
  fact-checking of, 188, 189
absorptive capacity, 39–45
accountability. *See* fact-checking; *tsek. ph*
administrative reforms. *See* electoral reforms
adultery, 316
adversities, 164–66
agricultural sector, 40, 44, 50, 52, 53. *See also* inflation
aid distribution, 45, 234–35
AIIB (Asian Infrastructure Investment Bank), 66
Alcantara, Jerome, 340–41
Alvarez, Pantaleon, 128
Amnesty International, 315
anger, 185. *See also* fear
Año, Eduardo, 100
antagonism, 90, 91
anti-communist insurgency campaign, 91–92
anti-poor programmes, 35, 40, 43, 47, 53. *See also* poverty
anti-terrorism campaign, 89–91
anti-US rhetoric, 69–72. *See also* United States
approval ratings, 47–48, 88, 240–42, 247, 278, 314
Aquino III administration
  China, case against, 61–62
  criticisms against, 278
  economy during, 34–35, 38
  reforms under, 204–7
Aquino, Corazon Cojuangco, 309–10
arbitral award, 61–62
armed forces, 92–95, 98, 104, 105, 128
ARMM (Autonomous Region in Muslim Mindanao), 122, 130
Arroyo, Gloria
  constitutional changes and, 120, 128–29, 135–37
  elections and, 214, 215, 222, 309–10
  South China Sea and, 66–67
artificial islands, 61, 75
Asian Infrastructure Investment Bank (AIIB), 66
Austin, Lloyd, 65
authoritarianism, 48, 51, 52, 54, 240–42
Autonomous Region in Muslim Mindanao (ARMM), 122, 130

Index

autonomy, 125, 139, 142, 236–40. *See also* centralization; federalism

B

Badoy, Lorraine, 189
Balikatan exercises, 70
Bangko Sentral ng Pilipinas (BSP), 51
Bangsamoro Autonomous Region in Muslim Mindanao (BARMM), 40, 122, 130, 211, 212
Bangsamoro Organic Law (BOL), 40, 130, 211
Bangsamoro Transition Authority (BTA), 211
Barangay and Sangguniang Kabataan Elections (BSKE), 212
barangay, 91, 156, 205, 239
BARMM (Bangsamoro Autonomous Region in Muslim Mindanao), 40, 122, 130, 211, 212
Bautista, Andres, 216
Bayanihan Constitution, 122–23, 136–37
Bayanihan to Heal as One Act, 45, 86, 238–39, 288
BBB ("Build, Build, Build") programme, 38–39, 45, 52, 64, 96
Beijing. *See* China
Bello, Walden, 176
Belt and Road Initiative (BRI), 65–66, 96
BES (Bureau of Employment Services), 336
blue economy, 75. *See also* environment
BOL (Bangsamoro Organic Law), 40, 130, 211
Boracay Island, 260, 264
BRI (Belt and Road Initiative), 65–66, 96

brutal deaths, 153–59. *See also* war on drugs
BSKE (Barangay and Sangguniang Kabataan Elections), 212
BSP (Bangko Sentral ng Pilipinas), 51
BTA (Bangsamoro Transition Authority), 211
Build Back Better Task Force (BBBTF), 289
"Build, Build, Build" (BBB) programme, 38–39, 45, 52, 64, 96
Bulay, Reynaldo, 217
bullying, 160–64
Bureau of Employment Services (BES), 336
Bureau of Internal Revenue, 125

C

cabinet appointments, 92–95, 98–100, 105
Cabochan III, Manuel, 128
calamities, 67. *See also* natural disasters
campaigning
 financial support for, 204, 215–16, 221
 laws regarding, 222–24
candidacy, 207–8, 219, 309
careening, 10–13
cartels, 50, 52. *See also* inflation
Casquejo, Marlon, 217
Catholic Church, 186
Cayetano, Allan Peter, 127
cease-fire, 91
Celis, Nelson, 223
censorship, 174–80
Center for Media Freedom and Responsibility (CMFR), 177
central-local relations, 230–31, 233–36
centralization, 232–36, 292. *See also* decentralization

CFO (Commission on Filipinos Overseas), 328
chambers of commerce, 101
charter change. *See* federalism
cheating, 205–6, 212–13, 214–15
China
   distrust towards, 61, 96, 103
   financial support from, 38
   pivot to, 63–68, 70–75, 85
China Energy Engineering Corporation, 66
China National Offshore Oil Corporation, 67
CHR (Commission on Human Rights), 315
Chua, Karl Kendrick, 37
Cimatu, Roy, 262
CIT (corporate income tax), 37
civil society organizations (CSOs), 277
civil-military relations, 92–95, 98–100, 105
climate change, 256, 260–61, 265, 266–70. *See also* natural disasters
CMFR (Center for Media Freedom and Responsibility), 177
coastal welfare, 75. *See also* environment
COMELEC (Commission on Elections)
   Duterte administration and, 207, 208, 216–17
   electoral process and, 213–21
   Marcos administration and, 218–19, 221–25, 321
   PNoy administration and, 204–7
Commission on Appointments, 216, 262, 267
Commission on Elections. *See* COMELEC

Commission on Filipinos Overseas (CFO), 328
Commission on Human Rights (CHR), 315
communist insurgency, 91–92
Communist Party of the Philippines (CPP), 91, 183, 192
Comprehensive Tax Reform Program (CTRP), 36–37
Conferences of Parties (COP), 261, 265, 268
Congress, 126–29, 136–38, 140–42
constitutional reforms. *See* electoral reform; federalism
cooperation narrative, 72–73
COP (Conferences of Parties), 261, 265, 268
corporate income tax (CIT), 37
Corporate Recovery and Tax Incentives for Enterprises (CREATE) Law, 37, 45
corruption, 67, 68, 238
cost-of-living crisis, 53. *See also* inflation
counterinsurgency, 91–92
counterrevolutionary politics, 176, 180
COVID-19 pandemic
   disaster response during, 288–89
   disinformation during, 184–88
   Duterte administration's handling of, 67–68, 234–35, 239, 241–42
   economic gains, impacts on, 37, 43–47, 53
   elections during, 217–18, 243–44
   under Marcos Jr. administration, 245–46
   migration, impact on, 329–30, 332–35, 337
   new normal after, 101–2

CPP (Communist Party of the Philippines), 91, 183, 192
CREATE (Corporate Recovery and Tax Incentives for Enterprises) Law, 37, 45
criminality, 64, 87–89
crisis, 46–47, 53–54, 329–30, 332–35
critical reporting, 178. *See also* media freedom
CSOs (civil society organizations), 277
CTRP (Comprehensive Tax Reform Program), 36–37
curfews, 67
Cusi, Alfonso, 210
cyber sphere. *See* social media
cyclones, 256, 277–78

D
Davao Death Squad, 158, 159, 315
DBM (Department of Budget and Management), 282
DDR (Department of Disaster Resilience), 260, 263, 282, 291
de Lima, Leila, 175, 315–16, 316–19
debates, 220–21
debt-to-GDP ratio, 34, 45–46. *See also* GDP
decentralization, 236–40. *See also* centralization
defence measures, 104–6
democracy
  defined, 175–76
  and Duterte, 207–13
  See also disinformation
DENR (Department of Environment and Natural Resources), 258–59, 261–62, 266, 267–68, 270
Department of Budget and Management (DBM), 282

Department of Disaster Resilience (DDR), 260, 263, 282, 291
Department of Environment and Natural Resources (DENR), 258–59, 261–62, 266, 267–68, 270
Department of Foreign Affairs (DFA), 340–41
Department of Health (DOH), 68, 86, 101, 245–46
Department of Information, Communications and Technology (DICT), 102
Department of Migrant Workers (DMW), 337–42
Department of Public Works and Highways (DPWH), 39
Department of the Interior and Local Government (DILG), 123, 124, 238, 288
Department of Transportation (DOTr), 39
deterrence, 74. *See also* internal security
devolution, 125, 138–43, 234, 239. *See also* decentralization; federalism
DFA (Department of Foreign Affairs), 340–41
DICT (Department of Information, Communications and Technology), 102
dictatorship, 48, 51, 52, 54, 240–42
digital economy, 44, 101–2
DILG (Department of the Interior and Local Government), 123, 124, 238, 288
Diño, Martin, 207
Diokno, Benjamin, 102, 131
diplomacy, 64–65, 72–73
disasters
  policy regarding, 282, 289–91, 291–94

prevention of, 276
   resilience towards, 260, 263
   response towards, 282–88
Disaster Response and Crisis
   Management Task Force
   (DRCMTF), 293–94
Disaster Risk Reduction and
   Management (DRRM) Law,
   276–77
Disaster Risk Reduction Network
   Philippines (DRRNetPhils), 277,
   290–91
disinformation
   2019 elections and, 181–84
   2022 elections and, 188–94
   COVID-19 pandemic and, 184–88
   defined, 172–73
   Duterte and, 15–17, 174–80
   gender gap and, 304–7
   gendered disinformation (*see*
      gendered disinformation)
   public trust and, 77
   See also democracy; misinformation;
      negative messaging
DMW (Department of Migrant
   Workers), 337–42
DOH (Department of Health), 68, 86,
   101, 245–46
Dominguez III, Carlos, 35, 37, 40, 45,
   46, 131
DOTr (Department of
   Transportation), 39
"Double Barrel". *See* war on drugs
DPWH (Department of Public Works
   and Highways), 39
DRCMTF (Disaster Response and
   Crisis Management Task Force),
   293–94
DRRM (Disaster Risk Reduction and
   Management) Law, 276–77

DRRNetPhils (Disaster Risk
   Reduction Network Philippines),
   277, 290–91
drug war. *See* war on drugs
Duterte administration
   authoritarianism, 240–42
   civil-military relations, 92–95
   COVID-19's economic impact
      during, 37, 43–47, 53
   democracy and, 207–13
   disaster policy of, 282, 289–91
   disinformation during, 15–17,
      174–80
   economic programmes of, 36–40
   environmental policy, 264–65
   failure of, 52–54, 129–39
   foreign policy during, 38, 63–68,
      70–75
   legacy of, 40–43, 265–66
   local governance (*see* local
      governance)
   migration policy of, 335–38
   misogyny (*see* misogyny)
   popularity of, 47–48, 88, 240–42
   promises of, 122–26, 258–61
   security policy, 87–92, 106
   war on drugs (*see* war on drugs)
Duterte, Sara, 166–67, 191–92, 218–19,
   247

E

e-commerce, 44, 101–2
Ease of Doing Business Act, 39–40,
   41, 53
economy
   Duterte's legacy of, 40–43
   gains to, 37, 43–47, 53
   liberalization of, 127–28
   programmes, 36–40
   recovery of, 246

Index 353

team dealing with, 51–52, 130–31, 138–39
version 2.0, 48–52
EDCA (Enhanced Defense Cooperation Agreement), 65, 76–77
education crisis, 46–47
Efficient Government Service Delivery Act, 39–40
Elago, Sarah, 186
Election Service Reform Act (ESRA), 205–6
elections
  in 2016, 305
  in 2019, 124–26, 181–84, 243–44
  in 2022, 95–96, 188–94
  access to, 205, 216, 222, 224
  commission of (*see* COMELEC)
  management of, 213–21
  offense relating to, 205–6, 212–13, 214–15
  process of, 207–13
  system of, 213, 214, 215, 221–22, 223
electoral reforms
  during Duterte administration, 207–13
  during Marcos Jr. administration, 219–20, 221–25
  See also federalism; institutional reforms
Emergency Events Database (EM-DAT), 274, 278
Energy Conservation and Efficiency Act, 263
energy crisis, 53–54
ENGOs (environmental non-government organizations), 261–62, 264
Enhanced Defense Cooperation Agreement (EDCA), 65, 76–77
entrapment narrative, 69–72

environment
  challenges relating to, 256, 260
  Duterte's promises to, 258–61
  expectations under Marcos, 266–70
  impacts on, 66, 75
  laws on, 257, 263
  legacy of, 265–66
  policy on, 264–65
environmental non-government organizations (ENGOs), 261–62, 264
ESRA (Election Service Reform Act), 205–6
European Union, 7, 64
evidence, 165–66
excise tax, 36–40, 53. *See also* onion fiasco; rice supplies; sugar fiasco
Exclusive Economic Zone, 61
Expanded Protected Areas Act, 263
external relations. *See* foreign policy
extrajudicial killings. *See* political violence

F
Facebook, 181, 182, 183, 188, 190. *See also* social media
fact-checking
  disinformation and, 188–94, 314
  in elections, 181–84
Fair Election Act of 2001, 208, 321
fake news. *See* disinformation
FDI (foreign direct investment), 34, 40, 41, 64
fear, 159, 160–64, 185
federalism
  congressional support, lack of, 136–38, 140–42
  economic team opposing, 130–31, 138–39
  leadership failure affecting, 129–30, 138–39

under Marcos Jr. administration, 140–43, 246–47
Mindanao, 89–91, 139–40, 142–43, 240
promises of, 122–26, 209, 211
public support, lack of, 131–36
See also autonomy
Ferolino-Ampoloquio, Aime, 217
financial assistance, 45, 234–35
food security, 41–42, 49–50, 53, 75
foreign direct investment (FDI), 34, 40, 41, 64
foreign ownership, 126–29
foreign policy, 38, 63–68, 70–75, 76
foreign trips, 50, 76, 102–3
fraud, 205–6, 212–13, 214–15
funds
    Maharlika Investment Fund, 51–52, 54
    mismanagement of, 68
    quick response fund (QRF), 283, 285, 288
    sources of, 102, 233–34

G
gadgets, 46–47
gambling industry, 64
Garcia, George, 220, 221–23
Garcillano, Virgilio, 214
GDP, 34, 40–41, 43, 46, 52, 53. *See also* debt-to-GDP ratio
gender gap, 304–7
Gender Social Norms Index (GSNI), 312
gendered disinformation, 305, 310–12. *See also* de Lima, Leila; Robredo, Leni
Gerbaudo, Paolo, 179
gig economy, 44, 101–2
Global Witness, 265–66
Go, Bong, 208

"golden age", 48–52, 74. *See also* Marcos Sr. Ferdinand
Gonzales Jr., Aurelio, 128
government spending, 38–39, 45, 64, 233–34
grief, 159–66. *See also* ungrievability
GSNI (Gender Social Norms Index), 312
Guanzon, Rowena, 217, 219–20
gunmen, 156–59. *See also* war on drugs

H
Habermasian public sphere, 187
Haiyan (typhoon), 277–78
Hameleers, Michael, 187
Hapilon, Isnilon, 89
hate speech, 176–77, 183, 185–86, 192. *See also* disinformation
health protocols, 218, 239. *See also* COVID-19 pandemic
Hello Garci scandal, 214
Herbosa, Teodoro, 245
hostilities, 74. *See also* internal security
House Committee on Constitutional Amendments, 124–29, 141
House of Representatives, 127–29, 137, 141–42, 210
human capital investments, 53
human rights, 87–89, 90, 315

I
IATF-EID (Inter-Agency Task Force for the Management of Emerging Infectious Diseases), 86, 230
ICC (International Criminal Court, 88–89, 151, 167
IFCN (International Fact-Checking Network), 181

Index   355

inclusivity, 205, 216, 222, 224
income tax, 36–40
inequality. *See* poverty
inflation, 41–42, 49–50, 53. *See also* cartels; rice supplies
information campaigns, 74, 77. *See also* disinformation
infrastructure development, 36–40, 45, 64
inoculation, 184, 194–95. *See also* disinformation
institutional reforms, 126–29. *See also* electoral reforms; federalism
institutional reproduction, 336, 339
Inter-Agency Task Force for the Management of Emerging Infectious Diseases (IATF-EID), 86, 230
Inter-Agency Task Force on Federalism and Constitutional Reform, 123–27
internal revenue allotment (IRA), 125, 142, 234, 285–86
internal security
  amidst 2022 elections, 95–96
  policy, 87–92, 97–98, 106
  See also deterrence; hostilities
International Criminal Court (ICC), 88–89, 151, 167
International Fact-Checking Network (IFCN), 181
International Organisation of Migration (IOM), 328
international relations, 38, 63–68, 70–75
international visibility, 50, 76, 102–3
Internet, 46–47, 60
Inting, Soccoro, 217
investment pledges, 50, 64, 68, 102–3
IOM (International Organisation of Migration), 328

IRA (internal revenue allotment), 125, 142, 234, 285–86

J
Janjan, Sangkay, 185
JFC (Joint Foreign Chambers), 101
JMSU (Joint Marine Seismic Undertaking), 66–67
"Jobs, Jobs, Jobs" online portal, 38–39
job loss, 42–44
Joint Foreign Chambers (JFC), 101
Joint Marine Seismic Undertaking (JMSU), 66–67
journalism, 174–80

K
Kadiwa stores, 48, 53
Kaliwa Dam, 38, 66
Kho Jr., Antonio T., 217, 220

L
labour migration, 335–42
Lakas-CMD, 219, 222
land use, 259–60, 263
Lao, Lloyd Christopher, 68
leadership failure, 129–30, 138–39
learning poverty, 46–47
legislative reforms. *See* electoral reforms
Leni Leaks, 313–14, 316–19. *See also* Robredo, Leni
LGUs. *See* local government units (LGUs)
Liberal Democracy Index, 11
livelihoods, 42–44
local governance
  central-local relations, 230–31, 233–36
  decentralization, 236–40
  Duterte's power over, 240–42

Local Government Code (1991)
  amendments to, 122, 125, 140, 142
  Duterte administration and, 232, 234, 236, 239, 249
local government units (LGUs)
  autonomy of, 125, 139, 142
  disaster response of, 277, 285–86, 288
lockdowns. *See* COVID-19 pandemic
logistics bottleneck, 49
Lopez, Regina Paz, 258–59, 261–62, 266, 270
Lorenzana, Delfin, 90

M
Macapagal-Arroyo, Gloria. *See* Arroyo, Gloria
Maceda, Ferdinand Ernesto, 223
Maharlika Investment Fund, 51–52, 54
Malaya, Jonathan, 124, 125, 126
Mandanas-Garcia ruling, 125, 139, 142, 233–34, 285–86
Mangiu-Pippidi, Alina, 180
Manila, 38, 39, 66, 238, 260, 264
Marawi City, 39, 40
Marawi Siege, 89–91
Marcos, Imee, 221–22, 291–92
Marcos Jr. administration
  challenges faced by, 52–54, 141–42
  climate change under, 266–70
  constitutional reforms under, 140–43
  COVID-19 pandemic and, 245–46
  debates, 220–21
  disaster policy of, 291–94
  disinformation during, 188–94
  drug war under, 166–67
  economy 2.0 of, 48–52
  electoral fraud, claims of, 205–6, 212–13, 214–15

foreign policy, 73–74, 76
  international visibility, 50, 76, 102–3
  migration policy, 335–38
  new normal under, 101–2
  reforms under, 219–20, 221–25, 246–48
  security policy, 95–96, 97–98, 106
Marcos Sr. Ferdinand
  disinformation and, 190–91, 310
  labour export policy of, 336
  nostalgia for, 48–52, 54, 74
marital infidelity, 316
martial law, 43, 74, 89–91, 190–91, 240
mask mandate, 246. *See also* COVID-19 pandemic
Maute, 89
MDT (Mutual Defense Treaty), 65
media freedom, 174–80
micro, small, and medium enterprises (MSMEs), 36, 37, 45
migration
  governance, 332–35
  of labour, 335–42
military and uniformed personnel (MUP), 92–95, 98, 104, 105, 128
military exercises, 70
military rule, 43, 74, 89–91, 190–91, 240
Mindanao, 89–91, 139–40, 142, 240. *See also* federalism
mining, 259–62, 266, 268–70
misinformation, 77, 172–73, 312. *See also* disinformation
misogyny, 306, 308–12. *See also* de Lima, Leila; Robredo, Leni
mobility restriction. *See* COVID-19 pandemic
modernization programme, 104
monetary assistance, 45, 234–35
morality, 316

Index   357

MSMEs (micro, small, and medium enterprises), 36, 37, 45
MUP (military and uniformed personnel), 92–95, 98, 104, 105, 128
Mutual Defense Treaty (MDT), 65

N
Naga Leaks, 313–14, 316–19. *See also* Robredo, Leni
"*nanlaban*" narrative, 150, 155–56. *See also* war on drugs
National Disaster Risk Reduction and Management Council (NDRRMC)
  establishment of, 276–77
  funding for, 282–85
  structure of, 289–90, 291–92
  See also Disaster Response and Crisis Management Task Force (DRCMTF)
National Election Summit, 223
National Food Authority (NFA), 36, 42
National Integrated Protected Areas System (NIPAS) Act, 263
National Land Use Act (NLUA), 259–60, 263
National Seamen's Board (NSB), 336
national security. *See* internal security
National Task Force to End Local Communist Armed Conflict (NTF-ELCAC), 91–92, 97–98, 106
national tax allotment (NTA), 234
National Union of Journalists of the Philippines, 175
Nationally Determined Contribution (NDC), 265
natural disasters
  funding for, 282–86, 288

  occurrences of, 256, 274, 277–82, 287–89
  resilience towards, 260
  See also calamities; climate change
natural gas reserves, 53–54
NDC (Nationally Determined Contribution), 265
NDRRMC. *See* National Disaster Risk Reduction and Management Council (NDRRMC)
negative messaging, 192, 314. *See also* disinformation
neutral policy, 71–72
new normal, 101–2, 245–46
New People's Army (NPA), 91
news literacy, 184, 194–95. *See also* disinformation
news organizations, 177–81
NFA (National Food Authority), 36, 42
NGOs (non-governmental organizations), 277, 278
NIPAS Act (National Integrated Protected Areas System Act), 263
NLUA (National Land Use Act), 259–60, 263
NOAH Project, 286–87
non-governmental organizations (NGOs), 277, 278
nostalgia, 48–52, 54, 74
NPA (New People's Army), 91
NSB (National Seamen's Board), 336
NTA (national tax allotment), 234
NTF-ELCAC (National Task Force to End Local Communist Armed Conflict), 91–92, 97–98, 106

O
ODA (Official Development Assistance), 38, 64

OEC (Omnibus Election Code), 206, 207, 216, 221–22, 224, 321
OEDB (Overseas Employment Development Board), 336
Office of the President, 291–92
Official Development Assistance (ODA), 38, 64
OFW (Overseas Filipino Workers), 44, 337–42
oil, 36, 41, 292–93
Omnibus Election Code (OEC), 206, 207, 216, 221–22, 224, 321
onion fiasco, 50, 52. See also inflation
online disinformation. See disinformation
online economy, 44, 101–2
online learning, 46–47
online narratives. See social media
ostracism, 160–64
oversea trips, 50, 76, 102–3
Overseas Employment Contracts, 335
Overseas Employment Development Board (OEDB), 336
Overseas Filipino Workers (OFW), 44, 337–42
Overseas Workers Welfare Administration (OWWA), 336
ownership access, 126–29

P

PAGASA (Philippine Atmospheric, Geophysical and Astronomical Services Administration), 284
Panelo, Salvador, 241
Pangarungan, Saideman, 220, 222
Pangilinan, Francis, 219
Pantawid Pamilyang Pilipino Program (4Ps), 35, 40. See also poverty
PAR (Philippine Area of Responsibility), 256
Paris Agreement, 261, 265, 268. See also climate change
Partido Demokratiko Pilipino-Lakas ng Bayan (PDP-Laban), 210–11
partisan politics, 128
Partners for Resilience (PfR), 277
party fragmentation, 210–11
PCA (Permanent Court of Arbitration), 61–62
PCIJ (Philippine Center for Investigative Journalism), 179
PCSD (Philippine Council for Sustainable Development), 257
PDEA (Philippine Drug Enforcement Agency), 150
PDP-Laban (Partido Demokratiko Pilipino-Lakas ng Bayan), 210–11
peace talks, 91
pension system, 53, 92–95, 105
Permanent Court of Arbitration (PCA), 61–62
Pernia, Ernesto, 131
perpetrators, 156–59. See also war on drugs
personal protective equipment, 67–68. See also COVID-19 pandemic
PEZA (Philippine Economic Zone Authority), 37
PfR (Partners for Resilience), 277
Pharmally Pharmaceutical Corporation, 68
Philippine Area of Responsibility (PAR), 256
Philippine Atmospheric, Geophysical and Astronomical Services Administration (PAGASA), 284
Philippine Center for Investigative Journalism (PCIJ), 179
Philippine Constitution (1987)
changes to, 120, 132–33, 135, 138–43

local government's autonomy and, 122–24, 236
women's role and, 309
Philippine Council for Sustainable Development (PCSD), 257
Philippine Drug Enforcement Agency (PDEA), 150
Philippine Economic Zone Authority (PEZA), 37
Philippine Institute of Volcanology and Seismology (PHIVOLCS), 287
Philippine National Oil Corporation, 67
Philippine offshore gaming operators (POGOs), 64
Philippine Overseas Employment Administration (POEA), 336, 339
PHIVOLCS (Philippine Institute of Volcanology and Seismology), 287
Pimentel III, Aquilino, 210
PNoy. *See* Aquino III administration
POEA (Philippine Overseas Employment Administration), 336, 339
POGOs (Philippine offshore gaming operators), 64
political dynasties, 204, 205, 243, 247, 309
political party reforms. *See* electoral reforms
political polarization, 128
political violence
  environmental advocates and, 265–66
  security policy and, 87–92, 106
  widowhood and, 153–59
  See also war on drugs

populism, 174, 240–42. *See also* Duterte administration: popularity of
poverty
  education and, 46–47
  rate of, 41–43
  reduction of, 53–54
  TRAIN's impact on, 36–37
  See also 4Ps (Pantawid Pamilyang Pilipino Program)
PPP (public-private partnerships), 38
press freedom, 174–80
Project NOAH, 286–87
proportional representation, 224–25
4Ps (Pantawid Pamilyang Pilipino Program), 35, 40. *See also* poverty
public administration, 92–95, 98–100, 105
public construction, 38–39, 45, 64, 233–34
public health emergency, 67. *See also* COVID-19 pandemic
public safety, 87–92. *See also* internal security
public trust, 77. *See also* disinformation
public-private partnerships (PPP), 38
Pulse Asia, 47, 48, 131–32, 141, 240

Q
quarantine, 67, 230, 245. *See also* COVID-19 pandemic
quick response fund (QRF), 283, 285, 288

R
Ranada, Pia, 177
Rappler, 177–79, 181, 184
reading proficiency, 46–47
recession. *See* COVID-19 pandemic

red-tagging, 90, 91, 183, 192. *See also* disinformation
reintegration, 341–42. *See also* migration
remittances, 44
renewable energy, 53–54
Reporters without Borders, 177
rice supplies, 36, 41, 42, 50, 52, 53, 66. *See also* inflation
Robredo, Leni
   disinformation about, 191–92, 313–14, 316–19
   electoral process and, 219
   online attacks against, 185, 186
Rodriguez, Rufus, 125, 126, 141
Roque, Harry, 175, 240
Russia, 49, 71–72

S

Safe Spaces Act, 311
Sangguniang Kabataan Reform Act of 2015 (SK Law), 205
satisfaction ratings, 47–48, 88, 240–42, 247, 278, 314
Scarborough Shoal, 61–62
school closures, 46–47
security policy. *See* internal security
Senate, 127, 128, 129, 137, 141–42
services sector, 44
sexist narratives, 310–12. *See also* gendered disinformation
Sinovac, 68
SK Law (Sangguniang Kabataan Reform Act of 2015), 205
SOCCSKSARGEN region, 90
social isolation, 160–64. *See also* widowhood
social media
   foreign policy, effects on, 74
   prevalence of, 60
   role in disinformation, 177–79, 181, 187–88, 305, 312, 314
   role in fact-checking, 188–94
social protection systems. *See* poverty
Social Weather Stations, 132, 184, 240, 314
SONA. *See* State of the Nation Address (SONA)
South China Sea
   arbitral award, 61–62
   defeatism in, 63–68, 70–75
   territorial disputes, 96
sovereign wealth fund, 51–52, 54, 102
Special Defense Economic Zones (SpeDEZ), 106
spending bottleneck, 39, 52
State of the Nation Address (SONA)
   by Duterte, 70, 73, 122, 123, 259, 260
   by Marcos Jr., 50, 97, 245, 268, 338
stigma, 160–64. *See also* widowhood
sugar fiasco, 50, 52. *See also* inflation
Supreme Court decision (2019), 125, 139
sustainable development, 257, 268, 269. *See also* environment
syndicates, 64

T

Task Force Bangon (Rise) Marawi, 89
tax laws, 36–40
Tax Reform for Acceleration and Inclusion (TRAIN Law), 36–37, 53
territorial disputes, 96
terrorism, 89–91
tokhang, 150, 156, 158, 161, 164
Torrefranca-Neri, Aimee, 220, 222
tourist destinations, 260, 264
traffic congestion, 38, 54, 238

TRAIN (Tax Reform for Acceleration and Inclusion) Law, 36–37, 53
tsek.ph
  during 2019 elections, 181–84
  during 2022 elections, 188–94, 314
turncoatism, 136
typhoons, 274, 277–81

U
Ukraine, 49, 71–72
UNDRR (United Nations Disaster Risk Reduction), 282
unemployment, 42–44
ungrievability, 155–56. *See also* grief
United Nations Convention on the Law of the Sea, 61–62
United Nations Disaster Risk Reduction (UNDRR), 282
United Nations Framework Convention on Climate Change, 261, 265, 268
United Nations Human Rights Council, 88, 90
United States
  alliance with, 76–77
  re-establish relations with, 102–3
  separating from, 63–65, 69–74, 85
United Vloggers and Influencers of the Philippines, 185
utang na loob (debt of gratitude), 73

V
vaccines
  distribution of, 235
  misinformation regarding, 184–88
  procurement of, 68

Varieties of Democracy, 11
Vera Files, 179, 181, 184, 188, 189
Vergeire, Maria Rosario, 101, 245
VFA (Visiting Forces Agreement), 65
violence. *See* political violence
virus. *See* COVID-19 pandemic
Visiting Forces Agreement (VFA), 65
vote padding, 214–15
voting registration, 205, 216, 218. *See also* elections
vulnerable population. *See* poverty

W
war on drugs
  criminality and, 87–89
  local government's role in, 237, 241, 242
  under Marcos Jr. administration, 166–67
  media reports on, 176, 177, 178
  tokhang, 150, 156, 158, 161, 164
  women affected by, 153–59
Washington. *See* United States
weaponization, 237–38
WEF (World Economic Forum), 102
West Philippine Sea, 66–67
widowhood, 153–59. *See also* grief
women in politics, 308–10. *See also* misogyny
World Economic Forum (WEF), 102
World Values Survey, 312

Y
Yang, Michael, 68
Yulo-Loyzaga, Ma. Antonia, 267–68

www.ingramcontent.com/pod-product-compliance
Lightning Source LLC
Chambersburg PA
CBHW040318300426
44111CB00022B/2941